Tyndale Old Testament Commentaries

Volume 2

TOTC

Exodus

For Matthew and Chelsee, Andrew and Khataya, with love

Tyndale Old Testament Commentaries

Volume 2

Series Editor: David G. Firth
Consulting Editor: Tremper Longman III

Exodus

An Introduction and Commentary

Paul R. Williamson

ivp

IVP
Academic
An imprint of InterVarsity Press
Downers Grove, Illinois

InterVarsity Press, USA
P.O. Box 1400 | Downers Grove, IL 60515-1426
ivpress.com | email@ivpress.com

Inter-Varsity Press, England
Studio 101, The Record Hall, 16–16A Baldwin's Gardens
London EC1N 7RJ, UK
ivpbooks.com | ivp@ivpbooks.com

InterVarsity Press® is the publishing division of InterVarsity Christian Fellowship/USA®. For more information, visit intervarsity.org.

Inter-Varsity Press, England, originated within the Inter-Varsity Fellowship, now the Universities and Colleges Christian Fellowship, a student movement connecting Christian Unions in universities and colleges throughout Great Britain, and a member movement of the International Fellowship of Evangelical Students. Website: www.uccf.org.uk.

USA ISBN 978-1-5140-1400-4 (paperback) | USA ISBN 978-1-5140-1624-4 (hardcover) |
USA ISBN 978-0-8308-9881-7 (digital)

UK ISBN 978-1-78974-541-2 (paperback) | UK ISBN 978-1-78974-599-3 (hardcover) |
UK ISBN 978-1-78974-542-9 (digital)

Typeset by Fakenham Prepress Solutions, Fakenham, Norfolk NR21 8NL

Printed in the United States of America ∞

Library of Congress Cataloging-in-Publication Data
A catalog record for this book is available from the Library of Congress.

British Library Cataloguing-in-Publication Data
A catalogue record for this book is available from the British Library.

33 32 31 30 29 28 27 26 25 | 12 11 10 9 8 7 6 5 4 3 2 1

CONTENTS

General preface   vii
Author's preface   ix
Abbreviations   xii
Select bibliography   xvi

Introduction   1
1. Exodus in the Pentateuch and beyond   1
2. Composition and date   2
3. Structure and thematic cohesion   6
4. Historical and archaeological issues   8
5. Theological themes in Exodus   30
6. Biblical-theological trajectories in Exodus   34

Analysis   37

Commentary   43

Additional notes
The revelation and meaning of the divine name   74
The hardening of Pharaoh's heart   85
The plagues as supernatural or natural phenomena   109
The origin(s) of Passover and Unleavened Bread   144
The size of the Israelite population at the time of the exodus   150
The chronological sequence of Exodus 19 – 24   218
Paul's interpretation of Moses' veil   367

GENERAL PREFACE

The decision to completely revise the Tyndale Old Testament Commentaries is an indication of the important role that the series has played since its opening volumes were released in the mid 1960s. They represented at that time, and have continued to represent, commentary writing that was committed both to the importance of the text of the Bible as Scripture and to a desire to engage with as full a range of interpretative issues as possible without being lost in the minutiae of scholarly debate. The commentaries aimed to explain the biblical text to a generation of readers confronting models of critical scholarship and new discoveries from the Ancient Near East while remembering that the Old Testament is not simply another text from the ancient world. Although no uniform process of exegesis was required, all the original contributors were united in their conviction that the Old Testament remains the word of God for us today. That the original volumes fulfilled this role is evident from the way in which they continue to be used in so many parts of the world.

A crucial element of the original series was that it should offer an up-to-date reading of the text, and it is precisely for this reason that new volumes are required. The questions confronting readers in the first half of the twenty-first century are not necessarily those from the second half of the twentieth. Discoveries from the Ancient Near East continue to shed new light on the Old Testament, while emphases in exegesis have changed markedly. While remaining true to the goals of the initial volumes, the need for contemporary study of the text requires that the series as a whole be updated. This updating is not simply a matter of commissioning new volumes to replace the old. We have also taken the opportunity to update the format of the series to reflect a key emphasis from linguistics, which is that texts communicate in larger blocks rather than in shorter segments such as individual verses. Because of this, the treatment of each section of the text includes three segments. First, a short note on *Context* is offered, placing the passage under consideration in its literary setting within the book as well as noting any historical issues crucial to interpretation. The *Comment* segment then follows the traditional structure of the commentary, offering exegesis of the various components of a passage. Finally, a brief comment is made on *Meaning*, by which is meant the message that the passage seeks to communicate within the book, highlighting its key theological themes. This section brings together the detail of the *Comment* to show how the passage under consideration seeks to communicate as a whole.

Our prayer is that these new volumes will continue the rich heritage of the Tyndale Old Testament Commentaries and that they will continue to witness to the God who is made known in the text.

David G. Firth, Series Editor
Tremper Longman III, Consulting Editor

AUTHOR'S PREFACE

The first time I studied the book of Exodus in any depth was during the final year of my undergraduate course at the Irish Baptist College. As the only student in this class, I had to translate and exegete all the select chapters myself, which introduced me first-hand to many of the book's exegetical challenges, as well as enriching my understanding of the book's theological significance. However, as I look back now, I realize that I had merely scratched the surface – there was so much more to glean from a detailed examination of this seminal Old Testament book. Accordingly, I was delighted when Philip Duce gave me the opportunity to do so by writing this commentary, especially as it was for a series that had proved so helpful personally when, unlike today, relatively few evangelical commentaries on Exodus existed.

Regrettably, this project took much longer than I had initially planned, but hopefully the commentary is so much the better for it. I have certainly benefited greatly from the numerous commentaries, books and articles on Exodus that have been published since I was an undergraduate student, and especially those that appeared during the period when I was working on this commentary. While I cannot claim to have read all these secondary sources, or even every Exodus commentary, from cover to cover, I have certainly read enough to know that it's impossible to do justice to this extraordinary book and the scholarly literature it has generated in so few words. However, I hope that there is enough to orientate readers to its key exegetical issues and biblical-theological significance, as well as to whet readers' appetites for the more detailed comment and reflection that can be found elsewhere.

Like any research project, this could not have been undertaken without the help and generosity of others, to whom I am greatly indebted. My employer, Moore Theological College, has contributed to the completion of this commentary by the generous provision of several study leaves. Without these, I would never have got the job finished, so I want to express my sincere thanks to principals John Woodhouse and Mark Thompson, to past and present members of the college council, and to all those who have served alongside me on the faculty, for facilitating my work on this extra-curricular activity. Thanks also to Philip Duce, and more recently Thomas Creedy, for their patience and willingness to extend my contract until the project was completed. Special thanks to David Firth who (along with Philip) gently prodded me from time to time at Tyndale Fellowship, and who also provided really helpful feedback and suggestions once the manuscript finally arrived. Special thanks are also due to Pieter van der Veen, who kindly sent me a copy of his co-authored *Keine Posaunen vor Jericho*, and to one of my students, Steph Larkin, for sharing her expertise in the production of the line-drawn map (p. 27), something that was way beyond my ability.

It would be remiss of me not to mention my wife, Karen, whose interest in my writing and whose loving support in so many ways made it possible to devote so many hours of my time to projects such as this.

Like ancient Israel, I truly have so much to thank the Lord for. Not only for how he has graciously delivered me from slavery and death, but also for his generous provision of everything I need for life and godliness. Moreover, despite my sinful tendency to forget and be ungrateful, to grumble and complain, indeed even to indulge in idolatry (albeit in more subtle ways than Israel's god of gold), he mercifully forgives my sins and continually proves himself faithful time after time. Such is the God who makes himself known to Moses and Israel in Exodus, and who has supremely made himself known to us through the Lord Jesus Christ – the ultimate deliverer who ransoms and consecrates us with his own blood and makes his home among us, both now and always.

Paul R. Williamson

ABBREVIATIONS

AB	Anchor Bible
ABD	D. N. Freedman et al. (eds.), *The Anchor Bible Dictionary*, 6 vols. (Garden City, NY: Doubleday, 1992)
AnBib	Analecta Biblica
AOTC	Apollos Old Testament Commentary
AUSS	*Andrews University Seminary Studies*
BASOR	*Bulletin of the American Schools of Oriental Research*
BHS	K. Elliger and W. Rudolf (eds.), *Biblia Hebraica Stuttgartensia* (Stuttgart: Deutsche Bibelgesellschaft, 5th edn, 1997)
BRev	*The Bible Review*
BSac	*Bibliotheca Sacra*
CAH	I. E. S. Edwards et al. (eds.), *The Cambridge Ancient History*, 3rd edn, 4 vols. (Cambridge: Cambridge University Press, 1970–75)
COS	W. W. Hallo et al. (eds.), *The Context of Scripture*, 3 vols. (Leiden: Brill, 1997–2003)
ed(s).	editor(s)
edn	edition
EVV	English versions
FS	Festschrift
HALOT	L. Koehler and W. Baumgartner, *The Hebrew and Aramaic Lexicon of the Old Testament*, tr. M. E. J. Richardson, 5 vols. (Leiden: Brill, 1994–2000)

Heb.	Hebrew
Int	Interpretation Commentary Series
ITC	International Theological Commentary
JBL	*Journal of Biblical Literature*
JETS	*Journal of the Evangelical Theological Society*
JPS	Jewish Publication Society
JSOT	*Journal for the Study of the Old Testament*
JSOTSup	Journal for the Study of the Old Testament Supplement Series
NAC	New American Commentary
NCBC	New Century Bible Commentary
NIB	L. E. Keck (ed.), *The New Interpreter's Bible*, 12 vols. (Nashville: Abingdon Press, 1994–2002)
NIBC	New International Biblical Commentary
NIDOTTE	W. W. VanGemeren (ed.), *New International Dictionary of Old Testament Theology and Exegesis*, 5 vols. (Grand Rapids: Zondervan; London: Paternoster, 1997)
NIVAC	NIV Application Commentary
NSBT	New Studies in Biblical Theology
NT	New Testament
OT	Old Testament
OTL	Old Testament Library
PNTC	Pillar New Testament Commentary
SBLMS	Society of Biblical Literature Monograph Series
SJOT	*Scandinavian Journal of the Old Testament*
TOTC	Tyndale Old Testament Commentaries
TynBul	*Tyndale Bulletin*
VT	*Vetus Testamentum*
VTSup	Vetus Testamentum Supplement Series
WBC	Word Biblical Commentary
WTJ	*Westminster Theological Journal*
ZAW	*Zeitschrift für die alttestamentliche Wissenschaft*

Texts and versions

AT	Author's translation.
CSB	The Christian Standard Bible. Copyright © 2017

NJB   The New Jerusalem Bible, published and copyright © 1985 by Darton, Longman & Todd Ltd and Doubleday & Co., Inc., a division of Random House, Inc., is used by permission.

NLT   The *Holy Bible*, New Living Translation, copyright © 1996. Used by permission of Tyndale House Publishers, Inc., Carol Stream, Illinois 60189, USA. All rights reserved.

NRSV   The New Revised Standard Version of the Bible, Anglicized Edition, copyright © 1989, 1995 by the Division of Christian Education of the National Council of the Churches of Christ in the USA. Used by permission. All rights reserved.

SP   Samaritan Pentateuch.

TNK   TANAKH: The Holy Scriptures. The New JPS Translation according to the Traditional Hebrew Text. Copyright © 1985 by the Jewish Publication Society.

SELECT BIBLIOGRAPHY

Alexander, T. D. (1999), 'The Composition of the Sinai Narrative in Exodus XIX 1 – XXV 11', *VT* 49: 2–20.

—— (2017), *Exodus*, AOTC (London: Apollos; Downers Grove, IL: InterVarsity Press).

—— (2022), *From Paradise to the Promised Land: An Introduction to the Pentateuch*, 4th edn (Grand Rapids: Baker Academic).

Alt, A. (1949), 'Das Verbot des Diebstahls im Dekalog', subsequently published in A. Alt, *Kleine Schriften zur Geschichte des Volkes Israel*, vol. 1 (Munich: C. H. Beck'sche, 1953), pp. 333–340. (Tr. into English by R. A. Wilson as *Essays on Old Testament History and Religion* [Oxford: Blackwell, 1966].)

Alter, R. (1981), *The Art of Biblical Narrative* (New York: Basic Books).

—— (2004), *The Five Books of Moses: A Translation with Commentary* (New York: Norton).

Arichea, D. C. (1989), 'The Ups and Downs of Moses: Locating Moses in Exodus 19 – 33', *The Bible Translator* 40: 244–246.

Ashby, G. (1998), *Go Out and Meet God: A Commentary on the Book of Exodus*, ITC (Grand Rapids: Handsel).

Assmann, J. (1997), *Moses the Egyptian: The Memory of Egypt in Western Monotheism* (Cambridge: Harvard University Press).

—— (2015), 'Exodus and Memory', in T. E. Levy, T. Schneider and W. H. C. Propp (eds.), *Israel's Exodus in Transdisciplinary Perspective: Text, Archaeology, Culture, and Geoscience* (Cham: Springer), pp. 3–15.

Athas, G. (2008), 'The Creation of Israel: The Cosmic
    Proportions of the Exodus Event', in B. S. Rosner and P. R.
    Williamson (eds.), *Exploring Exodus: Literary, Theological, and
    Contemporary Approaches* (Nottingham: Apollos), pp. 30–59.
Averbeck, R. E. (1996), מִזְבֵּחַ' (*mizbēaḥ*), *NIDOTTE* 2: 888–908.
Baden, J. (2012), *The Composition of the Pentateuch* (New Haven:
    Yale University Press).
Baker, D. L. (2009), *Tight Fists or Open Hands? Wealth and Poverty in
    Old Testament Law* (Grand Rapids: Eerdmans).
—— (2017), *The Decalogue: Living as the People of God* (Downers
    Grove, IL: IVP Academic).
Barclay, J. M. G. (1992), 'Manipulating Moses: Exodus 2.10–15 in
    Egyptian Judaism and the New Testament', in R. P. Carroll
    (ed.), *Text as Pretext*, FS Robert Davidson, JSOTSup 138
    (Sheffield: Sheffield Academic Press), pp. 28–46.
Barth, K. (1951), *Church Dogmatics*, vol. 3.4 (Edinburgh: T&T
    Clark, 1961; tr. from German).
Bartholomew, C. G. (2021), *The Old Testament and God*, Old
    Testament Origins and the Question of God 1 (London:
    SPCK).
Batto, B. F. (1983), 'The Reed Sea: Requiescat in Pace', *JBL* 102:
    27–35.
—— (1984), 'Red Sea or Reed Sea: How the Mistake Was Made
    and What *Yam Sup* Really Means', *Biblical Archaeologist Reader*
    10.4: 57–63.
Berman, J. A. (2017), *Inconsistency in the Torah: Ancient Literary
    Convention and the Limits of Source Criticism* (New York: Oxford
    University Press).
Bietak, M. (1991), 'Egypt and Canaan during the Middle Bronze
    Age', *BASOR* 281: 27–72.
—— (2006), 'The Volcano Explains Everything – Or Does It?',
    Biblical Archaeology Review 32.6: 60–65.
Bimson, J. J. (1981), *Redating the Exodus and Conquest*, 2nd edn
    (Sheffield: Almond Press).
Blackburn, W. R. (2012), *The God Who Makes Himself Known: The
    Missionary Heart of the Book of Exodus*, NSBT (Nottingham:
    Apollos).
Block, D. I. (2011), 'Bearing the Name of the LORD with Honor:

A Homily on the Second Command of the Decalogue (Exod 20:7; Deut 5:11)', *BSac* 168: 20–31.

Boda, M. J. (2009), *A Severe Mercy: Sin and Its Remedy in the Old Testament* (Winona Lake, IN: Eisenbrauns).

Brenner, A. (1985), *The Israelite Women: Social Role and Literary Type in Biblical Narrative* (Sheffield: JSOT Press).

Brin, G. (2001), *The Concept of Time in the Bible and the Dead Sea Scrolls* (Leiden: Brill).

Bruckner, J. K. (2008), *Exodus*, NIBC (Peabody, MA: Hendrickson).

Brueggemann, W. (1994), 'Exodus', *NIB* 1: 675–981.

Carpenter, E. E. (1997), 'Exodus 18: Its Structure, Style, Motifs and Function in the Book of Exodus', in E. E. Carpenter (ed.), *A Biblical Itinerary: In Search of Method, Form, and Content*, FS George W. Coats, JSOTSup 240 (Sheffield: Sheffield Academic Press), pp. 91–108.

Cassuto, U. (1967), *A Commentary on the Book of Exodus* (Jerusalem: Magnes).

Childs, B. S. (1974), *The Book of Exodus: A Critical, Theological Commentary*, OTL (Louisville: Westminster Press).

Chirichigno, G. C. (1987), 'The Narrative Structure of Exodus 19 – 24', *Biblica* 68: 457–479.

Ciampa, R. E., and B. S. Rosner (2010), *The First Letter to the Corinthians*, PNTC (Grand Rapids: Eerdmans; Nottingham: Apollos).

Cohen, J. M. (1999), 'The Fertility of the Early Israelites', *Jewish Bible Quarterly* 27: 195–198.

Cole, R. A. (1973), *Exodus: An Introduction and Commentary*, TOTC (Leicester: Inter-Varsity Press).

Collins, A. (2008), 'The Biblical Pithom and Tell el-Maskhuta: A Critique of Some Recent Theories on Exodus 1,11', *SJOT* 22: 135–149.

Collins, S. (2012), *Let My People Go! Using Historical Synchronisms to Identify the Pharaoh of the Exodus* (Albuquerque: Trinity Southwest University Press).

Currid, J. D. (1995), 'The Egyptian Setting of the "Serpent" Confrontation in Exodus 7:8–13', *Biblische Zeitschrift* 39: 203–224.

—— (2013), *Against the Gods: The Polemical Theology of the Old Testament* (Wheaton, IL: Crossway).

Davies, E. W. (1995), *Numbers*, NCBC (Grand Rapids: Eerdmans; London: Marshall Pickering).

Davies, G. I. (1974), 'The Hebrew Text of Exodus viii 19 (EVV 23): An Emendation', *VT* 24: 489–492.

Davies, J. A. (2004), *A Royal Priesthood: Literary and Intertextual Perspectives on an Image of Israel in Exodus 19.6*, JSOTSup 395 (London: T&T Clark).

Davis, D. R. (1982), 'Rebellion, Presence, and Covenant: A Study in Exodus 32 – 34', *WTJ* 44: 71–87.

—— (2006), *The Word Became Flesh: How to Preach from Old Testament Narrative Texts* (Fearn, Ross-shire: Christian Focus).

Davis, J. J. (1986), *Moses and the Gods of Egypt: Studies in Exodus* (Grand Rapids: Baker).

DeRouchie, J. S. (2017), *How to Understand and Apply the Old Testament: Twelve Steps from Exegesis to Theology* (Phillipsburg: P&R).

Dever, W. G. (1992), 'The Chronology of Syria-Palestine in the Second Millennium B.C.E.: A Review of Current Issues', *BASOR* 288: 1–25.

Dozeman, T. B. (2009), *Exodus*, Eerdmans Critical Commentary (Grand Rapids: Eerdmans).

Driver, G. R. (1973), 'Affirmation by Exclamatory Negation', *Journal of the Ancient Near Eastern Society* 5: 107–122.

Durham, J. I. (1987), *Exodus*, WBC (Waco: Word).

Enns, P. (2000), *Exodus*, NIVAC (Grand Rapids: Zondervan).

Exum, J. C. (1983), '"You Shall Let Every Daughter Live": A Study of Exodus 1:8 – 2:10', *Semeia* 28: 63–82.

Finkelstein, I., and N. A. Silberman (2001), *The Bible Unearthed: Archaeology's New Vision of Ancient Israel and the Origin of Its Sacred Texts* (New York: Free Press).

Firth, D. (2021), *Joshua*, Evangelical Biblical Theology Commentary (Bellingham, WA: Lexham).

Ford, W. A. (2006), *God, Pharaoh and Moses: Explaining the Lord's Actions in the Exodus Plagues Narrative* (Milton Keynes: Paternoster).

Fretheim, T. E. (1991a), *Exodus*, Int (Louisville: John Knox).

—— (1991b), 'The Plagues as Ecological Signs of Historical
Disaster', *JBL* 110: 385–396.

Friedman, R. E. (2003), *The Bible with Sources Revealed: A
New View into the Five Books of Moses* (San Francisco:
HarperCollins).

—— (2017), *The Exodus: How It Happened and Why It Matters* (New
York: HarperCollins).

Garrett, D. A. (2014), *A Commentary on Exodus* (Grand Rapids:
Kregel Academic).

Gehrig, A. G. (2024), *The Passover: A Literary and Theological
Analysis of Exodus 12:1 – 13:16*, Studies in Biblical Literature 185
(Lausanne: Peter Lang).

Greenberg, M. (1997), *Ezekiel 21 – 37: A New Translation with
Introduction and Commentary* (New York: Doubleday).

Greenstein, E. L. (2000), 'Recovering "The Women Who Served
at the Entrance"', in G. Galil and M. Weinfeld (eds.), *Studies
in Historical Geography and Biblical Historiography*, FS Zecharia
Kallai, VTSup 81 (Leiden: Brill), pp. 165–173.

Halpern, B. (1983), *The Emergence of Israel in Canaan*, SBLMS 29
(Chico, CA: Scholars Press).

—— (2003), 'Eyewitness Testimony: Parts of Exodus Written
within Living Memory of the Event', *Biblical Archaeology Review*
29.5: 50–57.

Hamilton, V. (2011), *Exodus: An Exegetical Commentary* (Grand
Rapids: Baker).

Harman, A. M. (1988), 'The Interpretation of the Third
Commandment', *Reformed Theological Review* 47: 1–7.

Hasel, M. G. (2004), 'The Structure of the Final Hymnic-Poetic
Unit on the Merenptah Stela', *ZAW* 116: 75–81.

Hendel, R. (2001), 'The Exodus in Biblical Memory', *JBL* 120:
601–622.

—— (2015), 'The Exodus as Cultural Memory: Egyptian
Bondage and the Song of the Sea', in T. E. Levy, T. Schneider
and W. H. C. Propp (eds.), *Israel's Exodus in Transdisciplinary
Perspective: Text, Archaeology, Culture, and Geoscience* (Cham:
Springer), pp. 65–77.

—— (2021), 'The Exodus as Cultural Memory View', in M. D.
Janzen (ed.), *The Exodus: Historicity, Chronology, and Theological*

Implications, Counterpoints (Grand Rapids: Zondervan), pp. 235–255 (also pp. 71–75, 124–128, 175–177, 228–230, 280–282).

Hendrix, R. E. (1992), 'A Literary Structural Overview of Exod 25 – 40', *AUSS* 30: 123–138.

Hess, R. S. (2007), *Israelite Religions: An Archaeological and Biblical Survey* (Grand Rapids: Baker Academic; Nottingham: Apollos).

—— (2016), 'Onomastics of the Exodus Generation in the Book of Exodus', in J. K. Hoffmeier, A. R. Millard and G. A. Rendsburg (eds.), *'Did I Not Bring Israel out of Egypt?' Biblical, Archaeological, and Egyptological Perspectives on the Exodus Narratives*, Bulletin for Biblical Research Supplement 13 (Winona Lake, IN: Eisenbrauns), pp. 37–48.

Hoffman, Y. (1989), 'A North Israelite Typological Myth and a Judaean Historical Tradition: The Exodus in Hosea and Amos', *VT* 39: 169–182.

Hoffmeier, J. K. (1997), *Israel in Egypt: The Evidence for the Authenticity of the Exodus Traditions* (New York: Oxford University Press).

—— (2005), *Ancient Israel in Sinai: The Evidence for the Authenticity of the Wilderness Tradition* (New York: Oxford University Press).

—— (2007), 'Out of Egypt: The Archaeological Context of the Exodus', *Biblical Archaeology Review* 33: 30–41, 77.

—— (2012), '"These Things Happened": Why a Historical Exodus Is Essential for Theology', in J. K. Hoffmeier and D. R. Magary (eds.), *Do Historical Matters Matter to Faith? A Critical Appraisal of Modern and Postmodern Approaches to Scripture* (Wheaton, IL: Crossway), pp. 99–134.

—— (2016), 'Egyptian Religious Influences on the Early Hebrews', in J. K. Hoffmeier, A. R. Millard and G. A. Rendsburg (eds.), *'Did I Not Bring Israel out of Egypt?' Biblical, Archaeological, and Egyptological Perspectives on the Exodus Narratives*, Bulletin for Biblical Research Supplement 13 (Winona Lake, IN: Eisenbrauns), pp. 3–35.

—— (2021), 'The Thirteenth Century (Late Date) Exodus View', in M. D. Janzen (ed.), *The Exodus: Historicity, Chronology, and Theological Implications*, Counterpoints (Grand Rapids:

Zondervan), pp. 81–108 (also pp. 53–59, 129–134, 166–171, 216–221, 261–267).

Hornung, E., R. Krauss and D. A. Warburton (eds.) (2006), *Ancient Egyptian Chronology*, Handbook of Oriental Studies (Leiden: Brill).

Hort, G. (1957), 'The Plagues of Egypt', *ZAW* 69: 84–104.

—— (1958), 'The Plagues of Egypt', *ZAW* 70: 48–59.

Houtman, C. (1990), 'On the Pomegranates and Golden Bells of the High Priest's Mantle', *VT* 40: 223–229.

—— (1993, 1996, 2000), *Exodus*, 3 vols., Historical Commentary on the Old Testament (Kampen: Kok).

Huffmon, H. B. (2004), 'The Fundamental Code Illustrated: The Third Commandment', in W. Brown (ed.), *The Ten Commandments: The Reciprocity of Faithfulness* (Louisville: Westminster John Knox), 205–212.

Hugenberger, G. P. (1994), *Marriage as a Covenant: Biblical Law and Ethics as Developed from Malachi* (Leiden: Brill; Grand Rapids: Baker).

Humphreys, C. J. (1998), 'The Number of People in the Exodus from Egypt: Decoding Mathematically the Very Large Numbers in Numbers i and xxvi', *VT* 48: 196–213.

—— (2000), 'The Numbers in the Exodus from Egypt: A Further Appraisal', *VT* 50: 323–328.

—— (2003), *The Miracles of Egypt: A Scientist's Discovery of the Extraordinary Natural Causes of the Biblical Stories* (London: Continuum).

Imes, C. J. (2018), *Bearing YHWH's Name at Sinai: A Reexamination of the Name Command of the Decalogue*, Bulletin for Biblical Research Supplement 19 (University Park: Eisenbrauns).

Janzen, J. G. (1997), *Exodus*, Westminster Bible Companion (Louisville: Westminster John Knox).

Janzen, M. (ed.) (2021), *The Exodus: Historicity, Chronology, and Theological Implications*, Counterpoints (Grand Rapids: Zondervan).

Kaiser, W. C. (2008), 'Exodus', in T. Longman and D. E. Garland (eds.), *The Expositor's Bible Commentary*, rev. edn (Grand Rapids: Zondervan), 1: 333–561.

Keil, C. F., and F. Delitzsch (1989), *Commentary on the Old*

Testament: The Pentateuch; Genesis, Exodus 1 – 11, tr. J. Martin (Peabody, MA: Hendrickson; repr. from edition published by W. B. Eerdmans [Grand Rapids], 1986).

Kitchen, K. A. (1993), 'The Tabernacle – A Bronze Age Artifact', *Eretz-Israel* 24: 119–129.

—— (2003), *On the Reliability of the Old Testament* (Grand Rapids: Eerdmans).

Kitz, A. M. (1997), 'The Plural Forms of *'Urim* and *Thummim*', *JBL* 116: 401–410.

Leveen, A. B. (2010), 'Inside Out: Jethro, the Midianites and a Biblical Construction of the Outsider', *JSOT* 34: 395–417.

Levine, B. (1989), *Leviticus: The Traditional Hebrew Text with the New JPS Translation*, JPS Torah Commentary (Philadelphia: Jewish Publication Society).

Levine, M. (1989), *The Tabernacle: Its Structure and Utensils* (London: Soncino).

Longman, T. (2009), *How to Read Exodus* (Downers Grove, IL: InterVarsity Press).

McGeogh, K. M. (2006), 'Birth Bricks, Potter's Wheels, and Exodus 1,16', *Biblica* 87: 305–318.

Meier, S. A. (1992), *Speaking of Speaking: Marking Direct Discourse in the Hebrew Bible*, VTSup 46 (Leiden: Brill).

Mendenhall, G. E. (1958), 'The Census Lists of Numbers 1 and 26', *JBL* 77: 52–66.

Meyers, C. L. (1996), *The Tabernacle Menorah: A Synthetic Study of a Symbol from the Biblical Cult* (Missoula, MT: Scholars Press).

—— (2005), *Exodus*, New Cambridge Bible Commentary (Cambridge/New York: Cambridge University Press).

—— (2008), 'Framing Aaron: Incense Altar and Lamp of Oil in the Tabernacle Texts', in S. Dolansky (ed.), *Sacred History, Sacred Literature: Essays on Ancient Israel, the Bible, and Religion in Honor of R. E. Friedman on His Sixtieth Birthday* (Winona Lake, IN: Eisenbrauns), pp. 13–21.

Milgrom, J. (1970), *Studies in Levitical Terminology I: The Encroacher and the Levite; The Term 'Aboda* (Berkeley: University of California Press).

—— (1990), *Numbers*, JPS Torah Commentary (Philadelphia: Jewish Publication Society).

—— (1991), *Leviticus 1 – 16*, AB (New York: Doubleday).

Millard, A. R. (2016), 'Moses the Tongue-Tied Singer', in J. K. Hoffmeier, A. R. Millard and G. A. Rendsburg (eds.), *'Did I Not Bring Israel out of Egypt?' Biblical, Archaeological, and Egyptological Perspectives on the Exodus Narratives*, Bulletin for Biblical Research Supplement 13 (Winona Lake, IN: Eisenbrauns), pp. 133–142.

Moberly, R. W. L. (1983), *At the Mountain of God: Story and Theology in Exodus 32 – 34*, JSOTSup 22 (Sheffield: JSOT Press).

—— (1992), *The Old Testament of the Old Testament: Patriarchal Narratives and Mosaic Yahwism*, Overtures to Biblical Theology (Minneapolis: Fortress).

—— (2011), 'Miracles in the Hebrew Bible', in G. H. Twelftree (ed.), *The Cambridge Companion to Miracles* (Cambridge/New York: Cambridge University Press), pp. 57–74.

Moran, W. L. (1963), 'The Scandal of the "Great Sin" at Ugarit', *Journal of Near Eastern Studies* 18: 280–281.

Morschauser, S. (2003), 'Potters' Wheels and Pregnancies: A Note on Exodus 1:16', *JBL* 122: 731–733.

Motyer, J. A. (2005), *The Message of Exodus: The Days of Our Pilgrimage*, The Bible Speaks Today (Leicester: Inter-Varsity Press).

Mullen, E. T. (1997), *Ethnic Myths and Pentateuchal Foundations: A New Approach to the Formation of the Pentateuch* (Atlanta: Scholars Press).

Noonan, B. J. (2016), 'Egyptian Loanwords as Evidence for the Authenticity of the Exodus and Wilderness Traditions', in J. K. Hoffmeier, A. R. Millard and G. A. Rendsburg (eds.), *'Did I Not Bring Israel out of Egypt?' Biblical, Archaeological and Egyptological Perspectives on the Exodus Narratives*, Bulletin for Biblical Research Supplement 13 (Winona Lake, IN: Eisenbrauns), pp. 49–67.

Noth, M. (1962), *Exodus: A Commentary*, OTL (London: SCM; Philadelphia: Westminster).

Novick, T. (2009), '*H'myn* in Jud 11,20 and the Semantics of Assent', *ZAW* 121: 577–583.

O'Brien, P. T. (2010), *The Letter to the Hebrews*, PNTC (Grand Rapids: Eerdmans; Nottingham: Apollos).

Paul, S. M. (1970), *Studies in the Book of the Covenant in the Light of Cuneiform and Biblical Law*, VTSup 18 (Leiden: Brill).

—— (1992), 'Exodus 1:21: "To Found a Family"; A Biblical and Akkadian Idiom', *Maarav* 8: 139–142.

Peels, H. G. L. (1994), 'On the Wings of the Eagle (Dtn 32,11): An Old Misunderstanding', *ZAW* 106: 300–303.

Polzin, R. (1975), '"The Ancestress of Israel in Danger" in Danger', *Semeia* 3: 81–97.

Propp, W. H. (1993), 'That Bloody Bridegroom (Exodus iv 24–6)', *VT* 43: 495–518.

—— (1999), *Exodus 1 – 18: A New Translation with Introduction and Commentary*, AB (New York: Doubleday).

—— (2006), *Exodus 19 – 40: A New Translation with Introduction and Commentary*, AB (New York: Doubleday).

Reinhartz, A. (1998), *'Why Ask My Name?' Anonymity and Identity in Biblical Narrative* (New York: Oxford University Press).

Rendsburg, G. A. (1988), 'Bilingual Wordplay in the Bible', *VT* 38: 354–357.

—— (1992), 'The Date of the Exodus and the Conquest/ Settlement: The Case for the 1100s', *VT* 42: 510–527.

—— (2001), 'An Additional Note to Two Recent Articles on the Number of People in the Exodus from Egypt and the Large Numbers in Numbers i and xxvi', *VT* 51: 392–396.

—— (2016), 'The Literary Unity of the Exodus Narrative', in J. K. Hoffmeier, A. R. Millard and G. A. Rendsburg (eds.), *'Did I Not Bring Israel out of Egypt?' Biblical, Archaeological, and Egyptological Perspectives on the Exodus Narratives*, Bulletin for Biblical Research Supplement 13 (Winona Lake, IN: Eisenbrauns), pp. 113–132.

—— (2021), 'The Twelfth-Century Exodus View', in M. D. Janzen (ed.), *The Exodus: Historicity, Chronology, and Theological Implications*, Counterpoints (Grand Rapids: Zondervan), pp. 183–209 (also pp. 66–70, 121–123, 172–174, 231–234, 274–279).

Rendtorff, R. (1998), *The Covenant Formula: An Exegetical and Theological Investigation* (Edinburgh: T&T Clark).

Reviv, H. (1989), *The Elders in Ancient Israel: A Study of a Biblical Institution* (Jerusalem: Magnes).

Robinson, B. P. (1997), 'Moses at the Burning Bush', *JSOT* 75: 107–122.

Rohl, D. (2015), *Exodus: Myth or History?* (St Louis Park, MN: Thinking Man Media).

Rosner, B. S., and P. R. Williamson (eds.) (2008), *Exploring Exodus: Literary, Theological and Contemporary Approaches* (Nottingham: Apollos).

Sailhamer, J. (2009), *The Meaning of the Pentateuch: Revelation, Composition and Interpretation* (Downers Grove, IL: InterVarsity Press).

Sarna, N. M. (1991), *Exodus*, JPS Torah Commentary (Philadelphia: Jewish Publication Society).

Seitz, C. R. (1998), 'The Call of Moses and the "Revelation" of the Divine Name: Source-Critical Logic and Its Legacy', in C. R. Seitz, *Word Without End: The Old Testament as Abiding Theological Witness* (Grand Rapids: Eerdmans), pp. 229–247.

Shead, A. G. (2000), 'Sabbath', in T. D. Alexander and B. S. Rosner (eds.), *New Dictionary of Biblical Theology* (Leicester: Inter-Varsity Press), pp. 745–750.

Siebert-Hommes, J. (1992), 'Die Geburtsgeschichte des Mose innerhalb des Erzählzusammenhangs von Exodus i und ii', *VT* 42: 398–404.

Smith, M. A. (2001), 'The Poetics of Exodus 15 and Its Position in the Book of Exodus', in L. Boadt and M. S. Smith (eds.), *Imagery and Imagination in Biblical Literature: Essays in Honor of Aloysius Fitzgerald*, Catholic Biblical Quarterly Monograph Series 32 (Washington: Catholic Biblical Association of America), pp. 23–34.

—— (2010), *Exodus*, New Collegeville Bible Commentary (Collegeville, MN: Liturgical Press).

Sohn, S.-T. (1999), '"I Will Be Your God and You Will Be My People": The Origin and Background of the Covenant Formula', in R. Chazan et al. (eds.), *Ki Baruch Hu: Ancient Near Eastern, Biblical, and Judaic Studies*, FS Baruch A. Levine (Winona Lake, IN: Eisenbrauns), pp. 355–372.

Sprinkle, J. M. (1993), 'The Interpretation of Exodus 21:22–25 (lex talionis) and Abortion', *WTJ* 55: 233–253.

—— (1994), *'The Book of the Covenant': A Literary Approach*, JSOTSup 174 (Sheffield: Sheffield Academic Press).

—— (2004), 'Law and Narrative in Exodus 19 – 24', *JETS* 47.2: 235–252.

—— (2006), *Biblical Law and Its Relevance: A Christian Understanding and Ethical Application for Today of the Mosaic Regulations* (Lanham, MD: University Press of America).

Steinmann, A. E. (2019), *Genesis*, TOTC (London: Inter-Varsity Press).

Stek, J. H. (1986), 'What Happened to the Chariot Wheels of Exodus 14:25?', *JBL* 105: 293–294.

Sternberg, M. (1998), *Hebrews between Cultures: Group Portraits and National Literature* (Bloomington: Indiana University Press).

Stuart, D. K. (2006), *Exodus*, NAC (Nashville: Broadman & Holman).

Thomas, K. J. (1976), 'Liturgical Citations in the Synoptics', *New Testament Studies* 22: 205–214.

Tigay, J. H. (1996), *Deuteronomy*, JPS Torah Commentary (Philadelphia: Jewish Publication Society).

Trible, P. (1989), 'Bringing Miriam out of the Shadows', *BRev* 5: 14–25.

Van Seters, J. (2003), *A Law Book for the Diaspora: Revision in the Study of the Covenant Code* (Oxford/New York: Oxford University Press).

Veen, P. van der (2018), 'Why Mount Horeb Is Not in Saudi Arabia and Why the Crossing of the Sea of Reeds Did Not Occur at the Gulf of Aqabah', Engl. tr. of Appendix B in U. Zerbst and P. van der Veen (eds.), *Keine Posaunen vor Jericho*, 3rd edn (SCM Hänssler), accessed 7 June 2024 via Academia: <https://www.academia.edu/108034936/Why_Mount_Horeb_is_not_in_Saudi_Arabia_and_why_the_crossing_of_the_Sea_of_Reeds_did_not_occur_at_the_Gulf_of_Aqabah?email_work_card=thumbnail>.

Waltke, B. K. (2007), *An Old Testament Theology: An Exegetical, Canonical, and Thematic Approach* (Grand Rapids: Zondervan).

Walton, J. H. (2006), *Ancient Near Eastern Thought and the Old Testament: Introducing the Conceptual World of the Hebrew Bible* (Grand Rapids: Baker Academic).

Webb, B. G. (2008), 'Heaven on Earth: The Significance of the Tabernacle in Its Literary and Theological Context', in B. S.

Rosner and P. R. Williamson (eds.), *Exploring Exodus: Literary, Theological and Contemporary Approaches* (Nottingham: Apollos), pp. 154–176.

Weems, R. J. (1992), 'The Hebrew Women Are Not Like the Egyptian Women: The Ideology of Race, Gender and Sexual Reproduction in Exodus 1', *Semeia* 59: 25–34.

Wenham, G. J. (1978), 'Law and the Legal System in the Old Testament', in B. N. Kaye and G. J. Wenham (eds.), *Law, Morality and the Bible* (Downers Grove, IL: InterVarsity Press), pp. 24–52.

—— (1980), 'The Religion of the Patriarchs', in A. R. Millard and D. J. Wiseman (eds.), *Essays on the Patriarchal Narratives* (Leicester: Inter-Varsity Press), pp. 157–188.

—— (1994), *Genesis 16 – 50*, WBC (Dallas: Word).

—— (2003), *Exploring the Old Testament: A Guide to the Pentateuch* (Downers Grove, IL: InterVarsity Press).

Wenham, J. W. (1967), 'The Large Numbers of the Old Testament', *TynBul* 18: 19–53.

Westbrook, R. (1994), 'What Is the Covenant Code?', in B. M. Levinson (ed.), *Theory and Method in Biblical and Cuneiform Law: Revision, Interpolation and Development*, JSOTSup 181 (Sheffield: Sheffield Academic Press), pp. 15–36.

Williamson, P. R. (2000), 'Promise and Fulfilment: The Territorial Inheritance', in P. Johnston and P. Walker (eds.), *The Land of Promise: Biblical, Theological and Contemporary Perspectives* (Leicester: Apollos), pp. 15–34.

—— (2007), *Sealed with an Oath: Covenant in God's Purpose*, NSBT 23 (Nottingham: Apollos).

—— (2008), 'Promises with Strings Attached: Covenant and Law in Exodus 19 – 24', in B. S. Rosner and P. R. Williamson (eds.), *Exploring Exodus: Literary, Theological and Contemporary Approaches* (Nottingham: Apollos), pp. 89–122.

—— (2025), '"Then They Will Know . . .": Hope for the World in Ezekiel 1 – 39?', in J. Grant, D. Firth and A. Lo (eds.), *Hope for the World*, FS J. G. McConville (Wilmore, KY: GlossaHouse), pp. 81–92.

Wright, C. J. H. (2021), *Exodus*, The Story of God Bible Commentary (Grand Rapids: Zondervan).

Yamauchi, E. M. (2004), *Africa and the Bible* (Grand Rapids: Baker).

Yee, G. A. (2009), '"Take This Child and Suckle It for Me": Wet Nurses and Resistance in Ancient Israel', *Biblical Theology Bulletin* 39: 180–189.

Youngblood, R. (1994), 'Counting the Ten Commandments', *BRev* 10: 30–35, 50, 52.

Zlotnick-Sivan, H. (2004), 'Moses the Persian? Exodus 2, the "Other" and Biblical "Mnemo-history"', *ZAW* 116: 189–205.

INTRODUCTION

1. Exodus in the Pentateuch and beyond

The title 'Exodus', meaning 'departure', derives from the ancient Greek translation of the Old Testament (LXX), which uses the genitive form of the Greek noun *exodos* to describe Israel's emancipation or 'going forth' (19:1; Heb. *lĕṣēʾt*) from enslavement in Egypt. The Christian title thus encapsulates one of the book's key concerns: the realization of God's promise to Abram that his offspring would be emancipated from servitude and mistreatment in a foreign land (cf. Gen. 15:13–14).

Like the rest of the Pentateuch, the book's Jewish title ('these are the names of') reflects its opening words in the Masoretic Text (*wĕʾēllê šĕmôt*), which refer to those who migrated with Jacob to Egypt generations earlier (1:1–4; cf. Gen. 46:8–27). As thus anticipated, the ensuing narrative in Exodus presents the sequel to the final section of Genesis (cf. Gen. 37:2), picking up the plot where Genesis ended (Gen. 50:24–25) and recounting key stages in its prophetic fulfilment – a focus that is maintained in the rest of the Pentateuch and beyond.

2. Composition and date

Exodus makes no direct claims about its author; thus any conclusions about its authorship and date of composition must be inferred from its contents or extrapolated from subsequent associations with Moses. On the basis of the latter (see especially Mark 12:26; Luke 2:22), Moses has traditionally been considered the author of Exodus (along with the rest of the Pentateuch; cf. 2 Kgs 14:6; Ezra 6:18; Neh. 13:1; John 7:23). However, Moses cannot have compiled its final/canonical form, as is clear from material that reflects a later time in Israel's history (Exod. 16:35–36; cf. Josh. 5:11–12).[1] This, along with the likelihood that most Old Testament references to 'the Book of Moses' (2 Chr. 25:4; 35:12; Ezra 6:18; Neh. 13:1), 'the Law of Moses' (Josh. 8:32; 1 Kgs 2:3; 2 Kgs 23:25; 2 Chr. 23:18; 30:16; Ezra 3:2; 7:6; Dan. 9:11, 13) or 'the Book of the Law of Moses' (cf. Josh. 8:31; 23:6; 2 Kgs 14:6; Neh. 8:1) refer only to the legislation now preserved in Deuteronomy 5 – 26 (or 5 – 30),[2] cautions against ascribing the composition of Exodus (and perhaps even a proto-Pentateuch) to Moses. Moreover, even some of the New Testament associations of the Pentateuch with Moses (Mark 12:26; Luke 2:22; 16:29, 31; 24:27, 44; Acts 13:39; 28:23) do not necessarily imply Mosaic authorship but could simply reflect his role or significance within the corpus, as when 'Moses' is employed as shorthand for the entire Old Testament (e.g. Rom. 10:19; 2 Cor. 3:15). Elsewhere, however, the writing of material is expressly ascribed to Moses (Mark 10:5; 12:19; Luke 20:28, 37; John 1:45; 5:46–47; Rom. 10:5). Admittedly, when this refers to specific things Moses is said to have recorded, authorship of the entire corpus cannot necessarily be inferred. Even so, according to explicit statements within Exodus itself (cf. 17:14; 24:4; 34:27–28),

---

1   While this is the only such text in Exodus, there are several other post-Mosaica scattered throughout the Pentateuch.

2   See Alexander (2022: 343–345), who nevertheless maintains that a written form of Deuteronomy, along with other 'pre-Pentateuchal' traditions, existed before the establishment of Israel's monarchy and Israel's earliest classical prophets.

Moses recorded at least some material that was subsequently incorporated into this book. In addition, the fact that he was the only eyewitness to several recorded events may further suggest that he contributed, albeit indirectly, to its contents. On this basis, conservative scholars have inferred that, whatever pre-existing material or subsequent compilation its canonical form reflects, Moses made some contribution to the contents of this book.

Critical scholars, however, typically reject any such authorial role for Moses, postulating for the Pentateuch much later oral traditions, literary sources (traditionally labelled J, E, D and P)[3] and editors/redactors who were responsible for combining such material at various stages in Israel's history. Thus understood, like the Pentateuch as a whole, the canonical book of Exodus is a composite of various traditions and written sources discernible in some cases by their discrete vocabulary or distinctive emphases, but more significantly, by the perceived disjointedness of the canonical text which may be resolved by isolating the different underlying sources. For the most easily accessible presentation of such a source-critical analysis of Exodus, see Friedman's colour-coded analysis with explanatory notations (2003: 119–189).

The speculative and subjective nature of such enquiry is highlighted by the lack of consensus among source critics over the number of such hypothetical sources, as well as their relative dating or content. For instance, while some (e.g. Propp 1999,

---

3 Formulated most influentially by Julius Wellhausen in his *Prolegomena to the History of Israel* (the original German edition, *Prolegomena zur Geschichte Israels*, was first published in 1878), the classic Documentary Hypothesis not only distinguished these four primary sources, but reconstructed an evolving history of Jewish religion on the basis of the relative dating and redaction postulated for them – J/E reflecting the most primitive stages, and P the most developed stage. Such historical reconstruction is eschewed by some contemporary advocates (e.g. 'neo-documentarians' such as Joel Baden [2012]), who are also critical of methodological flaws (such as the use of style and terminology to differentiate sources, or the assumption that different sources generally shared the same plots) reflected in the classical approach.

2006) still consider it possible to distinguish E from J in Exodus, most contemporary critics reject the independent existence of E altogether and allow for a much greater influence of the Deuteronomist in Exodus. Accordingly, Dozeman (2009: 48–51) distinguishes between two major sources in Exodus: the *P History* and the *Non-P History*. While the classical Documentary Hypothesis dominated such discussion for almost a century, since the 1970s there has been a significant shift away from the traditional source-critical analysis, with a variety of fresh attempts to explain how Exodus and the rest of the Pentateuch took shape. Rather than a gradual development over several centuries, some contemporary scholars (e.g. Mullen 1997; Van Seters 2003) posit a post-exilic composition for the book of Exodus, primarily addressed to Jewish exiles or diaspora whose situation was somewhat analogous to the literary scenario depicted in Exodus.

Such a theory, however, fails to account for the ubiquity of the Exodus traditions throughout the Old Testament (see section 4a below), which strongly suggests their antiquity unless all such material is similarly labelled post-exilic. Given its central significance for Israel's faith and worship, it is rather difficult to imagine pre-exilic Israelite Yahwism without an exodus at the core of its foundational beliefs.

A more fundamental criticism, however, relates to the dubious value of such source-critical discussion, including its revitalization by neo-documentarians. Not only has it failed to establish indisputable, objective criteria for discerning its putative sources, but it has arguably obstructed biblical interpretation by focusing on the prehistory of the text rather than on its final form. Diachronic approaches such as source criticism primarily focus on the process or stages through which a book was created, and thus tend to atomize the text rather than examine its canonical form as a work of literature. As wryly noted by Polzin (1975: 82–83):

> Traditional biblical scholarship has spent most of its efforts in disassembling the works of a complicated watch before our amazed eyes without apparently realizing that similar efforts by and large have not succeeded in putting the parts back together again in a significant or meaningful way.

In contrast, synchronic or discourse-orientated approaches focus on Exodus as a coherent work of literature, focusing on the parts in the light of the whole and vice versa. While it is sometimes assumed that diachronic investigation will complement such synchronic analysis, this seems seldom, if ever, true in practice. Rather, as Garrett (2014: 19) suggests:

> A distressing and inevitable outcome . . . is that it leads to commentaries that have more to say about the supposed sources of Exodus than they do about the canonical text. That is, we come away with little in the way of an interpretation of the one document that we know to be real, the book of Exodus.

Where source critics have often assumed literary disunity and rejected the theological integrity of the canonical text, more recent studies have sought to demonstrate a high degree of literary and theological coherence.[4] Though such studies may not necessarily dismiss source-critical analysis entirely, their more integrated reading of Exodus provides compelling evidence for the cohesion of its various parts, as well as unlocking important theological nuances that might otherwise be missed. Indeed, as Rendsburg (2016: 132) masterfully demonstrates in relation to Exodus 1 – 14: 'The partition of this material into its hypothesized J, E, and P components strips the narrative of its literary structure, belletristic artistry, textual interconnections, and at times its theological messages.'

Accordingly, this commentary will concentrate not on disparate (and hypothetical) underlying sources – whether oral or literary

---

4 E.g. Rendsburg's (2016) defence of the literary unity of Exod. 1 – 14. See also arguments for the coherence of the Passover narrative (Gehrig 2024), and likewise for the Book of the Covenant presented by Sprinkle (1994), Westbrook (1994) and Alexander (1999; updated and expanded in 2022: 302–330). For a recent and penetrating critique of the premises and methodological weaknesses of standard source-critical analyses, see Berman 2017.

– but rather on the canonical text and the theological message it communicates to its ancient and modern readers.

3. Structure and thematic cohesion

In terms of the book's overall structure, numerous suggestions have been proposed. For some, the geographical location or movement is key. Accordingly, some suggest a twofold division such as: (1) Israel's Departure from Egypt (1 – 18); (2) Israel's Encampment at Sinai (19 – 40). However, there is no consensus over where the exodus account ends (12:50; 14:31; 15:21 or 18:27?) and the second main part of the book begins. The book may also be divided into *three* main geographical sections, again understood in various ways: for example, (1) Israel in Egypt (1:1 – 13:16); (2) Israel's Journey from Sukkot to Sinai (13:17 – 18:27); Israel at Sinai (19:1 – 40:38). Alternatively, (1) Exodus from Egypt (1:1 – 15:21); (2) Testing in the Wilderness (15:22 – 18:27); Worship at Sinai (19:1 – 40:38). As these examples illustrate, discerning the book's structure on the basis of geography is not quite so straightforward as it may at first appear. Moreover, it generally overlooks the fact that some of the early material (2:16 – 4:28) is not actually set in Egypt at all, but in Midian and the Sinai region. Accordingly, a bipartite or tripartite division based on geography alone does not exactly match the book's contents.

Others have utilized more thematic analyses as the basis for a tripartite division. Thus Cassuto (1967) suggests: (1) Bondage and Liberation (1 – 17); The Torah and Its Precepts (18 – 24); The Tabernacle and Its Service (25 – 40); whereas Kaiser (2008) proposes: (1) Divine Redemption (1:1 – 18:27); (2) Divine Morality (19:1 – 24:18); Divine Worship (25:1 – 40:38); similarly, Davis (2006): (1) The God Who Delivers (1 – 18); (2) The God Who Demands (19 – 24); (3) The God Who Dwells (25 – 40). The obvious advantage of these more thematic approaches is that they draw out the major theological emphases of the book. The problem, however, is that they are too reductionistic, making the literary structure and theological focus more compact than it actually is.

Not surprisingly, therefore, still others provide more detailed outlines. For example, a sixfold division is suggested by Bruckner (2008: 2):[5]

I.   1 – 14   Exit from Egypt
II.   15 – 18   Journey to Sinai
III. 19 – 24   Ten Commandments and the Book of the Covenant
IV.   25 – 31   Tabernacle Instructions
V.   32 – 34   Golden Calf Crisis and God's Forgiveness
VI.   35 – 40   Tabernacle Built and God's Dwelling Presence

In a similar vein Fretheim (1991a: ix–xii) proposes a ninefold division:

1 Growth and Bondage in Egypt (1 – 2)
2 Moses and God: Call and Dialogue (3:1 – 7:7)
3 The Plagues (7:8 – 11:10)
4 From Passover to Praise (12:1 – 15:21)
5 The Wilderness Wanderings (15:22 – 18:27)
6 Law and Covenant (19:1 – 24:18)
7 The Plan of the Tabernacle (25:1 – 31:18)
8 The Fall and Restoration of Israel (32:1 – 34:35)
9 God Fills the Tabernacle (35:1 – 40:38)

Though these are certainly more complete outlines of the book's contents, they are arguably less helpful in expressing its theological cohesion (i.e. the thematic links or connections between the various parts) and could unfortunately give the impression that the book is somewhat disjointed. To address this problem, it is perhaps best to employ a combination of primary and secondary headings, which together articulate *both* the narrative progression *and* the primary theological foci that unfold within the book. For instance:

---

5   Blackburn's structure (2012) is almost identical (1:1 – 15:21; 15:22 – 18:27; 19 – 24; 25 – 31; 32 – 34; 35 – 40), although he uses different titles, especially for the first three sections.

I: Enslavement and Exodus (1:1 – 13:16)

1. Oppression and the promise of deliverance (1:1 – 4:31)
2. Pharaoh's recalcitrance in the face of Yahweh's mighty acts of judgment (5:1 – 11:10)
3. Redemption and consecration of Israel's firstborn (12:1 – 13:16)

II: Deliverance and protection (13:17 – 18:27)

4. Rescue and triumph at the Sea (13:17 – 15:21)
5. Yahweh's provision and instruction in the wilderness (15:22 – 17:7)
6. Victory over the Amalekites (17:8–16)
7. Response and advice of Jethro (18:1–27)

III: Covenant and worship (19:1 – 40:38)

8. Theophany at Sinai (19:1–25)
9. Israel's covenant obligations disclosed (20:1 – 23:33)
10. The sealing of the covenant (24:1–18)
11. Yahweh's instructions for worship (25:1 – 31:18)
12. The covenant broken and re-established (32:1 – 34:35)
13. Construction and consecration of Yahweh's tabernacle (35:1 – 40:38)

4. Historical and archaeological issues

a. The historicity of the narrative

In a post-Enlightenment world, the idea of a God who intervenes directly in human affairs might well be dismissed as intellectually naïve. A series of natural disasters may be less difficult to imagine in the twenty-first century, although the scale, timing, discriminating effects and their manipulation by a shepherd's rod must seem more at home in the world of fiction. As for water being transformed into blood, wooden sticks becoming living reptiles, fresh water gushing from a dry rock or seas piling up into walls – all this may suggest the realm of fantasy rather than the world as we know it. On account of these and other extraordinary features in the biblical account,[6] the historical veracity of Exodus is often

---

6   See the relevant sections of the commentary for a more detailed discussion.

dismissed, especially by those of an anti-supernaturalist mindset. However, it is not just the miracles of Exodus that have come under such sceptical scrutiny. So too has the major event it recounts (Israel's deliverance from oppression in Egypt) and related details.

Some contemporary scholars question whether such an exodus happened at all, pointing to its absence in extant Egyptian records and the complete lack of archaeological corroboration. However, neither objection is compelling: (1) Official Egyptian records, like most ancient texts, emphasize military success rather than humiliating defeat. Thus, Egypt's official annals or royal inscriptions would not typically record an event like the exodus, or else would depict it very differently (in terms of an Egyptian triumph rather than an embarrassing defeat). (2) The climate in the eastern Nile Delta and the Sinai wilderness is not conducive to the long-term survival of material remains, including non-inscriptional records on parchment or clay tablets. It is thus unreasonable to expect archaeological evidence for a particular contingent of Semitic slaves who, after their hasty departure, dwelt only in perishable tents until they settled in Canaan. Admittedly, a large-scale military *conquest* would undoubtedly leave some evidence behind (e.g. a stratigraphical layer of destruction). However, according to the biblical record only three Canaanite cities were actually destroyed (Jericho [Josh. 6:24], Ai [Josh. 8:28] and Hazor [Josh. 11:11]).[7] Moreover, the initial Israelite settlement in Canaan was a somewhat limited and protracted affair (cf. Josh. 13 – 19). Consequently, large swathes of the land (e.g. the coastal plain and the Jordan valley) remained occupied by Canaanites and in some measure under the control of Egypt for some considerable time. All these factors have a significant bearing on the nature and amount of corroborating evidence we should expect for the biblical accounts of Israel's exodus and settlement.

Moreover, there are also good reasons for concluding that the biblical account is reliable: (1) It is most unlikely that any

---

7 While archaeological excavation has unearthed various destructive layers, some of these locations and their exact historical timeline have been disputed.

people would invent such a story of their national origins: as slaves oppressed by a powerful neighbour. (2) The Egyptians employed large numbers of Semitic slaves in the second millennium BC to make bricks for their building projects. (3) Authentic place names (e.g. Ram[e]ses) are unlikely to have been remembered centuries later. (4) Tent-shrines such as the tabernacle are attested in Egypt and Canaan from the second millennium BC.

While none of these observations prove that the biblical account is true, they certainly suggest that the level of scepticism reflected in some circles today is unwarranted. This is especially so in the case of those who contend that Israel's origin story is nothing more than 'a brilliant product of the human imagination',[8] but it also applies to those who view it as a 'cultural memory',[9] that is, a mixture of history and fiction which 'distorts, omits, and fiction-alizes aspects of the past'.[10]

Not all of today's sceptics, however, deny the exodus account entirely. Some discern a historical basis of some kind, but radically downplay its significance – either turning it into a trivial event that was grossly inflated by Israel's later myth-makers, or claiming that the escape/expulsion motif was borrowed or appropriated from other people groups such as the Hyksos, Semitic foreigners who ruled over Lower Egypt from Avaris from c.1650 BC until they were successfully expelled by Ahmose I (1550–1525 BC), who established the New Kingdom. Thus understood, some kind of Semitic departure(s) from Egypt did actually take place, but certainly not on the scale or significance that the biblical narrative implies, and not incorporating all, if indeed any, of Israel's tribal predecessors.

Along such lines Friedman (2017) argues that a historical exodus involved just Levites, who (he claims) alone attest Egyptian personal names (Moses, Hophni, Phinehas, Hur) and

---

8   Finkelstein and Silberman 2001: 1.
9   See Assmann (1997, 2015) and Hendel (2001, 2015, and in Janzen 2021).
10 Hendel (in Janzen 2021: 235).

only *subsequently* became part of Israel;[11] by reciting and celebrating this exodus tradition (cf. Deut. 6:21) every Israelite came to accept it as their own. Though a critical scholar's defence of a historical exodus is welcome, and Friedman's 'historical exodus' may address some of the usual objections, his proposal leans heavily on a number of exegetical inferences and source-critical assumptions that are open to debate. Perhaps most glaring is the fact that Hur does not appear to have been a Levite (Exod. 31:2; 35:30; 38:22) or – if this is a different Hur from the one associated with Moses and Aaron back in chapters 17 and 24 – was clearly not an exclusively Levite name.

However, the major problem for all such theories is the ubiquitous biblical attestation of *Israel*'s exodus tradition: 'it is the most frequently mentioned event in the OT', mentioned outside Exodus itself some 120 times, and across almost every literary genre.[12] As Hoffmeier (in Janzen 2021: 81) observes, the answer to the prophet's rhetorical question 'Did I not bring Israel up from Egypt?' (Amos 9:7) is obvious, and evidently something his audience did not dispute. This is hardly surprising in view of the prominence and significance of this 'out of Egypt' motif throughout the Old Testament. Excluding within Exodus itself, this or a closely parallel expression is used 114 times with respect to Israel's exodus. On top of this there are numerous allusions (cf. Lev. 18:3; Deut. 5:15; 11:2–4; 24:18; Josh. 9:9; 1 Sam. 2:27; Neh. 9:9–12; Pss 66:6; 78:11–54).[13] The exodus is thus the defining

---

11 While others (e.g. Hoffmeier 2016) also note a predominance of Egyptian names among Levites, they do not support Friedman's more radical conclusion. Hess, who is not convinced that all such names reflect an Egyptian etymology, significantly concludes that all are 'appropriate to the time when the events of the exodus and the surrounding narrative took place' and that none appears only in the first millennium, and so cannot 'be used to support the argument for the narrative's being a fictional account written by scribes in the middle of the first millennium BC' (2016: 47).

12 Hoffman 1989: 170.

13 For all the relevant texts, see Alexander 2017: 5–6.

event in Israel's national identity and lies at the heart of Mosaic Yahwism. It underpins Israel's theological exclusivity (Exod. 20:2–3; Hos. 13:4), as well as God's covenantal demands (Deut. 24:18, 22; Jer. 31:32) and Israel's obligations (Exod. 22:21; 23:9; 23:15). Simply put, little if any of the Old Testament makes much sense without Israel's exodus from Egypt.

A second major obstacle to discounting the exodus account as gross fabrication is the number of authentic features it reflects. For example, archaeological excavation in the north-eastern Nile Delta has uncovered artefacts and burial customs attesting to a preponderance of *Asiatics* (Semitic-speaking foreigners of Syro-Canaanite ethnicity) during the second millennium BC. After the expulsion of the Hyksos from this area,[14] Egyptian rulers re-established themselves in the delta and several pharaohs undertook major mudbrick building projects. Many POWs were forced into hard labour in the manufacture and hauling of such bricks, as well as into other manual labour such as ploughing fields and harvesting crops.[15] Such minority groups adapted and assimilated to their culture over time – as was the case with the earlier Hyksos, who had adopted Egyptian names and titles. This would explain the Egyptian names borne by some prominent members of the exodus generation (including Moses, Aaron, Miriam, Phinehas and Hur), as well as the multiple Egyptian terms used to describe the tabernacle's furnishings and utensils, and the priestly regalia.[16]

---

14 The most likely connection with the biblical exodus is that Semites who remained in Egypt after the Hyksos expulsion would have been considered a national security threat, and thus treated accordingly (cf. Exod. 1:9–10). The biblical narrative implies that the pharaoh whom Joseph served (Gen. 46:28–34), the pharaoh who enslaved the Hebrews (Exod. 1:8–10) and the pharaoh confronted by Moses (Exod. 8:26) were ethnic Egyptians.

15 The skilled labourers would typically have been Egyptian, as both the biblical and extra-biblical testimony suggests.

16 See Hoffmeier (in Janzen 2021: 91–93); see also Hoffmeier 2016; for a less positive appraisal of the suggested Egyptian etymology for several such personal names in Exodus, see Hess 2016.

The volume of these and other Egyptian terms used in the exodus and wilderness traditions (i.e. 1.172% of lexemes, *not* including proper nouns) strongly points to an Egyptian provenance. Given the comparative figure for Persian-period biblical compositions (1.445% of distinct lexemes), Noonan (2016: 56) pointedly concludes:

> If we acknowledge Old Iranian linguistic influence on the books of Esther and Ezra-Nehemiah and the implications it has for these books' dates and composition, we should similarly acknowledge Egyptian linguistic influence on the exodus and wilderness traditions and implications it has for their date and composition.

The plethora of authentic topographical and geographical data may further support such a conclusion.[17] Thus Hoffmeier (2021: 103) opines:

> Many of the details . . . would not and possibly could not have been known to the Hebrew author(s) had the biblical texts been composed in the seventh through fifth centuries BC. And if they were somehow known, these seemingly trivial Egyptian minutiae would have been meaningless to a Jewish audience in the Babylonian-Persian period. All of this is relevant as we seek to date the writing of the text and the date of the exodus itself.

b. The date of the exodus

Even those who embrace the veracity of the biblical account differ significantly over the timing of the event it describes: some date this event in the fifteenth century BC, whereas others prefer a much later date, in the thirteenth or even the twelfth century BC. The issue is quite complex and not easily resolved, as each position draws on relevant biblical and extra-biblical data to validate its case, with several key issues subject to different interpretation. This includes not only extant archaeological evidence for occupation and/or destruction of sites associated with Israel's settlement in Canaan

---

17 See further, Hoffmeier 2021: 94–103.

(such as Jericho and Ai), but also germane Old Testament texts (e.g. Exod. 1:11; 1 Kgs 6:1) and Egyptian inscriptions (e.g. the Merneptah Stele), the relevance of the Hyksos in Egypt and the Habiru in Canaan, and even the historical chronology of the New Kingdom (i.e. Egypt's Eighteenth to Twentieth Dynasties; see Table 1).

Table 1: Comparison of high and low Egyptian chronologies (with suggested exodus pharaohs italicized)[18]

Dynasties & pharaohs	Period	High chronology (CAH)	Low chronology (ABD)
Eighteenth Dynasty	Middle Bronze II 2000–1550		
Ahmose I		1570–1546	1550–1525
Amenhotep I	Late Bronze I	1546–1526	1525–1504
Thuthmose I	1550–1400	1525–1512	1504–1492
Thuthmose II		c.1512–1504	1492–1479
Queen Hatshepsut		1503–1482	1479–1457
Thuthmose III[19]		1504–1450	1479–1425
Amenhotep II		1450–1425	1427–1400
Thuthmose IV		1425–1417	1400–1390
Amenhotep III	Late Bronze IIA	1417–1379	1390–1352
Amenhotep IV (Akhenaten)	1400–1300	1379–1362	1352–1336
Neferneferuaten		1364–1361	1338–1336
Tutankhamun		1361–1352	1336–1327
Ay		1352–1348	1327–1323
Horemheb		1348–1320	1323–1295
Nineteenth Dynasty			
Ramesses I		1320–1318	1295–1294

18 For more on the chronology of Egypt's New Kingdom, see Hornung 2006: 197–217.

19 The young Thuthmose III was initially co-regent with his aunt, Hatshepsut, who died in her early fifties.

Seti I	Late Bronze IIB	1318–1304	1294–1279
Ramesses II	1300 –1200	1304–1237	1279–1213
Merneptah		1236–1223	1213–1203
Amenmesse (usurper)		1222–1217 (?)	1203–1200 (?)
Seti II		1216–1210 (?)	1200–1194
Siptah	Iron I	1209–1200 (?)	1194–1188
Queen Tausret	1200–1000	1209–1200 (?)	1188–1186
Twentieth Dynasty			
Setnakht		1200–1198	1186–1184
Ramesses III[20]		1198–1166	1184–1153

The historical conundrum could well have been avoided had the Egyptian kings depicted in the exodus narrative been named – but this is something the author deliberately avoids doing for theological reasons.[21] Even the royal title (pharaoh) applied to these kings reflects later usage, and so offers no help in resolving this ongoing scholarly debate. The case for each position will therefore be summarized below, along with some critical appraisal.

i. The case for a fifteenth-century exodus
Generally referred to as the 'early date', Israel's exodus is located by many conservative scholars in the fifteenth century, usually *c.*1446 BC.[22] Such a date is inferred from a number of biblical

---

20 The Twentieth Dynasty continued in a long period of decline down to Ramesses XI (either 1113 – 1085 or 1099 – 1069), but this table concludes with the last pharaoh associated (by Rendsburg 1992; cf. Janzen 2021) with Israel's exodus.

21 See commentary on Exod. 1:15.

22 Approaches to the early dating of the exodus are not uniform. While most advocates understand this to have taken place *c.*1446 BC (i.e. the middle of the Late Bronze I period), others postulate a slightly later date (1406 BC is suggested; Collins 2012: 104–132), or, more radically,

texts, but primarily from 1 Kings 6:1. Here the construction of the Jerusalem temple commences in 'the second month [of] the fourth year of Solomon's reign over Israel' (c.967 BC; AT), and this is correlated with the 'four hundred and eightieth year after the Israelites came out of Egypt'.[23] Taking these ordinal numbers at face value, as would be expected, and thus adding 479 years to 967 BC, locates the exodus in 1446 BC.

Further corroboration of a mid fifteenth-century exodus is often adduced from Jephthah's claim that Israelites had occupied the Transjordan for three hundred years (Judg. 11:26) – again suggesting that the exodus took place in the fifteenth century, some 340 years prior to Jephthah's leadership (most commonly dated c.1100 BC).[24]

An early exodus has also been extrapolated from the genealogy of temple musicians presented in 1 Chronicles 6:33–37, a sequence of eighteen generations from Heman (a contemporary of David) back to Korah (a contemporary of Moses). Adding a nineteenth generation for Solomon's generation, and assuming that each biblical generation was around twenty-five years, suggests a period of 475 years between Korah and the reign of Solomon, tying in approximately with 1 Kings 6:1.

In terms of extra-biblical corroboration, the most significant objection to a fifteenth-century exodus relates to the Israelite invasion and occupation of Canaan. Not only were some key sites (e.g. Jericho) unoccupied between c.1550 BC and the Iron Age, but Israel's presence in Palestine during the fourteenth century is unattested. However, this depends on Kenyon's revised dating

---

revise the traditional archaeological periods and/or royal chronology to correlate the exodus with the end of the Middle Bronze Age (Bimson 1981; cf. Rohl 2015: 71–85).

23 So Hebrew; LXX reads 'four hundred and fortieth year', explaining the slightly later date mentioned in the previous footnote.

24 However, such an approximate date for Jephthah is simply a calculated guess, which therefore should not be used to compute the date of the exodus.

of Jericho being correct,[25] and how one interprets other relevant material.

In recent decades Kenyon's widely accepted chronology for Jericho has been challenged. Somewhat analogous to Bimson's (1981) proposed redating of the Middle Bronze Age to 1400, Bietak (1991) and Dever (1992) have argued that the transition from the Middle to the Late Bronze Age was much longer than generally understood, and that some degree of overlap exists between transitional phases. As Alexander (2017: 29) tentatively suggests, this might possibly accommodate the destruction of Jericho towards the end of the fifteenth century, as the early date requires.

Insofar as attestation of Israel's presence in fourteenth-century Canaan is concerned, much is made of the Habiru described in the Amarna Letters (dated c.1370 BC), and the reference to Israel in the Merneptah Stele (dated c.1200 BC). The former, discovered in 1887 at Tell el-Amarna in Egypt, contain pleas from Canaanite rulers to their Egyptian overlords, Amenhotep III and Akhenaten, to stem the tide of the 'Habiru' by whom their city-states were being overrun. Some of these Habiru could well have been the Israelites and others who left Egypt with them (Exod. 12:38).[26] Thus understood, the Amarna Letters may provide indirect support for an Israelite occupation of Canaan by the early fourteenth century.

Such early occupation is arguably confirmed by the Merneptah Stele, a 2-metre-tall granite monument commemorating the Egyptian king's victory over an encroaching Lybian

---

25 After major excavation of Tell es-Sultan (the site of ancient Jericho) in the mid twentieth century, Kathleen Kenyon redated the city's cataclysmic destruction to c.1550 BC in the Middle Bronze Age, challenging the later date (1400 BC) proposed by Garstang in the 1930s.

26 The biblical term for 'Hebrews' is possibly unrelated; in any case, 'Habiru' encapsulates a more diverse people who are attested from the eighteenth to the twelfth centuries, making it clear that they cannot simply be equated with the Israelites.

army during the fifth year of his reign (*c.*1208 BC), which also
claims that Merneptah's triumphs included three city-states
(Ashkelon, Gezer and Yenoam), plus Israel: 'Israel is laid waste,
his seed is not.' Significantly, a determinative marker used in
this inscription arguably designates Israel 'not as a territory that
corresponds to Canaan . . . [but] as a socioethnic entity within
the region Canaan/Hurru in the same way that the three city-
states are sociopolitical entities in the same geographical region'
(Hasel 2004: 80–81). Thus understood, Israel must have been
already resident in Canaan for some time before this, which,
as Alexander (2017: 21) points out, would place the exodus no
later than *c.*1248 BC and Moses' birth (cf. Exod. 7:7; cf. Acts 7:23)
around 1328 BC – a date which places the king 'to whom Joseph
meant nothing' (i.e. the pharaoh of the oppression; Exod. 1:8–9)
and the construction of the store cities (Exod. 1:11) well before
the reigns of either Seti I or Ramesses II. Moreover, at least one
of these cities (i.e. Pi-Ramesse) was expanded by Ramesses II to
incorporate the location of a much older city, known originally
as Rowaty, and subsequently Avaris and possibly Peru-nefer;
the entire complex was then renamed Pi-Ramesse after its
development by Ramesses II. Therefore, the name 'Rameses' in
Exodus 1:11 (and also 12:37; Num. 33:3, 5) should probably be
understood as an anachronism (cf. Gen. 47:11), applied by the
biblical author, which cannot be used as evidence to date either
the oppression or the exodus.

ii. The case for a thirteenth-century exodus

An exodus occurring during Egypt's Nineteenth Dynasty was the
consensus view of mainstream scholarship until the historicity
of the exodus came under sharp critique in recent decades, with
radically different explanations for Israel's historical origins and
settlement.[27] Nevertheless, a thirteenth-century exodus is still
upheld by a significant number of conservative scholars, including
Egyptologists such as Kitchen and Hoffmeier.

---

27 E.g. a partial exodus from Egypt; a gradual and mainly peaceful
    migration; a revolt by indigenous Canaanites.

Unsurprisingly, the allusion to Egypt's most prolific royal architect in Exodus 1:11 is considered of key significance. Rather than a biblical anachronism, the reference to 'Rameses' should be interpreted literally, indicating that the Israelites were still enslaved in Egypt in the thirteenth century. The city of Pi-Ramesse (now identified as Tell el-Dab'a) was established as a vast city complex in Egypt's northern frontier, principally constructed by Ramesses II (1279–1213) but later expanded by Ramesses III (1184–1153).[28] Ramesses II relocated his royal residence and government from Thebes in Egypt's south to this newly constructed city in the Nile Delta, and it remained the east Delta's centre of pharaonic rule for almost a century. This huge ancient city was clearly named after its primary architect, Ramesses II. While there is evidence for some earlier construction (i.e. a citadel and military compound) during the Eighteenth Dynasty, back then there would have been no Delta capital from which fleeing Israelites could make their hasty exit (Exod. 12:37).

Since such a thirteenth-century exodus does not correlate with a literal interpretation of 1 Kings 6:1, the 480-year period suggested there should be understood as a schematic figure – perhaps representing twelve generations (conventionally or symbolically set at forty years each).[29] Given that the time from the birth of one generation to the next would in reality have been twenty-five years

---

28 NB Identifying Ramesses II (1279–1213 BC), as some late-date advocates do, as both the pharaoh of the oppression *and* the pharaoh of the exodus conflicts with the biblical text (Exod. 2:23; cf. 4:19).

29 As an alternative explanation for the figure in 1 Kgs 6:1, Kitchen (2003: 308–309) creatively opines that the author may have selectively used the chronological information from Exodus–Judges to calculate Israel's *ideal* (i.e. unoppressed) era from the exodus to Solomon's fourth year. While this may seem somewhat arbitrary, it is worth noting with Kitchen that if all the biblical chronological data for this period is included, this results in a total span of 554 years (*plus* an unknowable number of years for the leadership of Joshua, Samuel and Saul), which advocates of both an early and a late date must compress in some way to correlate with the interpretation of 1 Kgs 6:1.

or less, the actual period envisaged by this symbolic 12x40 figure is less than three hundred years; hence the exodus took place *c*.1270. Such a date may be further corroborated by the genealogy in 1 Chronicles 6:3–8, in which the high priest Zadok (a contemporary of David) is only ten generations from Aaron.[30]

Even though it is not a multiple of 40, Jephthah's three hundred years (Judg. 11:26) could likewise represent some seven or eight generations. However, it may simply be a grossly exaggerated figure or an inaccurate guess by Jephthah,[31] who may have neither known nor cared exactly how long Israel had been resident in Canaan. Thus understood, Judges 11:26, like 1 Kings 6:1, should not be used to establish the actual timeline of Israel's migration from Egypt.

Extra-biblical data appears to validate such a conclusion. During the Eighteenth Dynasty the Egyptian capital was in the city of Thebes (in Upper Egypt), a considerable distance (*c*.800 km [500 miles]) and travelling time (*c*.2–3 weeks) from Goshen (in the north-eastern Delta). This makes difficult the frequent interaction between Moses and Pharaoh in Exodus, unless one speculates that the royal residence Moses frequented was either in Memphis (just south of the Delta) or somewhere much closer to Goshen. However, no such speculation is necessary in the thirteenth century, when Ramesses II's residence was near Goshen, at Pi-Ramesse in Egypt's northern frontier.

There is also the archaeological evidence relating to destruction and settlement in Canaan. At least some of the destructive layers *c*.1200 in Palestine (e.g. attesting to the complete destruction of Hazor) correlate well with the biblical record of Israelite invasion,

---

30 The five generations from Nahshon to David (Ruth 4:20–22) are understood as incomplete/telescoped.

31 While the significance of Judg. 11:26 for historical reconstruction must not be overstated, Jephthah's claim should arguably not be dismissed as worthless. Although he (or the book's author) was apparently sketchy on Ammonite worship (Judg. 11:24; cf. Num. 21:29; 2 Kgs 23:13), he is more sure-footed when it comes to Israel's history (Judg. 11:15–22). Even so, there is still the problem of knowing when, exactly, Jephthah lived (see n. 24 above).

in marked contrast to the lack of such support *c.*1400 on conventional dating. Moreover, the sudden appearance of settlements in the Ephraimite hill country around the same time (at the beginning of Iron Age I) similarly stands out, again in sharp contrast to the lack of such evidence for an Israelite presence at the earlier time.[32] As well as corroborating a late-date exodus and conquest, this also underlines one of the most serious objections to an earlier exodus: how did the Israelites remain archaeologically invisible for some two hundred years?[33]

A further issue concerns the city of Shechem: according to the Amarna Letters and archaeological excavations, this was a strong city around 1400 BC, yet there is no hint of it being a major stronghold that was destroyed or conquered by the Israelites; rather, the impression given in Joshua is that the location was militarily inconsequential (cf. Josh. 8:30–35; 24:1–32). The latter scenario best fits Shechem in Late Bronze IIB, after the city had lost all its former importance, having been destroyed and become a location of no great significance.

For these and other reasons,[34] a thirteenth-century exodus certainly warrants consideration, and should not be discounted

---

32 Advocates of a late (13th or 12th century) exodus maintain that there are too many differences in the data provided by the Amarna Letters and Joshua–Judges to identify the biblical Hebrews with the Amarna Habiru.

33 If, however, the Israelites lived largely in tents or occupied existing Canaanite dwellings (cf. Deut. 19:1), and/or used pottery that was similar to that of the Canaanites, the archaeological evidence would have been minimal. Still, to leave no distinctive footprint for two centuries would seem rather odd.

34 E.g. Kitchen argues that the structural arrangement of covenant material in Exodus and Deuteronomy shows significant correspondence with the typical Ancient Near Eastern treaty forms of the thirteenth century. However, suggested parallels between biblical texts and Ancient Near Eastern treaty documents are at best suggestive; biblical texts (which are not treaty documents) do not conform exactly to any such treaty forms. Accordingly, such formal comparison is a somewhat tenuous basis on which to date the material so precisely.

simply because it rejects the most straightforward interpretation of
1 Kings 6:1. As Garrett (2014: 91–92) illustrates from the rabbinic
(and Pauline, Gal. 3:16–17; cf. Acts 13:17–20) interpretation of the
430 years in Exodus 12:40:

> there is an ancient tradition of interpretation that reconstructs
> the chronology of biblical history in a way that would never
> occur to modern, western readers. We are not required to
> choose between the apparently literal meaning of Exod. 12:40
> and the apparently literal meaning of Gal. 3:16–17. Rather, we
> should be careful about assuming that we know exactly how
> biblical numbers have been computed and are meant to be
> used. Either Exodus, or Galatians, or both may compute the
> 430 years in a way we do not understand.

iii. The case for a twelfth-century exodus
Working on the assumption of a 'combination theory' of
settlement in Canaan (i.e. Israel pursued a twin-track approach
of military conquest and peaceful infiltration), Rendsburg (2021)
accepts only the essential historicity of the biblical account (i.e.
there was a historical exodus, but the biblical narrative is replete
with 'epic qualities'). However, he dates the exodus a century
later than most scholars, during the reign of Ramesses III. While
similarly discounting the relevance of 1 Kings 6:1, he rejects
its symbolic interpretation (i.e. 480 = 'twelve generations') on
the grounds that, however each generation should actually be
counted, twelve is still too many. Rather than reconstructing the
date of the exodus using such exaggerated biblical figures,[35] he
maintains that (some) biblical genealogies offer a more reliable
basis for calculation. Key for Rendsburg is the lineage appearing

---

35 Other suggested examples of such a feature, typical of ancient epic
    tradition, include the inflated ancestral lifespans (Gen. 25:7; 35:28;
    47:28), the idealized (Egyptian) 110-year lifespans of Joseph (Gen. 50:26)
    and Joshua (Josh. 24:29), and even round numbers (esp. multiples of 40)
    more generally: Gen. 15:13; Exod. 7:7; Deut. 29:5; 34:7; Judg. 3:11, 30;
    5:31; 2 Sam. 5:4; 1 Kgs 11:42; cf. also Judg. 11:26.

in Ruth 4:18–22,[36] which bridges the exodus and the tenth century by tracing David's genealogy five generations back to Nahshon, a member of the exodus generation according to Exodus 6:23 and Numbers 1:7. Assuming that the average generation should be counted as thirty to thirty-five years (rather than the lower figure of twenty to twenty-five suggested by most scholars), Rendsburg estimates Nahshon lived between 150 and 175 years before David, placing the exodus somewhere between 1175 and 1150 BC, during the twelfth-century reign of Ramesses III.

Such a date may also explain an otherwise anomalous fact: that the grandsons of both Moses and Aaron are still alive and active at the end of Judges (18:30; 20:28), not long before the time of Samuel. Although the timeline of the Judges 'appendix' (chs. 18–21) may not necessarily follow the same chronological sequence as the rest of the book, it is nevertheless possible to infer from the events recorded in Judges 18 (Danite migration) and 20 (civil war with Benjaminites) that the period between the exodus and the beginning of the monarchy was much shorter than generally assumed.

Other biblical texts, along with extra-biblical data, may provide further corroboration. If Exodus 13:17 suggests that some sort of military conflict, involving the Philistines, was currently taking place along the coastal route north of Egypt, this correlates well with the invasion of the Sea Peoples around 1180 BC. Unlike earlier, less significant invasions back in the thirteenth century, during the reign of Merneptah, the Philistines were now involved, if not actually leading this coalition of Sea Peoples that threatened Egypt's sovereignty.[37] A Philistine presence in the Levant at the time of the exodus (cf. Josh. 13:2–3) may also be inferred from their mention alongside Edom, Moab and Canaan in Exodus 15:14–15, although

---

36 Rendsburg discounts the much longer Davidic genealogy in 1 Chr. 2:5–15 on the premise that lineage lengthening is more common than lineage telescoping.

37 Some, though not all, of the relevant inscriptions place the Philistines at its head.

this could simply be an anachronism.[38] Somewhat more speculatively, Amos 9:7 might possibly imply that the Israelite exodus from Egypt, the Philistine migration from Caphtor and the Aramean migration from Qir[39] were contemporaneous events, again throwing significant light on the problem envisaged in Exodus 13:17.

Corroborating archaeological data for a twelfth-century exodus includes evidence of extensive new settlement in the central hill country in the early Iron Age (1175–1000 BC), compared with relatively few such settlements in the Late Bronze Age (1500–1175 BC). As well as this marked numerical increase, Rendsburg considers even the layout of these new settlements significant: resembling modern Bedouin encampments, the layout is eminently suited to Israelites, who are biblically portrayed as nomadic pastoralists.

An obvious archaeological problem for such a late-date exodus is the reference to Israel on the Merneptah Stele (see above). While Rendsburg does not doubt the historicity of Merneptah's claim (cf. *Me-Neptoah* in Josh. 15:9; 18:15), he offers a radically different interpretation. Rather than signalling Israel as a foreign location (as the other entities are so marked), the use of the people-determinative most likely identifies Israel as a people group presently *living in Egypt* but associated with these other entities because of their Canaanite origin. Alternatively, it may simply refer to semi-nomadic pastoralists encountered in Canaan 'who never experienced the eisodus, slavery, and exodus' (Janzen 2021: 193). In any case, the main point for Rendsburg is the apparent absence of Israelites in Canaan at a time when there certainly were Egyptians present: how can one envisage the Israelites being there

> without ever encountering the Egyptian presence in the land? . . . It is far better to assume that the Israelites left Egypt during the reign of Ramesses III, during the turmoil generated by the Sea Peoples invasion (ca. 1190 BCE), thereby bringing them to the land of Canaan about twenty-five years later, at the very

---

38 As could also be true of Exod. 13:17, though Rendsburg evidently rejects such a suggestion.

39 Nothing is known about either Aramean origins or the location of Qir.

point when there was no longer a strong Egyptian presence in the land. This would explain why the Bible never mentions the Egyptians beyond Exod 14 – 15 . . . people of all sorts are encountered – Amalekites, Edomites, Moabites, Ammonites, and Canaanites – but not Egyptians.

(2021: 195–196)

iv. Appraisal

The various dates suggested above for the biblical exodus are partly supported by a literal interpretation of at least some of the relevant biblical texts: the number in 1 Kings 6:1 (as well as the genealogy of 1 Chr. 6:33–37) computes to *c.*1446 BC; Exod. 1:11 (along with 1 Chr. 6:3–8) suggests the era of Ramesses II; the genealogy in Ruth 4:18–22 (along with Judg. 18:30; 20:28) implies the following century, during the reign of Ramesses III.[40] Clearly it is impossible to interpret all these texts at face value, and therefore some of these texts must be otherwise understood. In most cases an alternative reading is feasible, especially if the chronologies in the book of Judges are overlapping or some of the relevant genealogies (e.g. Ruth 4:18–22) are incomplete. However, given that the number in 1 Kings 6:1 is syntactically an ordinal (the 480th year) rather than a cardinal (480 years),[41] and is used in conjunction with another ordinal number (Solomon's *fourth* year), anything other than a literal meaning seems counter-intuitive. Nevertheless, in the light of how Paul interprets the 430 years figure in Exodus 12:40–41 (Gal. 3:17; cf. Acts 13:20), some caution is arguably warranted.

---

40 One could also argue that the chronology of Joshua–Judges–Samuel points to an extremely early date (*c.*1590 BC), which resolves an otherwise problematic conundrum (e.g. Jericho's unoccupied status until the Iron Age after its catastrophic destruction, often dated [after Kenyon's excavation in the mid twentieth century] *c.*1550 BC).

41 For the same syntax, see Ezra 3:8; Esth. 1:3; Jer. 51:59; 52:31. Note also that 'in the year of X . . .' is how ordinal figures – referring to a specific reference point in someone's reign – are introduced throughout 1 & 2 Kings.

In terms of the extra-biblical evidence, each position can likewise lay claim to at least some corroboration: the Habiru crisis of the Amarna Letters and the mention of Israel in Merneptah's Stele (early date); the location of Pi-Ramesse and the destruction of Hazor (late date); central hill country population explosion (very late date). But each also faces significant objections: the archaeology of Jericho, Hazor and Shechem on conventional dating, plus lack of any clear evidence for an Israelite presence in Canaan during the fourteenth century (early date); except for Hazor, lack of evidence for an Israelite conquest at the end of the Late Bronze Age (late date); the mention of Israel in Merneptah's Stele as a people group *in* Canaan by 1200 BC, plus the non-occupation of Jericho (very late date). Moreover, like the relevant biblical texts, some of the extra-biblical evidence is open to different interpretations.

Clearly some involved in this debate lean more heavily on biblical texts than others, but with the exception of Rendsburg's caveats, all affirm the historical veracity of the canonical account. Nevertheless, it is clear that the present evidence, arguably including 1 Kings 6:1, remains inconclusive, so this perennial debate over the date of Israel's exodus from Egypt will most likely continue unless (or until) evidence is uncovered that finally resolves it beyond all reasonable doubt.

c. The route of the exodus

Another bone of scholarly contention, especially among those who understand the narrative to be factual, is where, precisely, the geographical place markers reported in Exodus should be located on a regional map; the exact location of several of these places is somewhat uncertain and thus debatable. Indeed, this is especially so for the two most significant places mentioned in Israel's itinerary (see Fig. 1): the body of water described as the *yam sûf* (traditionally, 'the Red Sea', but arguably, 'Lake of Reeds');[42] and the mountain referred to as Sinai (traditionally situated

---

42 The Hebrew noun *yam* may denote both sea and lake, so is not decisive for locating this body of water. For the precise significance of *sûf*, see discussion below.

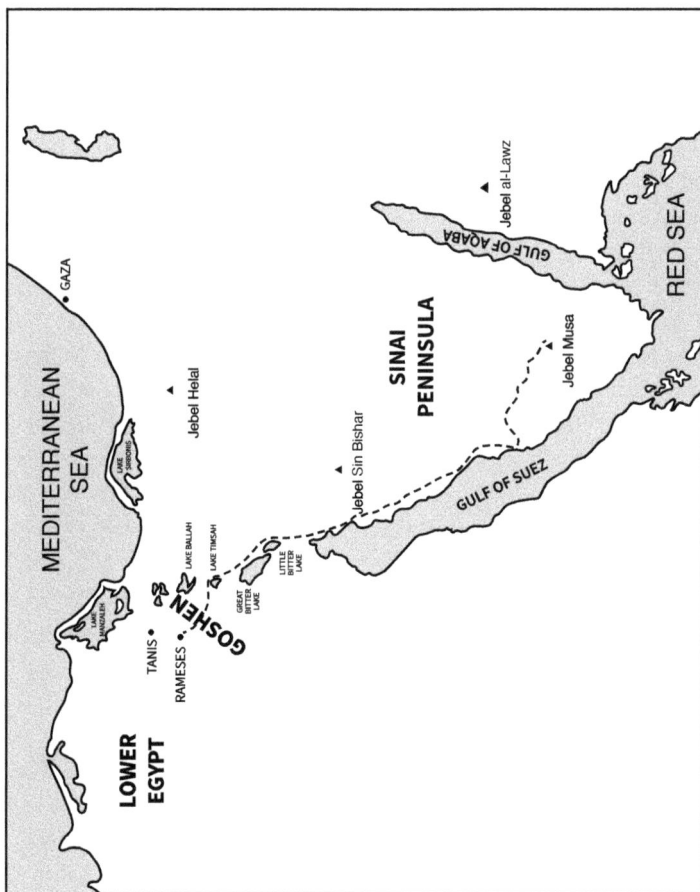

Figure 1: The route of the exodus

somewhere on the peninsula that lies between northern Egypt
and the southern Levant), where God manifested himself in a
theophany and communicated his instructions through Moses.[43]

i. The location of the yam sûf
While some suggest a northern location, either Lake Manzaleh
or Lake Sirbonis, both skirting the Mediterranean, most scholars
locate the *yam sûf* further south. Either the Ballah or Timsah
lake,[44] or one of the many reedy marshes further south, is thus
widely believed to have been the 'Sea/Lake of Reeds' which Israel
traversed safely but which engulfed the pursuing Egyptians. Such
an identification is supported by the standard interpretation of the
Hebrew term *sûf* as papyrus reeds (cf. Exod. 2:3 and the cognate
Egyptian word for marsh plant, *twf*). Since such papyrus does not
grow along the banks of the Red Sea, most scholars conclude that
the *yam sûf* was one of the freshwater marshy lakes in the eastern
Delta region north of Suez.

Older English versions followed the LXX in translating 'Red
Sea', suggesting a crossing far to the south, at the Gulf of Suez
– one of the Red Sea's northern extensions. While the terminology is apparently used in the Old Testament to refer to Suez
(e.g. Num. 33:10), this is possibly distinguished from the body
of water through which the Israelites had miraculously passed
(Num. 33:8).[45] To complicate matters further, *yam sûf* is also used

---

43 For a detailed discussion of both, see Hoffmeier 2005: 75–148.
44 Following Hoffmeier (2007: 40), Alexander (2017: 264) importantly notes
    that 'in the second millennium the Mediterranean coastline was some
    20 miles (32 km) south of its present location', making it much closer
    to Ballah lake(s) – the obvious topographical significance of which was
    diminished by its drainage by the mid-nineteenth-century construction
    of the Suez Canal. This suggests a possible location of the *yam sûf* in an
    area that might well have been susceptible to a king tide or tsunami.
45 Admittedly, however, this might be explained by a coastal itinerary:
    once they had crossed the northern part of the Gulf of Suez, they
    travelled due south until they eventually returned to the water's edge
    (see map).

in the Old Testament to refer to the Gulf of Aqaba (1 Kgs 9:26; and probably Num. 21:4 and Deut. 2:1), the other northern arm of the Red Sea. It can be inferred from this that, when used in combination with *yam*, *sûf* may not necessarily carry its normal connotation of papyrus reeds. Indeed, some (e.g. Batto 1983, 1984) have even challenged the consensus on the meaning of the term *sûf*, suggesting that the parallel between the Egyptian and Hebrew words is inexact – the former (*twf*) referring to an area of papyrus but never to a body of water. Moreover, they also maintain that the Hebrew term is related to a Semitic root meaning 'end' (cf. Heb. *sôf*), thus suggesting the translation 'the sea of the end' (i.e. the waters to the far south at the end of the land; viz. the Gulf of Suez). Without evidence suggesting that another body of water in the Delta region was ever known as the *yam sûf*, the Red Sea or one of its northern arms might thus seem feasible. However, Hoffmeier (2005: 85) insists that New Kingdom Egyptian texts do attest to a body of water or swampy region known as *p3 twfy* (sea of reeds), suggesting that the *yam sûf* of the exodus narrative lay further north than the Gulf of Suez.

ii. The location of Mount Sinai
After crossing the *yam sûf*, the Israelites entered the Wilderness of Shur (Exod. 15:22; Num. 33:8) in the north-west Sinai Peninsula (1 Sam. 15:7; 27:8), from which they proceeded to Sinai. Despite the apparent clarity of many Bible atlases, the precise location of the latter is again uncertain. At least three different possibilities have been suggested: Jebel Helal in the north of the peninsula, Jebel Sin Bishar in the middle, and Jebel Musa (the traditional site) in the far south.

As a result of the above possibilities, at least three different routes for the exodus have been proposed:

1 A northern route, taking the Israelites by the Way of the Sea, across Lake Manzaleh or Lake Sirbonis, and south to Jebel Helal;
2 A central route, taking them through the Ballah or Timsah lakes and on to somewhere in north-west Saudi Arabia, beyond the Gulf of Aqaba;

3 A southern route, taking them through/past the Bitter Lakes
   or across the northern point of the Gulf of Suez and then
   south to Jebel Sin Bishar or even further south to one of the
   other mountains near the bottom of the peninsula (e.g. Jebel
   Musa, the traditional site).[46]

As Durham (1987: 187) concludes:

> the best clue we have to the route of Israel's exodus from
> Egypt has to do . . . not with its location but with its purpose
> . . . Yahweh guided his people away from the shortest and most
> logical route and into an eccentric series of turns designed to
> depict confusion, first of all because of an intention to trick and
> then to defeat Pharaoh, and second, because he was not ready in
> any case to take his people on to the land he had promised them.

For the first and subsequent readers of this book, what matters
most was not *when* the exodus took place, nor *how* we should
trace Israel's journey immediately afterwards, but rather *why* these
events took place and *what* God teaches us through them (i.e.
the theological significance of the events related in this book).
Accordingly, to this more important matter we now turn our
attention.

5. Theological themes in Exodus

While a major topic of the book is Israel's 'exodus' or departure
from Egypt, this is really only the beginning of the story, covered
in the first third of the book (Exod. 1:1 – 15:21); the larger part
of the book (15:22 – 40:38) concentrates on what happens next:
Israel's journey to Sinai and what transpires there afterwards.
But what unites all the material is its overarching focus on

---

46 Objections to the traditional location of Mt Sinai include the following:
    (1) there was a significant Egyptian presence due to mining activities in
    this area; (2) it was a good area to fish, yet Num. 11:5 implies that they
    had had no fish since leaving Egypt. So Milgrom 1990: 280.

the divine–human relationship between the LORD/Yahweh (see notes on ch. 3) and Israel, Abraham's offspring and heirs to God's promises. This unique relationship with Israel's ancestors motivates the LORD's gracious response to Israel's plight (cf. 2:24–25; 6:5–8; 32:13–14), and his special relationship with Israel explains both his treatment of Pharaoh (4:22–23; 9:17) and the goal of the exodus (29:46). But this relationship is not an end in itself; it is a means to the LORD's greater objective to make himself known. Thus, his actions are not simply for the benefit of Egypt (7:5, 17; 8:10, 22; 9:14, 29; 11:7; 14:4, 18) and Israel (6:7; 10:2; 16:6, 8, 12; 29:46; 31:13), but also for the rest of the nations (cf. 9:16; 15:14; 33:16; 34:10), who will be blessed through Abraham and his seed (Gen. 12:1–3; cf. Exod. 19:6).

Chapters 1–2, in which God seems largely absent, highlight his faithfulness to the covenant promises he made to Israel's ancestors (cf. Gen. 15:13). Chapters 3–15 emphasize this still further by the measures the LORD takes to punish the oppressive Egyptian regime and emancipate Abraham's descendants (cf. Gen. 15:14). Through word and action, the LORD makes himself known as the holy and incomparable God, sovereign over history and creation, far superior to the deities that others worship (12:12; 15:11). The following section (15:22 – 18:27) further underlines this: the LORD demonstrates his incredible ability to sustain and protect the people he has rescued, and this culminates in Jethro, Moses' non-Israelite father-in-law, recognizing the LORD's might and supremacy over all other gods (18:10–11).

The first eighteen chapters of the book show Israel *why* the LORD, as saviour, deserves their service and worship; the remaining chapters reveal *how* the Israelites should serve and worship him exclusively as their divine king. The strict preparations necessary before God's appearance on Mount Sinai again underscore his holiness (ch. 19; cf. 3:5). Direct access to God is highly restricted: Israel must initially approach the LORD through a designated mediator. In the first instance, this mediator is Moses, through whom the LORD makes known Israel's covenant obligations and how to apply them (chs. 20–23). These covenant obligations are primarily Israel's grateful response to the LORD's saving work (19:4; 20:2). However, they are also a means by which Israel's unique status as the LORD's special people would become evident (19:5–6). The LORD's presence among the Israelites also reflects Israel's extraordinary status (cf. 29:45–46; 33:15–16), so they need an appropriate structure to accommodate such close proximity between a holy God and his imperfect people. In contrast to Aaron's golden calf and the idolatry which jeopardized the LORD's plans for dwelling with Israel (chs. 32–34), the divinely decreed means of worship involves a special, consecrated tent (the tabernacle) with consecrated personnel (Aaron and his priestly descendants). This enables Israel to live with the LORD among them and expresses their unique relationship with him as a holy nation.

As Exodus 3:14–15 might lead us to expect, within this narrative theology of the book a number of significant truths about God are disclosed, some – such as his holiness – for the first time in the Pentateuch. While God's sanctifying of the seventh day has already been noted in Genesis (Gen. 2:3), Exodus not only further elaborates on this (16:23; 20:8–11; 31:13–15; 35:2–3), but also places considerable emphasis on God's intrinsic holiness (15:13) and its 'transferability' to places (3:5; 19:23; 26:33; 28:35; 40:9–10), objects (29:37; 30:10; 30:29a, 36–37) and people (19:6; 22:31; 28:36; 30:29b; 31:13; 39:30).

Another divine attribute mentioned for the first time in Exodus is God's jealousy (20:5; 34:14). Unlike human jealousy, which so often is tainted by the sin of envy (e.g. Gen. 26:14; 30:1; 37:11), divine jealousy – like that of a husband/wife with respect to an unfaithful spouse – is evoked purely by God's right to exclusivity in his relationship with his covenant partner. Accordingly, in such a context, any form of polytheism or idolatry is proscribed (20:3–6; 23:13, 24) and constitutes a very serious transgression (22:20; 32:7–10, 21, 30–35).

The most concentrated focus on God's nature comes in Exodus 34:6–7, where – as anticipated in 33:19 – God causes all his goodness to pass before Moses and proclaims his name, the LORD, in his presence. Here a fuller account of God's *mercy, compassion* and *grace* is disclosed – namely, that he is slow to anger, abounds in love and faithfulness, maintains love to thousands, and forgives every kind of sin. In the immediate and wider context, this is very good news for Israel, whose 'great sin' with the golden calf has evoked a significant problem for both themselves and God. Nevertheless, as the caveat in 34:7 underlines, despite God's assurances to forgive sin, his mercy and compassion must not simply be assumed nor taken for granted. Though God will show such to whomever *he* pleases (cf. 33:19), this does not mean that he will leave the guilty unpunished; rather, justice will indeed be carried out, as the cross-generational consequences of sin make very clear. Accordingly, Israel should not repeat the folly of Pharaoh and the Egyptians in the earlier part of the book, but rather glean from such the need to take God at his word (of both promise and warning) and respond accordingly.

In addition to these divine attributes, Exodus also introduces other key Old Testament motifs, such as Yahweh being a *warrior* (Exod. 15:3). While this is especially highlighted by the victory song of Exodus 15, it is also implicit in the arsenal of weapons (divine 'strikes') unleashed by God's *mighty hand* (3:19–20; 6:1, 6; 13:14, 16) against Egypt in the earlier Yahweh–Pharaoh contest narrative (cf. 9:14–15), culminating in *judgment on all the gods of Egypt* (12:12; cf. 12:29–30), the plundering of the Egyptians after the death of their firstborn (3:21–22; 11:1–3; 12:33–36) and Israel's military-like departure from Egypt (6:26; 7:4; 12:41, 51). Such imagery is clearly evident in chapter 14, when Yahweh employs military tactics to lure Pharaoh into a trap, and victory is credited solely to the fact that Yahweh fights for Israel (14:14, 30–31), something even the trapped Egyptians acknowledge (14:25). Egypt is not the only object of such divine wrath in Exodus, with the Amalekites (17:8–16) serving as a precursor for the divine warfare to which the inhabitants of Canaan were later exposed. Significantly, however, Exodus makes clear that even Israel was not immune from such divine attack, should circumstances demand it (5:3; 32:10, 34–35; 34:7b). Thus, in Exodus we have the beginning of a theological theme that not only permeates the Old Testament, but culminates in that great Day when God will execute his righteous judgment on all who dare to stand against him.

6. Biblical-theological trajectories in Exodus

As noted above, Exodus is part of the unfolding theological account that began in Genesis and continues in the books that follow. In terms of the promise–fulfilment theme that pervades the Bible, Exodus is therefore of key importance. Not only does the LORD begin to fulfil his promises to Abraham, but the book is foundational for several theological trajectories that run through the rest of Scripture. Three examples will suffice.

a. Israel's emancipation as the paradigm of salvation

Israel's deliverance from Egypt becomes the major paradigm of salvation in the Old Testament. So it is not surprising that later Old Testament books anticipate a new exodus after Israel ends up in exile – this time because *they* harden their hearts and rebel against the LORD (cf. Isa. 11:10–16; Jer. 23:1–8). Consequently, the LORD's temporal emancipation of Israel from Pharaoh's oppressive regime foreshadows God's eternal emancipation of his people in the New Testament: Jesus is the ultimate Passover lamb (John 1:29; 19:36; 1 Cor. 5:7) through whom God's people are redeemed (1 Pet. 1:18–19) from the sin that enslaves them (John 8:34; Rom. 6:6, 17, 20).

b. Covenant as the framework of divine–human relationship

The Sinai covenant establishes the framework for the divine–human relationship reflected in the rest of the Old Testament. Despite their initial enthusiasm and avowed commitment (Exod. 19:8; 24:3, 7), the Israelites fail to keep this covenant – not just as the LORD officially hands over the tablets of the Ten Commandments (cf. Exod. 32), but throughout Israel's subsequent history. Such perennial failure and its tragic consequences lead to the hope of a new covenant, in which people internalize the LORD's covenant requirements (Jer. 31:33) by the work of his Spirit (Ezek. 36:27). Jesus inaugurates this new covenant; the echo of Exodus 24:8 in the Last Supper accounts implicitly reflects this, and various epistles explicitly underline it (e.g. 2 Cor. 3; Heb. 8 – 10). Consequently, God's people are no longer required to keep the obligations of the Sinai covenant, but the obligations of the new covenant.

c. Immanuel as a present reality and future hope

The goal of the exodus – the LORD's dwelling among his people in the tabernacle – is subsequently expressed through Solomon's temple but is likewise jeopardized when the nation's rebellion and idolatry eventually force the LORD to abandon this earthly dwelling and destroy it. Nevertheless, the Old Testament never abandons the prospect of the LORD's dwelling among his people; its prophetic hope is an even more glorious temple to come. Once again, Jesus fulfils this hope (cf. John 1:14), and God's people constitute his dwelling place (2 Cor. 6:16), a reality that will ultimately be experienced in the new heaven and new earth (Rev. 21:3).

When read in its literary and theological context, therefore, Exodus is much more than a story of miraculous intervention or divine concern for an oppressed people. Rather, it recounts a very significant stage in the fulfilment of God's promises to Israel's ancestors – promises through which God would eventually realize his purpose for all creation. Both Exodus as a whole and its opening chapters in particular are primarily concerned with these promises and the outworking of their fulfilment.

ANALYSIS

I. OPPRESSION AND THE PROMISE OF DELIVERANCE (1:1 – 4:31)

A. Enslavement, genocide and the rescue of Moses (1:1 – 2:10)
  i. Oppression (1:1–14)
  ii. Genocide (1:15–22)
  iii. The rescue of Moses (2:1–10)

B. Moses' exodus to Midian (2:11–22)

C. God hears Israel's cry for help (2:23–25)

D. Theophany and proof-signs (3:1 – 4:17)
  i. Theophany at the mountain of God (3:1–22)
  ii. Proof-signs for Moses (4:1–17)

E. Moses' return to Egypt and the Israelites' response (4:18–31)
  i. Departure from Midian (4:18–20)
  ii. Israel, Yahweh's firstborn son (4:21–23)
  iii. Bridegroom of blood (4:24–26)
  iv. Rendezvous with Aaron (4:27–28)
  v. Israel's response to Aaron and Moses (4:29–31)

2. **PHARAOH'S RESPONSE TO YAHWEH'S DEMANDS AND DIVINE REASSURANCE FOR MOSES (5:1 – 7:7)**
   A. Pharaoh's refusal, and recriminations against Moses (5:1–21)
      i. Pharaoh's refusal to obey Yahweh's demands (5:1–14)
      ii. Recriminations against Moses (5:15–21)
   B. Moses' complaint, Yahweh's reassurance and Israel's incredulity (5:22 – 6:9)
      i. Moses' complaint (5:22–23)
      ii. Yahweh's reassurance (6:1–8)
      iii. Israel's incredulity (6:9)
   C. Further instruction to confront Pharaoh (6:10 – 7:7)
      i. Yahweh's commission and Moses' response (6:10–12)
      ii. Levitical genealogy (6:13–27)
      iii. Aaron, a prophet for Moses (6:28 – 7:7)

3. **PHARAOH'S RECALCITRANCE AND YAHWEH'S MIGHTY ACTS OF JUDGMENT (7:8 – 10:29)**
   A. A miraculous sign for Pharaoh (7:8–13)
   B. Yahweh's mighty acts of judgment: strikes 1 to 9 (7:14 – 10:29)
      i. Blood (7:14–24)
      ii. Frogs (7:25 – 8:15)
      iii. Gnats (8:16–19)
      iv. Flies (8:20–32)
      v. Livestock (9:1–7)
      vi. Boils (9:8–12)
      vii. Hail (9:13–35)
      viii. Locusts (10:1–20)
      ix. Darkness (10:21–29)

4. **PASSOVER AND EXODUS (11:1 – 13:16)**
   A. The tenth plague announced (11:1–10)
   B. Instructions for Passover and Unleavened Bread (12:1–28)
      i. Yahweh's instructions concerning the original Passover (12:1–13)
      ii. Yahweh's instructions for the annual commemoration (12:14–20)

    iii. Communication of the instructions (12:21–28)

C. The death of Egypt's firstborn and Israel's hasty departure (12:29–51)

D. Consecration of the Israelites' firstborn (13:1–16)

5. DELIVERANCE AT THE SEA (13:17 – 15:21)

A. The crossing of the Sea (13:17 – 14:31)

    i. Israel's path out of Egypt (13:17–22)

    ii. The trap set by Yahweh (14:1–4)

    iii. The Egyptian pursuit (14:5–9)

    iv. Israel's panic and Moses' faith (14:10–15)

    v. Safe passage for the Israelites (14:16–22)

    vi. Drowning of the Egyptians (14:23–28)

    vii. Israel's fear of Yahweh and confidence in Moses (14:29–31)

B. Celebratory praise (15:1–21)

6. PROVISION AND PROTECTION ON THE JOURNEY TO HOREB (15:22 – 17:16)

A. Provision of water and food (15:22 – 17:7)

    i. Water at Marah and Elim (15:22–27)

    ii. Quail and manna in the Desert of Sin (16:1–36)

    iii. Water from the rock at Rephidim (17:1–7)

B. Divine protection in the face of Amalekite aggression (17:8–16)

7. THE RESPONSE AND ADVICE OF JETHRO (18:1–27)

A. Jethro's response to testimony about Yahweh (18:1–12)

B. Jethro's advice to Moses (18:13–27)

8. PREPARATIONS FOR COVENANT-MAKING WITH GOD (19:1–25)

A. Encampment at Sinai and Israel's 'declaration of intent' (19:1–9)

B. Consecration of the people (19:10–15)

C. Yahweh's descent on Sinai and instructions to Moses (19:16–25)

9. ISRAEL'S COVENANT OBLIGATIONS
DISCLOSED (I): THE DECALOGUE AND
ISRAEL'S TERRIFIED RESPONSE (20:1–21)
A. The Decalogue (20:1–17)
B. The community's response (20:18–21)

10. ISRAEL'S COVENANT OBLIGATIONS DISCLOSED
(II): THE BOOK OF THE COVENANT (20:22 – 23:33)
A. Regulations for worship, manumission and social
responsibilities (20:22 – 22:20)
    i. Regulations for Israelite worship (20:22–26)
    ii. Regulations for the manumission of Hebrew
    bondservants (21:1–11)
    iii. Regulations for various social responsibilities (21:12
    – 22:20)
B. Reflecting God's care for the oppressed (22:21 – 23:9)
    i. Loving the disadvantaged (22:21–27)
    ii. Living to please God (22:28–31)
    iii. Maintaining justice (23:1–9)
C. Israel's ritual obligations (23:10–19)
    i. The sabbatical year and sabbath day (23:10–13)
    ii. Annual pilgrimage festivals (23:14–19)
D. Hortatory epilogue (23:20–33)
    i. Yahweh's trailblazing angel and Israel's loyalty (23:20–26)
    ii. Yahweh's promise and Israel's task (23:27–33)

11. THE SEALING OF THE COVENANT (24:1–18)
A. The covenant-making ceremony (24:1–11)
B. Moses' ascent to receive the covenant tablets (24:12–18)

12. DIVINE INSTRUCTIONS FOR WORSHIP (I): THE
TABERNACLE'S DESIGN (25:1 – 27:19)
A. Collection of the raw materials (25:1–9)
B. Gold furniture and accessories (25:10–40)
    i. The ark (25:10–22)
    ii. The table (25:23–30)
    iii. The lampstand (25:31–40)
C. The sacred tent (26:1–37)

D. The bronze altar (27:1–8)

E. The courtyard (27:9–19)

13. DIVINE INSTRUCTIONS FOR WORSHIP (II): THE PRIESTHOOD (27:20 – 30:38)

A. Oil for the lampstand (27:20–21)

B. Vestments for the priests (28:1–43)

    i. General instructions for the priestly garments (28:1–5)

    ii. The ephod (28:6–14)

    iii. The breastpiece (28:15–30)

    iv. The robe (28:31–35)

    v. The emblem (28:36–38)

    vi. The tunic and sash (28:39–41)

    vii. The undergarments (28:42–43)

C. Consecration of the priests (29:1–46)

D. Priestly service in the tent of meeting (30:1–38)

    i. The golden altar (30:1–10)

    ii. Atonement money (30:11–16)

    iii. The bronze basin (30:17–21)

    iv. Anointing oil (30:22–33)

    v. Incense (30:34–38)

14. DIVINE INSTRUCTIONS FOR WORSHIP (III): THE SKILLED WORKERS, THE SABBATH AND THE COVENANT TABLETS (31:1–18)

A. Bezalel and Oholiab (31:1–11)

B. Sabbath rest (31:12–17)

C. Reception of the covenant tablets (31:18)

15. THE COVENANT BROKEN AND RE-ESTABLISHED (32:1 – 34:35)

A. Israel's 'great sin' with the golden calf (32:1 – 33:6)

    i. Israel's idolatry and Yahweh's response (32:1–10)

    ii. Moses' intercession and Yahweh's forbearance (32:11 – 33:6)

B. Moses' mediation and the covenant restored (33:7 – 34:35)

    i. Moses' tent of meeting (33:7–11)

    ii. Moses' request to see Yahweh's glory (33:12–23)

       iii. The covenant re-established (34:1–28)

       iv. Moses' radiant face (34:29–35)

16. MANUFACTURE OF THE TABERNACLE AND PRIESTLY GARMENTS (35:1 – 39:43)

A. Sabbath regulations (35:1–3)

B. Preparations for construction (35:4 – 36:7)

       i. Materials for the tabernacle (35:4–29)

       ii. Designated skilled workers (35:30 – 36:3a)

       iii. Restrained generosity (36:3b–7)

C. The manufacture of the tabernacle and its furniture (36:8 – 38:31)

       i. The ornate tent of meeting (36:8–38)

       ii. The ark of the covenant (37:1–9)

       iii. The table for showbread (37:10–16)

       iv. The seven-branched lampstand (37:17–24)

       v. The incense altar (37:25–29)

       vi. The altar for burnt offerings (38:1–7)

       vii. The basin for washing (38:8)

       viii. The surrounding courtyard (38:9–20)

       ix. The official inventory (38:21–31)

D. The priestly garments (39:1–31)

       i. Production of the priestly garments (39:1)

       ii. The ephod (39:2–7)

       iii. The breastpiece (39:8–21)

       iv. The robe (39:22–26)

       v. The tunics, turban, caps, undergarments and sash (39:27–29)

       vi. The sacred emblem (39:30–31)

E. The workmanship inspected (39:32–43)

17. THE TABERNACLE ERECTED AND FILLED WITH YAHWEH'S GLORY (40:1–38)

A. Yahweh's final instructions to Moses concerning the tabernacle (40:1–16)

B. The faithful implementation of Yahweh's instructions (40:17–33)

C. Yahweh's glorious and guiding presence (40:34–38)

COMMENTARY

PART 1: RESCUE FROM EGYPT (1:1 – 13:16)

The first part of the book of Exodus (1:1 – 13:16) focuses on Israel's oppression in Egypt (1:1 – 2:25),[1] Moses' encounter with Yahweh and his divine commission (3:1 – 4:31), the protracted conflict between Yahweh and Pharaoh (5:1 – 11:10), and, finally, the death of Egypt's firstborn and Israel's hasty departure (12:1 – 13:16). The total period covered (cf. 1:1; 12:40) is 430 years, although most of the material covers an eighty-year period: from Moses' birth to Israel's exodus (cf. 2:2; 7:7).

---

1 Siebert-Hommes (1992) argues for a sevenfold symmetrical structure of 1:1 – 2:25 which centres on the birth of Moses.

1. OPPRESSION AND THE PROMISE OF DELIVERANCE (EXOD. 1:1 – 4:31)

A. Enslavement, genocide and the rescue of Moses (1:1 – 2:10)

Context

Exodus must be read against the backdrop of the book of Genesis and the outworking of the promises made to Israel's ancestors. Accordingly, the book is much more than a story of deliverance or divine action on behalf of an oppressed people. Rather, it recounts a very significant stage in the fulfilment of the promises God made to Abraham, Isaac and Jacob – promises through which God's goal for creation would eventually be realized. It is with the initial outworking of this divine plan that the book of Exodus is primarily concerned. Its narrative thus commences with a brief recap of material recorded in the final chapters of Genesis – the migration of Jacob and his extended family to Egypt. The proliferation of Jacob's descendants and a change in Egypt's leadership since the demise of the original migrants precipitates a crisis for the present generation, for whom the prospect of deliverance anticipated by Joseph (Gen. 50:24–25) has not yet materialized. The opening chapter highlights the perilous situation they now face, while also subtly underlining how God's promises to Abraham are coming to fruition.

Comment
i. Oppression (1:1–14)

1–4. Picking up the story of Israel's period in Egypt from the book of Genesis, Exodus begins its account with a literary flashback. This opens with the exact words of Genesis 46:8, where a more comprehensive list of Jacob's extended family immediately follows (Gen. 46:9–25) using the following maternal sequence: Leah (vv. 8–15); Zilpah, Leah's maidservant (vv. 16–18); Rachel (vv. 19–22); Bilhah, Rachel's maidservant (vv. 23–25). Here in Exodus 1, however, a chiastic arrangement (Leah, Rachel, Bilhah, Zilpah) is adopted (Hamilton 2011), similar to that reflected in Genesis 35:23–26, where the context is the demise of the previous generation and God's command for Jacob's family to 'be fruitful and increase in number' (Gen. 35:11) in order that his covenant promises might be fulfilled. It is on the fulfilment of this command and the non-fulfilment of the related promises that these opening two chapters are primarily focused.

5. While *seventy* may be a round number (cf. Gen. 46:27) rather than a purely symbolic figure, some symbolism could nevertheless be intended. If, for example, there is a deliberate allusion to Genesis 10 (the seventy that constitute the 'table of nations'), Israel may well be presented here as a microcosm of humanity (Wenham 1994: 442). The LXX (followed by Acts 7:14) has 'seventy-five', but this is almost certainly a later attempt to incorporate the immediate descendants of Ephraim and Manasseh. Despite these textual differences, the inner consistency of both the MT and LXX highlights the continuity between the end of Genesis and the start of Exodus.

6–7. Despite the (peaceful) demise of the generation who migrated to Egypt, God's plans have clearly been coming to fruition: the prolific growth of Jacob's family in Egypt bears eloquent testimony to this fact (1:7; cf. Gen. 13:16; 15:5; 17:2, 6; 22:17). Thus, the book opens on a very positive note: Israel is experiencing God's blessing. The mandate God had given humans at creation (Gen. 1:28) and had reiterated to Noah (Gen.

9:1, 7) and subsequently to Jacob (Gen. 35:11) has clearly been fulfilled.[1] Jacob's offspring had been extremely fruitful and had multiplied greatly, and now the land (*'ereṣ*) was filled with them. Therefore, God's creative and redemptive purposes are in some sense being realized here through Abraham's descendants.

8–10. Ironically, however, this divine blessing that Israel was experiencing evoked a crisis. These verses introduce a complication into the unfolding plot: Israel's phenomenal population explosion was seen as a threat to national security by the new pharaoh. The precise identity of this *new king*, like that of the other pharaohs referred to in the Pentateuch, remains unclear,[2] rendering any precise correlation with Egyptian history problematic and open to debate. The *new king* almost certainly alludes to the end of an entire dynasty, not just the death of his immediate predecessor, but the precise identity of the dynasty in question is impossible to determine for sure. While some have tried to link the Israelite migration and subsequent expulsion with the Hyksos period – during which a large Semitic population resided and even exercised power in Egypt – such a connection is tenuous at best. Others date the beginning of Israel's oppression centuries later, identifying this new king as Seti I, founder of Egypt's Nineteenth Dynasty, but this is also uncertain (see Introduction 4b, 'The date of the exodus'). Since the narrator was obviously driven by other concerns and did not consider such information essential, the identity of this pharaoh/dynasty should not distract readers from the more important focus of the narrative.

The fact that this king 'did not know Joseph' (v. 8, AT) seems to imply more than just personal ignorance (cf. the later pharaoh's confessed ignorance of Yahweh, 5:2). Rather, this new king/ regime had no obligations to protect the favoured status formerly

---

1   An obligation to be fruitful and multiply is also reflected as promises elsewhere in the patriarchal narrative (cf. Gen. 17:2, 6; 17:20; 26:4, 24; 28:3; 48:4).
2   The first pharaoh actually named in the OT is Shishak (1 Kgs 11:40), a contemporary of Solomon.

conferred on the Hebrews: Joseph's actions and kinsfolk *meant nothing* to this new dynasty.

Israel's alarming population growth served only to stir up paranoid fears. Whether Pharaoh was suggesting that they were simply expanding too rapidly, or were already threatening to outnumber the indigenous population, the net effect was the same: sooner or later the Israelites would be beyond Egyptian control. The grammatical echoes ('Come, let us . . .') and conceptual parallels (obstructing divine objectives) between Pharaoh and Babel's tower-builders (Gen. 11:3–4) suggest to the attentive reader that Pharaoh's plans will be similarly frustrated. Ironically, Pharaoh's main concern was that Israel might 'go up from the land' (AT) – the very thing that Yahweh promised to do for them through the agency of Moses (cf. 3:10) and subsequently achieved (13:18). This renders less likely the suggestion that Pharaoh's immediate fears related not to the Israelites' actual departure, but to the possibility that they might unite with Egypt's enemies and, having formed some sort of fifth column, 'take possession of the land' (Stuart 2006: 66). But whatever the perceived threat, it was apparently groundless: other than Pharaoh's delusional fears, there is nothing to suggest that the Israelites were intent on either overthrowing the Egyptians or leaving the country anytime soon.

In an attempt to curb the perceived threat Pharaoh introduced a number of radical measures. While Pharaoh thought he was being shrewd (cf. v. 10), in fact he was acting foolishly – attempting to thwart the fulfilment of God's set plan and purpose. Thus, the stage is set for the ensuing struggle between Egypt's pharaoh and Israel's God.

11. Corvée labour – in which sectors of the community were conscripted for large public works (cf. 1 Chr. 22:2; 2 Chr. 2:17–18) – was the first of several attempts at population control. The *slave masters* or project managers were evidently Egyptian (cf. 5:14), but, as the latter text shows, some responsibilities were delegated to Israelite supervisors (cf. the use of *Kapos* in Nazi concentration camps). Pharaoh's initial policy was a fairly straightforward one of containment. It was evidently his intention to break the Israelites' spirits and so keep these immigrants firmly under Egyptian control. The precise location of *Pithom* and *Rameses* has generated considerable debate (cf. Hoffmeier 1997: 116–122; Kitchen 2003:

254–259; Collins 2008).[3] Both were apparently in the Delta region, in the vicinity of Goshen where the Israelites lived (cf. Gen. 45:10). Even more controversial is the significance of the second named city. While many link this to Ramesses II, a pharaoh renowned for his building enterprises in the region, others argue that the name is used anachronistically (cf. Gen. 47:11), similar to saying that the Romans built York – a much later name for the city they founded as Eboracum. Despite its initial promise, therefore, this text does not indisputably settle the question of the date of the exodus (see Introduction 4b, 'The date of the exodus'). As English translations suggest, both cities were storage facilities (not fortifications),[4] presumably for commodities collected as royal taxes – here and elsewhere in the Old Testament such cities are associated with royal activity (Hamilton 2011).

12–14. However strange it must have seemed for the Israelite victims of such oppression, this brutal treatment by the Egyptians was actually part of God's plan. After all, this was an aspect of his promise to Abraham (cf. Gen. 15:13). To the Israelites in Egypt, it may have seemed that God had simply forsaken or abandoned them, and that God's promises had failed. But even in these dire circumstances God was at work, bringing his plans to fruition and fulfilling the promises he had made to Israel's ancestors. Not surprisingly, therefore, this hard-labour policy failed miserably (v. 12a). Almost comically, Pharaoh's brutal oppression seemed merely to exacerbate the problem of population control. Moreover, now the Egyptians really did have something to worry about (v. 12b): here in their midst was an expanding community which they had deliberately alienated and aggrieved. Whatever threat these Hebrews had posed to national security beforehand, it must have seemed much greater now that Egypt had subjected them to such injustice – hence Egypt's new-found *dread* of the Israelites,[5] and

---

3   The debate is closely linked to the chronology controversy; see Introduction 4b, 'The date of the exodus'.

4   The LXX mistakenly translates *miskĕnôt* as 'fortified'.

5   While the verb *qûṣ* can mean 'loathe' (when followed by the preposition *bĕ*), followed by *mippĕnê* it means 'dread' (cf. Num. 22:3; Isa. 7:16).

their determination to carry on, and even intensify (Exum 1983: 69 n. 9), this new domestic policy despite its initial failure (vv. 13–14). With the fivefold use of *worked/labour* (Heb. *'ābad*), a key motif is introduced. Now reduced to harsh servitude in Egypt, the Israelites would subsequently be called to serve/worship (Heb. *'ābad*) Yahweh at Sinai. Thus, this exploitative and degrading activity imposed by Pharaoh stands in sharp contrast not only to work as God intended (cf. Gen. 2:15), but also to the service Yahweh would demand. God's creative and redemptive purposes are therefore both under direct assault, as Egyptian animosity towards Abraham's descendants intensifies.

ii. Genocide (1:15–22)

Despite popular (Egyptian!) support, Pharaoh's initial policy clearly failed to deliver. Given the reality of the situation depicted here, this is unsurprising. It was God's decreed will that his people should be fruitful, multiply and fill the earth. Moreover, God had promised that all the nations of the earth would be blessed through Abraham's seed. Thus, no pharaoh, however shrewd, could thwart God's sovereign plan. However, he could resist it; and resist it he did. Pharaoh now implemented an even more radical policy – one all too familiar today and somewhat euphemistically labelled 'ethnic cleansing'. This was the first of many attempts at a 'final solution' to a perceived threat posed by Abraham's descendants.

15–16. Pharaoh surreptitiously enlisted the help of two *Hebrew midwives* to implement a rather crude form of 'birth control'.[6] Whatever is intended by the *delivery stool*,[7] the king's diabolical intentions are crystal clear: males (perceived to be the main

---

6 Some witnesses (e.g. LXX; Vulgate; Josephus) suggest that they were Egyptians (i.e. midwives *to* the Hebrews), but the Hebrew grammar clearly presents them *as* Hebrews.

7 Lit. 'two stones'. While some interpret this euphemistically for testicles, or in terms of a form of prenatal examination (Morschauser 2003), the majority understand this as some form of birthing equipment. For more on the latter, see McGeogh 2006.

threat; cf. 1:10) were to be subjected to some form of involuntary euthanasia. How only two midwives could achieve this when apparently serving so many[8] is not immediately obvious. Possibly Shiphrah and Puah served in a regional or supervisory capacity (cf. 1:19b), although this is somewhat speculative and apparently of little concern to the author – unless his intention was to illustrate further the stressful conditions the Israelites faced (Hamilton 2011). That these two ladies are named is unusual, especially since neither name is particularly significant,[9] nor do we ever hear of them or their families again. However, there is probably a deliberate contrast between these two characters and the nameless pharaohs in this book; unlike those who despised Abraham's offspring and brought God's curse upon themselves and their families (cf. Gen. 12:3), these women are not only blessed themselves (cf. vv. 20–21) but are remembered by posterity.

17. These women courageously refused to participate in Pharaoh's devious plans, because they *feared God* (more so than the king of Egypt; cf. Acts 4:19). Here another recurring theme in Exodus is introduced (cf. 9:30; 14:31; 18:21; 20:20): fearing God and behaving appropriately are inextricably linked (cf. Gen. 20:11). The midwives' response appears to be instinctive – possibly reflecting a common standard of morality (cf. Gen. 20:9) that Pharaoh was blatantly ignoring.

18–19. Faced with an irate Pharaoh, the midwives make their excuses, exploiting Pharaoh's preconceived ideas in the process (Weems 1992). Perhaps there is more truth to their explanation than is often acknowledged. After all, if these Israelites were

---

8   Some eighty years later, Exod. 12:37 suggests a total population of some 2 to 3 million people. While the accuracy of such a huge figure has been questioned (e.g. Humphreys 1998, 2000; cf. Rendsburg 2001), for an attempt to explain how such rapid growth between Jacob's migration and Israel's exodus is feasible, see Cohen 1999.

9   Meaning something like 'fair' and 'girl' respectively, neither name has any obvious connection to the plot; hence a symbolic connotation seems rather unlikely.

swarming like flies (1:7; cf. Gen. 1:21; 8:17),[10] and there were only two midwives to deal with the entire population, many of the Israelite women could well have given birth before a midwife arrived on the scene. However, the text does not deny that they have been holding out on Pharaoh (it is highly unlikely that they were late for all such births); nor does it suggest that these women were blessed because they answered the king's accusation deceitfully. Rather, it is explicitly because they *feared God* that he *gave them families of their own* (v. 21). Here God was working out his purposes through God-fearing, but certainly not sinless, individuals.

20–21. Though certainly not motivated by self-interest or the like, the midwives' actions were divinely rewarded, an example of God honouring those who honour him (1 Sam. 2:30). Thus, because they refused to implement Pharaoh's murderous instructions, God dealt favourably with these women (v. 20). The irony should not be missed. God blessed these Hebrew women with the very thing that Pharaoh was seeking to deny them: the establishment of their own families (Paul 1992). Rather than Pharaoh thwarting the plan of God, here God is already thwarting the plans of Pharaoh.

22. Despite these setbacks, and his uncritical acceptance of the midwives' explanation, Israel's nemesis was not prepared to concede defeat quite so easily. Rather, he now devised an even more ruthless strategy for dealing with the perceived problem. However, this time, no subtlety or duplicity is involved. The second phase in his infanticide policy amounted to state-sanctioned mass murder: all male Hebrew babies were to be exposed to the Nile;[11] whether the intended meaning here is 'thrown into' (cf. Gen. 37:20–24) or simply 'abandoned beside' (cf. Gen. 21:15; Ezek. 16:5),

---

10 Hamilton (2011) tentatively suggests an ethnic slur (cf. 'breeding like rabbits') is expressed in Exod. 1:19b. However, attractive as this may be, his alternative pointing of the consonantal text is purely conjectural.

11 While the ethnicity of the victims is not specified in the Hebrew text, English versions are undoubtedly correct in linking the infanticide to newborn *Hebrew* boys.

the result is surely the same. As previously, only female infants would be allowed to live, possibly with a view to subsequent intermarriage with Egyptians (cf. Gen. 12:12).[12] The designated means of disposal was probably a matter of mere convenience rather than having any religious significance. The chapter thus ends on a rather ominous note and begs the question: how will Abraham's descendants possibly survive, and what will become of God's promises?

iii. The rescue of Moses (2:1–10)

It is into these perilous circumstances of state-sponsored infanticide (1:22) that Moses, the human channel of Israel's future deliverance, is born. Against all the odds, Egypt's later antagonist not only survives Pharaoh's homicidal decree, but finds shelter and protection in the most unlikely of places – within the confines of the royal household. Once again, Pharaoh's murderous machinations are foiled and, interestingly, once more women are involved. First it was those fertile Hebrew women; then it was those duplicitous midwives; and now it is the child's mother, the child's sister and, ironically, even Pharaoh's daughter![13] Given Pharaoh's preoccupation with the opposite gender, it is surely ironic that his policy should repeatedly be subverted by women.

There are several parallels between this account of Moses' deliverance in Exodus and several 'exposed infant' legends of the Ancient Near East (see Currid 2013: 75–87), perhaps simply reflecting a common ancient custom (Longman 2009: 54–56). However, the legend of the Akkadian king Sargon I is particularly close, suggesting to some a literary dependence (Smith

---

12 So Hamilton 2011, who further suggests this rationale may lie behind the later pharaoh's insistence that women (and children) remain in Egypt (Exod. 10:10–11).

13 Interestingly, none of the three women in 2:1–10 are named, which may focus attention on their 'typified roles' in this narrative (Reinhartz 1998: 106).

2010).[14] However, if drawing on the Akkadian legend, the biblical narrator (certainly not Moses) is apparently employing such polemically: rather than demonstrating Moses' royal origins (as in the Sargon legend), Exodus is exposing Moses' humble (Hebrew) origins.

For others, a more significant parallel is an Egyptian legend, the Myth of Horus, core elements of which predate the New Kingdom period, the biblical setting for the events recounted in Exodus. As Currid helpfully illustrates (see tabular comparison, 2013: 81–82), Moses' birth account in Exodus closely echoes the tale of Horus's birth, even sharing specific Egyptian vocabulary. However, this makes the differences all the more striking (not only the non-mythical setting of the biblical account, but its ironical twist in the plot: Moses, not Pharaoh, is the Horus-like victim of oppression, and Pharaoh is the Seth-like persecutor rather than the embodiment of Horus). Thus Currid (2013: 86) plausibly infers that the biblical author polemically 'takes the famous pagan myth and turns it on its head in order to ridicule Egypt and . . . the Egyptian Pharaoh'.

At any rate, here in Exodus 2 the narrative fosters further confidence in God's sovereignty and providence: it is Pharaoh's plans, not those of God, that are frustrated. Behind all this apparent happenstance God was evidently at work. However, somewhat typically the biblical narrator makes no explicit mention of this. Indeed, other than the cameo appearance in 1:20–21, there is no mention of God until Moses' potential as Israel's deliverer has apparently been circumvented by an act of folly that led to his own mini exodus and self-imposed exile in Midian.[15]

---

14 Sargon the Great reigned about 2334–2279 BC, but the legend was written long after his reign, perhaps as royal propaganda during the reign of his late eighth-century namesake (Sargon II), but possibly earlier. A mythic parallel with Cyrus has also been suggested (Zlotnick-Sivan 2004), but this is heavily dependent on a Persian dating for the biblical tradition.

15 In a number of ways Moses foreshadows the subsequent experience of the Israelites.

1–2. The new development in the plot begins with the birth of a son to a *Levite* couple. The significance of such parentage is not yet disclosed, but this will become apparent as the larger Pentateuchal narrative unfolds. This unnamed couple is traditionally understood to be Amram and Jochebed (Exod. 6:20; cf. Num. 26:59), although these may have been the ancestors, rather than the biological parents, of Aaron and Moses (cf. comments on 6:20).[16] Under normal circumstances, there would be nothing unusual about the birth depicted here. However, in view of Pharaoh's edict (1:22), this birth notice introduces significant tension: we wait with bated breath to see what's going to happen next – will this Hebrew boy fall victim to Pharaoh's murderous decree? Well, not if his mother can help it (v. 2b). According to the text, she was prompted to act as she did because 'she saw that he was good' (AT) – which the LXX translates as 'beautiful', giving the impression that she was motivated primarily by the child's appearance: he was a fine-looking (or healthy) baby.[17] Not surprisingly, a more theological rationale than this has been sought, some suggesting a possible allusion to the Genesis creation narrative, in which God repeatedly pronounces his creation 'good'. Thus understood, the birth of Moses constitutes the beginning of a new creation – the birth of a deliverer for God's people. However, the inclusion of the predicate here (i.e. '*he* was good'; cf. the absence of such in the refrain of Gen. 1) makes this allusion less likely. Rather, a much closer parallel is found in Genesis 6:2 (Hamilton 2011), where the Hebrew adjective almost certainly conveys the idea of physical beauty or attraction. However, rather than suggesting that Moses was a 'special' or 'favoured' child, the idiom may simply convey the

---

16   The fact that Jochebed was Amram's aunt bears testimony to the historicity of the narrative, as any such marriage was subsequently prohibited by the Mosaic law (cf. Lev. 18:12–14).

17   However, the semantic range of this adjective (*asteios*) was wider than just physical attractiveness, so perhaps some other quality is (also) being alluded to (cf. O'Brien 2010: 429). Acts 7:20 suggests he was 'beautiful *to God*' (AT).

idea that 'she liked him' or 'she wanted to keep him' (Stuart 2006). Thus understood, the text is not necessarily implying that this child was somehow exceptional or unusual; rather, the attempt to hide him was prompted simply by parental love.[18] In any case, by this action both the life of this child and the future of the nation were providentially preserved.

3. The preparation of a *papyrus basket* (lit. 'ark', but not the word employed subsequently in Exodus for *the ark* [i.e. chest] *of the covenant*) suggests that God's saving purposes are at stake here. This is the only occurrence of this Hebrew term (*tēbâ*) other than in the flood story, where a much larger ark is similarly waterproofed before sheltering its occupants from the deluge that followed. Like the flood survivors, the baby is safely located in this saving flotation device. Ironically, this is then deposited at the very river of execution (1:22), the reeds of which may ominously foreshadow the later fate of the Egyptians in the *yam sûf* (traditionally, the 'Red Sea'; cf. 15:4).[19]

4. The fact that his sister (presumably Miriam; cf. 15:20; Num. 26:59) monitored the situation to see what would transpire may suggest that subsequent events were not entirely unexpected. Moreover, given the duty of care exercised thus far, it seems quite likely that the location where the ark was left was carefully selected. Thus understood, the baby's mother may well have been entrusting her child not simply to God, but also to Pharaoh's daughter (Hamilton 2011).

5–6. Since the river was infested with crocodiles, it could not have been very long before Pharaoh's daughter arrived on the scene. In any case, the baby was quickly discovered – an ominous development were it not for the fact that Pharaoh's daughter was clearly unlike her father; whereas he had heartlessly decreed that such babies be drowned (or at least abandoned to their fate), his daughter's compassion dictated otherwise – and so this child was spared.

---

18 The action is ascribed to both parents in Heb. 11:23.

19 See brief discussion of the route taken in Introduction 4c, 'The route of the exodus'.

7–10. In an extraordinary turn of events, Pharaoh's daughter allows the baby's older sister to arrange a foster home and pays his mother to be a wet nurse for her own child.[20] Rather than depicting this Egyptian princess as hopelessly naïve or foolish (cf. Yee 2009), this is surely further testimony to her compassion for those her father so despised. Anyhow, Pharaoh ends up supporting one of the very infants he had condemned. Indeed, not just one of them, but the one who, under God, would bring about the very thing he was most opposed to: the departure of the Israelites from Egypt (cf. 1:10).

Once weaned, the child is formally adopted as Pharaoh's daughter's son, presumably with all the privileges that entailed. As the narrator informs us with some sort of play on the boy's name,[21] this 'drawn-out' child is none other than Moses, the human instrument God raised up to deliver his people from captivity; the one whose personal deliverance from the reeds (*sûf*) of the Nile foreshadowed an even greater deliverance ahead, when Israel would be delivered from the *yam sûf* (cf. ch. 14).[22]

Meaning
By tracing the radical changes that have taken place in Israel's circumstances in Egypt since the original migration of Jacob and his family, the author has subtly highlighted the extent to which God's promises have thus far been fulfilled, suggesting that

---

20 Yee (2009) offers some interesting insights on the role of a wet nurse in antiquity, although most of her information reflects a much later period than the narrative setting of Exodus.

21 Both the provenance and meaning of Moses' name are debated. Most understand it to be Egyptian (cf. Ah-mose, Thut-mose, the Egyptian deity's name having been deleted in the case of Moses); Kitchen (2003: 296–297), however, suggests an original *Māšû* ('one drawn out'), later changed to *Mōšeh* ('one drawing out'). Following Sternberg (1998: 335), Hamilton (2011) suggests a double etymology, with an allusion to the similar-sounding Egyptian word for 'son' (*mesu*).

22 However, see discussion of the meaning and identity of the *yam sûf* in the Introduction 4c, 'The route of the exodus'.

everything is working out according to God's plan. This is further underlined by the sinister developments that unfold subsequently, since such oppression was precisely what God had foretold back in Genesis 15:13. Therefore, while Israel's situation may seem rather stark by the end of chapter 1, the thread of fulfilment running through it implies otherwise: despite appearances, Israel's future is nevertheless secure; God's covenant promises are sure. This is further highlighted at the start of chapter 2, where God's sovereignty and providence are further underlined: once again, it is Pharaoh's plans that are frustrated, ironically by those whose lives his murderous decree has spared. Moreover, the one who in time would become Egypt's arch-nemesis is brought up within its royal place. Behind all this apparent happenstance God was very evidently at work.

B. Moses' exodus to Midian (2:11–22)

Context

This next episode could arguably begin with the heading 'Forty years later', since that is the time-lapse according to Acts 7:23; there Stephen claims that this new twist in the tale took place when Moses was about forty years old. Between 2:10 and 2:11, therefore, the narrator has skipped over the early chapters of Moses' life. It is now four decades since Moses escaped the jaws of death in a watery grave and was adopted by the Egyptian royal family. According to Jewish tradition, in the meantime Moses has received an education with Egypt's finest. Again, Stephen claims that 'Moses was educated in all the wisdom of the Egyptians, and was powerful in word and action' (Acts 7:22, AT). Philo and Josephus concur, adding that he surpassed all his peers, and started to carve out a major political career. Such extra-biblical accounts may reflect some degree of embellishment and pious fiction, but whatever the facts, these formative years are clearly of no importance to the writer of Exodus, who skips over them without comment. The storyline resumes when the boy has become a man, and the man is about to make some career-changing decisions.

Comment

11. This next episode begins with an inspection of the royal building site. However, it was not the construction that interested Moses, but the Hebrew labourers. Significantly, the verb used here for Moses' 'going out' is later used to describe Israel's departure from Egypt (cf. 12:41). Moses is thus embarking here on his own mini exodus, leaving the palace and exposing his personal sympathies. To all appearances, he was undoubtedly an Egyptian (cf. 2:19), but like his adoptive mother he was clearly moved by the plight of *his own people*. Whether or not he was aware of his true identity at this stage is not spelt out (although cf. Acts 7:25), but by his actions Moses was taking the first tentative steps in his monumental 'refusal to be called the son of Pharaoh's daughter, choosing rather to be mistreated with the people of God than to enjoy the fleeting pleasures of sin' (Heb. 11:24–25, AT).

12. It was apparently concern for *his own people*, rather than just compassion for other human beings, that propelled Moses into action when he witnessed the brutal treatment of one of his fellow Hebrews. His action in killing the Egyptian supervisor has been variously explained. Since the causative Hebrew verb (Hiphil *nākâ*, 'to strike') does not necessarily imply a fatal blow, this was arguably a rash, impulsive act rather than intentional homicide. Understood thus, Moses intended merely to intervene in this situation and give the Egyptian a little of his own medicine. However, in the heat of the moment, Moses overdid it, inadvertently killing him. Alternatively, Moses' action can be seen as more calculated and deliberate, possibly prompted by the fact that there was no-one else to avenge the victim of this assault.[23] Thus understood, Moses was acting in a judicial rather than a homicidal manner, foreshadowing the subsequent action of Yahweh himself (3:20; 12:12–13). However, while the latter may certainly be true,

---

23   With others, Hamilton (2011) infers from analogous language used in Isaiah (59:16; 63:5) that Moses *looking this way and that* (2:12) does not necessarily express a concern to avoid detection. However, given the circumstances here in Exodus, this seems somewhat contrived – who else might Moses have expected to intervene in this particular situation?

Moses' actions both immediately before and after the killing suggest that the killing was somewhat impulsive. Indeed, given the apparent absence of any other witnesses,[24] the Hebrew assault victim probably survived (cf. 2:14), making Moses' reaction clearly disproportionate. However, whether Moses actually intended to kill the Egyptian or simply beat him up is more difficult to ascertain, especially since no weapon is mentioned in either assault. In any case, this deed severed all ties with Pharaoh; by striking someone whose actions were officially sanctioned, Moses was clearly aligning himself with Pharaoh's enemies. But while fear of reprisal may explain Moses' actions to some extent, the narrative implies that Moses did exactly as he intended. It is doubtful, therefore, that Moses thought he had used excessive force. Rather, as Stephen explains, seeing one of his brothers being mistreated, Moses 'went to his defence and avenged him by killing the Egyptian. Moses thought that his own people would realise that God was using him to rescue them, but they did not' (Acts 7:24–25).

13–14. Such lack of comprehension quickly manifested itself. When Moses again intervened in a fracas – on this occasion *two Hebrews* were brawling (cf. 21:22) – he experienced rejection and rebuke.[25] Rather than being accepted as Israel's deliverer, Moses' authority is challenged: *Who made you ruler and judge over us?* The irony should not be lost on the attentive reader; this is precisely the role to which Yahweh subsequently called Moses. Yet there is nothing in the preceding verses to suggest that Moses was acting on divine impulse or commission. Moreover, even if he was aware that God had preserved his life for such a purpose (cf. Acts 7:25), he seems here to have jumped the gun and acted on his own initiative. Not surprisingly, therefore, his misguided attempt to rescue the Israelites by his own hand ends in abysmal failure. Clearly Moses had yet to learn that if these people were going to

---

24 Unless the idea is that there were no other *Egyptians* in the vicinity to witness the event.

25 On top of verbal rejection, according to Acts 7:27 Moses was also physically manhandled.

be delivered, it would not be through human strength – not even that of a prince of Egypt; rather, deliverance would come only through Yahweh's mighty hand and Yahweh's outstretched arm (cf. 3:19).

The immediate problem for Moses, however, was not his rejection by the Hebrews, but his alienation from the Egyptians. News of his previous subversive behaviour had leaked, despite his diligent efforts to bury the evidence. Either the Hebrew victim of the previous day's assault had told others (Hamilton 2011), or else – assuming that Moses' precautionary glance (2:12) related to potential *Egyptian* witnesses – some of the Israelite workforce had in fact seen what Moses had done and spread the word. While admittedly conjectural, it is also possible that the present scenario (2:13–14) took place within earshot of Egyptian taskmasters; this would certainly explain Moses' new-found fear and anxiety. But however the news spread, it was clearly evident to Moses that he was now in a rather precarious situation.

15. It quickly transpires that Moses had every reason to be afraid. Given what we know of this pharaoh so far, his hostile reaction comes as no great surprise. Indeed, if he were already aware of Moses' origins, perhaps this simply gave him the excuse he'd long been waiting for. Whatever the reason, Pharaoh's reaction was swift and his intent clear: he sought *to kill Moses.* Once again, however, his plans to kill this particular Israelite were foiled, this time by the swift response of Moses himself. Realizing his situation in Egypt was fraught with danger, Moses made good his escape. The New Testament suggests that he was motivated by faith rather than by fear (cf. Heb. 11:27), although this may arguably be alluding to subsequent events at the time of the exodus. Understood in this manner, Hebrews 11:28–29 is expanding on 11:27, rather than reflecting a chronological sequence of events. Alternatively, the more positive take in Hebrews is simply due to the LXX, which avoids any embarrassment by describing Moses' flight in terms of a tactical withdrawal (Barclay 1992).[26] Located in

---

26 Rather than *pheugein* (flee), the more obvious equivalent of Heb. *bāraḥ*, the LXX here employs *anechōrēsen* (depart/withdraw).

the north-western part of the Arabian Peninsula, *Midian* was dry, uncultivated land, very different from that of the irrigated Nile Delta. It is unclear whether Midian was his intended destination or was simply where he happened to end up. If the former, it may have been because the Midianites, a nomadic people, were distant relatives (cf. Gen. 25:2–4). However, arguably Moses' movements reflect another example of divine providence. Indeed, given the parallels between the following incident and the earlier experience of Jacob,[27] it seems that God was continuing to direct and overrule in what otherwise might seem a rather ordinary affair. The following incident should therefore not be dismissed as either trivial or insignificant.

16–19. Once again (the third time within a few verses), Moses actively expresses a concern for the oppressed – a concern which, as we'll soon discover, is shared by God himself. This time the dispute is over watering rights. We are not told why the shepherds behaved as they did – perhaps it was simply a matter of male dominance rather than any entrenched animosity – but it's implicit from the subsequent dialogue between Reuel and his daughters that this was a frequent, if not daily, occurrence. However, on this occasion the shepherds meet more than they bargained for; an Egyptian stranger comes to the girls' aid and ensures that their flock gets watered.

Like most of the characters in the plot, Moses' future father-in-law is not initially introduced by name (v. 16), although this is disclosed in 2:18 as *Reuel* ('friend of God' or 'God is a friend'). Unless either Jethro or Reuel is a clan name (cf. comment on 3:1), it seems that Moses' father-in-law had more than one name.[28] Anyhow, here attention is drawn to his occupation; he was a *priest of Midian.*[29] From this, and his later interactions with Moses and the Israelites in chapter 18, some have inferred that Moses'

---

27 Following Alter (1981: 47–62; esp. 56–58), many identify this as a biblical 'type-scene of betrothal'.

28 Other biblical examples include Uzziah/Azariah and Saul/Paul.

29 For the possible significance of this, and Jethro's contribution to the OT concept of an 'outsider', see Leveen 2010.

father-in-law exercised a significant influence on Israel's subsequent faith. However, according to Exodus 18 (cf. esp. vv. 10–12), it was the Midianite's faith that was impacted by Moses and his testimony of what the Lord had accomplished for Israel.

Moses' mistaken identification as an Egyptian (v. 19) is presumably explained by his appearance and language. Such assimilation to Egyptian culture is not surprising for a Hebrew brought up in the royal palace but was not atypical for any Semite involved in the upper echelons of Egyptian bureaucracy (cf. Gen. 42:8).

20–22. Having been rejected by his own people and having exchanged his life in the palace for life in the desert, Moses – a foreigner – is now embraced by these foreigners. His acceptance by Reuel and his family was evidently sealed by marriage to Zipporah. Unlike the similar accounts in Genesis, there is no mention of either special virtues (cf. Gen. 24) or a romantic interest (Gen. 29) to explain why, of Reuel's seven daughters, Zipporah was singled out. Indeed, the impression given is that the selection was made entirely by Reuel; both Moses and Zipporah play a rather passive role. In any case, the narrator seems much more interested in the name Moses gave to their son, reflecting Moses' sociopolitical status as *a foreigner in a foreign land.*

While the rationale given by Moses could possibly refer to his previous status in Egypt (i.e. 'I have *been* a foreigner in a foreign land'), it seems more likely here to describe his present status (i.e. 'I have *become* a foreigner in a foreign land'). Since this is the only time during this episode that Moses actually speaks, it's obviously not an insignificant detail. Indeed, the previous section ends on a similar note, which only heightens its importance. Possibly the ambiguity in Moses' explanation of Gershom's name is intentional; Moses may have both scenarios in mind. Whether back in Egypt or here in Midian, he is a stranger, a resident alien; his true homeland is elsewhere – in the land that Yahweh had promised to Abraham. As Hebrews 11 puts it, 'Moses considered the reproach of Christ greater wealth than the treasures of Egypt, for he was looking to the reward' (i.e. the better country – the Promised Land). However, it appears with the passing of time that Moses seems to lose sight of this fact; certainly, the next time we encounter him he has settled entirely into the life of a nomad, with no great aspirations and apparently little concern for anything other than his father-in-law's sheep. In this respect Moses' flight and temporary exile from Egypt differ markedly from the story of Sinuhe, an early second-millennium historical fiction with a somewhat similar plot to this passage in Exodus (see Currid 2013: 89–95). Unlike Moses, however, Sinuhe truly is a son of Egypt, longing to return there. Indeed, when he finally does so, he and his pharaonic nemesis are completely reconciled. From this comparison Currid again discerns a polemical twist, by which the biblical author 'taunts Egypt and her nationalistic fervor: Moses doesn't crave Egypt or her kingly deity; he longs only to serve Yahweh' (2013: 95). However, while the former is clearly so, there is no evidence at this point for the latter.

Meaning

This is not just a nice story about macho Moses rescuing some pretty damsels in distress. Together with the previous episode, this incident foreshadows the even greater deliverance that lies ahead. Just as these antagonistic shepherds *drove away* Reuel's daughters, so the Egyptians would *drive away* the Israelites. Just as Moses *delivered* these girls and watered their sheep, so later Yahweh through Moses would *deliver* his people and quench their thirst. The rescue that Moses accomplishes here foreshadows the even greater deliverance to come, as is further highlighted by the way Reuel's daughters describe what happened: 'An Egyptian *rescued* us from the hand of the shepherds' (AT); later the almost identical clause describes how 'Yahweh *rescued* [the Israelites] from the hand of the Egyptians and from the hand of Pharaoh' (14:30, AT). What we have here is the exodus in microcosm. And as such, this incident alludes to the fact that despite Moses' clumsy efforts, God's plans are still on track. Nothing that has happened has upset the divine apple cart. Rather, God is still at work behind the scenes, bringing his sovereign plans to pass and putting into effect his unchanging purpose. It might look as if Moses had thoroughly messed things up; but he hadn't. God's plans are still intact. Indeed, all this is an essential part of Moses' training, his preparation for ministry. Moses had to learn that deliverance for Israel would not be the result of mere human strength; flexing his muscles might be enough to rescue a few sheep, but this would not be enough to rescue God's flock. This was something only God could do. And yet, as this incident with the shepherds reminds us, God could use even an imperfect vessel such as Moses to accomplish this task. The Israelites might have rejected Moses, but God had not rejected him; rather, God was moulding and shaping him, preparing him to accomplish his purposes in his way and at his time.

C. God hears Israel's cry for help (2:23–25)

Context
This transitional paragraph switches the focus back to the situation in Egypt and signals the most significant change in Israel's circumstances thus far. An undisclosed period of time is passed over in relative silence, although according to the New Testament it was another period of some forty years (cf. Acts 7:30). During this time there had been some significant changes: for one thing, the pharaoh who instigated the oppression of the Israelites had died. Despite this, however, their circumstances remained the same. However, this would not be the case for much longer, for their cry for help had been heard by God. Thus, for the reader at least, hope is now revived.

Comment
23. While Moses was making a new home for himself in Midian, the oppression in Egypt continued unabated – even after the death of the reigning pharaoh. Whatever forlorn hope of relief the latter might possibly have engendered, the harsh reality of the situation soon became evident: no radical changes to Egyptian domestic policy were imminent. Rather, the status quo would continue for the foreseeable future. For the first time, however, the reaction of the Israelites to their enslavement is mentioned: not surprisingly, they groan and cry out. While their cries for help here are not explicitly directed towards God (or indeed anyone) specifically (although cf. Num. 20:16; Deut. 26:7), they reach him nonetheless. This contrasts markedly with Pharaoh, who deliberately remains deaf to Israel's subsequent cries (cf. 5:8–9).

24–25. At last, a note of relief is breathed into the narrative: 'God heard . . . God remembered . . . God looked . . . and God was concerned' (lit. 'knew'; AT). After his relative and somewhat disturbing absence in these two chapters,[30] God finally takes centre stage, from this point on becoming the central character in the plot. At long last, God acknowledges the Israelites' plight and remembers his covenant with their ancestors; he is thus about to act. Such is the significance of God 'remembering'; the idea is not that he has somehow forgotten to act previously, but rather that – because of a prior commitment he has made – he is now about to act. Thus, God is not primarily motivated by a concern for social justice – though it would be misleading to suggest that such is not part of the equation – but by covenant obligation and responsibility. 'Even if life in Goshen had been serene and idyllic, God still would have delivered them' (Hamilton 2011: 42). And so hope is again renewed; finally deliverance for Israel is somewhere in sight.

Meaning
Moses had apparently put his past and the Israelites' plight behind him during his prolonged stay in Midian. This, however, was premature for, unlike Moses, God had not forgotten them. As this final paragraph informs us, the situation for Israel was about to change. While, humanly speaking, deliverance may seem as far away as ever, God has finally entered the unfolding drama, and with covenant fulfilment on top of his agenda, more positive developments can now be expected.

D. Theophany and proof-signs (3:1 – 4:17)

Context
According to Stephen (Acts 7:30), this next incident took place when Moses was around eighty, after living in Midian some forty years. Apparently, since settling into his new life as a nomad,

---

30 Other than the passing mention in 1:20–21, this is the first explicit mention of God in the story so far.

little has changed for Moses. Despite the passing of time, he still appears to be dependent on his father-in-law for his livelihood. But this does not seem to bother him; Moses seems quite content with his new lifestyle, however alien it once was. Moreover, it would appear that he has absolutely no plans for returning to Egypt; seemingly that period in his life has finally been put behind him. At least, so he thought – his situation is about to change dramatically. The narrator has already given notice of this at the end of chapter 2. 'During those many days' (2:23, AT) a significant development had taken place. Despite a change in leadership, not much had happened politically and socially; the situation of the Israelites remained much as it was. However, there had been a theological watershed. The desperate groans of God's people had reached heaven itself; God had heard; God had remembered his covenant; and finally, the time has come for God to act. And so, here in chapter 3, God begins to put the next stage of his plan into action. The event anticipated back in Genesis 15:14 is fast approaching: Israel's deliverance is now at hand. Consequently, the day has dawned for Moses to step into his divinely appointed role.

Comment

i. Theophany at the mountain of God (3:1–22)

1. As suggested above, the fact that after forty years Moses is still tending *the flock of . . . his father-in-law* may imply a lack of independence. The unexpected name-switch to *Jethro* (cf. 2:18) is not elucidated in the text and has given rise to various theories.[31] For some, this anomaly reflects the use of different underlying sources in the compilation of the narrative. However, this fails

---

31 To complicate things further, 4:18 refers to him as 'Jether', he is arguably called 'Hobab' in Num. 10:29 and Judg. 4:11, and in some texts he is identified as a Kenite (cf. Judg. 1:16; 4:11) rather than a Midianite. However, each of these is fairly easy to explain: 'Jether' is simply a variant of 'Jethro', 'Hobab' probably refers to Jethro's son (cf. *NIDOTTE* 2: 327), Moses' brother-in-law, and Midian refers to a coalition of peoples that included the Kenites.

to do justice to the integrity of the compiler/editor, who was obviously aware of such 'inconsistencies' in the text. Still others conclude that the diversity reflects a use of the clan name in some texts, rather than the personal name of Moses' father-in-law. However, the simplest explanation (i.e. that he had more than one name) is probably the best.

There is nothing to suggest that the route that Moses took on this occasion was unusual,[32] nor does the description of Horeb as *the mountain of God* suggest some kind of pilgrimage. Rather, the latter description derives from the fact that God manifests his presence there – first to Moses (here in ch. 3), and subsequently to Israel (chs. 19–40). There is no suggestion that God actually dwelt on this mountain (see 15:13). As with Jethro, it appears that the mountain was known by more than one name (cf. 19:18–23) – unless one name denotes something different from the other (a single peak as opposed to a mountain range). The precise location of this mountain is unknown. Its traditional site (Mt Musa) is in the central, southern region of the Sinai Peninsula, but nearby (Mt Serbal) or more northerly (Mt Sin Bishar) sites are also feasible, as the precise route taken by Israel is uncertain (see Introduction 4c, 'The route of the exodus').

2–3. What probably started as a fairly ordinary day became something else when Moses came across a bush-fire – one that, despite being relatively contained, was extremely unusual.[33] It was not the fire itself, but rather the fact that the bush was not consumed by the flames, that drew Moses' attention to this *strange sight*. Scholarly attempts to explain this phenomenon naturalistically, however ingenious, strangely miss the point: this sight was so unusual that it caught the attention of a seasoned nomad and

---

32 'Desert' and 'wilderness' conjure up misleading associations of arid wasteland, whereas here *midbār* denotes uncultivated, remote grazing land; cf. Exod. 34:3 (Hamilton 2011: 45).

33 Even the term used for 'bush' (*sĕnê*) is unusual; its only other occurrence is in Deut. 33:16. It has clear similarities with 'Sinai' (Heb. *sînāy*), and thus subtly anticipates the subsequent theophany that would take place there (Exod. 19).

drew him closer to investigate. Unlike Moses, of course, readers are alerted to what is actually happening from the outset: these were no ordinary flames; rather, this supernatural fire was a theophany, a means through which God was manifesting his presence to Moses. Here *the angel of the LORD* (see Additional note below on the revelation and meaning of the divine name) seems to be synonymous with the actual flames of fire; hence the GNT's '*as* a flame . . .' (emphasis added) better captures the sense. Thus understood, here the angel of the LORD is simply a vehicle for divine communication. Elsewhere in the Old Testament, however, this figure apparently assumes a human form (e.g. Judg. 6:11–22; 13:2–22; cf. Gen. 18:1–2), leading some to explain the motif as a Christophany (a pre-incarnate manifestation of Christ). However, this is problematic, both exegetically and theologically: whatever form the manifestation takes, this angel is closely identified with God (and so speaks with divine authority), while at the same time being carefully distinguished from God (i.e. he remains a 'divine messenger' and is not to be confused with the LORD himself; cf. 23:20).

4–6. Having captured Moses' attention, the LORD now begins to communicate with him verbally. It seems unlikely that the switch halfway through verse 4 was designed to identify the speaker as the aforementioned angel (so Hamilton 2011), as 'the angel' rather than 'God' would have made this more obvious. While possibly stylistic, it may also highlight the perilous nature of the situation: Moses was standing in the presence of God (cf. vv. 5–6).[34] The double vocative (*Moses! Moses!*) is not unusual in such divine communications (cf. Gen. 22:11; 1 Sam. 3:10); like other such examples (cf. 2 Sam. 18:33; 2 Kgs 2:12; Ps 22:1 [MT 2]), the sense is emphatic. Having responded in a conventional manner,[35] Moses now discovers what readers already know: this is an encounter with none other than God. As such, steps must be taken to ensure Moses' safety. As was later true for Israel (cf. ch. 19), Moses must maintain a safe distance and take appropriate

---

34 Interestingly, apart from v. 7, *God* is used consistently of the divine speaker up until the revelation of the divine name.

35 Cf. Gen. 22:1, 11; 27:1; 31:11; 37:13; 46:2; 1 Sam. 3:4, 5, 6, 8, 16; Isa. 6:8.

action before a holy God. The removal of his sandals may be just
a reverential act (cf. Muslim practice entering a mosque), but was
possibly designed to avoid 'contaminating' holy space (i.e. ground
that had been set apart by God's manifest presence) with anything
that might be defiling or unclean.[36] The somewhat unusual
singular noun at the end of the phrase *I am the God of your father* (v.
6; but cf. 15:2) may well have a collective nuance (cf. 3:13, 15–16)
or be echoing the ancestral promise of Genesis 46:3. In any case,
whether God introduces himself as the deity of Moses' *father* or
'fathers' (as attested in SP, some Greek witnesses and Acts 7:32), the
explicit mention of Abraham, Isaac and Jacob makes it abundantly
clear that Moses was standing in the presence of Israel's ancestral
deity – something that Moses obviously realized was fraught with
danger (cf. Gen. 32:30; Exod. 33:20), prompting him to hide his
face before God (cf. the similar action of the seraphs in Isa. 6:2).

7–8. Whatever his apprehensions, Moses had nothing to fear;
God meant him no harm. All he wanted was to share some
information and make Moses aware of his plans to rescue Israel.
And so, beginning with what we, the readers, already know (v. 7;
cf. 2:24–25), God makes his intentions clear, fleshing out what it
meant for God to have *remembered* his covenant (2:24). Not surprisingly, God's plan involves rescuing Abraham's descendants from
Egyptian oppression (v. 8a; cf. Gen. 15:14)[37] and bringing them
safely back to Canaan (v. 8b; cf. Gen. 15:16), thus fulfilling the
covenant promises of Genesis 15. The description *flowing with milk
and honey* is undoubtedly figurative speech involving hyperbole;
significantly, the twelve spies brought back grapes, pomegranates
and figs to illustrate the land's fertility (Num. 13:23, 27). Thus
understood, it is not entirely beside the point whether *milk* (*ḥalab*)

---

36 As Hamilton (2011) observes, the absence of any mention of footwear in
    Exod. 28 and 39 (chapters dealing with priestly clothing) may indicate
    that priestly service in the tabernacle was conducted barefoot.

37 As mentioned above, the verb (Hiphil *nāṣal*) used here of God's act of
    deliverance is the same verb used by Jethro's daughters to describe their
    'rescue' by Moses. It is also used several times of God's deliverance of
    Israel in Exod. 18.

should be understood as 'fat' (*ḥeleb*) or the *honey* (*děbaš*) as sweet syrup produced from fruit (e.g. grapes, date and figs);[38] the main idea is that this land is extremely fertile, a pastoralist's dream. As elsewhere, the extent of Israel's territorial inheritance is delineated by a representative list of its indigenous inhabitants. While the numbers in such lists vary considerably,[39] this probably reflects different levels of exactitude (i.e. some lists differentiate between the various people groups more precisely than others) and possibly in some cases a desire to represent the Canaanites symbolically.

9–10. As the repetition (cf. v. 7) indicates, Israel's plight has prompted God to act; it now becomes clear how this also involves Moses: he has been selected to confront Pharaoh and play a significant role in this divine deliverance. As so often in Scripture, God does not act alone, but uses human instruments to bring his plans to fruition.

11. Not surprisingly, Moses found this divine commission quite incredible. After all, there were several issues that God seemed to have overlooked: (1) his refugee status – technically, he was still a fugitive from justice; (2) his track record – his previous attempt to rescue his fellow Israelites had ended in rejection and failure; (3) and his advanced age – at eighty years old, surely he wasn't the ideal candidate for this formidable task. But whatever thoughts may have been on Moses' mind, the question he asks (*Who am I . . . ?*) makes it abundantly clear that his focus was solely on himself.

12. As God's response underlines, Moses was ignoring the most important detail: this time, he would not be acting alone; rather, God would be with him. God's assurance here (*I will be with you*) is later given to Joshua, Moses' successor (cf. Deut. 31:23; Josh. 1:5; 3:7), and the concept also appears elsewhere in the Old Testament, usually in relation to those God has raised up for a particular task (Jer. 1:8, 19; 15:20; cf. Isa. 43:2; Jer. 20:11; 30:11; 46:28). The verbal form used in the assurance here in Exodus 3:12 (*'ehyê*) may deliberately foreshadow the revelation of the divine name

---

38 Explicit OT references to bee honey are uncommon (e.g. Judg. 14:8–9; cf. also 1 Sam. 14:26–27).

39 Cf. Gen. 13:7; 15:19–21; Num. 13:29; Deut. 7:1.

that immediately follows (cf. vv. 14–15), which arguably reflects a closely related verb (Heb. *hāvâ*, 'to become' [Aramaic, 'to be']; cf. Heb. *hāyâ*, 'to be'). If so, this verse may throw some light on the meaning and significance of the latter revelation (see discussion below). Not only is Moses assured of God's divine presence, however; he is also assured that the entire assembly (the *you* of the final clause in the verse is plural) will worship God at this very place. The latter seems somewhat strange as a *sign* designed to bolster Moses' confidence, prompting some commentators to suggest that this *sign* must actually refer to something else (e.g. the burning bush). However, it is probably best thought of as a 'fulfilment sign' which both encouraged faith in the present and provided retrospective reassurance in the future (Stuart 2006). Its anticipatory nature readily explains why it failed, on this occasion, to eradicate Moses' present anxieties and fears. As Cole (1973: 68) comments, 'Self-distrust is good, but only if it leads to trust in God. Otherwise, it ends as spiritual paralysis, inability and unwillingness to undertake any course of action.' Thus, instead of pressing forward in faith, Moses responded with objection number 2.

13. Moses' first objection focused on his inadequacy; this next one focuses on his ignorance: rather than asking, 'Who am I?' he now asks, 'Who are you?' He frames the question, however, with a hypothetical, yet realistic, scenario: *Suppose I go to the Israelites and say to them, 'The God of your fathers has sent me to you,' and they ask me, 'What is his name?' Then what shall I tell them?* This seems to be a perfectly legitimate question, especially if Moses himself was ignorant of the divine name. Understood in this way, Moses was concerned with how he could possibly convince the Israelites that *their* God had spoken to *him*, especially if he was unaware of their deity's name. However, while this explanation seems more plausible than the argument that – until now – the divine name had not been disclosed to anyone,[40] it is still somewhat inadequate. Mere

---

40 Apart from having to assume an anachronistic usage of the name in Genesis, this idea fails to explain how Moses could prove his prophetic credentials by presenting himself to the Israelites in the name of a deity that was hitherto unknown to anyone.

acquaintance with the name of the Hebrew deity would not necessarily prove that Moses had personally encountered this God at Sinai, still less that God had given Moses this particular task; less incredible explanations for Moses' familiarity with God's name would probably have seemed more obvious.[41]

However, if the divine name was already familiar to both Moses and his fellow Israelites, then what are we to make of the hypothetical question that Moses anticipates here and his implied ignorance of the correct answer? The key to the most likely solution is found in the interrogative pronoun which Moses uses. Rather than the idiomatic '*Who* is your name?' Moses asks, '*What* is your name?'[42] Waltke thus concludes that, 'Within the context of the narrative, Moses is really anticipating this question from the Israelites: "Given all the suffering we have been through, what does I AM mean anyway?"'[43] Along similar lines, Blackburn (2012: 37) argues that Moses is anticipating misgivings on Israel's part over the success of the proposed mission. Accordingly, Moses is enquiring here about the *character* as opposed to merely the *appellation* of Israel's God (cf. Neh. 9:10).

14–15. Not surprisingly, therefore, rather than simply answering, 'My name is Yahweh' (as would presumably have sufficed if a mere epithet was the focus of Moses' enquiry), God unpacks the meaning and significance of this name, responding: 'I will be who I will be', or as most English versions render this notoriously enigmatic phrase, *I am who I am* (see Additional note

---

41 Such knowledge would hardly have seemed extraordinary for an educated person such as Moses, especially given the interest he had already shown in these Hebrew slaves.

42 As Waltke (2007: 365) points out, 'In biblical Hebrew *mî* . . . is the animate, interrogative pronoun that focuses on the person. Thus, *mî šemekâ* (lit., "Who is your name?") is used to ask for someone's name (Judg. 13:17). The inanimate pronoun *mah* is used when the focus is on the circumstance rather than the person. Thus, *mah šemekâ* (lit., "What is your name?") seeks the meaning of the name (Gen. 32:28).'

43 Waltke 2007: 365. Waltke uses 'I AM' rather than 'the LORD' to translate the divine name YHWH.

on the revelation and meaning of the divine name).[44] Thus God does not simply supply Moses with the divine name here; rather, he discloses something of his character that is bound up in the name. The revelation, therefore, concerns something about the name's significance of which both Moses and his fellow Israelites were presently unaware, and which Moses is to communicate to the Israelites.

Interestingly, a similar use of an 'I am who I am' statement is reflected in an Egyptian mythical text, the Book of the Heavenly Cow,[45] which Currid (2013: 97) takes to be an example of polemical theology by the ancient Egyptians in response to a major tenet of Hebrew theology. Scholars have highlighted various parallels between this text and Exodus, the most astounding being the *idem per idem* use of the verb 'to be' (the cognate Egyptian root is *yw*) found in Re's edict to destroy rebellious humankind: 'I am that I am [*ywy ymy*]. I will not . . .' This is arguably the earliest attested extra-biblical use of the divine epithet,[46] preceding other such non-Israelite examples (e.g. the Moabite Stone) by several centuries. But it employs the key phrase with reference to the god Re, of whom Pharaoh was considered the human embodiment, sovereign over all creation. Given how the significance of Yahweh's name is gradually disclosed in the conflict between Moses and Pharaoh in Exodus, it is perhaps unsurprising that the

---

44 Yahweh (he is/he will be?) is probably the third-person form of the verb *hwh* (Heb. 'to become'; Aramaic, 'to be/become'). A very similar verb (even more so in Hebrew, where the middle consonants are more alike), *hyh* (also meaning 'to be'), is used in the sentence, 'I am/will be who I am/will be'), subsequently abbreviated to 'I am/will be'. See further, Athas 2008: 41–47.

45 As Currid explains (2013: 99), the name derives from the way Amon-Re's creation of the cosmos is depicted 'as a cow being uplifted by the god Shu, the deity of air and light, with the help of eight other deities'.

46 Some suggest an even earlier reference in a list from the reign of Amenhotep III (fourteenth century BC), in which 'the land of Shosu-Yhw' designates a geographical location, and may not refer to the God of Israel at all (especially if a late date for the exodus is correct).

Egyptians might appropriate it as a means of denying Yahweh's claims and asserting the supremacy of Re and Pharaoh, akin to how Moses had appropriated the pharaonic phrase 'Thus says the pharaoh' and applied it to Yahweh.[47]

Additional note: the revelation and meaning of the divine name

The commentary above has argued that (1) the divine name is not revealed here for the first time; and (2) that some theological information, pertinent to Moses and Israel's circumstances, is being disclosed. Neither of these conclusions is universally accepted. Indeed, the sheer volume of secondary literature pertaining to Exodus 3:13–15 attests to how exegetically challenging and controversial this material in Exodus actually is. In terms of the first issue, many scholars have argued that this text does indeed suggest that the name of God (YHWH) is here revealed for the first time.[48] The difficulty with this, however, is not only its prior usage in Exodus (cf. 3:2, 4, 7), but also the numerous times that it has been

---

47 While one could argue that 'I am that I am' was simply another phrase the Hebrews polemically appropriated from Egypt, this would depend on Exodus 3 being the first use of the epithet by them. For the problems with this, see Additional note on the revelation and meaning of the divine name.

48 The divine name is sometimes referred to in scholarly literature as the 'Tetragram' or 'Tetragrammaton' (i.e. 'four letters'). Uncertainties with respect to its correct pronunciation have led to a reluctance on the part of many to supply any vowels at all (YHWH). The traditional pronunciation (Jehovah) is certainly incorrect, deriving from the scribal combination of the consonants of YHWH and the vowels of *Adonai* (the word traditionally substituted to avoid misusing God's name). Many scholars (and some modern translations) suggest 'Yahweh', although this too is not without problems (e.g. technically speaking, this would probably mean 'He causes to be', hardly appropriate as a revelation for Israelites currently under Egyptian oppression). Modern Jewish practice is simply to refer to 'the name' (Heb. *haššēm*; cf. Lev. 24:11).

used in Genesis. To account for the latter, mainstream scholarship has often resorted to source criticism, concluding that usage in Genesis reflects an underlying source ('J') that differs from that reflected in Exodus 3 and Exodus 6:3 ('P').[49] This, however, builds on the unlikely premise that there was no consensus in ancient Israel over such a fundamental issue. Alternatively, some (e.g. Wenham 1980; Moberly 1992; Bartholomew 2021) argue that the use of the divine name prior to Exodus 3 is deliberately anachronistic, designed to identify Yahweh as the God of the primeval and patriarchal narratives. However, while it is true that the divine name is mostly employed by the narrator (rather than the characters) in Genesis, this is not always the case (cf. Gen. 4:1; 9:26; 14:22; 15:2; 16:2, 5, 11; 18:14; 19:13; 22:14; 24:3, 7, 12, 27, 31, 35, 40, 42, 44, 48, 50, 51, 56; 26:22, 28–29; 27:20, 27; 28:16, 21; 29:32–33, 35; 30:24, 27, 30; 31:49; 32:9; 49:18; cf. also Gen. 4:26; 12:8; 21:33; 26:25).[50] Others thus conclude that while God's name was known before Exodus 3, its theological significance was not appreciated or understood.

The latter, however, has also generated considerable controversy. The explanatory phrase ('I am/will be who I am/will be') has been understood as stressing God's existence, sovereignty, creative power or presence; indeed, it has even been seen as deliberately evasive (cf. Gen. 32:29; Judg. 13:18), amounting to a curt refusal to answer Moses' question. However, this seems inappropriate in the present context, where the credibility of Moses as a divinely sent ambassador is at stake. It is much more likely that 'I will be who I will be' is drawing attention to the fuller revelation of Yahweh that Moses and Israel are about to experience in his

---

49 Previously, scholars distinguished a third putative source ('E'), allegedly underlying Exod. 3:13–15.

50 Admittedly, on the lips of some characters (e.g. the entourage from Gerar in 26:28–29), the mention of Yahweh may well be rhetorical; moreover, to 'call on the name of the LORD' may simply be an idiom for offering acceptable worship. This does not significantly detract from the numerous texts suggesting patriarchal familiarity with the divine name.

mighty acts of deliverance (Seitz 1998). Thus understood, the revelation given to Moses, to be passed on to Israel, amounted to an exposition of the divine name in terms of who he is, as would be demonstrated in what they were about to see him do.

16–17. Something of the divine character that is bound up in the divine name is further unpacked as Moses' commission is reiterated and amplified (vv. 16–22). Through what Moses is about to disclose, the Israelites will learn more about Yahweh, who has *appeared* (v. 16) as such to Moses (cf. 4:1; 6:3). They will discover that he is not only one who speaks, but one who saves.

Moses' mission will begin with a declaration of Yahweh's concern and intent (cf. vv. 7–8) to Israel's *elders*. The fact that there were such in the Israelite community suggests some degree of social autonomy and organization. Elders were recognized leaders in many ancient societies (cf. Gen. 50:7; Num. 22:7), often due to their position as heads of their tribes, clans or households.[51]

18–19. In view of God's assurance here of a positive response, Moses' subsequent objection (4:1) seems inexcusable – although even Yahweh seems prepared to concede that some initial reluctance may have to be overcome (cf. 4:8). But however the Israelites might respond, there is no mistaking the fact that Moses will come up against an immovable obstacle: Pharaoh will obstinately refuse to let the people go. The specific request – for a three-day journey into the desert – may seem strange or even disingenuous in view of the ultimate objective and destination (cf. vv. 8, 17). Most likely, however, this was simply a conventional expression for a short journey (i.e. a figure of speech readily understood within Ancient Near Eastern culture which no-one would have taken literally; cf. Firth 2021: 71–75).[52] Alternatively, it may have

---

51 For a detailed discussion of elders in the OT, see Reviv 1989.

52 For more on this, with some comparable expressions in modern English, see Stuart 2006: 124–125. It is nevertheless interesting that the only temporal reference highlighted in the itinerary of Num. 33 is the 'three days' it took for the people to reach Marah (Num. 33:8) – possibly throwing some light on Israel's impatience with Moses at that point in the journey.

been a bartering technique, making a fairly small request to determine how much (or otherwise) Pharaoh was prepared to concede. Whatever the case, Pharaoh would not be compelled by mere human persuasion (v. 19). While most English translations assume that the 'strong hand' (AT) is Yahweh's, Stuart (2006) argues that it is better to translate the last part of verse 19 as 'not even by a strong hand', which refers here to mere human strength in contrast to the kind of power that Yahweh will exercise against him (v. 20).

20. Yahweh would therefore have to exercise his powers of persuasion; this time it would be Yahweh's hand that would *strike* the Egyptians (cf. 2:12), and by performing *wonders* (i.e. the subsequent plagues) he would secure Israel's deliverance. The final outcome of this enterprise was absolutely certain: however much he might resist, Pharaoh would eventually capitulate and let Israel go.

21–22. As well as receiving 'exit visas', these emancipated slaves (cf. Deut. 15:12–18) would not leave *empty-handed*. Rather, in fulfilment of the promise of Genesis 15:14, they would 'come out with great possessions'. Other than the fact that Yahweh would make the Egyptians *favourably disposed* towards the Israelites, the motivation for such 'generosity' is not really explained either here or in 11:2–3. However, it is clear from 12:33 that their motivation was not entirely altruistic: fear for their lives contributed significantly to the desire to see the back of these troublesome Israelites, and thus facilitate their speedy departure in whatever way possible. By this means Israel would *plunder the Egyptians*. Most likely this alludes to booty taken by the victors in battle. However, it may also suggest that, as well as being emancipated, these Israelite slaves will receive some measure of compensation for their hard service (cf. 1:13).

ii. Proof-signs for Moses (4:1–17)
Despite the assurances already offered, Moses remains unconvinced. He continues to focus on how the Israelites *might* respond to his extraordinary claims. However, while the situation envisaged by him here is clearly hypothetical, subsequent events (4:29–31) suggest that Moses' misgivings were not entirely unfounded: the

performance of the signs (4:30) seems to imply that Moses was indeed challenged to validate his testimony after all.

1. The issue now is one of incredulity: how will anyone believe such extraordinary claims?[53] Nevertheless, while Moses' objection may seem quite reasonable, the fact that he is verbally denying what Yahweh has already said (cf. 3:18) should not be missed. It seems that Moses is simply unable to move beyond the first perceived obstacle (i.e. convincing his fellow Israelites); there is no suggestion (contra Hamilton 2011) that he thought persuading Pharaoh might be any easier.

2–5. Amazingly, this bold contradiction of Yahweh's previous reassurance does not evoke an immediate rebuke or divine anger (cf. v. 14). Rather, Yahweh continues to exercise great patience with his reluctant servant, offering him some proof-signs to shore up his faith and disclose how any necessary persuasion will be done. The idea that the first of these sign-acts – involving Moses' staff – was some kind of conjuring trick that Moses had learnt in Egypt is clearly belied by his personal reaction: an inanimate object had temporarily changed into a slithering snake, prompting a hasty retreat. Clearly it was God, not Moses, who was responsible for this amazing metamorphosis. This transformation demonstrated Yahweh's sovereignty over a creature revered in Egypt and even used, along with a staff, to symbolize Pharaoh's authority.[54] Along with the following two signs (vv. 6–9), it was also a subtle reminder that Yahweh has ultimate authority over all creation. Here, however, it primarily served to authenticate Moses' claim that Yahweh, the God of Israel's ancestors, had indeed appeared to him (v. 5; cf. v. 1).

6–9. The same was true in the case of the two subsequent signs, both of which again involved a miraculous transformation:

---

53 The Hebrew preposition may suggest the focus is more on the credibility of Moses' claims than his personal trustworthiness (Novick 2009, cited in Hamilton 2011: 69), though the difference is surely rather semantic.

54 For more on the latter, see comment on the use of Moses' and Aaron's rod in their initial confrontation with Pharaoh (Exod. 7:8–13).

normal skin changing to abnormal skin,[55] and back again; and water changing into blood.[56] Only the first of these additional signs was apparently 'pre-viewed' at this stage by Moses. Indeed, it is unclear whether the third sign was even necessary to eradicate any Israelite scepticism (4:30). In any case, its description here seems to distinguish it clearly from the implementation of the 'plague of blood' recounted in Exodus 7:14–24. While Moses' subsequent performance of at least two of these three signs convinced his fellow Israelites (cf. 4:30), the first and the third (albeit on a much larger scale) were insufficient to persuade Pharaoh.

10–12. Ironically, the same was also true in the case of Moses. Despite these extraordinary 'sign-acts' – which underline that it is not Moses, but Yahweh, who will do the persuading – Moses remains sceptical about his ability to carry out the task that Yahweh is giving him.

Moses' fourth objection (v. 10) involves a switch in focus from Yahweh and the Israelites to himself and his perceived inadequacies – more precisely, his inability to communicate clearly or effectively. It is hard to know how we should interpret this fourth objection. After all, according to Stephen, Moses 'was powerful in *speech* and action' (Acts 7:22; emphasis added), which might seem to undermine any suggestion that 'heavy of mouth and heavy of tongue' (AT) alludes to some form of speech impediment (cf. 6:12, 30) or language barrier (cf. Ezek. 3:5–6). The latter, however, seems most unlikely since Moses would have spoken Egyptian for some forty years before his exile in Midian, and he is never portrayed as requiring an 'interpreter' (cf. Gen. 42:23). Possibly

---

55 The description of the transformed skin clearly suggests some form of severe skin disease (e.g. psoriasis), but arguably not the medical condition we know today as leprosy (i.e. Hansen's disease).

56 Here, unlike in Exod. 7:14–24, it is difficult to see how *blood* can possibly be construed as contaminated or discoloured water (i.e. water that simply looks like blood). If understood in terms of an unusual chemical reaction between the water and the sand on the ground, it is hard to see how this would conceivably prove persuasive, as it could quite easily be replicated by others.

Moses is simply referring here to his general communication skills (or lack thereof), claiming that he had never been very articulate (a man of words), but generally found himself 'tongue-tied' in the presence of others. For Moses, that such was true even in the present context may have been a case in point, although the irony of Moses boldly arguing with God cannot be lost on the reader. Nevertheless, it is clearly Yahweh who does most of the talking here, and his response to Moses' objection suggests that Moses' claim was not unwarranted. Moreover, a close reading of the ensuing narrative in Exodus and beyond lends significant support to the suggestion that Moses did indeed have some sort of speech issue such as an acute stammer, necessitating communicative assistance from others (Millard 2016; see p. 100 n. 10 below). But whatever the precise problem – and significantly Yahweh does not deny that such existed – Moses is still making the same fundamental mistake; once again, he's focusing in the wrong direction: looking at himself and his own inadequacy, rather than at Yahweh and his sufficiency.

Not surprisingly, therefore, Yahweh responds (vv. 11–12) by redirecting Moses' focus, answering a series of rhetorical questions with, *Is it not I, the LORD?* By this means Yahweh again encourages Moses to get his eyes off himself and onto the one who gives people their faculties, and on whom the success of this mission ultimately depends. What actually matters is not Moses' abilities or lack thereof, but the fact that – as stated back in 3:12 – Yahweh would accompany him. Moses could therefore boldly go and carry out this task, knowing that Yahweh would both *help* [him] *speak and . . . teach* [him] *what to say.*

With all his objections duly answered, we might expect that Moses would finally submit to the divine commission and carry out the task assigned to him. However, it now becomes clear that all these objections sprang from the fact that Moses simply did not want to do so.

13. This time, rather than raising another objection, Moses curtly refuses to go. He introduces this negative response respectfully ('Please, my Lord', AT), and phrases it as diplomatically as possible: *Please send someone else* is literally, 'Send by the hand you will send' (i.e. 'Send whomever you please, so long as it's not me').

Even so, this does little to soften what amounts to unbelief and disobedience. Whether or not Moses really thought there might be a more suitable candidate is beside the point; he was clearly not prepared to carry out this assignment.

14–16. Not surprisingly, this evoked God's anger. Though God is *slow to anger* (34:6), disobedience inevitably arouses God's wrath – as the Israelites themselves would later discover. It was thus at this stage of the divine encounter that Moses was clearly in the greatest danger; but unlike some other cases in the Old Testament where God's anger is directed against individuals (cf. 2 Sam. 6:7), Moses does not lose his life. Rather, despite his divine anger,[57] God continues to deal with Moses graciously and patiently, again addressing his insecurities by providing a practical solution to the lack of communication skills raised previously. Yahweh had apparently anticipated Moses' need for assistance in effective communication; hence his brother Aaron, a skilled orator, was already on his way to meet Moses. His description here as *the Levite* (cf. 2:1) probably anticipates the later significance of both Aaron and his tribe in Israel's worship (cf. 28:1; 32:29), but in the immediate context his role was merely to serve as Moses' assistant. It is subsequently made clear that Aaron had been similarly called by Yahweh to embark on this journey (cf. 4:27); thus the circumstances and timing of their brotherly reunion were divinely orchestrated. Aaron would function as Moses' mouthpiece or, as God later puts it (cf. 7:1), as Moses' *prophet*; Moses would be *God* to him (i.e. he would communicate Yahweh's thoughts and will) in the same way that he would subsequently represent Yahweh before Pharaoh. Together Moses and Aaron would communicate Yahweh's message. But, as the final instruction (see v. 17) implies, the work of persuasion would be done by Yahweh himself. It wasn't really Moses *or* Aaron who would do the convincing. That was God's responsibility. All Moses had to do was to carry out Yahweh's instructions, and trust Yahweh to do the rest.

---

57 As Stuart (2006: 137) suggests, a better translation might be: 'Although God's anger raged against Moses, he said . . .'

17. Moses' *staff* has now become the symbol of his divine authority. While it was used only in connection with the first of the aforementioned signs (vv. 1–9), the use of the plural here (*the signs*) implies that it will be used more extensively in subsequent events. During these later events it appears that Aaron kept possession of the staff (cf. 7:8, 10, 12, 19; 8:5, 16; cf. 7:17; 9:23; 10:13; 14:16); thus understood, there is no discrepancy between Yahweh's instructions here and the implementation of these signs in the narrative that follows. Whether associated with Moses or Aaron, it is this one staff that is in view throughout.

Meaning

The opening two chapters have raised readers' expectations that God is about to intervene on behalf of Abraham's descendants and that Moses will have a significant role to play in this. Unfortunately, however, Moses is not particularly interested in the job; he has no great desire to return to Egypt; and he certainly has no wish to incur the wrath of another pharaoh. Whatever the frustrations of his dead-end job in the desert, at least there he was safe; he had apparently been able to put his past troubles behind him – and he clearly wished to remain doing so.

However, this was no longer possible; whether Moses liked it or not, he was God's chosen instrument, the one through whom God would deliver his people. Moreover, the time had come for God's promise of Genesis 15:14 to be fulfilled. However, as this encounter repeatedly stresses, this anticipated deliverance would not be achieved by human strength, but rather by divine might; Moses (and Aaron) were merely the human instruments through whom Yahweh would make himself known, whether to Israel, Egypt or other nations.

E. Moses' return to Egypt and the Israelites' response (4:18–31)

Context

Having exhausted his protests, it seems that Moses has finally been persuaded to carry out the divine assignment. His final argument will resurface again later – after the initial efforts to persuade Pharaoh have failed (cf. 6:12, 30) – but for now Moses appears ready to comply with Yahweh's instructions. And so, as we approach the conclusion of this chapter, it seems that the matter has finally been resolved and Moses has fully submitted to Yahweh's command. Apparently, however, there remains a significant problem which must be addressed before Moses begins his mission.

Comment
i. Departure from Midian (4:18–20)

18. While requesting such 'leave of absence' in such circumstances would have been a matter of Ancient Near Eastern etiquette,[58] this report of Moses doing so clearly indicates his assent to Yahweh's instructions. Admittedly, Moses may seem somewhat coy about the goal of his mission – in view of what Yahweh has said already (cf. 3:7–10, 16–22), what are we to make of the rationale Moses offers Jethro here? Does this reflect some degree of lingering doubt in Moses' mind? Or is he simply side-stepping what would inevitably have been an awkward conversation? 'I need to take some time off. God appeared to me in the desert and told me to pick a fight with the most powerful man in the world.' However, it seems preferable to interpret this verse in the light of Moses' previous attempt to rescue Israel (cf. 2:11);[59] thus understood, Moses now intends to complete the task he had initiated some forty years earlier; this time, however, he would do so in God's time and in God's way.

19. Translating the first verb of verse 19 as a pluperfect (*Now the LORD had said to Moses in Midian*), as the context seems to suggest, is certainly possible. In this case, verse 19 would constitute a short parenthesis or flashback. Alternatively, since the rationale given by Yahweh here is new, it is possible to interpret the verse as a further nudge by Yahweh to ensure that Moses did not procrastinate. In any case, rather than suggesting that it is now 'safe' for Moses to return

---

58 Seeking such permission to leave is best understood in terms of parting on amicable terms, rather than acrimoniously.

59 Significantly, both these verses refer to Moses going to see his brothers.

because the previous Egyptian leaders have died, verse 19b may well be indicating that the process of deliverance has begun with the death of Moses' adversaries. Thus understood, this is a further indication that the fulfilment of God's purposes is now back on track; God's time has arrived, so Moses can return to Egypt and fulfil his destiny – the task of leading God's people out of Egypt.

20. And so off Moses goes, back to Egypt, with his family in tow and that all-important staff of God in his hand (cf. v. 17). Mention of *sons* is surprising, since only one son has been mentioned previously (cf. 2:22) and only one son is spoken of in the enigmatic incident that follows (cf. 4:24–26). Nevertheless, it is subsequently disclosed that Moses and Zipporah had two sons (cf. 18:2–4), whom Moses sent (with Zipporah) back to Jethro at some stage between his 'near-death experience' (4:24–26) and the family reunion recounted in chapter 18. Whether this separation took place after the incident related in the next few verses (4:24–26) or at some later stage (either to keep them out of harm's way, or, more probably, to herald the arrival of the Israelites at Sinai) is impossible to determine.[60] Whatever the circumstances, there is little in the text to support any suggestion of an acrimonious separation (cf. 18:2–4).

ii. Israel, Yahweh's firstborn son (4:21–23)

21. While possibly hinted at earlier (cf. 3:19), it is now clearly indicated that Egyptian compliance was not the short-term objective. The *wonders* that Yahweh had given Moses the power to initiate refer to the extraordinary phenomena that culminated in the death of Egypt's firstborn (cf. 3:20; 7:8 – 11:10). Although there is clearly some overlap with the *signs* that Moses performed before the Israelites (4:1–9, 30), it seems that the latter were designed to stimulate faith, whereas the *wonders* (i.e. the plagues) primarily functioned as acts of judgment designed to induce repentance. However, any such repentance on the part of Pharaoh would not last, because Yahweh would *harden his heart* – the first mention of a recurring theme throughout the narrative in chapters 7–14 (see Additional note on

---

60 This is one of several 'blanks' in the narrative of Exodus which the narrator has not filled in.

the hardening of Pharaoh's heart). Therefore, despite these portents that Egypt would experience, Pharaoh would persist in his refusal to comply with Yahweh's demands, thus bringing dire consequences not only on his own family, but on all of Egypt.

22–23. Consequently, the time would inevitably come for Moses to announce the ultimate judgment that Yahweh would bring on those who refused to release his *firstborn son*: the life of their firstborn would be forfeit. These two verses clearly rehearse the speech that Yahweh (through Moses) will declare to Pharaoh *at the climax* of the ensuing conflict (cf. ch. 11), just prior to the final blow in the series.

Additional note: the hardening of Pharaoh's heart

As noted above (see comment on 4:21), one of the recurring themes in Exodus 4 – 14 is the hardening of Pharaoh's heart, for which three different Hebrew verbs are employed, with different subjects and in a variety of ways (prediction, action or disposition; see Table 2).

Table 2: Verbs used to describe Pharaoh's heart

Nuance of the verb used	Prediction	Action	Disposition
The LORD makes Pharaoh's heart:			
firm/strong (*ḥāzaq*)	4:21; 14:4	9:12; 10:20, 27; 11:10; 14:8 (cf. 14:17)	
heavy (*kābēd*)		10:1	
difficult (*qāšâ*)	7:3		
Pharaoh makes his heart:			
firm/strong (*ḥāzaq*)		13:15 (heart implied)	
heavy (*kābēd*)		8:15, 32; 9:34	
Pharaoh's heart is/becomes:			
firm/strong (*ḥāzaq*)			7:13, 22; 8:19; 9:35
heavy (*kābēd*)			7:14; 9:7

While on some occasions Yahweh is said to be responsible for
the hardening of Pharaoh's heart, at other times Pharaoh is said
to harden his own heart, or his heart is simply described as being
or becoming hard. Back in 3:19 it appeared that Pharaoh himself
was wholly responsible for his anticipated intransigence, but
Yahweh would apply some persuasion by means of the wonders
he would perform in Egypt. In 4:21, however, Yahweh seems to be
responsible for Pharaoh's intransigence, and these wonders either
fail to persuade or are the very means by which Yahweh hardens
Pharaoh's heart.

Various solutions to this crux have been proposed, concisely
summarized by Ford (2006: 5–10). For source critics, the
'discrepancy' is largely due to different explanations reflected in
the underlying sources. Others attempt to resolve the tension
by foregrounding the role of either Pharaoh or Yahweh. Thus,
some maintain that Pharaoh is always responsible, so statements
attributing the hardening to Yahweh have either a permissive
nuance (Yahweh *allowed* rather than *caused* the hardening), or
reflect the mindset of authors who attributed everything to God
without denying human agency. Conversely, others argue that
Yahweh is always responsible for the hardening, with Pharaoh
never really acting independently of Yahweh's influence, but
rather in terms of the mysterious interplay between divine
sovereignty and human responsibility. Still others maintain
that some kind of progression can be traced in the narrative –
either in terms of Pharaoh's psyche, the reader's understanding
or Yahweh's response. Thus understood, responsibility shifts
from Pharaoh to Yahweh at some stage in the sequence of
events, either because Pharaoh has gradually 'lost control',
or to emphasize that Yahweh is now judging Pharaoh for his
persistent intransigence. Either way, there is a progressive self-
hardening which culminates in, or is ultimately explicable by, a
divine hardening.

Arguably, however, the conundrum can be resolved by paying
close attention to the actual circumstances of such hardening in
the narrative. Certainly, in the case of the plagues, it is only after
relief from such that Pharaoh is said to harden his heart. Thus,
God's *gracious* action in granting respite seems to have had the

negative effect of prompting *Pharaoh* to stiffen his resolve. Even in the Sea incident, Yahweh created the circumstances (Israel's apparent confusion; cf. 14:1–4) which led to the hardening of Pharaoh's heart and Egypt's final humiliating defeat. Accordingly, rather than controlling Pharaoh as some kind of puppet, or yielding his sovereignty to human whim and happenstance, Yahweh simply utilized the changing circumstances (including Pharaoh's intransigence) to execute his plans and purposes. Thus understood, the problem of Pharaoh's hardened heart is best explained in terms of a disposition that became Pharaoh's undoing when Yahweh's actions stiffened his resolve (from 9:12) not to let Israel go. And so an inflexible, insensitive and unresponsive king became even more resistant to Yahweh's will, while at the same time ensuring that God's purpose for Pharaoh (9:16) would indeed be realized. Rather than hardening Pharaoh's heart directly, Yahweh did so indirectly (by his acts of mercy and grace) and is thus in no way implicated in the sin for which Pharaoh is solely responsible.

But whatever the explanation of this interpretative crux, we must not lose sight of the overarching point: it is Yahweh, not Pharaoh, who is ultimately in control – as indicated by the recurring phrase *as the LORD had said* (7:13; 8:15, 19; 9:12, 35). God's sovereign control of these affairs does not absolve Pharaoh of blame because, like all sinners, Pharaoh remains fully accountable for his stubborn refusal to obey God (Rom. 9:16–18).

iii. Bridegroom of blood (4:24–26)

24–26. At this stage the narrative flow is unexpectedly inter-rupted by one of the most enigmatic passages in all of Scripture – this bizarre incident concerning Zipporah and the rite of circumcision. Like 3:13–15, the paragraph continues to attract considerable scholarly attention with little consensus over its meaning. There are several exegetical difficulties: the ambiguous use of Hebrew pronouns makes the object of key clauses unclear (i.e. both the object of Yahweh's hostility and the owner of the 'feet' Zipporah touched); the only indisputable fact is that Zipporah somehow knows to circumcise her (unnamed) son to avert the implementation of Yahweh's death threat. The context suggests that Moses is the target of the latter,[61] and that it is his 'feet' (perhaps a euphemism for genitals) that Zipporah touches with the foreskin of their son (Gershom?). This action appears to have a vicarious effect, compensating in some way for Moses' implied 'offence' – his failure to apply the covenant sign of circumcision to his son (cf. Gen. 17:1–14). This may have been due to some reluctance or opposition to this cultic rite on the part of Zipporah (v. 25b), although this is dependent on how her enigmatic 'bloody bridegroom' declaration should be understood.[62] While this is often interpreted as a derogatory statement expressing Zipporah's revulsion over the rite of circumcision, the precise meaning of these words (and who Zipporah is describing) is another one of the many exegetical challenges these verses present. Some (e.g. Fretheim 1991a; Hamilton 2011) are therefore reluctant to portray Zipporah as the villain of the story, seeing her rather as the heroine who saves Moses from God's wrath. However, whether directed towards God or Moses, it is difficult not to detect some sort of negative vibe in what she says.

Apart from these knotty exegetical issues, there is also the problem of its literary and theological significance; what purpose does this enigmatic account serve? Having finally persuaded Moses to return to Egypt, why should Yahweh now seek to kill him? It is clear that this incident emphasizes the importance of circumcision for being counted among Israel, God's firstborn son. However, it may also highlight the significance of this rite (and/or the obedient faith it expressed), not just for Israel as a whole, but for each family within Israel. Ignoring God's command meant exposing oneself to divine hostility; such wilful neglect would have dire consequences in relation to the divine judgment that had just been anticipated for the Egyptians (v. 23).

---

61 The most immediate antecedent is Pharaoh's firstborn, but clearly this cannot be Yahweh's target in 4:24. Prior to 4:21–23, Moses is the main subject, and his 'absence' in 4:24–26 would be anomalous (the father would normally have been responsible for circumcising his son; cf. Gen. 17:23; 21:4).

62 For the various possibilities, see Propp 1993.

iv. Rendezvous with Aaron (4:27–28)

27–28. After Moses' extraordinary brush with death, the main narrative resumes with what appears to be a flashback: God's command for Aaron to go and meet Moses (cf. v. 14), followed by a brief account of their subsequent reunion at the mountain of God (cf. 3:1). Presumably this was their first meeting in decades, although it is possible that the narrator has deliberately gapped any previous encounters. The use of the verb *command* here (in connection with *signs*) may deliberately allude to the basic struggle, by contrasting Yahweh's demands with those of Pharaoh (cf. 1:22; 5:6).

v. Israel's response to Aaron and Moses (4:29–31)

29–31. As Yahweh had directed, Moses and Aaron cooperate in announcing the good news to Israel's elders. Possibly the Israelites did require some convincing, hence the performance of the afore-mentioned signs; while it is Aaron who now carries out Yahweh's instructions, including the performance of these signs, he clearly acts with Moses' authority and as his intermediary. Interestingly, however, the Israelites' response is explicitly related not to what they *saw*, but to what they *heard*, which may suggest that they were a lot less sceptical than Moses had anticipated. In any case, the good news that Moses brought them was received in an attitude of acceptance and grateful adoration.

Meaning

After his initial reticence, Moses has finally been persuaded to carry out his divinely appointed task. Compliance, however, does not mean that it will all be plain sailing. Rather, Moses must carry out Yahweh's instructions knowing that Pharaoh will refuse to comply. Still, this human intransigence was not something that Yahweh had somehow overlooked or failed to take into account. Rather, even this was something through which God could and would work out his purposes. Nevertheless, it was also something for which Pharaoh (and Egypt) would be divinely judged – a divine judgment that would encompass others also, including Moses, should they fail to implement Yahweh's instructions. True to his word, Yahweh not only supplies Moses with the assistant he needs, but also empowers both to convince the Israelites that their circumstances are about to change. However, this was only the first hurdle, overcome only temporarily; as the following chapter plainly demonstrates, Moses and Aaron are still a very long way from 'mission accomplished'.

2. PHARAOH'S RESPONSE TO YAHWEH'S DEMANDS AND DIVINE REASSURANCE FOR MOSES (5:1 – 7:7)

A. Pharaoh's refusal, and recriminations against Moses (5:1–21)

Context

With the acceptance of Yahweh's revelation by the Israelite elders (4:29–31), the stage is now set for the confrontation between Moses and Pharaoh, and between Yahweh and the so-called gods of Egypt. The positive responses to Yahweh's wishes with which the previous chapter concludes place the negative response of Pharaoh in sharper relief.

Comment

i. Pharaoh's refusal to obey Yahweh's demands (5:1–14)

1. The fact that Moses and Aaron have apparently got ready access to Pharaoh is probably not to be explained by Moses' royal upbringing, but rather by a narrative gap on the part of the author: presumably a royal audience was secured by first of all going through the appropriate channels (i.e. the bureaucratic protocols).

In any case, this is one of many details that the biblical writer obviously saw no need to explain. In using the messenger formula ('Thus says X'), Moses and Aaron employ a speech form with which Pharaoh was undoubtedly familiar.[1] Pharaoh could easily have assumed that the message was from the Israelites' human leader had 'Yahweh' not been qualified by *the God of Israel*. Nor was Pharaoh left in any doubt about what this deity wanted: he was making demands of Pharaoh![2] While Moses does not initially seem to follow Yahweh's instructions to the letter (i.e. relating Yahweh's precise instructions, accompanied by the elders; cf. 3:18), to infer negligence (Motyer 2005) or impertinence (Hamilton 2011) on the part of Moses and Aaron may be reading too much into this. As Enns (2000) observes, the focus of this narrative is not so much on what Moses did (or failed to do), but on how Pharaoh responded. Moreover, the latter's belligerence is never attributed to the confrontational stance adopted by Yahweh's envoys; rather, Pharaoh's negative reaction was inevitable, even if a more courteous and diplomatic approach had been adopted (cf. 3:18–20).

2. Pharaoh's initial response highlights a major theme in the first part of Exodus: the king of Egypt does not *know* Yahweh (cf. 1:8), a deficiency that will be addressed in the ensuing narrative. Pharaoh's ignorance of Yahweh can be understood in terms of (1) simple unfamiliarity ('I've never heard of this deity before') or (2) defiant rejection ('Why should *I* care what your god demands?'). However, while Pharaoh may well have been unacquainted with Yahweh, it is clear from what follows that the identity of Israel's deity is not the issue; Pharaoh does not recognize his authority, and thus has no intention of complying with his demands.

---

1   The Amarna Letters (correspondence between Egyptian pharaohs and various minor Ancient Near Eastern kings dating between 1400 and 1360 BC) are replete with this expression that highlights that the messenger is repeating verbatim the words of the person who sent him. The formula is later used extensively by Israel's prophets to introduce the oracles Yahweh has charged them to deliver.

2   Rather than the softer cohortative ('let us go'; cf. 3:18), this opening salvo employs the imperative (lit. 'Send!').

3. As noted above, this subsequent request – for a three-day journey – is probably not intended literally but is a figure of speech (cf. 3:18). Significantly, Moses offers no promise to return, and Pharaoh never really expected such (cf. 10:24; 14:5). The request alludes to the earlier sign of assurance that God had given to Moses (cf. 3:12), but significantly underlines the inevitable consequences of disobeying or defying Yahweh – an implicit warning that is unfortunately lost on Pharaoh.

4–5. Rather than granting their request, Pharaoh puts his own spin on what Moses and Aaron are doing: all this talk of Yahweh and his demands was simply impeding the construction programme being carried out for Pharaoh. Given the priority of the latter, this Israelite workforce was going nowhere – for however short or long. Interestingly, like his predecessor, this pharaoh also draws attention to the way the 'peasants' have multiplied.[3] But unlike the earlier pharaoh who instituted the oppression, apparently this was no longer seen as a problem to be solved but as an opportunity to be exploited. However, while the current pharaoh's rationale may have been different, he too responds by pitting himself against God's plan and purpose.

6–9. Thus, rather than granting this labour force permission to leave, Pharaoh intensifies their workload (by no longer supplying the straw needed to reinforce the clay bricks) – probably a clever ploy to drive a wedge between the people and Moses. Certainly, this was its inevitable effect (cf. vv. 19–21). In any case, by misconstruing their *crying out* as a symptom of laziness (cf. 2:23; 3:7), and diabolically dismissing their claims about Yahweh as *lies* that should be ignored (cf. Jer. 27:9–10, 14, 16), Pharaoh sets himself in direct conflict with the God who has claimed the Israelites as his own. Pharaoh's hard heart may well be alluded to in the harder work he here imposed (the same verbal root is used for both the Hebrews' *harder* service and Pharaoh's *hardened* heart).

---

3   Such is probably the derogatory significance here of *the people of the land*. The Samaritan Pentateuch, however, suggests that the latter refers to native Egyptians, who are now outnumbered by Israelite labourers.

10–14. The messenger formula with which Pharaoh's edict is introduced in verse 10 seems to be a deliberate echo of 5:1 (cf. 4:22), further highlighting the nature of this conflict as a struggle involving competing claims of sovereignty. While the text appears to suggest that Egyptian slave drivers and the Israelite overseers collaborated in introducing Pharaoh's new construction policy (vv. 10–11), it seems possible (especially in view of the ignorance the Israelite overseers express in vv. 15–16) that those mentioned in verses 6 and 10 are in fact Egyptian, and are to be distinguished from the *Israelite* overseers explicitly described as such in verses 14–16. Whether the latter were simply berated or physically beaten,[4] this group bore the brunt of the Egyptian abuse that followed the inevitable reduction in productivity.

ii. Recriminations against Moses (5:15–21)

15–16. Their appeal (lit. 'they cried out'; cf. v. 8) to Pharaoh and their implied ignorance of his edict suggests that these Israelite overseers were not already privy to the information contained in verses 6–9. Thus, they ascribe responsibility for this construction crisis to others, namely, *your* [Pharaoh's] *own people*.

17–18. Once again, however, the 'crying out' of the Israelites falls on deaf ears. Rather than relating it to his oppressive regime (cf. 2:23; 3:7, 9), Pharaoh again belligerently ascribes it to Israelite laziness, for which this additional workload is the obvious remedy. Significantly, Pharaoh's command here (lit. 'Go, serve!', v. 18) will later be repeated, but in a different tone and with a different focus (cf. 10:8, 24; 12:31).

19–21. The sobering reality of the situation has now dawned on the Israelite overseers. Such a hostile reaction on the part of Pharaoh had clearly not been anticipated – not even by Moses himself (cf. vv. 22–23). In one sense, therefore, the overseers' response is understandable, however misguided: Moses' actions may have been the catalyst for more intense suffering, but the ultimate responsibility for such clearly lay with Pharaoh and the

---

4   The Hebrew verb may denote verbal as opposed to physical harassment in vv. 14 and 16 (Hamilton 2011).

Egyptians. Moses was not the cause of their oppression; rather, he was God's chosen instrument to end it (Enns 2000).

Meaning
The initial confrontation with Pharaoh did not result in Israel's immediate emancipation, but rather in further and heightened oppression. Instead of humbly submitting to Yahweh's demands, Pharaoh has boldly challenged both Yahweh's authority to issue such a decree and Israel's motivations in wishing to obey him. Pharaoh does not simply reassert his own supremacy but does so in a way that sets himself not only against Yahweh's will, but also as a rival to Yahweh himself. Both Pharaoh and Yahweh claim authority over the Israelites and demand their service, although the nature of such service contrasts markedly. Thus, in the battle for supremacy that follows, the basic issue at stake is this: to whom does authority in Egypt ultimately belong, and thus whom will Israel serve?

B. Moses' complaint, Yahweh's reassurance and Israel's incredulity (5:22 – 6:9)

Context
Previously, Israel's and Pharaoh's response to Yahweh's revelation has been set in bold relief. Perhaps now we expect Moses' response to be set in similar relief to that of Israel. Initially, however, Moses appears to be going down a similar trajectory: as the Israelite overseers had placed the blame squarely on Moses and Aaron (5:21), so Moses now pins it on Yahweh himself. It is only subsequently (after further reassurances by Yahweh) that some measure of hope is rekindled.

Comment
i. Moses' complaint (5:22–23)
22–23. Moses was clearly knocked back by the sinister developments that his announcement to Pharaoh had precipitated. Consequently, he too had serious doubts about what was going on and thus *returned to the LORD* (v. 22). Whatever this means, evidently he did not return to Mount Sinai; presumably he went somewhere private where he could meet with God, possibly the tent that was subsequently used for such a purpose (cf. 33:7–11). Wherever

this divine–human encounter took place, there the 'blame game' continued. Just as the Israelites had blamed Moses for their troubles, so Moses blames Yahweh, accusing him of bringing trouble on (lit. 'doing evil to') this people rather than rescuing them. While not absolving Pharaoh of any responsibility, Moses clearly believes that Yahweh – the one who set this state of affairs in motion – is ultimately responsible. However, while this is not something that Yahweh denies, Moses is clearly demonstrating a misapprehension of what Yahweh had previously told him. After all, the situation was developing just as the latter had forewarned; Moses should not have expected immediate success (cf. 3:19). However, he had evidently not anticipated that Israel's situation would actually deteriorate.

ii. Yahweh's reassurance (6:1–8)

Rather than rebuking Moses for insolence, Yahweh gently reassures his deflated servant, reminding him how Israel's deliverance will be secured (cf. 3:20) and thus encouraging him to be patient and to persevere.

1. Deliverance might not presently look like a distinct possibility but, given Yahweh's plan to exercise a 'strong hand' (AT), it was nevertheless inevitable – something that no mere pharaoh could possibly prevent. Hence, whatever resistance he might offer initially, Pharaoh would eventually capitulate to Yahweh's demands.

2–5. To drive home this point, Yahweh reminds Moses of his covenant commitment to Israel's ancestors. The deity who was presently guaranteeing Israel's imminent deliverance from Egypt was none other than Yahweh, the God who had partially disclosed himself to Abraham, Isaac and Jacob as El-Shaddai,⁵ and made a sworn agreement (or *covenant*) to give them the land in which they

---

5   Genesis explicitly attests to this only in the case of Abraham (17:1) and Jacob (35:11), although Isaac (28:3), along with Jacob (43:14; 48:3), uses 'El-Shaddai' in dialogue. Following the LXX (*pantokratōr*) and Vulgate (*omnipotens*), this divine epithet is often understood as 'God Almighty' (e.g. NIV). If *shaddai* is related to the Akkadian noun *shadu*, it means 'God of the mountain' (Hamilton 2011). However, such an epithet would seem more appropriate after the Sinai theophany than before.

had lived as resident aliens. Responding to the groaning of his oppressed people, Yahweh was now about to put his covenant oath into effect (cf. Gen. 15:13–14) and reveal himself much more fully through his actions. Therefore, despite the sinister turn of events that confrontation with Pharaoh had precipitated, there was no need to panic; Pharaoh was merely a pawn in the hand of the God who was about to fulfil his covenant promise. The fact that Yahweh had established this covenant with Israel's ancestors constituted a firm basis for confidence in imminent deliverance (cf. Rom. 4:21).

The interpretation of verse 3 (cf. 3:13–15) is highly controversial; did God make himself known to Israel's ancestors as Yahweh or simply as El-Shaddai? While 6:3 at first glance appears to suggest that the patriarchs knew God only as El-Shaddai and not as Yahweh,[6] the use of the Tetragrammaton in Genesis seems to suggest otherwise, prompting many scholars to draw source-critical conclusions (see Additional note on the revelation and meaning of the divine name). Admittedly, the divine name is seldom found on the lips of the patriarchs themselves (however, see Gen. 14:22; 15:2, 8; 22:14; 24:3, 7; cf. 4:1; 5:29; 9:26; 16:2, 5; 24:12, 42), who seem to use the 'El' epithet much more often. Thus, some conclude that the name 'Yahweh' is used anachronistically in Genesis, the point being to identify the God of the patriarchs as the same deity who later made himself known to Moses as Yahweh. However, the frequency and usage in Genesis (according to Hamilton [2011], 148 times, 96 by the narrator) suggests to others that Exodus 6:3 is not claiming that the patriarchs were altogether ignorant of the Tetragrammaton (i.e. that they were unaware of this divine epithet); rather, the point is that God had not disclosed its meaning and significance to them, as he was now about to do in the time of Moses. The US edition of the NIV is probably correct, therefore, in suggesting that while appearing to Israel's ancestors as El-Shaddai, God had not made himself *fully known to them* as Yahweh – as he was now about to do in the days of Moses. Thus understood, this enigmatic verse should be read in the light of the declaration that follows (vv.

---

6   The attempt by Driver (1973: 109) to read the statement as a question ('Did I not . . . ?') has attracted little scholarly support.

6–8), which articulates how Yahweh will make himself known to Israel. God had established a covenant with Israel's ancestors (vv. 4–5), revealing himself as a promise-making God. He would now fulfil these promises for their descendants, and in so doing, would become known to Israel in a way not hitherto experienced (cf. v. 7b).

6–8. Moses was thus to go and reassure the Israelites accordingly. Bracketing the message with 'I am Yahweh' (vv. 6a, 8c; AT) may well serve to emphasize not only the identity of the one sending this message, but also the fact that Yahweh intends to make himself known in what he is about to do on Israel's behalf. Thus, Yahweh's anticipated actions – liberating the Israelites from Egyptian slavery, redeeming them with outstretched arm and mighty judgments, establishing a special relationship with them, bringing them to and granting them possession of the Promised Land – are all revelatory. Particularly significant is the language of redemption and adoption, both of which attest to a unique divine–human relationship. Acting as their kinsman-redeemer, Yahweh will first restore liberty to the Israelites, before entering into an intimate relationship with them and granting them possession of the land sworn to their ancestors.

Verse 7 clearly echoes the so-called covenant formula(ry) ('You will be my people and I will be your God'; cf. Rendtorff 1998), an oft-repeated phrase deriving from Ancient Near Eastern marriage and adoption formulas (Sohn 1999), which articulates the unique relationship between Yahweh and Israel anticipated back in Genesis 17:7–8. There is thus significant emphasis in these verses not only on Yahweh as the one who fulfils his promises, but also on the special relationship that Israel would have with him.

iii. Israel's incredulity (6:9)

9. Although Moses was reassured (albeit temporarily) by Yahweh's word, the rest of the Israelites were clearly not impressed. Whether due to impatience or discouragement,[7] their response was

---

7   Lit. 'shortness of breath/spirit' (cf. Job 21:4; Mic. 2:7), which the LXX understands as 'discouragement' rather than 'impatience' (cf. the possible antonym in Eccl. 7:8).

similar to the earlier reaction of Moses himself: they could not see past their initial disappointment and adverse circumstances (cf. 5:22–23). It seems that they, like Pharaoh (cf. 3:19), needed to be persuaded by more than mere words (cf. 14:21).

Meaning
Rather than fixating on the adverse circumstances of the present, the challenge for Moses (and Israel) here is to persevere in obedient faith, remembering who Yahweh is and what he has promised. It is by doing so that confidence in God is renewed and hope for the future is restored. Such is clearly the significance here for the original and later readers as well.

C. Further instruction to confront Pharaoh (6:10 – 7:7)

Context
While it is possible to take 6:10–12 as the conclusion of the previous subsection, there are several reasons for taking it as the introduction to what follows: the MT isolates these verses as a distinct unit; together with 6:28 – 7:7, these verses appear to be part of the frame that surrounds the genealogy introduced in 6:14–25;[8] and the fact that 6:10–12 and 6:28–30 are essentially the same suggests some kind of resumptive repetition in the narrative. Most significantly, however, the focus shifts in this unit from what Moses must say to Israel to what he must say to Pharaoh.

---

8   This section appears to be arranged in two parallel panels as follows:
    A. Yahweh's commission to Moses (6:10–11)
       B. Moses' response (6:12)
          C. Genealogy of Moses and Aaron (6:13–25)
             D. Moses and Aaron's compliance (6:26–27)
    A. Yahweh's commission repeated (6:28–29)
       B. Moses' response repeated (6:30)
          C. Yahweh's solution repeated (7:1–5)
             D. Moses and Aaron's compliance repeated (7:6–7)

Comment
i. Yahweh's commission and Moses' response (6:10–12)

10–12. The adverse response of the demoralized Israelites has evidently brushed off on Moses, whose focus has again shifted to himself and his perceived inadequacies. When God instructs him to repeat his demands to Pharaoh (vv. 10–11), he understandably responds: 'If the Israelites won't listen to me, why should Pharaoh?' For good measure, he then throws in the same problem that he had introduced previously: his *faltering* [lit. 'uncircumcised'] *lips* (v. 12; cf. 4:10). While this might simply refer to Moses' ineloquence or tendency to get 'tongue-tied' (cf. 4:10, 14),[9] it more likely alludes to some form of serious speech impediment such as a severe stammer (see Millard 2016).[10] But whatever the issue was, it explains and necessitates the supporting role of Aaron (7:1; cf. 4:14–16).

ii. Levitical genealogy (6:13–27)

13–27. Somewhat abruptly, at this point the narrative is interrupted with a genealogy,[11] prompting the question: why is it placed here, and what function does this incomplete genealogy serve?[12] The immediate context, and its particular emphasis on Aaron's side of the family (see below), suggests that a primary function is to highlight Aaron's suitability as a leader alongside

---

9 Here the LXX renders 'uncircumcised' *alogos* ('wordless'), although in 6:30 it translates it as *ischnophōnos* ('weak-voiced').

10 Millard infers from the Exodus–Deuteronomy narrative that Moses consistently required a spokesman to communicate any public address (even when this is not explicitly stated), but (like King George VI in the 2010 film *The King's Speech*) could overcome this impairment when singing (e.g. Exod. 15; cf. also Exod. 32:18; Num. 10:35–36; Deut. 32).

11 As noted above, vv. 28–30 constitute a resumption of the main narrative, an almost verbatim repetition of vv. 10–12. This genealogy thus disrupts the main narrative thread.

12 A close analysis suggests that, like many other biblical genealogies, this one is telescoped (i.e. several gaps are reflected, such as between Kohath [cf. Gen. 46:11] and Amram).

Moses. A focus on Aaron is especially evident from the way it is concluded (vv. 26–27; cf. v. 13) – the usual sequence (i.e. 'Moses and Aaron') is notably inverted (*Aaron and Moses*). The genealogy itself is primarily concerned with the descendants of Levi (Reuben and Simeon are mentioned only in passing, before zooming in on Jacob's third-born son), as is demonstrated by the inclusions of lifespans (cf. vv. 16, 18, 20) in the most important lineage (i.e. Levi→Kohath→Amram). However, the fact that the genealogy does not terminate with Moses or his descendants, but rather with Phinehas, Aaron's illustrious grandson (cf. Num. 25:7–8), again shifts the main focus on to Aaron rather than Moses.[13] The fact that the genealogy terminates with Phinehas may draw attention to the covenant faithfulness of this priestly line – possibly necessary in view of Aaron's subsequent behaviour during the golden calf episode (Exod. 32). Indeed, the other branch traced here (Levi→ Kohath→Izhar→Korah→Korahite clans) may further emphasize the special calling of Aaron and *his* descendants.

The disruption of the narrative flow by this genealogy of Moses and Aaron seems therefore to illustrate that Moses and Aaron – the latter in particular – were deemed to be suitable persons to carry out this God-given mission (vv. 26–27).[14]

Amram and *Jochebed* (v. 20) may have been ancestors, rather than the biological parents, of Aaron and Moses. Whatever their relationship to Moses and Aaron, the fact that they were so closely related (according to v. 20, Jochebed was Amram's paternal aunt) attests to the text's historical veracity; such a proscribed marriage (cf. Lev. 18:12; 20:19) would hardly have been 'invented' by post-Mosaic authors of a literary fiction.

Kohath, born at least 350 years before Moses (Gen. 46:11; cf. Exod. 12:40–41), is too old to have been his grandfather, as verse

---

13 Note also the inclusion of spouses in 6:23, 25 (cf. 6:20), further demonstrating that the main focus of this genealogy is on Aaron's lineage.

14 In addition, however, it may also attest to the fulfilment of God's promises to Israel's ancestors (so Hamilton 2011), although this depends to some extent on a questionable alignment of the generations listed and the 'fourth generation' mentioned in Gen. 15:16.

20 (cf. Num. 26:59; 1 Chr. 6:3) might otherwise imply. As with other biblical genealogies (cf. Gen. 10; Matt. 1), this one is apparently selective, placing the spotlight on more significant members of the ancestral line.

Unlike Amram, *Aaron* (v. 23) did not marry into the levitical tribe: Elisheba's father, *Amminadab*, and her brother, *Nahshon*, are of Judahite lineage (cf. Num. 1:7), both being named in the genealogy of David (Ruth 4:20; cf. 1 Chr. 2:10–11) and hence also that of Jesus (Matt. 1:4; Luke 3:32–33). In the marriage of Joseph and Mary, this mixing of lineage is repeated, albeit in reverse (cf. Luke 1:5, 36).

The term *divisions* (v. 26) has military connotations, as reflected, for example, in the divine title 'Yahweh of *hosts*' (i.e. 'armies'). Here, as elsewhere in Exodus (cf. 12:41, 51), its use in relation to Israel conveys the idea that Israel will march out of Egypt triumphantly, as if in military formation.

iii. Aaron, a prophet for Moses (6:28 – 7:7)

28–30. As noted above, the last three verses of chapter 6 pick up where the story left off, repeating almost verbatim what we already know from verses 10–12. It is doubtful, therefore, that there is any significance in the slightly different sequence: the problem Moses raises is the improbability of Pharaoh paying any attention to a speaker such as Moses.

7:1–2. This time, however, the narrative continues by highlighting God's solution to the objection that Moses has raised. Previously, Moses had drawn attention to his deficiency in the context of declaring God's word to the Israelites (4:10). Now he does so in the context of addressing God's word to Pharaoh. But God's solution to the problem remains the same: Aaron will function as Moses' prophet (i.e. a spokesperson for someone else; cf. 4:16; Deut. 18:18). Just as earlier Moses functioned as God to Aaron (cf. 4:16), so now he would function as such to Pharaoh (7:1). Aaron would thus again assume the role of a prophet by faithfully transmitting the divine message (as communicated by Moses) to the intended audience.

3–5. Nevertheless, speaking with such divine authority was no guarantee of a receptive audience; Pharaoh would not be prepared to listen to and obey Yahweh's voice, even when the authenticity of the message was validated by multiple *signs and wonders* (an allusion to the transformation of Aaron's staff and subsequent events; 7:8 – 11:10). However, securing Pharaoh's compliance was not God's immediate objective. Rather, the latter was to harden Pharaoh's heart (cf. 4:21), so that Israel's freedom might finally be secured through *mighty acts of judgment* – alluding to the death of Egypt's firstborn and the ensuing destruction of Egypt's elite chariot force. By such a display of his power and authority, the Egyptians would have no choice but to acknowledge Yahweh and his sovereignty over them – a recurring motif in the narrative that follows (cf. 7:17; 8:22; 9:14; 11:7; 14:4, 18). Thus, despite what Pharaoh or others may have thought, refusal to comply with Yahweh's demands was simply ensuring that his ultimate plans would indeed materialize. These initial hurdles that had so demoralized Israel and Moses were part of God's plan and purpose. It may have looked as if God's plans were being thwarted by Pharaoh, but in fact everything was working out precisely as God had intended.

6–7. Reassured by Yahweh's words, Moses and Aaron faithfully carried out their divine commission. The significance of the fact that both were already octogenarians is unclear, since each of them lived for another forty years (cf. Num. 33:39; Deut. 34:7). But whether it emphasizes their heroic faith or the special strength that Yahweh gave them, age did not become an obstacle in following God's instructions and again confronting the most powerful man in the world.

Meaning
Despite the setbacks experienced thus far, God's plan remained on track. Whatever others may have thought – including Moses himself – both he and Aaron were eminently qualified for the task. This did not mean that their efforts would be crowned with instant success – indeed, the answer to Moses' question (6:12, 30) is that Pharaoh would not listen, at least initially. Nevertheless, the ultimate outcome was never really in any doubt; thus even the Egyptians would eventually be forced to acknowledge who Yahweh is, as finally will everyone (cf. Phil. 2:11).

3. PHARAOH'S RECALCITRANCE AND YAHWEH'S MIGHTY ACTS OF JUDGMENT (7:8 – 10:29)

This next section of the book depicts the signs and wonders that Moses has been told to anticipate (7:3; cf. 3:20; 4:21), and through which Yahweh will demonstrate his superior power to Pharaoh and the Egyptians (cf. 9:16). The first of these wonders (7:8–13) involves no real threat to either people or the economy, yet it is an important precursor to the ensuing contest between Yahweh and Pharaoh. Despite the truth of Yahweh's superiority staring him in the face, Pharaoh refuses to yield, thus setting the stage (and the pattern) for the series of disasters that would cripple Egypt's economy and eventually bring the nation to its knees.

A. A miraculous sign for Pharaoh (7:8–13)

Context
Although not one of the plagues,[1] this 'wonder' performed by
Moses and Aaron before Pharaoh serves as a kind of prelude
to what follows: Yahweh demonstrates his power, but Pharaoh
foolishly refuses to take the theological lesson on board. In
view of what Yahweh has just told Moses (7:3–4; cf. 4:21),
Pharaoh's negative response is hardly surprising. However, it may
be further explained by relevant Egyptian background, which is
often overlooked. As Currid (2013: 111–117) explains, the usage of
a wooden staff (Heb. *maṭṭê*; cf. Egyptian *mdw*) in Egypt parallels
its usage in the biblical narrative: 'they were both used in the
context of the common, everyday life of the herdsman, as an
instrument of travel, and as a symbol of the power of a deity' (114).
Such rods were thought by Egyptians to be imbued with divine
power, thus their magicians used them to perform their dark arts,
including transforming them into snakes. Accordingly, for Moses
to do likewise may not have impressed Pharaoh much, especially
since his own magicians were able to do the same with a highly
esteemed Egyptian emblem.

In any case, this Egyptian background throws significant light
on this incident in Exodus, which portrays 'a heavenly combat – a
war between the God of the Hebrews and the deities of Egypt'
(Currid 1995: 206).

Comment
8–10. Whereas previously this phenomenon was one of the
three *signs* designed to convince the Israelites of Moses' divine
authority (cf. 3:13; 4:1–5),[2] here its function is to demonstrate

---

1 Some commentators, however, conclude otherwise, further suggesting
that Exod. 11 and following should be treated as distinct from the
preceding narrative. However, this first phenomenon is clearly distinct
from the judgment-laden phenomena which follow.

2 Whereas the 'staff becoming a snake' and the 'hand becoming leprous'
are designated as *signs* (4:8–9), the 'water becoming blood' is not

Yahweh's power to Pharaoh (and the Egyptians). Perhaps this explains why a different noun (*tannîn*, 'serpent') is employed to describe the creatures into which the staffs metamorphosed on this occasion (cf. *nāḥāš*, 'snake', in 4:3–4). Interestingly, however, the reptile into which Moses' staff was transformed is described as a *nāḥāš* in 7:15. Unless we differentiate between Moses' staff and that of Aaron (however, see comments on 4:17), this would seem to indicate that the two nouns are synonyms here in Exodus 7, as in Isaiah 27:1 (cf. Deut. 32:33; Ps. 91:13, in which it is used in parallel with 'cobra'). Accordingly, it is probably mistaken to interpret *tannîn* as 'crocodile', even though the reptiles here may be somewhat more sinister than before; the noun is most often associated with primordial monsters of chaos (Job 7:12; Pss 74:13; 148:7; Isa. 27:1; 51:9), but on two occasions symbolizes the despotic power of Pharaoh (Ezek. 29:3; 32:2). Perhaps the latter image derives from the fact that the king cobra was used as an insignia of Pharaoh's power. In any case, this association between Pharaoh's power and reptilian creatures makes Yahweh's demonstrated supremacy over such all the more pointed: this was surely an object lesson that no sentient Egyptian could simply ignore.[3]

11–13. Unlike the Israelites, who were convinced by this and the other signs they witnessed (cf. 4:30), Pharaoh remained unimpressed – even more so when his magicians were able to replicate the feat by their *secret arts*. Rather than referring to a subgroup of Egypt's mantic priests (i.e. the *wise men* and *sorcerers* summoned in v. 11), *magicians* may simply be a functional term for these recognized specialists in signs and wonders. However, since

---

explicitly described as such, and here in ch. 7 a variation of that last demonstration of Yahweh's power is the first of the plagues. Nevertheless, readers are most probably meant to infer from ch. 4 that there were three signs, that all three were presented before an Israelite audience (4:30), and that these are to be distinguished from the 'wonders' performed subsequently before Pharaoh.

3   For more on this, see Currid's informative and insightful discussion of the way Moses' rod is used to critique Egyptian practice and claims (2013: 111–119).

'wise men' is the more generic term for professional specialists in the royal court (cf. Gen. 41:8), *magicians* probably refers to those within this larger body with a particular skill set (i.e. the aforementioned sorcerers, whose expertise involved dabbling in the occult). In any case, these Egyptian magi offer an impressive display of their proficiency in paranormal activity. Whether their *secret arts* alludes to some kind of visual illusions (employing sleight of hand etc.) or genuine occult activity is beside the point;[4] Yahweh's superiority is demonstrated by the fact that Aaron's staff swallowed up theirs – a portent of the ultimate triumph of Yahweh over Pharaoh, when the latter's elite chariot force is likewise 'swallowed up' (*bāla'*) by the earth (15:12). This object lesson, however, was evidently lost on Pharaoh, whose unyielding response was just as Yahweh had envisaged. Significantly, at this stage there is no mention of an agent hardening Pharaoh's heart – whether Yahweh or Pharaoh himself – implying that no further hardening yet took place; Pharaoh simply responded according to character.[5]

'Just as Yahweh said' (AT) is a recurring refrain in the plague narrative that follows (cf. 7:22; 8:15, 19; 9:12, 35), further emphasizing Yahweh's sovereignty over Pharaoh.

Meaning
This incident offers a snapshot of the ensuing conflict between Yahweh and Pharaoh: Yahweh demonstrates the superiority of his power, but Pharaoh foolishly dismisses this revelation. Given the significance of serpents in Egypt (e.g. cobras representing Egyptian/pharaonic power), as well as the Egyptians'

---

4 The suggestion that cobras can become catatonic when held in a particular manner (Kitchen 2003: 249) overlooks the fact that the narrative does not suggest that either Aaron or the Egyptian magicians were expert 'snake handlers'. Moreover, it clearly depicts staffs becoming slithering serpents rather than serpents becoming rigid-like 'staffs'.

5 While some versions suggest that Pharaoh's heart *became hard* (e.g. NIV), the verb (*ḥāzaq*) may simply be translated 'was hard', indicating a settled condition rather than a further development.

understanding of magic rods imbued with divine power, this was a clear illustration of Yahweh's supremacy over Pharaoh. As Enns (2000: 197) observes, 'This sign and the ten plagues display one by one Pharaoh's impotence, despite his grandiose self-image, and Yahweh's unquestionable and unconquerable might.' Somewhat ironically, this is further demonstrated in Pharaoh's hard-hearted response to the revelation he had been given.

B. Yahweh's mighty acts of judgment: strikes 1 to 9 (7:14 – 10:29)

Context
In response to Pharaoh's refusal to comply with Yahweh's demand, the aforementioned striking of the Egyptians (cf. 3:20) commences with a sequence of ten extraordinary disasters or 'plagues' (11:1). The stated purpose of these phenomenal events, however, is not primarily to be a means of punishment but a vehicle of revelation through which Yahweh might demonstrate his universal presence and sovereign power (cf. 8:22; 9:14–16, 29), and impress this truth upon his people (10:2).

Comment
As many commentators point out, the first nine disasters seem to constitute a distinct literary unit, comprising several subsets, organized in three groups of three:

> The first sign-and-wonder in each triad (bloody water, flies, hail) has the same format, with the pharaoh being warned of the impending calamity in the morning when he is on his way to the river. The second sign-and-wonder in each set (frogs, pestilence, locusts) mentions a warning, and the confrontation with the pharaoh appears to take place in the palace. The third sign-and-wonder in each set (gnats, boils, darkness) comes about abruptly, with no warning or indication of locale. (Meyers 2005: 78)

The apparently deliberate arrangement of this material reflected by these and other features suggests to some that the 'plague' narrative should not be read simply as a straightforward account of how they actually transpired.[6] Even so, only the most sceptical doubt that the narrative attests to a series of ecological disasters that actually took place.

As Ford (2006) observes, some sort of progression in the series is discernible: both the first and the seventh appear to introduce a new phase in Yahweh's dealings with Pharaoh. Not only are they introduced with similar points (cf. 7:14–17a; 9:13–17), but only these two conclude with double observations on Pharaoh's heart (cf. 7:22–23; 9:34–35) and include the idea of 'setting one's heart upon' something as an appropriate response to divine revelation (cf. 7:23; 9:21).[7] Some progression in the series seems also to be marked by the fourth plague (the beginning of the second triad), at which point Israel becomes exempt from the plagues, which become more serious (lit. 'heavy') and permanent in their effects. Thus understood, there is an increasing severity reflected in the three phases: the first phase was more an irritation and temporary inconvenience; the second was more discriminatory and significantly affected the land, livestock and people; the third phase threatened to ruin the Egyptian economy and make any productivity impossible.

Additional note: the plagues as supernatural or natural phenomena

Some have attempted to explain these divinely orchestrated disasters in naturalistic terms (i.e. rather than being supernatural occurrences, these events can be interpreted in terms of sequential

---

6   Not all scholars (cf. Childs 1974: 130) accept that this arrangement into three groups of three was intentional or throws any light on the meaning of the final composition. However, for a tentative approach to the latter, see Ford 2006: 135–137.

7   Both are also immediately preceded by a comment on Pharaoh's heart – the first simply drawing attention to its intrinsic hardness (7:13); the second reintroducing Yahweh's role in such hardening (9:12; cf. 4:21; 7:3), although the significance of this is unclear.

natural phenomena). It has been suggested, for example, that the series could form a sequence of unusually severe ecological events:[8] (1) excessive August rains wash down red earth and organisms, creating conditions which kill fish; (2) the decomposing fish both cause frogs to leave the river and infect them with a deadly organism; (3 & 4) the stagnant waters left as the river retreats breed mosquitoes and flies; (5) the dead frogs cause the cattle disease anthrax; (6) the flies spread skin anthrax; (7) hail destroys the early flax and barley harvest; (8) locusts, whose breeding was encouraged by the initial heavy rain, destroy the later wheat harvest; (9) the annual sandstorm which hits Egypt in February–March is made far worse by the fine red dust from the mud deposits and brings intense darkness.

While such an explanation of these phenomena is initially appealing (and could arguably explain why Pharaoh chose to dismiss their theological significance – especially if his royal advisers discerned 'natural causation' behind these disasters), it is not without difficulty. Both the timing (in response to Moses' words and actions) and the discriminatory nature of several of the plagues are difficult to account for in terms of mere natural disasters: geography alone cannot explain why gnats would affect the entire land while the region of Goshen would be immune from the flies or locusts. Moreover, there is no naturalistic explanation for the tenth plague; given its extremely selective basis, it cannot plausibly be linked to any particular disease. Whatever the explanation of these 'signs and wonders', God obviously used the elements of his created world. But the prediction, precise timing and unusual severity of the phenomena make them clearly miraculous. Moreover, 'to see them simply as sequential natural

---

8   E.g. Hort 1957, 1958. Hoffmeier (1997: 146–149) offers a concise (and positive) summary; cf. also Kitchen (2003: 250–251) and Humphreys (2003: 111–149). Such a naturalistic sequence of events is partly reflected in the 2014 film *Exodus: Gods and Kings*, which employs mass crocodile attacks to explain how the river water became blood and initiated the ecological crises that followed, and has one of Ramesses' magicians articulate a typical naturalistic account of this series of events.

occurrences is to ignore their presentation as deliberate, super-natural or hypernatural [i.e. nature in excess] events and to deprive them of their theological significance' (Meyers 2005: 79).

i. Blood (7:14–24)

The first of these sign-acts strikes at the very heart of Egyptian life and economy: the life-sustaining waters of the Nile. Like each of the following catastrophes, it demonstrates Yahweh's identity as Lord of creation (7:17), further reflected in the subtle 'de-creation' theme that permeates the series (see Fretheim 1991a), and constitutes judgment on the Egyptians for refusing to submit to Yahweh's demands.

14. The verb (*kābēd*, 'to be heavy/weighed down') now employed to describe Pharaoh's heart (cf. 4:21; 7:13 [*ḥāzaq*]; 7:3 [*qāšâ*]) is used several times in chapters 7–14 with the sense of 'harden/is heavy' (cf. also 1 Sam. 6:6, where it describes the analogous action of the Philistines). As in the previous verse (7:13), no agent is explicitly mentioned here as the cause of this heart condition, but Pharaoh himself is clearly culpable: *he refuses to let the people go*.

15–19. Moses is thus commanded to meet Pharaoh beside the river (presumably as Pharaoh goes there to bathe; cf. 2:5), with staff in hand (cf. 4:17), and announce a further wonder, this time unsolicited, through which Yahweh would be made known (cf. 5:2; 7:5). This phenomenon would have immediate (albeit temporary) repercussions for the ecology of Egypt, which was so dependent upon the Nile (v. 18; cf. v. 24). Whether *blood* suggests a chemical transformation or, as seems much more likely, is simply a phenomenological depiction of contaminated water (cf. v. 24),[9] the extent of the pollution thus described was evidently widespread,[10] with dire consequences for Egypt's fresh-water supply.

---

9   Cf. the similar description of the Nile in the Egyptian text *The Admonitions of Ipuwer*: 'Indeed, the river is blood, yet one drinks from it' (§2:10, *COS* 1: 94).

10 Modern translations generally assume that *wood and stone* (v. 19) alludes to *vessels* (so NIV) holding water. Possibly, however, this phrase simply refers to more remote areas or to building materials, either of which

20. Once again, the emphasis on the compliance of Moses and Aaron (cf. vv. 6, 10) sets the defiance of Pharaoh in sharper relief.

21. The impact of this disaster on the *Egyptians* is repeatedly noted (cf. v. 24), which could be taken to imply that, as with some later plagues, the Israelites were somehow sheltered from its effects. Against this, however, there is no explicit mention of Yahweh making any such distinction between the Egyptians and the Israelites until 8:22, where it seems to be introduced as a new development.

22–24. As before, the activities of Pharaoh's magicians encouraged him to ignore the significance of what had taken place and thus helped foster his recalcitrance: as with the previous manifestation of Yahweh's power, these Egyptian magi proved able to replicate the phenomenon by their secret arts. This implies, however, that there was still access to some unpolluted water, which is possibly explained in verse 24. This verse suggests that the polluted water was naturally filtered by sand on the riverbank; presumably it was such 'filtered' water that the Egyptian magicians subsequently transformed by their secret arts. Alternatively, perhaps the original transformation of water into blood employs some degree of hyperbole (i.e. despite the repeated use of 'all' and 'every', we are not to press such language literally; cf. 9:6, 19; 11:5). This, along with the temporary nature of these circumstances, may help explain why no relief from this particular disaster was requested or subsequently described.

ii. Frogs (7:25 – 8:15)

25. The next confrontation takes place a week later, giving Pharaoh ample time to repent before further trouble is inflicted on Egypt – an opportunity squandered by Egypt's recalcitrant king (cf. Rev. 9:20–21; 16:11).

8:1–4. Once again, Moses is to reiterate Yahweh's demand (v. 1), on this occasion followed by a conditional warning (v. 2). The scale of the threatened disaster is again widespread, with *frogs*

---

may simply be highlighting the all-pervasive nature of this plague (Hamilton 2011).

encroaching everywhere and on everyone (vv. 3–4).[11] Significantly, the verb used here in relation to the frogs (*nāgap*) is later used of Egypt's firstborn (12:23, 27), thus foreshadowing the final and decisive divine strike in the series.

5–7. As before (7:19–20), the onset of the plague swiftly follows its announcement, giving Pharaoh no time to respond before Aaron initiates yet another disaster. While this may reflect a narrative gap in both places, it more probably indicates that Pharaoh has made his mind up already: he has no intention of backing down at this stage. Yet again the magicians were able to replicate the phenomenon by their secret arts, although in doing so, they were ironically making a bad situation even worse. Perhaps it is not surprising, therefore, that by this stage their actions did not prove quite so reassuring; an ability to eradicate the problem might have been much more impressive.

8. Rather than hardening his resolve (as previously), for the first time Pharaoh acknowledges Yahweh's power; indeed, his request that Yahweh be implored to remove the frogs is a tacit admission of Egyptian impotence in the face of this crisis. Moreover, he also raises the possibility of emancipation, although 'may/might' probably captures the sense better than *will* (most EVV). Thus understood, Pharaoh is merely expressing a willingness to negotiate; he is not yet prepared to submit to Yahweh's demand.

9–11. To remove any doubt about the supernatural nature of this phenomenon, and thus the supremacy of Yahweh, Pharaoh is allowed to determine when Moses would intercede on Egypt's behalf and thus when this intolerable situation would end. The choice reflected in most English translations (i.e. *Tomorrow* rather than 'today') certainly seems strange, as it implies that Pharaoh was somehow willing to tolerate these adverse circumstances for one more day. It is much more likely, however, that he is requesting that the frogs be removed as soon as possible, thus here the noun (with prepositional prefix: *lĕmāḥār*; cf. 34:2; Ps. 30:5 [MT 6]) probably denotes '*by* tomorrow' (Hamilton 2011).

---

11 This Hebrew noun (*sĕp̄ardēaʿ*) occurs only here (7:27 – 8:9 [EVV 8:2–13]) and in later references to this 'plague' (Pss 78:45; 105:30).

12–14. Why Moses (and Aaron) left Pharaoh's presence before praying for the removal of the plague is not explained, but this may have been to avoid any notion that Yahweh could be manipulated by certain words or actions (Milgrom 1991: 588, 660). Whatever the motivation, Moses' private crying out to Yahweh on Pharaoh's behalf results in immediate relief (cf. Pharaoh's negative response to Yahweh, Moses and Israel). Presumably the frogs had abandoned their natural habitat (cf. vv. 9, 11) because the Nile was so contaminated. The demise of these frogs may thus have resulted from bacterial infection and/or an unsuitable environment. If so, the death of these frogs (rather than their complete removal) may have seemed like a natural development to Pharaoh and his officials. That other frogs are said to remain (and survive) in the Nile suggests that the river water was no longer contaminated.

15. Relief from the affliction, however, simply prompted Pharaoh to renege on his earlier readiness to negotiate – so hardening his heart and refusing to listen, just as Yahweh had already anticipated.[12]

iii. Gnats (8:16–19)

16–17. Like others coming third in the triad (see above), no notice of this third attack is given to Pharaoh. Rather, it comes hard on the heels of Pharaoh's rejection of Yahweh's demands. While it is impossible to determine which variety (or varieties) of parasite is intended ('lice', 'gnats' and even 'mosquitoes' have been suggested),[13] some kind of insect larvae seems likely if this and the following plague are causally related. In any case, the precise identity of these pests is unimportant. More significant is

---

12 This is the first time that Pharaoh is said to harden his heart. Prior to the plague narrative Yahweh is said to harden it (4:21; 7:3), and after the previous two phenomena no agent is explicitly mentioned (cf. 7:13, 22).

13 The Hebrew noun *knm* is found only here and in Ps. 105:31 (a reference to this plague) and Isa. 51:6. In the present paragraph, both a masculine plural and a collective form (attracting fem. sing. verb forms) are used of these pesky creatures.

the extensive nature of the problem that is again underlined (vv. 16b, 17b),[14] suggesting that the entire population of Egypt suffered under the effects of this epidemic.

18–19. For the first time, however, the Egyptian magicians proved unable to manage this wonder. It is not quite clear whether they were attempting to replicate what Aaron had done (as the identical 'Thus they did' to depict both actions suggests), or were actually attempting to eradicate the problem, as the ambiguous 'to bring out' may imply (Alter 2004: 354). Either way, their efforts failed, forcing them to concede the exceptional nature of this phenomenon. While not quite an acknowledgment that *Yahweh* was responsible, *the finger of God* (cf. 31:18; Deut. 9:10; Luke 11:20) clearly attests to some supernatural power that was beyond their ability to manipulate or control. However, despite this rather embarrassing confession of defeat, the magicians make no recommendations to Pharaoh (cf. 10:7), who is as unsettled by their spectacular failure as he was by Aaron's phenomenal success; his heart remains as hard as ever. Unlike his magicians, Pharaoh was not prepared to concede defeat just yet, again demonstrating the intransigence that Yahweh had anticipated and further amplifying the extent of the latter's dominion.

Thus, the first round in this second phase of the confrontation with Pharaoh ends in stalemate, even though both Pharaoh and the Egyptians have made tentative concessions along the way.

iv. Flies (8:20–32)

The first of the second triad of disasters is distinguished from the preceding in a number of ways: (1) the magicians no longer respond to Yahweh's actions; (2) the focus of the plague is much more discriminatory; (3) Pharaoh begins to negotiate, making partial concessions to Yahweh's demands.

20–21. Like the first triad, the second begins with Yahweh

---

14 However, *'all* the dust' (v. 17 [MT 13]) is undoubtedly hyperbole; cf. 9:6, 25.

instructing Moses to confront Pharaoh in the morning,[15] on his way to the river (cf. 7:15). Yahweh's core demand is reiterated once again, followed by yet another conditional warning – again threatening widespread disruption for Egypt.[16]

22–23. A new twist in the plague narrative is now explicitly introduced: while Egypt will be inundated with these flies, the land of Goshen – and hence the people of Yahweh – will escape this disaster, a distinction that will cogently illustrate Yahweh's presence (and Pharaoh's impotence) in the land.[17] While 'the land' (AT) could possibly refer to all Egypt, it seems more likely – given its immediate antecedent – to refer to the land of Goshen. In any case, Yahweh will somehow protect his people from the effects of this plague,[18] a differentiation designed to leave Pharaoh in no doubt about these uncanny circumstances, significantly described here as a *sign* for the first time since 7:3. As Keil and Delitzsch (1989: 484) suggest, this may address the incomplete confession of the magicians in the previous episode by highlighting that these events should not be attributed to any Egyptian deity, but rather to the God of the Hebrews. It certainly attests to Yahweh's complete control over these disasters: just as only he can remove them, so also he can curtail their reach and effects.

---

15 This time, as at the beginning of the third triad (9:13), *'early* in the morning' is specified. While perhaps suggesting insomnia on Pharaoh's part, this may be reading far too much into an insignificant detail.

16 While modern interpreters understand the *swarm* to be flies, some early Jewish interpreters understood it to be wild beasts (see Durham 1987: 114).

17 NIV's '*this* land' (emphasis added) is interpretative; lit. 'that I, Yahweh, am in the midst of the land' or 'that I am Yahweh in . . .'

18 The MT's 'I will set a ransom [*pdt*] between . . .' is most likely the result of textual corruption, the *resh* (r) of an original *prdt* ('separation') having been unintentionally omitted due to its similarity with the following *dalet* (d). So G. I. Davies (1974: 491), Stuart (2006: 215 n. 70) and Hamilton (2011: 140). For the same phrase, cf. 2 Kgs 2:11; Ruth 1:17; Prov. 18:18.

24. For the first time in the sequence of disasters, no human agent or instrumentality is expressly mentioned. Rather, Yahweh seems to act independently or at least without explicit recourse to Moses and Aaron's staff (cf. also the fifth and tenth plagues).

25–27. In response to the disaster, Pharaoh initially suggested a compromise, subtly reducing Yahweh's demand to the perform-ance of religious ritual (*sacrifice*) which could surely be carried out in the land of Egypt. Such a compromise was apparently ill-conceived in terms of Egyptian sensitivities, the precise nature of which is debatable but seems to relate to an antipathy towards flocks and those who look after them (cf. Gen. 43:32; 46:34). As such, the sacrifices that Israel must offer to Yahweh (i.e. sheep and goats) would be detestable and intolerable to the Egyptians. More importantly, however, as Moses gently reminds Pharaoh, Yahweh had specified where Israel's worship was to take place; thus, this was not really open for negotiation.

28. Undeterred by Moses' unwillingness to bend, Pharaoh suggests a second alternative, this time making greater conces-sions, while still attempting to impose his own restrictions on the Israelites' freedom. His final words, however, indicate that Pharaoh's concession was motivated by self-interest and the desire to secure relief from the present disaster.

29. While Moses had no intention of looking this gift-horse in the mouth, thus embracing Pharaoh's request for intercession, it is at least implicit in the reproof that follows that any naïvety in his dealings with Pharaoh has by now been displaced by a justified degree of scepticism.

30–32. As before, Pharaoh's accommodating attitude quickly gave way to further intransigence as soon as the immediate crisis had passed. For the second time in the sequence (cf. v. 15), it is Pharaoh himself who hardens his heart (v. 32), again in response to the relief that Yahweh has graciously granted.

v. Livestock (9:1–7)

1–2. As previously, the announcement of the fifth disaster commences with a summons to reiterate Yahweh's basic demand, followed by a conditional threat. On this occasion the usual condi-tional clause – *If you refuse to let them go* – is uniquely augmented with 'and you keep holding on to them' (AT). Presumably the latter alludes to his hardened heart,[19] an allusion unfortunately lost in the NIV's paraphrastic *continue to hold them back*.

3–4. The ominous 'hand of Yahweh' (AT) is mentioned here for the first time since 7:4, and the imminent disaster is uniquely described as a severe pestilence (lit. 'a very heavy plague'). Pharaoh's hard(ened) heart is thus portrayed as directly responsible for Yahweh's heavy-handed response (cf. 3:19–20; 6:1). Moreover, the reciprocal nature of Yahweh's response is further highlighted by the unique use of the *hyh* participle.[20] However, only livestock (rather than people) would be afflicted by this plague, and only those of the Egyptians: once again, Israel would enjoy immunity from the effects of this plague (cf. 8:22–23). The latter seems to exclude normal diseases such as anthrax, although such is often suggested.

5–6. The fact that it is now Yahweh who sets the time (cf. 8:9–10) may further highlight that Pharaoh is increasingly losing control over his kingdom; despite being given prior notice (and thus time to repent), Pharaoh proves unable to preserve Egypt's livestock, in contrast to Yahweh, who ensures that no harm befalls the livestock of the Israelites. As the subsequent plague narrative makes clear (cf. the livestock mentioned in vv. 19–21), some measure of hyperbole is involved in describing the extensive impact of this plague (v. 6). The main point, however, is that unlike Yahweh, Pharaoh cannot preserve the livestock of his people – a contrast that is even more pronounced when it comes to protecting the people themselves.

7. Somewhat ironically, Pharaoh 'sends' (Qal *šlḥ*) to investigate the situation in Goshen, but – despite the clarity of the attested sign (Israel's exemption) – refuses Yahweh's basic demand to

---

19 The root (*ḥzq*) is frequently used with reference to Pharaoh's hardened heart in the Exodus account.

20 This is true whether it parallels just the anticipated 'seizing' by Pharaoh or conforms to the wider pattern of these statements about Yahweh's responses to Pharaoh's hypothetical refusals employing participial forms (cf. 7:17; 8:2 [MT 7:27]; 9:3; 10:4).

'release' (Piel *šlḥ*) Israel. The necessity of such an investigation suggests that Goshen was some considerable distance from the royal palace, or at least that the Israelite livestock were somewhat removed from the centre of the administrative bureaucracy. The fact that the Egyptian livestock had already been decimated undoubtedly explains why, on this occasion, there was no pleading for Moses to intercede so that Yahweh might grant any relief from this plague.

vi. Boils (9:8–12)

8–10. As with the first triad, the third plague in the second triad is introduced without any warning or opportunity to avert it. Moses and Aaron are once again given responsibility for initiating the disaster. They do so by tossing handfuls of 'furnace-soot' in the air. The Hebrew noun translated *soot* or 'ash' (*pîaḥ*) occurs only in these two verses. The type of *furnace* from which it came was used for metalwork (e.g. to mould gold or bronze doors) rather than the manufacture of bricks, which were sun-baked prior to use. The symbolic staff does not appear to have been utilized on this occasion. This was probably due to how the soot was manipulated (v. 10), although perhaps the presence of the staff and possibly its use are simply assumed (cf. 10:12–13).

11–12. The capitulation of the Egyptian magicians – who previously opposed Moses (cf. 2 Tim. 3:8) – is further underlined by their inability in the face of this plague to ward off its effects upon themselves, still less provide protection for the Egyptian population as a whole. Having failed to handle the gnats, they now reappear as victims of these debilitating *boils* (cf. Deut. 28:27, 35),[21] the first plague that explicitly harmed people rather

---

21 Cf. also Lev. 13:18; 2 Kgs 20:7; Job 2:7. While 'skin anthrax' (Tigay 1996: 263) and a 'dermatitis infection' (B. Levine 1989: 79) have been suggested, the precise identity of this ailment is unimportant; both the initial (a rash) and the fully developed symptom (blistering boils; Heb. *šĕḥîn*) made its victims painfully obvious. The use of the Aramaic cognate (*šḥn*) in the Prayer of Nabonidus (cf. *COS* 1: 286 n. 3) implies that the last king of Babylon may have suffered from a similar ailment.

than simply impacting their livestock or environment.[22] Once again, therefore, the inferiority of Pharaoh's magicians and the inadequacy of their secret arts are exposed. No longer can they even stand before Moses, far less stand against him. Once again, the magicians serve here as a foil to Pharaoh, whose stubborn resolve shows absolutely no sign of weakening, despite everything he has just witnessed – including the monumental humiliation of his magicians. Significantly, for the first time since 7:3, Yahweh is credited with hardening Pharaoh's heart – perhaps a further indication that Pharaoh's reaction here was both irrational and unnatural, and arguably implying that Yahweh's patience with Pharaoh was beginning to wear out. Thus understood, this marks an important watershed between persuasion and punishment: from this point on Yahweh is primarily focused on the latter. In any case, we are reminded once more that Pharaoh's refusal to yield took neither Yahweh nor Moses by surprise. Rather, events were working out exactly as Yahweh had planned: while Pharaoh seemed to be thwarting Yahweh's purposes, the reality of the situation was quite otherwise.

vii. Hail (9:13–35)

Interestingly, the final triad in the sequence is by far the longest, chiefly due to the additional details relating to Pharaoh's intransigence and his role in the purpose of God.

13–14. Once again, the triad begins with a commission to confront Pharaoh *in the morning* (cf. 7:15; 8:20), although the river is not explicitly mentioned in this instance.[23] Yahweh's familiar demand is again reiterated; however, this time the threat element

---

22 As such, this (presumably non-fatal attack) was a harbinger of things to come; Yahweh had already shown that he could kill Egypt's livestock; he now demonstrated that he could afflict the Egyptian population. These were lessons ignored at great national and personal cost.

23 Perhaps an indication that Pharaoh had stopped bathing in the Nile, maybe due to a lack of confidence in its supposed healing or purifying properties.

is intensified by the prospect of unleashing the *full force* of Yahweh's power (lit. 'all my plagues') against Egypt.

15. The latter, as this elaboration makes clear, refers to the annihilating impact that Yahweh's hand could have had on Egypt already, had Yahweh so intended.

16. Yahweh's rationale for exercising restraint is now explained. The ambiguity of the main verb (lit. 'I have caused you to stand') facilitates two quite different interpretations: traditionally it has been understood with the NIV text as *I have raised you up*, referring to Yahweh's sovereignty in manipulating Pharaoh's circumstances;[24] however, it could also mean 'I have spared you' (NIV margin), a reading that is at least equally and arguably more appropriate in the immediate context.[25] Either way, the reason why Yahweh has not exercised lethal force against Egypt thus far is so that Yahweh's mighty power might be personally disclosed and globally proclaimed.

17–19. Therefore, in view of Pharaoh's persistence in opposing Yahweh's people by his stubborn refusal to release them, a storm is coming – the scale of which is completely unprecedented in Egyptian history. Indeed, this hailstorm will prove fatal for any person or animal caught out in it. On account of its life-threatening nature, therefore, opportunity is given to shelter potential victims from its impact – a development that highlights the escalating scale of these disasters,[26] as well as Yahweh's concern to preserve rather than to extinguish life (cf. Ezek. 18:32; 2 Pet. 3:9).

20–21. This remarkable contrast between the actions of Pharaoh's officials who 'feared the word of Yahweh' and those who 'ignored the word of Yahweh' (AT) highlights the choice that was open to all, and the growing Egyptian recognition of

---

24 Such is how the text is interpreted in the NT (cf. Rom. 9:17).

25 See Ford (2006: 60–70) for a defence of this interpretation and a concise discussion of the interpretative issues involved.

26 This is the first plague that explicitly threatens human life. Like the other (firstborn), death is presented as inevitable only for those who do not find shelter.

Yahweh's supremacy. It also foreshadows even greater capitulation to follow (cf. 10:7).

22–26. As in most of the previous plagues, the staff of Moses is explicitly involved in the initiation of this meteorological disaster. Not surprisingly, the storm proved every bit as exceptional and lethal as had been anticipated, destroying everything in its wake. Only Goshen (cf. 8:22) escaped unscathed – further underlining that this deluge was no ordinary severe weather system or coincidental freak of nature, but an 'act of God' in the truest sense.

27–28. Presumably it was the forced recognition of the latter that prompted Pharaoh to make his greatest concessions thus far, acknowledging not only his (and his people's) fault, but also the legitimacy of Yahweh's demand. With his petition for prayer (cf. 8:28) and promise of liberation, it seems as if Pharaoh has now capitulated entirely.

29–30. Moses, however, clearly knew otherwise. His critical appraisal of Pharaoh's sincerity may have been due to the latter's track record thus far, and/or the fact that Yahweh had given Moses no reason to expect otherwise (cf. 11:1).

31–32. This parenthetical note qualifies the hyperbole used in verse 25 and explains how the forthcoming locust invasion proved so catastrophic even in the aftermath of the extensive destruction caused by the hail.

33–35. In keeping with the now-familiar pattern, once Moses secured relief from the plague, Pharaoh reneged on his end of the agreement and thus repeated his transgression (cf. v. 27). On this occasion his officials also – presumably those mentioned in verse 21, but possibly including those of verse 20 as well – are said to have hardened their hearts, underlining that they too (and not just their leader) were culpable. And so, despite Pharaoh's momentary capitulation, now that the crisis has passed both he and his officials remain adamant. However, as the final verse (v. 35) underlines yet again, the situation was unfolding precisely as Yahweh had anticipated.

viii. Locusts (10:1–20)

Like the account of the previous disaster, this one is considerably longer than others – due in some measure to the initial comment on Egyptian intransigence (10:1–2) and the subsequent hiatus prompted by the reaction of Pharaoh's servants (10:7–11).

1–2. The introduction to the eighth plague does not follow the previous pattern; rather, the initial exhortation (*Go to Pharaoh*) is immediately followed by a threefold explanation (to Moses) outlining why Yahweh has hardened the hearts of Pharaoh and his officials: (1) to facilitate the performance of these signs in Egypt; (2) to provide testimony about Yahweh's actions for future generations of Israelites; and (3) to enhance Israel's knowledge of Yahweh (cf. 6:7; 11:7). Moreover, on this occasion the first stage of the communication process (the reception of the specific message by Moses) is omitted, but its delivery to Pharaoh is included – a striking reversal of the previous pericopes. This unexpected shift from prophetic reception to prophetic proclamation may help signify that the climax of this series of disasters is now approaching (cf. Greenberg 1997: 513–514). It certainly paves the way for a focus on Pharaoh's response to the threat of a plague rather than the plague itself: this is the first time in the series where the former is explicitly recorded.

3–6. The message delivered to Pharaoh conforms more closely to the usual pattern, although this time the usual demand and conditional warning are preceded by a rhetorical question: *How long will you refuse to humble yourself before me?* (v. 3). While possibly an indication that Yahweh's patience is beginning to wear thin,[27] this question highlights the underlying problem: Pharaoh was refusing to acknowledge his proper place in the created order by asserting his own sovereignty over Yahweh's. This is the final time that Yahweh restates his core demand (cf. 5:1; 7:16; 8:1, 20; 9:1, 13), a further indication that the struggle is approaching resolution. The anticipated infestation of locusts threatens to wipe out whatever crops have survived the devastation caused by the previous plague (v. 5),[28] as well as overrunning their homes as the frogs had previ-

---

27 Cf. 16:28, where an analogous question expresses Yahweh's exasperation with the disobedient Israelites.
28 This is the only explicit reference to another plague in the series, which for Ford (2006: 158) signals an end to the mitigation that Pharaoh has thus far squandered.

124

EXODUS

ously (v. 6). Moreover, like the plague of hail, this locust invasion will be on an unprecedented scale. These features all point to the still escalating nature of the plagues in their intensity. The use of locusts (whether literal or figurative) to evoke repentance is reflected elsewhere in the Bible (cf. Joel 1 – 2; Amos 4:9; Rev. 9:1–11), albeit without much success – as ultimately proved to be true in this case also.

7. Clearly echoing Yahweh's exasperation with Pharaoh (cf. v. 3), the Egyptian officials now express similar sentiments (*How long . . . ?*) – ostensibly with respect to Moses, but there is clearly implicit criticism of Pharaoh himself, further articulated in the second rhetorical question they ask ('Do you not yet know . . . ?', AT). Capitulation to Moses' demands seems to be the only sensible course of action to take. While their position may reflect a lack of theological awareness,[29] and is certainly motivated by a vested interest in preserving what was left of the Egyptian economy, it nevertheless exposes further cracks developing (cf. 8:18–19; 9:11, 20–21) in what was proving to be a problematic domestic policy. Moreover, as their assessment ('Egypt is decimated', AT) inadvertently bears testimony, persistent rebellion against God has disastrous consequences for nations as well as individuals. As Ford (2006: 159) suggests, the gradual capitulation of Pharaoh's officials bears striking parallels with that of the magicians in the earlier part of the narrative. Moreover, their use of key terminology (i.e. 'know') suggests implicit acknowledgment of Yahweh's sovereignty over Egypt.

8. Whether he was simply bowing to his political advisers or had already drawn similar conclusions himself, Pharaoh again expresses a willingness to grant Moses' request, albeit with certain conditions clearly in mind – namely, that there should be restrictions imposed on who might be allowed to serve Yahweh, possibly prompted by his officials' appeal to let 'the men' go (v. 7, AT).[30]

---

29 They seem to place the blame on Moses, rather than paying sufficient attention to his ambassador status.

30 While Yahweh has repeatedly spoken of releasing *my people* (*'ammî*), Pharaoh's officials speak of releasing 'the men' (*hā'ănāšîm*). Whether this

Thus, while his earlier compromise related to *how far* they would be permitted to go (cf. 8:25–28), this one zooms in on *who* might be allowed to do so.[31]

9–11. Despite Pharaoh's protestations to the contrary (v. 11), Moses' insistence that the entire Israelite community must leave comes as no great surprise. However, it does evoke a negative reaction, with Pharaoh's appeasing-sounding 'Yahweh be with you' (AT) being abruptly followed by a statement of what he truly thought – that they had ulterior motives (lit. 'because evil is in front of your faces').[32] To interpret the latter clause more positively (i.e. expressing concern for the Israelites' well-being; cf. NIV footnote) would imply a level of concern that is displayed nowhere else in the narrative, and is diametrically opposed to the character of this and other pharaohs in Exodus. Thus, rather than reflecting any fluctuation of thought, Pharaoh's initial statement – probably spoken in a derisory tone – apparently bristled with sarcasm and was quite in keeping with his accusatory and hostile response that immediately followed. And so, even in the face of yet another disaster, Pharaoh digs in his heels: the Israelites may leave on his terms or not at all! The fact that Moses and Aaron are now forcibly expelled from Pharaoh's presence is a clear indication that patience on either side was wearing increasingly thin (cf. v. 3).[33]

12–15. While the staff is not explicitly mentioned in Yahweh's command (v. 12), the use of this instrument was evidently implicit

---

reflects an Egyptian male-orientated cultic practice or is simply a clever ploy designed to thwart Israel's escape, Pharaoh seems to press this idea when he restricts permission to adult males (*gĕbārîm*) in the negotiations that immediately follow.

31 The unusual repetition of the Hebrew interrogative (lit. '*Who and who* are going?') clearly emphasizes Pharaoh's main concern here.

32 An allusion to Pharaoh's god (Ra) has also been discerned, hence Cassuto (1967: 126) and Rendsburg (1988: 355) take the statement ('evil/ Ra is before you') as some kind of theological threat.

33 Significantly, the same verb (*gāraš*) was previously used to describe what Pharaoh would ultimately do to the Israelites (6:1) and is later used to describe their eventual release (12:31). See also 2:17.

(v. 13). The *east wind* may simply explain where such a huge swarm of locusts came from, but it may also anticipate Yahweh's final victory over the Egyptians at the crossing of the Sea (cf. 14:21; 15:10; cf. also 10:19). In any case, God's sovereign power is here displayed in his ability to control even the wind (cf. Ps. 135:7; Jer. 10:13; Matt. 8:23–27). As with some of the previous plagues, the extremity of the disaster is painted in the darkest of terms (v. 14), further highlighting the escalating scale of these events (cf. 9:18). The description here undoubtedly employs some degree of hyperbole, although the use of the merism (*Never before . . . again*; lit. 'not before it . . . nor after it . . .') clearly attests to its destructive intensity.[34] While locust invasion was a widespread phenomenon in the Middle East, the impact of such on an unprecedented scale is not hard to imagine.

16–17. It is thus a chastened and seemingly contrite Pharaoh who urgently summons Moses and Aaron a second time, acknowledges again that he has sinned – against both Yahweh and his envoys[35] – and urges Moses (and through him, Yahweh) to show clemency once more and remove *this deadly plague* (lit. 'this death') from Egypt. Pharaoh's willingness to accede to Yahweh's wishes is not stated explicitly but is clearly implied (cf. v. 20).

18–20. Moses complies without delay, but this time he adds nothing further by way of warning (cf. 8:29) or recrimination (cf. 9:30). Thus, the impression given is that by this stage Moses is simply resigned to Pharaoh's intransigence. Despite the latter, however, Yahweh again responds positively to Pharaoh's petition, and thus for the last time in the narrative Egypt is granted a reprieve from

---

34 See Brin 2001: 110. However, for other extraordinary phenomena similarly described, cf. Josh. 10:14; Matt. 24:21; Rev. 16:18.

35 In speaking of those he has sinned against, Pharaoh's confession here goes beyond that of 9:27. However, despite the theological correctness of its expression (in biblical perspective, sin is first and foremost against God; cf. Gen. 39:9; Ps. 51:4 [MT 6]; Luke 15:18, 21), Pharaoh's confession is superficial because, like Israel's first king (cf. 1 Sam. 15:24–27), he stops short of genuine repentance. For more on the latter comparison, see Hamilton 2011: 160.

the clutches of death. From this point on there is no intercession, and the spectre of the final and most ominous plague draws inevitably closer. Significantly, Yahweh eradicates the present problem by effecting a change in the wind's direction which drove the locusts into the sea. The exact location of this body of water is unclear (cf. 13:18; 14:2; see also Introduction 4c, 'The route of the exodus'), complicated by the general consensus that the Hebrew almost certainly denotes 'Reed Sea'. Such a description (a sea associated with reeds) is anomalous for the actual Red Sea (including both its northern extensions, the Gulfs of Suez and Aqaba). For this reason, alternative fresh-water locations have been proposed, although none has gained unanimous support. Whatever the sea's precise location, the locusts' fate seems in some way to foreshadow that of the Egyptian army (cf. 14:27). Once the present crisis has passed, however, Pharaoh once more recants and refuses to let the Israelites go – a hardening of resolve for which Yahweh is expressly credited with responsibility for the third time in the plague narrative (cf. 9:12; 10:1).[36]

ix. Darkness (10:21–29)

21–23. As before, the third plague in the group is introduced without notice or warning. Rather, Moses is simply commanded to *stretch out [his] hand towards the sky* and thus initiate a period of intense, preternatural darkness.[37] While not stated explicitly, its three-day duration and palpable intensity may imply that, like the previous two phenomena, this also was an unprecedented experience in Egypt's history. In any case, the darkness that shrouded the rest of Egypt did not affect the Israelites (v. 23)

---

36 The fact that these references to Yahweh hardening Pharaoh's heart are concentrated in the latter part of the plague narrative (cf. 9:12; 10:1, 20, 27; 11:10) suggests that a significant watershed is marked by the end of the second triad.

37 Elsewhere such terminology is associated with the Day of Yahweh (Joel 2:2; Zeph. 1:15; cf. Isa. 29:18; Amos 5:20). The possible allusion to Gen. 1:2 in Exod. 10:22b (Hamilton 2011) would imply that this was yet another de-creative act in the plague narrative (see p. 130 n. 42).

– again bearing eloquent testimony to Yahweh's presence in the land (8:22) and his ability to do as he pleased in the land of Re (the sun-god). As its discriminating nature makes abundantly clear, this intense and prolonged darkness was no mere naturally occurring phenomenon (i.e. the result of a severe sandstorm or solar eclipse), but rather another extraordinary circumstance controlled entirely by Yahweh.

24–26. It is unclear whether Pharaoh reopened negotiations during this period of darkness or immediately afterwards – there is no formal petition for its removal, nor is there any record of Yahweh doing so. However, this could well be explained by Pharaoh breaking off negotiations at the end of the three days, as soon as he saw that normality had been restored. Moreover, given his track record, it seems unlikely that Pharaoh would have summoned Moses once the situation had been resolved. It is thus more probable that, faced with a further crisis, Pharaoh is again prepared to comply – at least in part – with Moses' demands. He nevertheless still insists on imposing his own restriction that, as before, seems designed to obstruct Israel's permanent departure. However, as Moses somewhat comically observes, this constraint would also undermine and frustrate the major objective of their stated goal: sacrificial worship of Yahweh. Moses thus responds to Pharaoh's unreasonable imposition by an equally adamant (and outrageous) insistence that all their livestock must accompany them.[38] This all-or-nothing approach leaves no further room for compromise.

27. Clearly, if there is to be any resolution, it must come from Pharaoh. This, however, will never happen so long as Yahweh continues to harden Pharaoh's heart, as he does here and (with the exception of 9:34–35) throughout this last triad of plagues. While not stated explicitly, perhaps the catalyst was the end of the three days of darkness. In any case, the negotiations collapse as soon as Pharaoh's heart is hardened, and his resolve to retain his

---

38 Moses' logic – that they needed every last animal because they did not yet know which ones Yahweh required by way of sacrifice – makes little more sense than that of Pharaoh (Ford 2006: 162).

Hebrew slaves becomes more determined than ever. By now it is abundantly clear that Pharaoh has lost any personal control over how this situation will unfold.

28–29. Having reached an impasse, Pharaoh breaks off all future negotiations with Moses, threatening execution should he dare to confront him again. Although Pharaoh's threat and Moses' response may seem somewhat premature in the light of the subsequent narrative, it is possible to resolve the difficulty of an implausible narrative sequence by reading some of the material in chapter 11 as parenthetical, and the rest as resumptive repetition.[39] Alternatively, we should understand that despite what either party said in the heat of the moment, communications did not terminate immediately (nor even entirely; cf. 12:31–32).[40] Either way, more interaction took place than one might reasonably infer from these two verses.

Meaning
In terms of the theological significance of the plague narrative, some have discerned a subtle theological critique of various Egyptian gods and beliefs. Admittedly, there may be some support for this in the text itself (cf. 8:10 [MT 6]; 9:14),[41] especially in relation to the tenth and final plague in the series (12:12; cf. Num. 33:4).

---

39 So NIV (US edn), which renders the verbs in both 11:1 and 11:9 as pluperfects. The NIV (UK edn) and NLT do so only in the case of the latter, whereas the ESV translates both 11:1 and 11:9 using the simple past tense, arguably yielding the most contextually implausible narrative sequence in both places. Since there is no obvious syntactical support for a pluperfect in either verse, such a translation is surely questionable unless the context clearly demands it (see further discussion below).

40 Ford (2006) concludes that 11:1–8 is set immediately after 10:29, with 11:8 providing the note of departure that would otherwise be anomalously missing from such a dialogue (i.e. where Pharaoh speaks to Moses and Aaron *during* rather than *before* the plague).

41 While 'gods' are not mentioned explicitly in either text, references to such elsewhere in the book (12:12; 15:11; 20:2–5; 22:20; 23:32; 34:11–16) warrants their inclusion in such comparisons (Blackburn 2012: 43 n. 34).

However, it is probably mistaken to attempt to associate individual plagues with particular Egyptian deities; rather, while certain plagues may indirectly expose the impotency of the Egyptian pantheon, the text focuses much more explicitly on Yahweh's manifest sovereignty in Egypt and its corollary, his supremacy over Pharaoh. This contest or struggle is primarily between Yahweh and Pharaoh, each of whom claimed sole authority over the Israelites (cf. 5:2).

Yahweh's supremacy in this struggle is indicated throughout the plague narrative, not least by the gradual capitulation of Pharaoh's entourage and the discriminating nature of the majority of the plagues. Yahweh's sovereignty over Pharaoh is further reflected in the latter's irrational intransigence, which in reality served the interests of Yahweh and the Israelites, rather than those of Pharaoh and the Egyptians. Moreover, Yahweh's ultimate triumph over Egypt is foreshadowed when the intensity and severity of the disasters escalate as Yahweh unleashes his mighty hand in increasing measure.

Arguably throughout the plague narrative there is an under-lying 'reversal of creation' theme: Yahweh is unleashing the forces of creation against the Egyptians because of their anti-creational stance, and in some sense returning Egypt to a kind of pre-creation chaos.[42] In this light, the judgments that fall on Egypt are theologically reminiscent of the flood, and the deliverance and birth of the Israelite nation is a new creation (cf. Ps. 74:12–17).

However, while the plagues clearly did function as divine judgment on Pharaoh and the Egyptians, their primary role was revelatory, as suggested by their more common description as *signs* or *wonders*. As such, they graphically demonstrated Yahweh's supremacy over Pharaoh, over creation, and over all other gods, Egyptian or otherwise.

---

42 For more on this de-creation motif, see Fretheim 1991a and Athas 2008.

4. PASSOVER AND EXODUS (11:1 – 13:16)

A. The tenth plague announced (11:1–10)

Context

The tenth and final plague is announced in chapter 11, but its execution and consequences are not narrated until the second half of the following chapter (12:29–39). In between its announcement and its execution are instructions concerning the preparations for and the subsequent commemoration of the Passover festival (12:1–28). While some of this instructional material focuses on the original Passover night in particular, other sections focus more on its later, annual commemoration.

As previously noted, this final plague is announced to Pharaoh in a conversation that in most English translations appears to take place after negotiations have actually terminated (cf. 10:28–29). Enns (2000: 245) resolves this difficulty by concluding that

the announcement of this [climactic] plague should be read in light of 4:21–23, where God had previously told Moses what

would ultimately happen to Egypt. This also helps make sense
of the fact that Moses and Pharaoh apparently have a conversation in 11:4–8 after they have both vowed that they will never
see each other again . . . The conversation between Moses and
Pharaoh that follows [i.e. 11:4–8] is . . . simply a continuation of
the conversation of 10:24–29.[1]

However, while the latter conclusion is surely correct, it is
entirely feasible that Yahweh's previous revelation (4:21–23) should
now be reiterated and elucidated – as the wording of Moses'
message to Pharaoh in 11:4–8 surely implies. Thus understood,
having already carried out Yahweh's instructions of 4:21, Moses is
now told (11:1–2) – presumably while still standing before Pharaoh
– that it is time to enact the instructions of 4:22–23 and 3:22 (cf.
3:20–21). He thus proceeds to announce the final plague (11:4–8)
before negotiations are officially concluded.

Comment
1–3. However understood (see above), these verses record
Yahweh's disclosure of the tenth and last plague in the series,
along with instructions for 'plundering the Egyptians' (cf. 12:36).
Moses was thus made aware that this final catastrophe, which
transcended all preceding signs and wonders in its devastating
impact (cf. 11:6), would be effective in securing Israel's anticipated
deliverance; finally, Pharaoh would be all too eager to rid Egypt
of the Israelite menace.[2]

Such eagerness on Pharaoh's part would be matched only by that
of the Egyptian populace, whose enthusiasm (cf. 12:33) was to be
flagrantly exploited by the departing Israelites, thus facilitating the

---

1   By translating 11:1 as a pluperfect: 'The LORD *had said* to Moses' (i.e. for
    Enns, back in 4:21–23), the NIV (US edn, emphasis added) treats 11:1–3
    as a narrative flashback, with v. 3 being a parenthetical explanation of
    the Egyptians' anticipated response.
2   Pharaoh's eagerness is highlighted by the emphatic and somewhat
    repetitive Hebrew clause: lit. 'when he expels you, he will indeed drive
    you completely from here'.

fulfilment of the promise of 3:21–22 (cf. 12:35–36). As Ashby (1998: 50) suggests, this plundering of Egypt does not constitute theft or even recompense for services rendered, but is an expression of Yahweh's victory over Pharaoh and the Egyptians ('to the victor belong the spoils'): 'Egypt is now paying tribute to the people of Yahweh.' The parenthetical comment that follows (v. 3) clarifies that such plundering of the Egyptians was possible only because Yahweh made the Egyptians favourably disposed towards his people, and because of the respect that Moses had gained in the eyes of both Pharaoh's officials and the Egyptians in general – in sharp contrast to the hostility of Pharaoh[3] – and is thus a further indication of Egypt's progressive capitulation before Yahweh.

4–8. As suggested above, this paragraph records the conclusion of the conversation which had seemingly ended with 10:29. In keeping with Yahweh's earlier directive (4:21–23), the time had eventually come (11:1) for the execution of Egypt's firstborn: the series of wonders that Yahweh had given Moses the power to perform (4:21a) had run its course and, as anticipated from the outset, this had resulted in the providential hardening of Pharaoh's heart (4:21b). Now it was time for Yahweh to act directly rather than through the agency of Moses and Aaron (v. 4; cf. 12:12, 23). In some sense this last plague, from which no Egyptian firstborn would be immune, will serve as retribution for the suffering that Egypt has inflicted on Israel, God's firstborn (v. 5; cf. 4:22–23). As Enns (2000: 246) observes, 'Now it will be Egypt's turn to "cry" because of *their* oppression (the use of *šěʿāqâ* [cry] in v. 6 is an echo of Israel's cry in 3:7)' (emphasis his). The discriminating nature (v. 7) of this last plague, encompassing both people and animals, will be so effective that the Egyptians will actually beg the Israelites to depart (v. 8a).[4] Only then would Moses leave (v. 8b) and so never appear before Pharaoh again (cf. 10:29). And so, implicitly matching Pharaoh's own disposition, Moses angrily

---

3   The LXX, however, suggests that Moses also had such stature before Pharaoh.

4   Indeed, as already noted, they would eagerly assist them in any way possible (cf. 11:3).

leaves Pharaoh's presence for the last, or perhaps penultimate, time (v. 8c).[5]

9–10. In this final summary of all that has transpired so far, we are reminded once again that Pharaoh's refusal to cooperate throughout the wonders performed through Moses and Aaron was no great surprise; rather – in the providence of God – it had simply facilitated the multiplication of such wonders in Egypt (v. 9).[6] Pharaoh was merely an actor in a stage play that Yahweh was obviously directing. Thus, while Moses and Aaron had faithfully carried out their task, the ultimate effect on Pharaoh of all these wonders they had performed was merely to harden his resolve so that he stubbornly refused to let God's people go.

Meaning

Pharaoh remains as intransigent as ever, but Yahweh's patience has now been exhausted. Pharaoh's consistently negative response to his recurring experience of Yahweh's leniency (i.e. in complying with all Pharaoh's requests to end successive plagues) has secured the fate of Egypt's firstborn. Having hardened his heart, or having had his heart hardened in this way, Pharaoh's experience of Yahweh's righteous judgment was now inevitable (as anticipated in 4:22–23). The time for diplomacy had ended; it was now time for Pharaoh to experience the full force of Yahweh's mighty hand. Pharaoh would thus learn the ultimate folly of defying God and resisting his will – not simply the fact that God's plan would finally prevail, but the sobering reality that God's patience, while extensive, is not limitless, so persistent human defiance inevitably evokes God's judgment and wrath.

---

5 A further appearance can be inferred from 12:31–32, although some commentators conclude that on that occasion Pharaoh communicated through official channels rather than meeting with Moses and Aaron personally.

6 While the preposition could arguably introduce a purpose clause here, the resultative sense seems more appropriate in the immediate context.

B. Instructions for Passover and Unleavened Bread (12:1–28)

Context

Once again, the pace of the unfolding drama slows down when we get to the beginning of chapter 12, where the instructions for the necessary preparations for the aforementioned climactic plague (11:1, 4–6) are given to and through Moses and Aaron. This chapter comprises a mixture of instructions for the original Passover night and regulations for its annual commemoration in the Passover meal and feast of Unleavened Bread. As Wenham (2003: 63) observes:

> This mixture of materials poses a number of problems for commentators and historians, but the very mixture illustrates perfectly the character of the book of Exodus: it is Torah, that is religious instruction. It is designed to instruct its readers about the past, but also to teach them about how to behave in the present. The Passover celebrates an event in the past, Israel's escape from slavery in Egypt, but it is also an annual festival, which must be kept in the approved manner if God is to continue to bless Israel. Thus while the storyline proceeds roughly chronologically detailing what happened when, it is interrupted from time to time with lengthy digressions on how the Passover must be celebrated for all time.

Part of our difficulty in reading this material, therefore, lies in discerning which instructions were unique to the original occasion (e.g. the smearing of blood on the doorposts and consuming the meal in haste) and which aspects apply rather to all future celebrations of it in the Promised Land (e.g. the extended festival, lasting for just over a week; cf. 12:25).

Comment

The first section (12:1–20), in which Yahweh gives his instructions to Moses and Aaron, contains two subunits: the first (vv. 1–13) relates primarily to the original Passover; the second (vv. 14–20) concerns its annual commemoration. The subsequent section

(12:21–28) then narrates Moses' communication of these instructions (at least, in part) to the people via their elders.

i. Yahweh's instructions concerning the original Passover (12:1–13)

1–2. The exodus constituted a new beginning for Israel – its birth or creation as a separate nation; thus from this point onwards it would mark the beginning of the nation's religious calendar. The *first month*, Abib (cf. 13:4),[7] was the spring month, corresponding to March–April in the Western calendar.[8]

3–4. The sacrificial animal (*śê*) could be either a lamb or a kid (cf. NIV footnote); therefore Durham's (1987) 'flock-animal' (cf. 12:5) is a better translation than the traditional 'lamb'.[9] In oriental flocks the difference was much less defined. The number of flock animals slain and consumed on the night of Passover was to be proportionate to the number of occupants per household. A later tradition set the minimum number for the latter as ten, but as Cole observes, 'this figure was reached by artificial exegesis . . . it seems to have been a question either of appetite, or the size of the sheep, rather than theology' (1973: 106). Evidently the underlying rationale for this ratio of meat to people relates to ensuring that there was sufficient for all, without any unnecessary wastage.

5. The reason why the flock animal had to be without defect is not spelt out at this point (cf. Lev. 22:18–25), but its typological significance, as reflected in the New Testament,[10] illuminates the theological ramifications of this particular stipulation: only an unblemished sacrifice would suffice. While there is no *explicit* connection here in Exodus between the Passover sacrifice and

---

7   This month was called Nisan after the exile (cf. Esth. 3:7), when the months received new names and the civil year began in autumn.

8   Exod. 23:16 and 34:22 refer to the end of the *agricultural* year – after the harvest.

9   Deut. 16:2 expands this to include calves, commensurate with the larger setting (sanctuary rather than individual households); see Tigay 1996: 153–154.

10 E.g. John 1:29; 19:36; 1 Cor. 5:7; 1 Pet. 1:19.

either sin or atonement, it clearly served as a substitute for the Israelite firstborn whom it delivered from death (vv. 13, 21–23, 27; cf. 13:13). Moreover, as Alexander (2017) and Gehrig (2024) have argued from the significant parallels between the Passover ritual and the priestly consecration of Aaron and his sons (Exod. 29; cf. Lev. 8), it apparently served a dual purpose: not only delivering Israel's firstborn from death by its shed blood, but also consecrating each Israelite household through the consumption of its flesh.

6–7. The entire community was to participate in the slaughter of the animals at dusk of the fourteenth day – the Hebrew phrase literally means 'between the evenings', most likely referring to twilight, the period between sunset and nightfall.[11] This collective involvement in the slaughter, as well as the application of the blood to the doorframes of each house in which the meat was subsequently consumed, closely identified the Israelite households with the animals that were slain. While this may further imply the substitutionary nature of the ritual, more likely this relates to consecration (see comment on vv. 3–4).

8–9. The regulations governing how the meat was to be cooked may possibly serve to distinguish this rite from any analogous ritual in Canaanite practice, but, more significantly, further suggests a close association between the Passover sacrifice and priestly consecration (cf. 29:31–34). The prohibition on 'boiling' may at first seem to be contradicted in Deuteronomy 16:7, which employs the same Hebrew verb when prescribing how the meat *is* to be cooked (i.e. 'boiling'). However, there the omission of 'in water' removes the apparent contradiction. The significance of the *bitter herbs* is not explained. Even though the same word for *bitter* is used of the Israelite service in 1:14, drawing an implicit link between these two chapters (cf. Mishnah Pesaḥim 10:5) seems rather tenuous. More likely is the suggestion that bitter herbs were selected because they were readily available and required the least amount of preparation (so Stuart 2006). This squares

---

11 For further discussion of this phrase, including the equivalent expression used in Deut. 16:6, see Alexander 2017: 224.

more logically with the immediate context, tying in with the consumption of unleavened bread (see below) – which is later explicitly related to the haste of the Israelites' departure (cf. v. 39).

10. No rationale is offered for the prohibition on subsequently eating the leftovers, but like the similar regulation governing other sacrifices (cf. 23:18), it was probably designed to prevent any profane use of sacred flesh. Such holy meat was not for personal consumption outside a sacrificial context.

11. *Passover* (introduced here for the first time) refers primarily to the victim, and secondarily to the feast. None of the various etymologies proposed for the Hebrew term (*pesaḥ*) is sufficiently convincing to replace that suggested by the use of the cognate verb in the text (v. 13), whatever the precise connotation of the latter (see comment on vv. 12–13). The Israelites are to eat the Passover 'dressed and ready to leave' (AT) – there being little time to pack or to make even the most basic preparations for the journey (cf. v. 39). Following Wellhausen, biblical critics have argued that the Passover was originally a cultic ceremony of nomadic shepherds in the spring which only later acquired this historical significance as a cultic representation of the exodus (see Additional note on the origin[s] of Passover and Unleavened Bread). However, this fails to account for the 'haste' factor mentioned here.

12–13. In striking down Egypt's firstborn Yahweh will execute *judgment on all the gods of Egypt.* This is the only explicit reference to such activity (i.e. targeting Egyptian deities) in the narrative, and clearly envisages a collective judgment rather than anything more specific. Thus, Egyptian perceptions of the firstborn son of Pharaoh or the association of a firstborn bull with the Apis cult are arguably beside the point. Rather, the death of all firstborn – whether human or animal – would be the ultimate demonstration that Egyptian deities were no match for Yahweh; they could protect neither people nor livestock as Yahweh alone could. Thus, with the tenth plague, Egypt's deities would be utterly exposed as worthless idols that, in contrast to Yahweh, inevitably fail.[12] In contrast to

---

12 NB 'I am Yahweh' (AT) at the end of v. 12 is a further allusion to the significance of the divine name.

such impotent deities, Yahweh would not only execute judgment but also provide protection from such. The blood of the Passover animal, duly applied to the doorframes of each house (cf. v. 7), marked out the houses that Yahweh would *pass over*. Although the precise meaning of the latter verb is disputed, it arguably denotes 'to stand watch over'. The basic meaning is arguably to 'stand still' (cf. 1 Kgs 18:21, where NASB has 'hesitate'), whether because movement is impeded (cf. 2 Sam. 4:4; Lev. 21:18) or undesirable (cf. Isa. 31:5, which speaks of God *protecting* Jerusalem). The LXX translates the verb with *skepazō* ('to cover/shelter') in Exodus 12:13 and 12:27, although inexplicably employs *parerchomai* ('to skip over/ pass by') in 12:23. As Hamilton (2011) suggests, 'stand/watch over' seems appropriate for all three verses. Accordingly, the image is probably that of Yahweh shielding occupants from the impact of the destructive plague that would strike all unprotected households. Significantly, ethnicity alone would not protect Israelite households from this final plague in the series; deliverance was possible only if the blood of the flock animal had been appropriately applied. In this sense the blood was a sign for Israel, signifying the obedience of faith to which Yahweh would graciously respond. Blackburn (2012: 50) infers from this (and the fact that some Egyptians had followed Yahweh's instructions previously) that some Egyptian households were likewise protected. However, this seems unlikely, since the instructions here are to be communicated to *the whole community of Israel* (v. 3), and such is precisely what Moses does (v. 21). There is no explicit communication with the Egyptians until *after* the plague has struck.

ii. Yahweh's instructions for the annual commemoration (12:14–20)

14. The focus now shifts to how this event was to be commemorated by future generations: it was to be perpetually celebrated as one of Yahweh's special festivals (cf. 23:14–17). For biblical instances of its subsequent commemoration, see Numbers 9:1–5; Joshua 5:10; 2 Kings 23:21–23; Ezra 6:19–22; Matthew 26:17–19; Luke 22:1; John 11:55.

15–16. A seven-day period is prescribed during which all bread consumed must be unleavened. The dough for a day's bread was normally mixed and left to stand before being baked, so that a small quantity of the fermented dough from the previous day's batch could 'leaven' (raise as yeast) the new batch. In this instance such fermented dough or leaven must be removed on the first day and a total ban imposed; anyone consuming leavened bread during this restricted period would be committing a serious offence – being *cut off from Israel* arguably denotes divinely imposed death (see Wenham 1978), rather than simply self-exclusion, excommunication or even execution by human hand (although the last-mentioned is clearly suggested in Exod. 31:14–15; cf. 35:2; Num. 15:32–36). Whatever the 'cutting off' penalty entailed, the application of a punishment usually reserved for serious cultic or moral offences is due to the fact that such defiant behaviour (like the non-observance of sabbath) sharply distinguished offenders from the rest of the Israelite community who had faithfully complied with Yahweh's instructions, demonstrating the respect and honour he deserved.

The temporary prohibition on leaven was not due to the negative associations we find expressed in the New Testament (e.g. 1 Cor. 5:6–8; cf. Matt. 16:6; Mark 8:15; Luke 12:1), but to permit subsequent worshippers to replicate the experience of those who had insufficient time to make anything but unleavened bread (cf. 12:39). Removal of leaven on the first day may thus have been more a ritual act than a means to ensure that no leaven was available during the festival. However, Hamilton's suggestion (2011: 187) that the leaven was not destroyed but sealed and stored elsewhere during this time is both conjectural and difficult to square with Paul's symbolic use of the imagery in 1 Corinthians 5:6–8.

The *sacred assembly* of the first and seventh days presumably marked the official beginning and conclusion of this sabbatical week, during which any work (other than food preparation) was also prohibited.

17. This week-long festival is now named *Unleavened Bread*, but its rationale is explicitly tied to the exodus. Therefore, whatever pre-history such a spring festival may have had in Israel's cultic calendar before this (see Additional note on the origin[s] of Passover and Unleavened Bread), its significance from this point onwards is not in doubt.

18. This verse seems to suggest that the festival of Unleavened Bread was to begin on the evening of the fourteenth day and cease on the evening of the twenty-first. However, other passages indicate that it began on the fifteenth day, the day *after* Passover (cf. Lev. 23:5–6; Num. 28:16–17). The simplest solution to this crux is to understand the reference to the fifteenth day in Leviticus and Numbers as commencing with sunrise, rather than sunset. While the Jewish day began at sunset in the post-exilic period, the dating formula in all Pentateuchal Passover texts implies a day starting at sunrise (as with the Egyptians). Moreover, reconstructions assuming a day beginning with sunset involve the difficulty of an apparently redundant day (i.e. a day with no particular significance, either at the beginning or at the end of the week). It seems best, therefore, to understand that while no leaven was to be consumed from the beginning of Passover at twilight on the fourteenth day, the feast of Unleavened Bread officially commenced on the morning of the fifteenth day and concluded on the evening of the twenty-first day with sacred assemblies.[13]

19–20. This complete ban on leaven extended to everyone (v. 19) and everywhere (v. 20) within Israel. Here a settled existence in the Promised Land is evidently assumed; there is no suggestion that the week-long feast of Unleavened Bread was celebrated after the original Passover night.

iii. Communication of the instructions (12:21–28)
Having been given this twofold set of directives by Yahweh, Moses now imparts them – in the same sequence – to Israel's elders. The only other occasions in Exodus where *all the elders* are explicitly involved are when Moses tells them about Yahweh's intentions (4:29) and during the fellowship meal with Jethro (18:12). On each occasion it was evidently important to stress that the entire community (as represented by its leadership) was involved in these events.

---

13 Significantly, there is no mention of 'twilight' or 'evening' in Lev. 23:6 or Num. 28:17.

21. The NIV's *Go at once* is somewhat misleading,[14] as it might give the impression that the Israelites were to select and sacrifice the Passover animal without delay. The translation offered by Stuart (2006) ('Round up') captures the sense much better: 'Round up and select for yourselves sheep [or 'a sheep'] for your families . . .'

22–23. Before the significance of the ritual is explained, Moses stresses the most important element: the application of the animal's blood to the Israelite doorframes, which would ensure Yahweh's protection.[15] The instruction is transparently the same as previously outlined (v. 7), although here Moses elaborates on the mechanics of the procedure: the texture of the hyssop plant apparently made it a natural applicator – a good substitute for a modern paintbrush or roller (see Lev. 14:4, 6, 49, 51–52; Num. 19:6, 18; Heb. 9:19; cf. Ps. 51:7). Crucially, this blood ritual would secure protection only for those who remained within the appropriately marked houses. In that sense Yahweh's redemptive act was clearly selective, having a particular rather than a general or even ethnic focus.

Though *the destroyer* (Heb. *mašḥît*) mentioned here in verse 23 (cf. the threat posed by 'a destroyer' in v. 13) has traditionally been understood in terms of a 'destroying angel' (Ps. 78:49; cf. 2 Sam. 24:15–16; 2 Kgs 19:35; 1 Cor. 10:10), it could simply be a personification of the plague itself (Enns 2000: 246 n. 3). Except for Exodus 12, the noun has always a human referent. Here, however, it seems to be either a hypostasis of Yahweh or a divine agent of some kind, as suggested by the parallel between Yahweh's going 'to strike' and the *mašḥît*'s entering 'to strike'. Accordingly, this agent of death is apparently distinguished in this verse from Yahweh himself, while at the same time being closely associated with him and evidently under his sovereign control.

24–27a. Moses now moves on to the instructions relating to subsequent commemoration of this event (Passover), after Israel

---

14 A more literal translation of the Hebrew verb is 'Go' or 'Draw out'.

15 There is no suggestion that the blood had any magical properties to ward off evil; rather, it served simply to designate the houses that Yahweh himself would protect from *the destroyer* (see below).

enters their territorial inheritance. Surprisingly, however, the focus at this point is exclusively on the Passover meal; there is no mention of the week-long festival of Unleavened Bread (cf. vv. 14–20). However, details of the latter festival are further outlined in the following chapter (13:3–10), sandwiched between Yahweh's instructions about Israel's firstborn (13:1–2) and Moses' communication of these instructions to the people (13:11–16). While possibly we are simply to assume a narrative gap between the end of Moses' speech and the narration of the Israelite response (12:27–28), it seems more likely that Moses delayed communicating Yahweh's further instructions (i.e. about Unleavened Bread) until *after* the Passover had taken place and the exodus had begun. In any event, the instructions relating to Passover were obviously of greater relevance in the present context of preparations for the original Passover night, so perhaps this is why it receives the primary focus at this point in the narrative as the ritual to be observed and explained to future generations (cf. 13:14).

27b–28. As they had originally reacted (back in 4:31), the Israelites respond positively to Moses' message.[16] Evidently the sequence of plagues through which Yahweh displayed his supremacy over Pharaoh has eradicated the fears and misgivings that had previously been expressed (cf. 6:9).

Meaning
The blood of the Passover animal evidently ensured the protection of Israel's firstborn from the effects of the plague, indicating that its death constituted a substitutionary sacrifice of some kind. New Testament authors such as the apostle Paul draw out its ultimate significance as a foreshadowing of Christ, our Passover lamb (1 Cor. 5:7). In that same context, however, Paul creatively uses the leaven and its physical removal to symbolize the Christian community's radical break with their old and corrupted way of life (1 Cor. 5:6–8). As noted above, in its original setting the

---

16 It is possible also that they serve, once again, as a foil to Pharaoh, whose stubborn refusal to listen to Moses has been a refrain throughout the plague narrative.

eradication of leaven was dictated by circumstances (the need for a hasty departure); it does not seem to be a symbol of what the Israelites were leaving behind in Egypt. Nevertheless, the idea of getting rid of the old and creating a new batch of dough ties in nicely with the concept of the new beginning reflected in Israel's exodus.

However, the striking parallels between the Passover ritual (involving the flock animal's death, blood and subsequent consumption) and the subsequent consecration of Aaron and his sons (Exod. 29; Lev. 8) suggest that as well as delivering each household from death by its blood, the Passover animal also consecrated the Israelites as God's holy people through its consumption. Accordingly, Passover constitutes the first ritual stage in the process of making Israel 'a holy nation and a royal priesthood' (19:6, AT).[17]

Additional note: the origin(s) of Passover and Unleavened Bread

For critical scholars the true origins of these distinctive festivals are to be found elsewhere. The Passover is considered to have originated in pre-Mosaic times as a domestic ceremony among nomadic shepherds – the ancestors of those who later became known as Hebrews or Israelites. It was a spring festival celebrated at the full moon of the vernal equinox. The blood rite – in which animal blood was allegedly sprinkled on the tent poles – was designed to ward off hostile, demonic powers (cf. 'the destroyer') which were thought to bring sterility or death in the night. Through freak coincidence (for those who allow some historicity to the biblical account of the exodus) a series of calamities in Egypt culminated in a severe epidemic which claimed the lives of many Egyptians at the time of the Passover. Exploiting this calamity which had fallen upon their Egyptian oppressors, the Israelites made their escape, despite a vain attempt by the Egyptians to recapture them.

---

17 For the most comprehensive analysis to date, see Gehrig 2024.

After settling in Canaan the Israelites adopted the agriculturist feast of Unleavened Bread from the native Canaanites. This was a spring harvest ceremony celebrated at the sanctuaries. As both Unleavened Bread and Passover were celebrated in the springtime, it was natural over time to combine them, 'historicizing' both feasts with the exodus tradition.

However, all of the traditions reflected in the Pentateuch connect Unleavened Bread (Exod. 23:15; 34:18; Deut. 16:3) or the Passover (Deut. 16:1, 6), or both (Exod. 12:23–27, 39 [allegedly 'J']; cf. 12:12–13, 17 [allegedly 'P']), with the exodus from Egypt. Exodus 12 connects them most closely, incorporating the rites for both feasts into the account of the exodus, and explaining their institution as specifically for the commemoration of the exodus event. Thus, the biblical text consistently presents Unleavened Bread and Passover as a dramatic ritual through which the Israelites celebrated and proclaimed their liberation from Egypt by Yahweh, and reaffirmed their faith in him. Other than scholarly conjecture and an unwarranted degree of historical scepticism, there is no reason for doubting the authenticity of this biblical tradition.

C. The death of Egypt's firstborn and Israel's hasty departure (12:29–51)

Context
After the detailed instructions for the institution of Passover and Unleavened Bread, and regulations for the subsequent commemoration of the exodus, the story of Israel's escape from Egypt is resumed. In a few brief paragraphs, we are informed that Yahweh makes good on his threat (v. 29), resulting in the anticipated anguish for every Egyptian household (v. 30), the total capitulation of Pharaoh (vv. 31–32) and the plundering of the Egyptians (vv. 33–36).

Comment
29–30. Finally, it is Yahweh's turn to 'strike' Egypt (cf. 2:11; 3:20). As anticipated (cf. 11:5), no Egyptian firstborn had immunity from this fatal blow, regardless of their social status or category.

Consequently, the entire Egyptian community – *Pharaoh and all his officials and all the Egyptians* – were rudely awakened to a living nightmare. This seems to stress the all-encompassing nature of its impact on Egypt; it is thus difficult to envisage (with Blackburn 2012: 50) that some Egyptian households escaped this tragedy. Moreover, it is far from clear how the Egyptians would have known what to do, since they were apparently not privy to the information conveyed by Moses to the Israelite elders.

31–32. In view of the way their last conversation ended (cf. 10:28), the irony of Pharaoh summoning Moses and Aaron into his presence again should not be lost on us.[18] Though Pharaoh is still issuing commands, however, his tone is rather different. He now capitulates totally to Yahweh's demands, as is emphasized by the synonymous phrases 'according to your words' and 'as you have spoken' (AT), and no longer seeks to impose any caveats with respect to distance, people or livestock (cf. 8:25, 28; 10:8–11, 24–27). In fact, as Alexander observes (2017: 237), 'his action is highly ironic, because it goes beyond what Moses and Aaron have repeatedly requested', granting them permission to leave Egypt permanently, rather than just go on a relatively short journey to worship Yahweh.[19] While often understood as ironic, Pharaoh's enigmatic request 'bless me also' (AT) is probably not a petition for blessing or a prayer request of some kind.[20] Indeed, even the suggestion that this constitutes a verbal acknowledgment that Israel's imminent departure would finally bring Pharaoh relief from the disasters that have befallen him is probably reading too much into what appears to be an idiomatic farewell greeting

---

18 *Pace* Stuart (2006), who speculates that here Pharaoh's words were delivered to Moses and Aaron via a royal communiqué. But even if there was no direct communication, Pharaoh is clearly the one who loses face by initiating contact in this way.

19 While a permanent departure was certainly their intent (cf. 3:8, 17), they never explicitly demanded this of Pharaoh.

20 Significantly, there is no record of Moses complying with Pharaoh's appeal, unlike earlier instances where Pharaoh clearly did ask Moses to intercede.

(cf. NIV footnote for Gen. 47:10). Thus understood, Pharaoh is basically urging Moses to 'bid him farewell'.

33–36. Pharaoh's urgency in seeing the back of this problem is exceeded only by that of the general populace, whose overwhelming fears are perhaps not altogether irrational – just somewhat uninformed. Urged on by the Egyptians, the Israelites leave in the anticipated manner (i.e. carrying their unleavened dough, using whatever means were readily available). Moreover, as anticipated, the Egyptians were all too eager to assist them however possible. This Egyptian generosity is again credited to Yahweh (cf. 3:21; 11:3), as was Pharaoh's earlier intransigence. Both were a direct human response to Yahweh's dealings with Egypt, but whereas Pharaoh had responded negatively to God's leniency, his subjects respond positively to his severity. Thus, Israel departs with its plunder (v. 36) – a further indication that Yahweh and his people have triumphed in this prolonged conflict with Pharaoh and his people. The link between Yahweh's 'rescuing' Israel and Israel's 'plundering' Egypt is more obvious in the Hebrew, which uses different stems of the same verb (*nṣl*).

37–38. The first stage of Israel's exodus itinerary, *from Rameses to Sukkoth*, was probably quite short, about a day's journey if Sukkoth is located somewhere between Lake Timsah and the Bitter Lakes (see Introduction 4c, 'The route of the exodus'). As its name (lit. 'booths') suggests, *Sukkoth* was simply a place where Israel found basic, temporary shelter, hence Hamilton's (2011) 'Shelterville' is probably an apt description. The number of Israelite men mentioned in verse 37 seems excessively large (implying a total population of 2 to 3 million), prompting many to come up with alternative interpretations (see Additional note on the size of the Israelite population at the time of the exodus). None of these, however, is without difficulty. Therefore, it is arguably better to remain somewhat agnostic on this particular issue. It seems clear from verse 38, however, that those who participated in the exodus were an ethnically diverse group: *many other people* – besides Jacob's descendants – accompanied the Israelites on this mass departure from Egypt. Presumably these were other Semites who, like the Hebrews, had been reduced to forced labour by the Egyptians. In any case, these diverse ethnic groups apparently remained with

the Israelites for some time (cf. Num. 11:4), during which there
was at least some degree of assimilation (Num. 12:1; cf. comment
on Exod. 18:27).

39. The reason why the Israelites had to eat unleavened bread
is now fully explained: given their hasty departure from Egypt,
there was insufficient time to prepare food and for the leaven to
do its work on their dough.

40. The period given for Israel's stay in Egypt (*430 years*) appears
to be an exact chronology. However, this is complicated by the
following:

1 Moses is presented as the third generation after Levi (Exod.
   6:16–20). However, as noted above, this genealogy, like many
   others (e.g. Matt. 1), is not exhaustive but selective.
2 Other figures are given: e.g. 400 years (Gen. 15:13; Acts 7:6);
   four generations (Gen. 15:16); 450 years (Acts 13:17–20 –
   covering the time in Egypt, the wilderness and the conquest,
   which agrees with 400 for Egypt). These may of course be
   approximate figures.
3 The SP and LXX understand the 430-year period as inclusive of
   the patriarchal period – but this may be inaccurate.

However these various figures may be reconciled, Durham (1987)
correctly underlines that the point not to be missed here is that
Yahweh kept his promise to Abraham.

41. The NIV's *to the very day* is unfortunately misleading. The
Hebrew idiom (lit. 'in the bone of this day') conveys the idea of 'on
that same day' (cf. ESV's 'on that very day') both here and elsewhere
in the Old Testament (e.g. Exod. 12:17). Thus understood, it refers
to the night of the Passover, which makes the transition to the
following verse with its focus on *that night* a lot smoother.

The militaristic depiction of these liberated people (cf. NIV's
divisions; also v. 51) is hardly intended literally; rather, this is an
ideological description, the theological significance of which
should not be lost: 'The Israelites march out of Egypt through the
front door, with dignity – not like dogs crawling through the back
fence, but like God's people. This exaltation of Israel is another
humiliation for Egypt' (Enns 2000: 250).

42. As suggested above, the material in this verse is not introduced as abruptly as may initially appear (esp. if following the NIV) but follows on from the reference to 'that same day' in the preceding verse. Thus, the time of Israel's departure from Egypt is to be perpetually commemorated by a night vigil – mirroring the night vigil of Yahweh by which he had secured their deliverance.

43–49. While again this prescriptive material might initially appear to interrupt the narrative, these regulations presumably elaborate on the most important element of the night vigil: the Passover meal. The additional restrictions and qualifications primarily focus on who may participate (vv. 43–45, 48–49), and could thus reflect the fact that non-Israelites took advantage of the situation and left Egypt along with the Israelites (v. 38); however, like so much in this chapter, they are obviously orientated towards the future – when the Israelites are settled in their own land (vv. 45, 48–49). While non-Israelites (whether household slaves or resident aliens) could also celebrate the Passover, they could do so only if they had formally identified with the Israelite community by embracing the covenant sign of circumcision (v. 48; cf. 4:24–26).[21] The prohibition on breaking the animal's bones (v. 46) has not been mentioned previously and is left unexplained but, like the stipulation that none of the meat should be taken outside the house, it was probably to ensure that the purity of the sacred meat was maintained and/or that the familial (or communal) nature of the meal was adhered to. The stipulation finds its full significance in the way that it foreshadows the ultimate Passover Lamb (cf. John 19:36), whose body did not see corruption or decay.

50–51. The chapter concludes with two further summary statements – the first highlighting Israel's explicit obedience, and the second again depicting the departing slaves not as disorientated

---

21 Several different nouns describe the non-Israelite in these verses: 'foreigner' (*nēkār*), 'temporary resident' (*tôšāb*), 'hired worker' (*śākîr*) and 'resident alien' (*gēr*). The middle two, *tôšāb wĕśākîr*, is probably a hendiadys (meaning 'resident hireling'), focusing on the occupation of *nēkār* or *gēr* in Israel.

refugees, but as a disciplined army, marching out in triumphant formation (cf. 13:18).

Meaning
At last Pharaoh and the Egyptians capitulate totally, and the Israelites not only get to leave, but do so in triumphant fashion – despite their considerable haste. Rather than inferring from this that the previous wonders failed, it is important to understand that they were all building up to this significant climax. From the outset (cf. 3:18–20; 4:21–23; 6:1, 6–8; 7:3–5), Yahweh had indicated that his contest with Pharoah would be prolonged, yet a successful outcome was never in any real doubt. Thus we see here that Yahweh not only makes good on his threat to Pharaoh, but also fulfils his covenant promise to Abraham and his descendants. This, therefore, was a night to be remembered, not only by Abraham's descendants, but also by all who wished to be aligned with them, whether at that time or in the future.

Additional note: the size of the Israelite population at the time of the exodus

As noted above, the biblical figure for the size of the exodus population seems excessively large, so much so that some have used such apparently inflated figures to challenge the historical credibility of the Old Testament. Others, however, have attempted to resolve the problem by interpreting the problematic numbers rather differently, focusing mainly on alternative interpretations of *'ellef*, the Hebrew noun for 'thousand' (e.g. 'families'; 'clans'; 'brigade'; 'warriors').[22] However, while there is some biblical support for understanding *'ellef* as a 'clan' (cf. Num. 1:16; Josh. 22:14, 21, 30; Judg. 6:15; 1 Sam. 10:19; 23:23), there is little evidence to corroborate other suggestions (i.e.

---

22 E.g. Mendenhall 1958; Wenham 1967; Humphreys 1998, 2000. In particular, such scholars have noted the total number of firstborn males listed in Num. 3:39 (22,000), which seems to project a much smaller population. The suggestion that this figure relates only to those born after the exodus is unsubstantiated by the text.

that it denotes a military unit or elite soldiers of some kind).[23] Perhaps the greatest obstacle to reducing the number to a more manageable figure lies in the census figures of Exodus 38:25–28, which clearly assume a literal interpretation of the 603,550 men (one half shekel per head yields the total of 100 talents, 1,775 shekels).[24] One might also infer such an extraordinarily large population from the concern that evoked Egyptian oppression (Exod. 1:9), and the similarly large number of livestock mentioned in subsequent texts (e.g. Num. 31:32–40). Attempts to reduce *six hundred thousand* (Exod. 12:37) on lexical grounds, therefore, seem to be ill-conceived. Nevertheless, perhaps the problem is due to later scribal confusion over the meaning of numerical sigla used in earlier texts, or the author is again employing hyperbole, arguably using these figures to make some sort of theological point rather than providing us with strict historical data. Thus understood, the idea may be that all Israel – even those at a much later time such as the early monarchy period – were incorporated in Yahweh's great redemptive act of the past: the exodus.

D. Consecration of the Israelites' firstborn (13:1–16)

Context
The final unit of this section repeats and expands the regulations relating to the feast of Unleavened Bread (13:3–10), sandwiched between regulations concerning the consecration of Israel's firstborn (13:1–2, 11–16).[25] As mentioned above (see comment

---

23 Lexical appeal is sometimes made to the fact that a cognate noun, *'allup*, is used in modern Hebrew for an army colonel. However, this has little, if any, significance for the biblical connotation of *'elep*. While other OT texts refer to '600 warriors' (cf. Judg. 18:11, 16, 17; 1 Sam. 13:15; 14:2; 27:2; 30:9; 2 Sam. 15:18), none of these employ *'elep*.

24 However, Alexander (2017) suggests that the figure includes all Israelite adults, not just men; for more on this, see my comment on 38:25–26.

25 For structural parallels between 13:1–16 and the previous chapter, see Hamilton 2011: 201. Hamilton does not really explore the significance of such, but it arguably places emphasis on the firstborn ritual (as ch. 12 did on the Passover).

on 12:24–27a), relaying the second part of Yahweh's instructions, those relating to Unleavened Bread (cf. 12:14–20), seems to have been intentionally postponed – at the very least, by the narrator – until after Israel's departure from Egypt. This may be explained in part by the future orientation of these regulations of the firstborn; they are explicitly related to when Israel enters their promised land (13:5, 7) and the uninformed ask about the meaning of the festival (13:8). This same future orientation is shared by the stipulation concerning Israel's firstborn – at least in Moses' communication of it to the Israelites (13:11–16). The location of this communication after, rather than before, the exodus may again be because this is precisely when these regulations were most appropriate. Like the consecration of the firstborn, the command to commemorate their escape by eating unleavened bread for a week would have made little sense and required much more explanation prior to the event. Previously, Moses had outlined how Israel should *commemorate* the exodus through the Passover ritual (12:24–27). Now, prompted by Yahweh's instruction in 13:1–2, he conveys how Israel must also commemorate their deliverance through Unleavened Bread and the consecration of the firstborn.

Comment

1–2. Unlike the regulations for Unleavened Bread (vv. 3–10) sandwiched between these instructions on the consecration of the firstborn, there is no indication that this material had been disclosed to Moses at some earlier point (i.e. in the context of 12:12–20). Both, however, find their significance only after the Passover and exodus have taken place, and thus the way they are tied together here is not surprising. While the only rationale offered for the ritual here is Yahweh's claim of ownership, this is elaborated by the information in verses 14–15, where Yahweh's redemption of Israel's firstborn explains Israel's duty to return such to Yahweh, either through their actual sacrifice or by a suitable substitutionary sacrifice or ransom payment. It is thus a means of reminding the Israelites to acknowledge their special status as belonging to Yahweh. Legislation on Israel's firstborn also appears later in Exodus (22:29–30 [MT 22:28–29]; 34:19–20), as well as in other Pentateuchal texts (Lev. 27:26–27; Num. 18:14–18;

Deut. 15:19–23).[26] While some have inferred from these and other texts (e.g. Gen. 22; Ezek. 20:25–26; Mic. 6:7) that Israelite religion originally incorporated sacrificial infanticide, the canonical text clearly indicates otherwise: any such activity never enjoyed divine approval (cf. Jer. 7:31).

3–4. *This day* which the Israelites must commemorate is identified as the day of their departure from Egypt, that is, the fifteenth day of the month. While here the restriction is simply on eating anything containing yeast, it is clear from verse 7 that even possessing this substance during the exclusion period was not permitted.

5–7. Unleavened Bread was to be celebrated when they entered the Promised Land, which seems to suggest that it was not celebrated for some forty years. Both here and in verse 11 Israel's territorial inheritance is described not only in terms of its present occupants, but also (and more importantly) in terms of the ancestral oath – again highlighting how Yahweh is acting to fulfil his covenantal promises.

8. The implied question of the children ('Why are you doing this?') expresses an ignorance on their part which suggests that they did not participate in the exodus. Such is confirmed by the answer they are to receive. Like Passover and the firstborn ritual, Unleavened Bread will inform *future* generations about Yahweh's deliverance, hence the importance of celebrating these traditions in the Promised Land (cf. 12:25; 13:5, 11).

9–10. The observance of this regulation thus serves as a kind of mnemonic device, a perpetual annual reminder of how Yahweh had rescued them from Egypt.

11–12. Attention now reverts to the instructions concerning the firstborn, which likewise are apparently to be implemented only after their arrival in the Promised Land. Yahweh's gift to Israel (v. 11) is now to be reciprocated by Israel's gift to Yahweh (v. 12a), although the latter is only what is now rightfully his in any case (v. 12b).

---

26 For a discussion of the variations in these texts, and their canonical significance, see Hamilton 2011: 202–203.

13. In some cases the firstborn must be *redeem[ed]* (or more accurately, 'ransomed' – the Hebrew verb *pādâ* denotes release through the payment of a ransom) by the substitution of a flock animal or other suitable payment. Rather than donkeys being singled out here as domestic pack animals, and hence of particular value, related texts (cf. Lev. 27:27; Num. 18:15) would suggest that they are simply representative of unclean animals, unsuitable for sacrifice. Whatever the case, the consequence for the non-ransomed donkey underlines the absolute necessity of such substitution for any Israelite firstborn, for on account of their deliverance from death on Passover night they belonged to Yahweh (vv. 2, 15; cf. Num. 3:13). As such, they have a holier status than the rest of the Israelite community. Subsequently, on account of their dedication to Yahweh in the golden calf fiasco (cf. Exod. 32:27–29), the Levites took the place of firstborn sons (Num. 3:11–13), serving Yahweh in relation to the tabernacle (Num. 3:14 – 4:49), but a financial payment was substituted for any firstborn sons exceeding the number of those ransomed by the Levites (Num. 3:15, 39–51; cf. Num. 18:16).

14–15. The ignorance expressed by the questioner apparently relates to both the consecration and the redemption of the firstborn, as is evident from the fairly comprehensive answer offered in response.

16. As with Unleavened Bread, this ritual serves to remind Israel of their deliverance from Egypt by Yahweh's mighty hand.

Meaning
The firstborn ritual relates to the terrible slaughter that had secured Israel's deliverance from Egypt. Yahweh had afflicted Egypt's firstborn because of the treatment shown to Israel, Yahweh's firstborn son (4:22–23). Yahweh's claim on Israel's firstborn vividly memorializes the divine act that claimed the lives of Egypt's firstborn but had delivered Israel's firstborn by the death of flock animals in their place. As those belonging to Yahweh, Israel's firstborn had either to be offered up in sacrifice or (in the case of humans and unclean livestock) ransomed by a suitable substitute. The firstborn ransom ritual was thus a perpetual reminder of (1) the terrible cost of Israel's redemption,

(2) Yahweh's unique claim of ownership, and (3) the only way that their lives would not also be forfeit – this last point foreshadowing the ultimate substitutionary sacrifice offered by God's unique firstborn son (Heb. 1:6).

PART 2: LESSONS ON THE JOURNEY TO HOREB (13:17 – 18:27)

The next block of Exodus (13:17 – 18:27) narrates the first major leg of Israel's journey from Egypt to Canaan (i.e. from Sukkoth [cf. 12:37] to Sinai). As a comparison between 13:20 and 12:37 shows, this material takes up the narrative where the latter verse had left off. There are two main sections: the first (13:17 – 15:21) focuses on Israel's exodus from Egypt and Yahweh's climactic victory over the Egyptians at the Sea.[1] The second (15:22 – 18:27) recounts the ups and downs of the Israelite journey from the Sea to their encampment at Rephidim (in the vicinity of Horeb; cf. 18:5). As Motyer (2005: 156) helpfully summarizes, 'Exodus 1 – 13 is the record of how the Lord *came to his people* in their distress; Exodus 13 – 18 is the record of how the Lord *went with* his people on their pilgrimage' (emphasis his).[2]

---

1 For more on the identity and location of the body of water described in the MT as the *yam sûf*, see Introduction 4c, 'The route of the exodus'.

2 Motyer identifies 13:21–22 (esp. v. 21a) as the keynote in this second part of the book; cf. 3:7–8 in the first part.

In terms of time, the period covered by these five chapters is approximately two months, from which six incidents have been recorded. The first of these is undoubtedly the most significant. This material, dealing with Israel's deliverance and the destruction of the Egyptian chariot force at the Re(e)d Sea, comprises two main subsections: the narrative of the event (13:17 – 14:31) and Israel's subsequent celebration in song and dance (15:1–21).

5. DELIVERANCE AT THE SEA (13:17 – 15:21)

A. The crossing of the Sea (13:17 – 14:31)

Context
Here the narrative resumes its account of Israel's travelogue from where it left off in 12:37 (cf. 13:20). However, before outlining this next stage of the journey, it provides the theological rationale for what might otherwise appear to be a very strange route – thus setting the stage for Pharaoh's ultimate folly in his dealings with Yahweh and his people.

Comment
i. Israel's path out of Egypt (13:17–22)
17–18. As Enns (2000: 268) observes:

> The use of the verb *šlḥ* (to release, let go) in verse 17 is surely intentional. It is what Moses has been demanding of Pharaoh from the very beginning of their confrontation (5:1) and what God said would happen as far back as 3:20 . . . Indeed, 13:17

brings us to the threshold of the consummation of God's deliverance of Israel.

However, now that Pharaoh has submitted to Yahweh's demand, the story takes an unexpected twist: rather than following the 'Way of the Sea' (the *Via Maris* [Mediterranean] ancient trade route), the most straightforward (and shortest) route out of Egypt, the Israelites are led by Yahweh on a more circuitous route. 'Putting it bluntly, where the people expected to go north, they turned south and ended up in the wilderness!' (Motyer 2005: 178). The rationale given for this roundabout journey was to avoid military conflict (v. 17b), presumably reflecting the threat posed by fortifications dotted around the northern highway to protect Egypt's borders. Yahweh's concerns may seem somewhat strange given recent events and the militaristic imagery used to describe these liberated slaves in the following verse (v. 18).[1] Moreover, this alternative route almost immediately involved an even greater test of faith – the escaping Israelites quickly found themselves hemmed in between Pharaoh's army and the body of water described as the 'Re(e)d Sea'. However, Yahweh's concern over a military confrontation was focused particularly on its potential for reversing the exodus: *they might change their minds and return to Egypt*. As it turns out, whatever misgivings the Israelites expressed during the ensuing crisis (cf. 14:10–12), there was certainly no talk of turning back at this stage (cf. Num. 14:3–4). Besides, Israel had a very passive role in the subsequent encounter, having only to stand still and watch while Yahweh dealt with their Egyptian adversaries.

19. Once again, the exodus story connects with the ancestral stories (and, hence, the covenant promises) in the book of Genesis; in particular, the hope of future deliverance held out by Joseph (Gen. 50:24–25). In the removal of Joseph's bones 'we have another reminder that the departure from Egypt is part of a larger plan that God has been orchestrating for hundreds of years and that is now coming to its climax' (Enns 2000: 270).

---

1   However, see comments on 12:41 and 12:51.

20. *Sukkoth . . . Etham.* Despite these and other places subsequently named in the narrative (cf. 14:2), Israel's itinerary from Egypt is extremely difficult to reconstruct with a great degree of confidence. The precise location of the campsites associated with the exodus is largely a matter of scholarly dispute, as is also true of the two major topographical markers (i.e. the Re[e]d Sea and Mount Sinai). All reconstructions of the route of the exodus and Israel's itinerary to Sinai are thus somewhat conjectural. For further discussion, see Introduction 4c, 'The route of the exodus'.

21–22. These two verses emphasize Yahweh's accompanying and guiding presence: the *pillar of cloud* and the *pillar of fire* probably refer to the same phenomenon as viewed during daylight and night-time respectively. Like the burning bush (3:2–3) and the subsequent blazing fire on Mount Sinai (19:18; 24:17), this was clearly a theophany, a manifestation of God's presence with his people, leading and directing them on their journey. Led by Yahweh in this manner, the Israelites had every reason to be confident of safe passage. However, with the start of chapter 14, the narrative takes another unexpected turn when Yahweh issues his next directive to Moses: an 'about-turn' that apparently brought Israel to the brink of disaster.

ii. The trap set by Yahweh (14:1–4)

1–2. Under normal circumstances Israel's next move amounted to military suicide: marching the Israelites towards the sea cut off an escape route from any who might be following in hot pursuit. The locations of both *Pi Hahiroth* and *Migdol* are uncertain (cf. 13:20),[2] but an Egyptian papyrus locates *Baal Zephon* near Lake Manzaleh (*c.*30 km [20 miles] east of Rameses; see note on 1:11). This suggests that the infamous body of water referred to in this chapter was located at the southern end of Lake Manzaleh, some

---

2   *Migdol* is probably related to the Hebrew noun for a watchtower or fortress (*migdāl*). As such, it was apparently used of several sites in the Delta region, just as the OT attests to the use of *migdāl* in compound names for various sites (cf. Gen. 35:21; Josh. 15:37; 19:38; Judg. 8:9, 17).

60 km (40 miles) above the northern tip of the Gulf of Suez (see notes on 10:19; 13:20).

3–4. However, while the strategy may have looked foolish in military terms, Yahweh was laying the trap that would result in the climactic humiliation of Pharaoh – whose heart he was about to harden still further. As before, the latter seems to be a direct consequence of Yahweh's activities (in this case, placing the Israelites in a 'vulnerable' position that would induce Pharaoh to change his mind); thus again divine sovereignty (Yahweh's manipulation of the situation through the directions he gave) and human responsibility (Pharaoh's treacherous decision with respect to Israel) are working in tandem to secure God's intended purpose: *I will gain glory for myself through Pharaoh and all his army, and the Egyptians will know that I am the LORD* (v. 4).[3] Such recognition of Yahweh has been a recurring motif in the plague narrative (7:5; 8:10, 22; 9:14, 29; 11:7), and here presumably applies to the Egyptian populace as a whole and not just Pharaoh's chariot force immediately prior to their destruction. However, analogous uses of this recognition formula elsewhere (e.g. Ezek. 25:7; 26:6) suggest that the elite Egyptian chariot force was certainly included in such recognition of Yahweh, which does not signify coming to faith but rather recognizing Yahweh's sovereignty in the execution of his judgment.[4]

iii. The Egyptian pursuit (14:5–9)

5–9. Since Pharaoh had granted the Israelites permission to leave (12:31–32), the first clause in verse 5 is somewhat surprising. Given his earlier negotiations with Moses, it seems unlikely that it is only now dawning on Pharaoh that his Hebrew slaves have no intention of returning. Rather, what is probably in view here is a progress report. But whatever the explanation, the socio-economic

---

3 As Ford (2006: 178) observes, ultimately Pharaoh's *hard* heart, described several times in the plague narrative as *kābēd* (although not here in Exod. 14), brings *kābôd* (glory) to Yahweh.

4 For more on the use of the recognition formula and its significance in Exodus and Ezekiel, see Williamson 2025.

realities prompt Pharaoh and his officials to set about recapturing the fleeing Hebrews, who have trapped themselves in the desert with no possible means of escape; see 14:3, where Pharaoh waxes poetical on Israel's situation: 'Trapped, they are, in the land; closed them in (has) the desert' (AT). In reality, it is Pharaoh and his forces who are rushing headlong into inescapable peril, and it is Israel who will wax poetical as a result (ch. 15).

The chariot force was probably deployed primarily for speed, whether or not the *six hundred* chariots selected,[5] along with appropriate personnel,[6] implies a certain degree of urgency in the mission. In any case, the picture of Pharaoh marshalling this elite military force to round up these emancipated slaves is somewhat ironic – all the more so since his conflict is not primarily with these Hebrew slaves but with the God who has claimed them as his own and has already demonstrated that no human force is any match for him. However, as verse 8 reminds us, the folly of such action was clearly lost on Pharaoh, whose heart had once again been divinely hardened. Thus, as precipitated by Yahweh,[7] these Egyptian forces catch up with their quarry encamped and vulnerably exposed beside the Sea.

iv. Israel's panic and Moses' faith (14:10–15)

10–12. Although everything is working out according to God's purpose, the Israelite reaction to these sinister-looking developments is unsurprisingly one of terror (v. 10). Still, in view of how Yahweh had responded to their previous cry for help (2:24–25; 3:7), the sentiments expressed towards Moses in their panic-stricken cry are less excusable. Indeed, it quickly becomes clear that faith had succumbed to fear, and any confidence in Yahweh and/or Moses

---

5   It is unclear whether the six hundred chosen chariots constitute only some or all of Egypt's chariot force, since the following clause could be governed by an explicative *waw* ('*that is*, all Egypt's chariots').

6   The precise connotation of *šālîšîm* (NIV: *officers*) is uncertain, but arguably it refers to those who were in charge of these chariots (cf. 15:4). For other suggestions, see Hamilton 2011: 211.

7   Note the repetition of place names from v. 2.

has quickly dissipated in the face of this crisis, giving place to bitter recriminations (vv. 11–12). Even though Israel's previous verbal response was not explicitly recorded earlier in the narrative (cf. the gloss inserted in 6:9 by the SP), there is no reason to doubt that such sentiments had indeed been expressed (cf. the similar 'citation' in Jon. 4:2). As before (cf. 5:21), Moses is accused of making their situation worse, rather than improving it. Significantly, their shift in viewpoint echoes that of Pharaoh and his officials,[8] further betraying where their true allegiance lies: 'It is Pharaoh that Israel fear and him that they choose to serve' (Ford 2006: 177). Such lack of respect for Yahweh in the light of all that has taken place is startling, and a harbinger of things to come. Israel's natural tendency to grumble at every hurdle is one of the recurring motifs in the ensuing narrative, both in Exodus and beyond.

13–14. In contrast to the Israelites, Moses' confidence in Yahweh remains steadfast – undoubtedly bolstered by the revelation that Yahweh had already given him concerning this otherwise alarming situation (cf. v. 4). Thus, faced with this ominous Egyptian onslaught, Moses shifts Israel's focus back to Yahweh, boldly anticipating Israel's forthcoming deliverance and Egypt's imminent demise (v. 13; cf. 2 Chr. 20:17, which seems to cite Moses' words when Jehoshaphat is similarly encouraged in the face of such overwhelming odds). Moses' assurance, that *the LORD will fight for you*, is the first instance of a theme that will become prominent in Israel's subsequent history. As the divine warrior (cf. 15:3), Yahweh fights on Israel's behalf – usually in such a manner that secures for him the exclusive glory (23:20–30; Hab. 3:3–15; Hag. 2:21–22; Zech. 14:3–15; cf. Rev. 19:11–16). While English translations might imply that Moses is advocating simply staying where they are (e.g. *you need only to be still*, NIV), the idea is probably that of 'keeping silent' (i.e. doing nothing) in the context of the ensuing conflict (cf. Ps. 46:10).

15. In another strange turn of events, Moses' rebuke of the Israelites for their lack of faith (vv. 13–14) is immediately followed

---

8   Several commentators draw attention to the verbal parallelism between
     Egypt's question (14:5) and Israel's (14:11–12).

by a similar reprimand of Moses by Yahweh himself. Either there is another gap in the narrative (i.e. Moses did indeed cry out to Yahweh even though this has not been explicitly recorded) or, more probably, Moses is so closely identified with the people he represents before God that their guilt becomes his by association. In any case, this was not a time for prayer but for action: to move on as divinely directed.

v. Safe passage for the Israelites (14:16–22)

16–18. Once again, Moses' staff is to be utilized – presumably to highlight the true power behind Moses' action by demonstrating the continuity between the plagues that had afflicted Egypt and this final act securing Israel's deliverance at the Sea. However the forthcoming phenomenon is to be explained (see below), the Israelites will be enabled to traverse the sea on dry ground. It is implicitly by means of these unusual circumstances that Yahweh will harden the hearts of the Egyptians, and so induce them to pursue the Israelites into this precarious situation. Again (cf. v. 4) we are reminded that the ultimate goal is twofold: that Yahweh will be glorified, and that the Egyptians will have no choice but to recognize his supremacy (vv. 17b–18).

19–20. Before the trap is finally sprung, steps are taken to keep the two groups apart. For those who discern different underlying sources (e.g. Smith 2010), this material reflects a different, less dramatic version of Israel's deliverance, which later compilers have merged with the better-known one involving Yahweh's supernatural suspension of water to facilitate Israel's escape. However, details from both 'versions' are clearly necessary in order to explain Israel's escape and Egypt's destruction, and any alleged discrepancies in the canonical account seem to be the result of a forced or extremely literalistic interpretation of particular details.

The angel of God is closely associated with the column of cloud and fire (v. 19), and thus with Yahweh himself (cf. 13:21; cf. 3:2–4). The two (i.e. the cloud and the angel), however, are not necessarily synonymous. While the NIV adds an interpretative gloss (*also*) to the text of verse 19, Stuart's contention (2006: 340) that the angel of God and the pillar of cloud 'were the same thing' is debatable. His case would be stronger had the text employed an explicative *waw* in the second clause. However, the fact that the pillar's relocation is separately described (by the same *wayyiqtol* verb as before) suggests that the two are not identical entities. Rather, the movement of the cloud seems to be precipitated by the movement of the angel. The moving column is clearly a visible manifestation of God's presence with his people, which should have allayed their fears to some extent: the God who had demonstrated his power in Egypt, and who was presently displaying his presence in this manner, could surely be relied upon to secure the deliverance Moses had anticipated. In any event, although the details are somewhat unclear (cf. ESV for a more literal translation of the Hebrew text), the cloud evidently served the interests of the Israelites while thwarting the intentions of the Egyptians. Possibly, as some English translations (e.g. NIV) suggest, it did so by supplying light to the former while simultaneously imposing darkness on the latter. Thus understood, the similarity of its effects with the ninth plague (which immediately preceded a mass slaughter of Egyptians) highlights its ominous nature for Pharaoh's forces. It is not clear if the resulting separation served primarily to protect the Israelites from immediate attack while they made their way to safety, or to lure the Egyptians into their watery grave, or possibly both.

21–22. Under the cover of the cloud, Yahweh drove the sea back with a *strong east wind* and the Israelites were thus enabled to cross over on dry ground. Some have attempted to explain this miracle along purely naturalistic lines (encouraged to some extent by the mention of what appears to be a 'natural cause' – the strong east wind blowing throughout the night). Thus understood, the hot wind sufficiently dried up a marshy lagoon or an area of mudflats to enable the Israelites to cross over relatively easily. In a similar vein, others suggest that the wind was strong enough to uncover a subterranean ridge on which the Israelites were able to get across. Yet it is hard to imagine how people could survive in such circumstances, never mind traverse a relatively narrow platform safely. In any case, such a dichotomy between natural and supernatural events would have been foreign to an Ancient Near Eastern mindset. Admittedly, the extent to which the language here should be interpreted literally is another matter entirely. There are no grounds, however, for a mythological reading, despite such associations of the verb *bāqaʿ* ('split') in some Ugaritic texts. As Hamilton (2011: 218) observes, 'Exodus 14 is not about God's victory *over* the sea, but it is about God's victory *at* the sea' (emphasis his).

The concept of a physical *wall* of water standing on either side of the Israelites is considered by many to be a phenomenological impossibility, so other less dramatic explanations of the event described here (e.g. involving unusually low and high tides, or even tsunamis) have been proposed. Some such explanations are tied to particular identifications of the 'Re(e)d Sea' and thus involve further presuppositions and assumptions.[9] Although the term used here for 'wall' (*ḥômâ*) generally depicts a large wall (usually city walls some 6 or more metres high), it may also be used metaphorically – usually for protection (cf. 1 Sam. 25:16; Jer. 1:18; 15:20; Zech. 2:5 [MT 2:9]). However, there is nothing in the text of Exodus to indicate that the description here is intended metaphorically. Hence, other than the sheer difficulty of fathoming such vertical bodies of water, supernaturally suspended and defying the normal forces of gravity, there is no reason for rejecting the biblical account at face value. But whatever 'natural' phenomena God may or may not have used on this occasion, the timing and circumstances of this event clearly point to a supernatural phenomenon. Thus, even if the scene is not envisaged precisely as depicted in illustrated Bible storybooks or presented by cinematic portrayals, some kind of miraculous event is certainly presented here.

---

9   One such proposal depends on identifying the Red Sea with the Gulf of Aqaba, with the crossing taking place at the Straits of Tiran. This particular location as the site of the Red Sea crossing has most recently been defended by Humphreys 2003 and (albeit more cautiously) Garrett 2014: 104–135; however, for an archaeologist's critical appraisal of this proposal, which locates Mount Sinai in Arabia, see van der Veen 2018.

vi. Drowning of the Egyptians (14:23–28)

23–28. With the sea still held back, the Egyptians plunge towards their fate. Ironically, the very symbol of their strength – their chariots – becomes their downfall (v. 25; cf. Judg. 4 – 5). Whether the wheels fell off, or simply got bogged down in the seabed,[10] the chariots became immobilized and thus offered no help whatsoever to the panic-stricken Egyptians. With the grim theological reality of the situation at last dawning on them (v. 25; cf. v. 14), Pharaoh's army attempts to escape its inevitable fate. Most English translations exacerbate the Egyptian mayhem by suggesting that, when the parted waters were returning, the Egyptians were actually fleeing *towards* the deluge (v. 27). However, as Stuart correctly points out (2006: 345), such a translation is misleading; they were actually fleeing 'from' or 'before' it (cf. NRSV). And so, swept into this watery grave like the earlier locusts (10:19), 'Pharaoh's entire army' (AT) is lost (v. 28).[11] Like the flies and locusts that had earlier plagued Egypt (8:31 [MT 27]; 10:19), not one Egyptian remained. Although this may be yet another example of hyperbole, it probably refers more strictly to the elite chariot force that Pharaoh had dispatched to recapture the Israelites and which had pursued Israel into the sea. The humiliation for Pharaoh and Egypt would nevertheless have been extreme, and not likely to be recorded in any of their official annals. In this final defeat

> Egypt has finally paid the ultimate price for the ultimate transgression. Their king has been contending with God, thinking that he was his equal. He set out to destroy God's beloved son, Israel. Now, finally, once mighty Egypt understands that this was a mistake.
>
> (Enns 2000: 278)

---

10 LXX, Syriac and SP all suggest 'jamming', whereas the MT's 'turned aside' seems to suggest 'removing'; however, see Stek 1986.

11 Note the stark contrast between the Israelites (not one perished) and the Egyptians (not one survived).

vii. Israel's fear of Yahweh and confidence in Moses (14:29–31)
29–31. In sharp contrast to the Egyptians, the Israelites traversed the sea successfully, divinely protected from the water that effectively flanked them. And so Israel is saved from the *hand* of the Egyptians by the *hand* of the LORD – a contrast more obvious in the original than in our English translations. Not surprisingly, this mighty act of Yahweh instilled within the Israelites not only a healthy fear of God, but also renewed confidence in both Yahweh and his servant, Moses.

Thus, with the conclusion of chapter 14, God's promise to the patriarchs – or at least one very important dimension of it – has at last been kept; Abraham's descendants have escaped their servitude to Pharaoh and are finally on their way towards the service of Yahweh.

Meaning
The exodus from Egypt was only the first stage in Israel's deliverance, which was not complete until the Egyptian threat was finally removed and the Israelites' journey to the Promised Land could continue unimpeded by Pharaoh. This final humiliation of Egypt, secured through a further blending of divine sovereignty and human responsibility, constituted the most effective self-revelation of Yahweh to date – not only to the defeated Egyptians but also to the delighted Israelites: Yahweh revealed himself as one who could fight on behalf of his people and prevail over all their enemies, however formidable. Yahweh, not Pharaoh, was thus the one who should be feared; moreover, he was also the one who, along with his servant Moses, could be fully trusted.

B. Celebratory praise (15:1–21)

Context
This predominantly poetic section, often referred to as 'the Song of Moses and Miriam' or, perhaps better, 'the Song at the Sea',[12]

---

12 Thus distinguishing the song(s) here from the Song of Moses recorded in Deut. 32.

celebrates Yahweh's climactic victory over the Egyptians at the Re(e)d Sea. Its location at the conclusion of the preceding narrative account of this event is therefore apposite, setting out the appropriate human response.[13] However, whereas the first part of the song (vv. 1–11) recounts the victory at the sea, the second (vv. 12–18) seems to be a celebration of its sequel: Yahweh's imminent defeat of those who oppose Israel's settlement in the Promised Land. Grammatically there is little change between verses 1–11 and verses 12–18 (cf. NRSV),[14] although it is possible to interpret the verbs in the latter section as 'rhetorical *qatals*' and 'non-perfective preterites', depicting future events as having already transpired.[15] Alternatively, the canonical form of the song postdates the conquest and thus the original composition was changed (and arguably expanded) to become the version of the song passed down to us. This would explain how such a rhetorically complex piece might have evolved (rather than being a totally 'ad hoc' composition), and might also account for other peculiarities in the song, such as the mixture of 'archaic' and standard grammatical forms. It is quite conceivable, therefore, that – like several classic Christian hymns – parts of the original composition have necessarily been altered, updated and possibly even supplemented over centuries of use. Unless one insists that the canonical form must be identical with the original spontaneously composed and sung at the Sea, there is no reason why

---

13 According to Sailhamer (2009: 36–37, 333, 572–573), this is one of four major poems in the Pentateuch (cf. Gen. 49:1–27; Num. 22 – 24; Deut. 32 – 33), all of which mark the end of major narrative blocks. Thus understood, this song brings to conclusion the first part of Exodus, dealing primarily with Israel's deliverance from Egypt, by emphasizing Yahweh's kingship and eternal reign – something which in the other three poems is a more eschatological prospect.

14 Throughout the song both *qatal* and *yiqtol* verb forms are used. While alternating, both are apparently used in the song to describe past events (i.e. many of the *yiqtols* appear to be preterites), as well as events which (in the immediate context of the exodus, at least) are still future.

15 Previously, grammarians described such forms as 'prophetic perfects' designed to highlight the certainty of fulfilment.

Moses (or others) could not subsequently update or expand the song as deemed appropriate. In any case, there is nothing of substance in the canonical version that Moses could not have sung or recorded.[16] Indeed, the majority of scholars agree that this song is one of the earliest compositions contained within the Old Testament.[17]

As noted above, the subject matter is apparently twofold. This is marked by the concluding refrains in verses 11 and 18. However, the song seems to have several stanzas (v. 1; vv. 2–5; vv. 6–11; vv. 12–18). The first three climax with Egypt's destruction in a watery grave, whereas the last climaxes with Israel's safe arrival at their intended destination.

Although some feminist interpreters (Brenner 1985; Trible 1989) may disagree, there is no reason for supposing that male editors have downplayed Miriam's role in the composition of the song by attributing it primarily to Moses. The biblical narrator focuses primarily on its performance, and in this Miriam's role seems most significant: it is apparently Miriam who, on this occasion, calls Israel to worship Yahweh, using the words of this song; and it is certainly Miriam's voice that challenges subsequent readers to do likewise. To infer that female voices are being muted or that women are being sidelined in some way is thus rather curious and unconvincing. It is noteworthy, nevertheless, that, contrary to normal biblical convention, it is not just women who celebrate with victory songs here; rather, all Israel, male and female alike, join together to acknowledge their victorious Lord.

Comment

1. According to this opening verse the song is sung by Moses and the Israelites, whereas in verses 20–21 it is Miriam who does the singing, accompanied by timbrel and dance. The striking correspondence between Miriam's lyrics (v. 21b) and these opening lyrics of Moses' song (cf. v. 1b) has led to

---

16 As noted below, the nations' responses to Israel are framed in a rather idealistic manner.

17 Noth (1962) is one of the few scholars who argue for a late date.

some discussion of the nature of the song and the identity of its composer. Possibly the song was sung antiphonally, with Miriam singing in alternation with the rest ('to *them*' in v. 21a is a masculine form [cf. 1:18], which may well suggest that the group she addressed [perhaps as cantor] was either a male or mixed-gender 'choir'). Alternatively, Miriam encouraged others to join in the singing of Moses' song (in its entirety) by rephrasing its opening line as an invocation. While both scenarios can find some support in the biblical text, such hypotheses are admittedly quite speculative. However, although in one sense the issue of who sang what and how is of no great significance, the canonical placement of Miriam's exhortation – inviting others, including the book's readers, to join in the song – suggests that this celebration is one in which all generations of God's people should participate.

Rather than celebrating the exodus in general (i.e. Israel's deliverance from Egyptian servitude), the song focuses on one aspect in particular: Yahweh's annihilation of the Egyptian chariot force in the sea. This theme permeates the song from the outset, as does the divine warrior imagery. If pressed in a woodenly literal manner, some of the images in this poetic material contradict those of the preceding narrative. For instance, does Yahweh 'hurl both horse and rider into the sea' (v. 1b), or does he engulf them with water as they try to reach the safety of the other side (cf. 14:26–28)? As Enns (2000: 297) observes, to identify such inconsistencies is to 'misread the song . . . We must resist the temptation to impose our own modern expectations on a text, which ancient texts are not always prepared to shoulder.' In any case, we must allow for 'poetic licence': the details of Israel's subsequent experiences (vv. 13–16) do not match up exactly with the narrative accounts either. Nevertheless, to acknowledge that the poetic account here may be somewhat idealized or embellished is certainly not to concede that it is simply 'fictitious'.

2–5. The song continues by elaborating on who Yahweh is and what he has done, focusing first on Yahweh's might and the deliverance wrought by it. Many English translations render the second word used to describe Yahweh here as 'song', but the parallelism with the previous word suggests to many commentators that 'my

strength and my might' (NRSV) is a more appropriate translation,[18]
hence NIV's *my strength and my defence*. In any case, the main point is
that it is through Yahweh's superior power and assistance that Israel's
deliverance has been secured. By means of synonymous parallelism,
the second couplet reiterates the link between the Israelites and their
ancestors, primarily Jacob or Abraham,[19] and thus alludes once again
to Yahweh's covenant faithfulness. The concept of Yahweh as a
warrior (cf. 14:14) adds specific content to the *name* by which he had
revealed himself (cf. 3:14–15). It was as such a warrior that Yahweh
had fought on Israel's behalf and wrought victory over Egypt, the
details of which are now recalled (vv. 4–5). Significantly, neither here
nor in the narrative account is Pharaoh himself – or his infantry
– said to have perished in the Sea. Nevertheless, it was not a few
reservists but the Egyptian military elite that reportedly perished,
along with their formidable chariots. While admittedly poetic, the
description of their demise suggests that they drowned in deep
water, rather than a relatively shallow mudflat or marshy lagoon.

6–8. Continuing the same theme – Yahweh's victory over Egypt
– the focus narrows to Yahweh's destructive fury. Yahweh's sheer
power, with which he *shattered the enemy*, is highlighted in verse 6,
with metaphorical references to Yahweh's *right hand* – the double
reference to which echoes his earlier words to Moses (cf. 3:19–20;
6:1; 7:4–5). The parallelism in the following verse underlines that
Yahweh's majesty and wrath are not polar opposites or mutually
exclusive ideas, but rather the former can be given expression by
the latter. The judgment imagery, however, is obviously not to
be pressed literally, as the mixed metaphors already underline.[20]

---

18 The underlying Hebrew word could derive from one of two homonyms.
    To complicate matters further, both homonyms are used elsewhere in
    close proximity to words for strength or might.
19 The singular *father* is admittedly unusual (although cf. 3:6 MT), but seems
    here to be alluding to one of the patriarchs rather than to the biological
    father of the speaker(s).
20 Stuart's suggestion (2006: 352–353) – that the underlying metaphor (i.e.
    'swallowing') links what the Sea did to the Egyptians and what fire does
    to stubble – seems a little forced.

Rather, like elsewhere in Scripture, it graphically portrays the terrible consequences faced by those who oppose God. The east wind of the previous chapter is now metaphorically depicted as *the blast of* [*Yahweh's*] *nostrils* – possibly suggesting the supernatural nature of the phenomenon that turned the sea into dry ground (i.e. this was no ordinary east wind that blew all night long). While the metaphorical language might arguably extend to the following description of the waters 'standing up' *like a wall* (i.e. a dam or dyke; cf. Josh. 3:13, 16) and 'the deeps [congealing] in the heart of the sea' (AT), the terminology undoubtedly connotes an idea of depth that certainly concurs with a more literal interpretation of the events depicted in the previous chapter. In any case, as with the plague narrative, there are clear echoes here of the Genesis flood and a return to pre-creation chaos, with the watery forces of the deep engulfing those opposed to God and his purposes.

9–10. Shifting the focus to Yahweh's enemy (v. 9), the parlous situation that Israel had faced is again underlined: while some degree of poetic licence is probably involved, the battle would certainly have resulted in many casualties and loss of the plunder which they had carried with them from Egypt. It could be argued, however, that Pharaoh was intent primarily on eradicating the Israelites rather than simply recapturing his slave labour. If so, then verse 9 may be a rather accurate reflection of Egyptian sentiments. Whatever the reality of the situation, Egyptian aspirations were thwarted by Yahweh's *breath* (cf. v. 8) and the deluge it produced (v. 10). Thus, contrary to their somewhat naïve expectations, it was they (and not the Israelites) who suffered humiliating defeat.

11–12. Once again, Yahweh assumes centre stage, as the theological ramifications of his actions are underlined. While the emphasis in verse 11 is on Yahweh's uniqueness – in particular, his manifest superiority over any other deity (cf. Pss 35:10; 71:19; 89:6; Mic. 7:18) – there may also be an implicit suggestion here that his cataclysmic humiliation of the Egyptians also constituted a humiliation of their gods in particular (cf. 12:12). While such a rhetorical question should not be pressed as evidence of a polytheistic worldview, Enns's caution (2000: 300) about importing 'later idol polemics', such as Isaiah 44:6–20, into the present text is certainly valid. The idea here is simply that no other deity in the ancient world could realistically rival Yahweh – not because they were perceived as non-existent (cf. Deut. 4:35, 39), but because none had purportedly done anything like Yahweh.[21] The distinctive attributes highlighted here (*majestic in holiness, / awesome in glory, / working wonders*) set Yahweh apart from all others. Not surprisingly, one particular wonder – the supernatural destruction of his enemies – is singled out (v. 12). Interestingly, it is now Yahweh rather than Moses who stretches out his hand (cf. 14:26–27), again highlighting Moses' representative role. The substitution of *earth* for *sea* in the following clause (*the earth swallows your enemies*) may seem strange but is possibly explained by a metaphorical use of 'earth' ('*ereṣ*) here for 'underworld' (so Stuart 2006: 355). Alternatively, the allusion is to the later Korah incident (cf. Num. 16:28–34), and thus this verse marks the transition in focus from the sea crossing to Israel's subsequent experiences.

13–17. As noted above, the focus in these verses is on subsequent events in Israel's history – or at least, on events that lie ahead for the Israelites in the context of crossing the Sea. While this may reflect the earliest date for the composition of the song in its canonical form (so Enns), a prophetic interpretation of this material cannot be ruled out. Indeed, the lack of exact correlation between the somewhat idealistic reactions depicted here and the various responses recorded in the biblical narrative accounts may indicate that this part of the song reflects Israelite expectations rather than historical experiences. Whatever the case, the inclusion of this material after recounting Yahweh's victory at the Sea points to the theological links between the two events (i.e. Yahweh's triumph over Egypt and Yahweh's subjugation of Canaanites): each was necessary to fulfil Yahweh's covenant promises, and each was a marvellous demonstration of Yahweh's kingship.

---

21 Stuart's attempt (2006: 354–355) to excise the text of any hint of polytheism is unconvincing and unnecessary: whether or not these supernatural beings are conceived of as truly existing, they are no match for Yahweh.

As these verses remind us once again, redeeming (Heb. *gā'al*) this people (v. 13; cf. 6:6) was merely the first stage in Yahweh's covenant plan.[22] The next was that they should be brought to his *holy dwelling*. While this is possibly an allusion to Mount Sinai rather than the land of Israel/the city of Jerusalem/the temple,[23] the parallelism with verse 17 seems to make the latter much more likely, and certainly Mount Zion was their ultimate destination.[24] With Yahweh as their strong and reliable guide, there was nothing to fear. Rather, it would be their enemies – those who stood between them and their destination – who would be gripped with dread and terror (vv. 14–16). The same mighty power that had been unleashed against Egypt would be unleashed against all who would oppose Yahweh and his people, thus giving those Yahweh had purchased unrestricted access to their promised inheritance.[25]

18. The poetry fittingly concludes with Yahweh's kingship, highlighting the primary theme of the song throughout: Yahweh's supremacy over all. As suggested by Enns (2000: 305–306):

---

22 While *redeemed* may simply be synonymous with 'rescue', its use here (as in 6:6) probably implies that Yahweh is performing the role of Israel's guardian-redeemer (cf. Lev. 25:25; Ruth 3:9–13).

23 So Halpern 1983: 39; Smith 2001: 34; 2010: 64–65; Hamilton 2011: 232. However, while the Hebrew term (*nāwê*) is often used of temporary nomadic shelter, it can also refer to Yahweh's more permanent abode (cf. 2 Sam. 15:25; Jer. 25:30).

24 Hamilton (2011), however, suggests that the ambiguity may be intentional (allowing successive generations to appropriate it to their own circumstances), while taking the primary focus to be on Israel's more immediate future – their arrival at Sinai. Thus understood, the song encapsulates the two main foci in the book: victory over Egypt and worship at Sinai, and constitutes its literary fulcrum (Smith 2001). However, the language of 'bringing in', 'planting' and 'inheritance' seems more appropriate as a description of settlement in the Promised Land.

25 While it is also possible to understand the verb in v. 16 as 'created' (NIV footnote), the parallelism with *redeemed* (v. 13) seems to favour the idea of 'purchased' or 'acquired' (cf. also Ps. 74:2).

if the Israelites are to learn anything from the death of the Egyptians, it is that the Exodus story is about more than the Exodus . . . The Exodus is about God and who he is. The focus of the song is not on what happens to the Israelites or the Egyptians, but on God, who 'will reign for ever and ever'.

19. This verse summarizes what has already been narrated in chapter 14. If read as the conclusion of the previous unit,[26] this verse reiterates the rationale for the song (cf. v. 1b): '*for* Pharaoh's horses . . . but the Israelites walked through the sea on dry ground'. However, it is probably better to take this verse as the protasis ('When . . .') that provides the setting for the action narrated in the following verses.

20–21. The narrative resumption is followed by the first explicit mention of Miriam in the book,[27] here described as 'the prophetess'[28] and *Aaron's sister*. Miriam's prophetic role (see comment on 7:1) is also alluded to elsewhere (cf. Num. 12:1–2; Mic. 6:4), although she is explicitly described as such only here in Exodus 15. As with most of the other women described as such in Scripture, little information is given as to what her prophetic role entailed.[29] Possibly it alludes to the role she exercises in calling

---

26 The MT includes this prose verse at the conclusion of the song, beginning the new paragraph with verse 20.

27 Cf. 2:4, 7. While the identity of Moses' elder sister is not revealed in chapter 2, the fact that Miriam is the only sister of Moses mentioned by name makes such identification most likely (cf. Num. 26:59; 1 Chr. 6:3).

28 With the NRSV and NLT, NIV translates as 'prophet', even though the Hebrew noun is clearly feminine in form.

29 Deborah's prophetic ministry (Judg. 4:4) seems largely confined to offering inspired directives (or rebuke) with respect to military activity (cf. Judg. 4:6–14), although she, like Miriam, is also closely associated with a victory song (Judg. 5). Huldah, however, seems to function very much like her male equivalents in declaring a message from Yahweh (2 Kgs 22:14–20). Of the others, it is impossible to know precisely what their 'prophetic ministry' might have entailed (cf. Neh. 6:14; Isa. 8:3; Luke 2:36; Acts 2:17; 21:9; 1 Cor. 11:5; Rev. 2:20).

Israel to worship, which may also explain to some extent why she is associated here with Aaron in particular (cf. Num. 26:59). More precisely, it may relate to her association with this song, which clearly constitutes a prophetic witness to Yahweh (cf. Deborah's association with such a song in Judg. 5). Whatever the case, it is clear that, along with her brothers, Miriam had some kind of official status; such can be inferred not only from Micah 6:4, but also from the fact that she receives a separate death notice (Num. 20:1) – an honour subsequently shared only by Aaron (Num. 20:28) and Moses (Deut. 34:5–6) in the Pentateuch. Whatever the precise nature of Miriam's role, the repetition of the song (whether part or all of it) at this point most likely serves to link Yahweh's great act of deliverance in the past with ongoing celebrations of it in the present and future: Miriam's song begins with a masculine plural imperative ('Sing!'), a formulaic call to worship. As Enns (2000: 307) elaborates, 'The fact that [the song] is repeated so soon after its premiere performance [i.e. by Moses and the Israelites] hints that it should be sung not just once more, but again and again.'

Meaning
The main theological theme of this song – Yahweh's majestic power and sovereignty over all – is amply illustrated by his humiliation of the Egyptians and his (anticipated) subjugation of the Canaanites. Through such mighty acts Yahweh has made himself known as a deity without equal, and as a warrior king who reigns supreme, both now and for ever. His mighty acts not only bolster the confidence of his people, whatever challenges they may face, but are also to be celebrated by every generation.

6. PROVISION AND PROTECTION ON THE JOURNEY TO HOREB (15:22 – 17:16)

A. Provision of water and food (15:22 – 17:7)

Whatever the Israelites' exact route (see Introduction 4c, 'The route of the exodus'), it was not long before another crisis arose – in fact, a series of crises relating to their food and water supply. The latter is the focus of concern in the first and third incidents, sandwiched between which is the crisis involving the lack of food. These three incidents are bracketed by Yahweh's victory over the Egyptians and his victory over the Amalekites; thus, it is possible that the material has been deliberately arranged to highlight Yahweh's ability to provide as well as to protect:

A   Protection from Egypt (13:17 – 15:21)
   B   Provision of water (15:22–27)
      C   Provision of food (16:1–36)
   B' Provision of water (17:1–7)
A' Protection from Amalek (17:8–16)[1]

---

1   However, the significant imbalance of material in A and A' undermines the implied symmetry of the suggested chiastic pattern here.

Certainly, all three incidents recorded in 15:22 - 17:7 belong together and share a similar theme: Israel's grumbling and Yahweh's provision. The fact that they occur in rapid succession, and so soon after their miraculous deliverance from the Egyptians, is staggering – and undoubtedly intentionally so. Despite their renewed trust in Yahweh and his human representative (14:31), these emancipated slaves are clearly still walking by sight, rather than by faith. Yet, in a demonstration of amazing patience and grace, Yahweh responds with care and compassion, taking the opportunity to make himself known still further.

i. Water at Marah and Elim (15:22–27)
Context
The first crisis Israel faced related to their water supply. Having travelled some distance without finding water, eventually when they did locate an oasis, its water was undrinkable. This provided Yahweh with an opportunity to teach Israel an important lesson about himself as the God who maintains his people's welfare.

Comment
22. As with the places mentioned at the beginning of chapter 14, the precise location of the places mentioned here and in the next few chapters is uncertain. As a result, tracing the exact route taken by the Israelites from the Nile Delta is difficult, if not impossible. The details of Israel's itinerary are filled out in Numbers 33, where the *Desert of Shur* (i.e. fortress wall) is referred to as the 'Desert of Etham' (Num. 33:8). A close reading, however, suggests that Etham was actually on the edge of the desert (cf. Exod. 13:20); thus any contradiction is only apparent. Possibly the *three days'* duration of their desert trek may indicate why the Israelites stumble at the first major hurdle; they may well have expected to have reached their initial destination by now, believing that their journey there would be a relatively short one (cf. 3:18). More likely, however, here the three days simply highlights the serious nature of their dilemma: survival in the wilderness without fresh water was impossible; so, unless this problem was resolved fairly soon, they would all die.

23–24. Thus, their bitter disappointment, having arrived at this worthless but appropriately named oasis,[2] is perfectly understandable. Nevertheless, their subsequent reaction (i.e. grumbling against Moses) is completely inexcusable – all the more so if, at this point, they were still being visibly directed by the pillar of cloud/fire (cf. 13:21–22). Admittedly, however, this phenomenon has not been mentioned since their encounter with the Egyptians, and it is Moses who is expressly said to have directed them (lit. '*made* [Hiphil *nāsa'*] Israel journey') to this place (15:22). In any case, once again they are showing their true colours and exposing the fickleness of their faith: grumbling seems to have been the Israelites' default response to crises in the wilderness (cf. 16:2; 17:3; Num. 14:2; 16:11, 41). While ostensibly directed against Moses (and Aaron), in reality such grumbling was against Yahweh (cf. 16:7–8). However, in contrast to his later reactions to such behaviour (cf. Num. 11:4–34; 14:26–35; 16:41–50), here and in the immediately following episodes Yahweh responds graciously. Perhaps, as Hamilton (2011: 241) avers, this is to be explained by Israel's current pre-covenantal status. However, a more likely explanation is that at this stage Yahweh is still teaching Israel to trust him to provide, whereas in Numbers the people are deliberately ignoring everything that Yahweh had taught them about himself and are exhibiting blatant unbelief.

25a. Moses responds to the crisis as he had before (i.e. by crying out to Yahweh; 14:15; cf. 2:23), and God responds with yet another water spectacle – once again disclosing his control (as Creator) over nature. The MT literally reads: 'Yahweh *instructed* him a piece of wood',[3] which presumably means that Yahweh taught Moses

---

2 It is unclear whether it was already called 'bitter' (Heb. *mārâ*) or was subsequently so named by the Israelites. Some identify it as one of the Bitter Lakes, but modern Hawarah (a well some 80 km [50 miles] south of the northern tip of Suez) is more likely if the sea crossing took place somewhere along the Gulf of Suez.

3 While usually denoting a tree or trees, '*ēṣ* can also refer to a smaller piece of wood that can be held in someone's hand (cf. Ezek. 37:16, 19). Thus, here it probably means a stick or small branch.

about this wood (i.e. branch or bark), which may imply that it had chemical properties that made the brackish water palatable.[4] Such may also be implicit in the SP and LXX, which suggest that Yahweh *showed* Moses such a piece of wood. Either way, when Moses threw this wood into the water, the latter was transformed. However, whether this remedy involved some sort of ancient herbology or not, it was clearly unknown to Moses beforehand. Thus, this is not simply a case of Moses using his prior knowledge as an experienced desert nomad, but Yahweh providing for his people. Indeed, what we have here is almost the opposite phenomenon of the first plague: by means of a piece of wood in Moses' hand (i.e. his staff), God had previously made 'sweet' water 'bitter'; now, by means of a piece of wood in Moses' hand, he makes 'bitter' water 'sweet'.

25b–26. Such a connection with the earlier experience of Egypt is further expressed in the following divine directive through which Israel could avoid what Yahweh had inflicted on the Egyptians. Rather than alluding to some earlier legislation now lost (Sarna 1991: 85), or even anticipating the commands and decrees that will be disclosed in the following chapters, the substance of Yahweh's 'binding instruction' (AT; lit. 'statute and judgment')[5] is apparently spelt out in verse 26. Thus understood, the latter explains how Yahweh *tested* Israel at this time. Rather than functioning merely to examine Israel's heart, this instruction (as articulated in v. 26) was the means through which Yahweh *trained* his people. As Blackburn (2012: 66) maintains:

---

4   However, since any such plant is unknown to modern Bedouins, some conclude that the healing properties were not inherent in the wood; the latter was simply a symbolic means through which Yahweh performed this miracle. If so, the wood may allude to the tree of life (Gen. 2:9), and foreshadow the healing that Yahweh would eventually bring, not just to Israel, but also to the nations (Rev. 22:2).

5   The unusual combination of these two *singular* nouns (1 Sam. 30:25; although cf. Josh. 24:25; Ezra 7:10) may support Houtman's conclusion that the phrase here should be understood as a hendiadys, 'a binding statute' (1996: 313).

The traditional translation 'test' for the Hebrew root *nsh*, if simply seen as the Lord's seeking to know Israel's inclinations, is inadequate to the context of 15:25b. While there may be an element of seeking to know Israel's inclinations, the emphasis falls upon teaching or instruction.

This is clearly supported by the thrust of verse 26, and its climactic revelation of Yahweh as Israel's healer. For an instance where *nsh* carries a similar connotation, Blackburn (2012: 67 n. 5) cites 1 Samuel 17:39, where David declines Saul's armour because he has not *trained* with it.

It is thus made 'unmistakably clear that the liberation from Egypt does not lead to autonomy for Israel, but rather to an alternative sovereignty that imposes an alternative regimen on the liberated slaves' (Brueggemann 1994: 807–808). By keeping Yahweh's *commands* and *decrees* (beginning with those that follow in chapter 16, but obviously incorporating those subsequently revealed at Sinai), the Israelites would avoid the negative experiences of the Egyptians, described here in terms of 'diseases which Yahweh had brought upon them' (AT). Rather than referring to typical Egyptian ailments such as dysentery or elephantiasis, these *diseases* seem to allude to the earlier plagues. Even though the plagues are never described as such in the previous narrative, this noun is certainly associated with such plagues and disasters elsewhere (cf. 1 Kgs 8:37).

It is in this sense that Yahweh reveals himself here as the one who *heals* Israel.[6] The 'healing' in question is not the eradication of individual sickness or disease, but rather, as the immediate context suggests, the maintaining of Israel's welfare by adequately looking after their needs and keeping them from the kinds of terrifying disasters with which he had judged Egypt. It is clear from the conditional nature of verse 26, however, that such divine provision

---

6   The Hebrew verb *rāpā'* has a broader connotation than 'heal' may suggest; it may describe the repairing of an inanimate object (1 Kgs 18:30; Jer. 19:11) and, significantly, making bad or salt water drinkable (2 Kgs 2:21; Ezek. 47:8–9).

was not automatic, but contingent upon Israel's obedience: 'The corollary to the Lord's not visiting the disasters of Egypt upon Israel if she obeys is that he will bring disaster if she does not' (Blackburn 2012: 67). Indeed, this is spelt out plainly in the curses of Deuteronomy (cf. Deut. 28:60–61). To this extent, the use of *nsh* here in verse 25 is analogous to its use in 20:20; like the theophany there, the binding rule here is designed to instil a fear that would promote obedience. Thus 'the promise here was not that Yahweh would never allow those who place their faith in him to get sick. It was that the Israelites would be free from having to worry about the plagues' (Stuart 2006: 367–368). In other words, rather than lending support to the shallow prosperity teachings that plague modern Christianity, Yahweh's words serve more as a warning against the consequences of disobedience. Through obedience to Yahweh's commands Israel would escape the terrible judgments that had been experienced by the defiant Egyptians.

27. Yahweh's faithfulness in so providing for his people is further highlighted by Israel's subsequent encampment. In sharp contrast with the bitter experience at Marah, Elim – with its twelve springs and seventy palm trees – illustrates Yahweh's generous provision and serves as a foretaste of the blessings to come: those that an obedient Israel could anticipate when they entered the Promised Land, and ultimately those of God's restored world (cf. Ezek. 47; Rev. 22:1–5).

Meaning
As with the other crises Israel faced on their journey to Sinai, the lack of drinkable water at Marah served as a test of Israel's faith and an opportunity for further instruction about the God who had delivered them from Egypt. Coming so soon after their positive reaction to the events at the Sea (14:31), their negative response here (grumbling against Moses) is perhaps surprising, but not unusual for those whose natural inclination is to walk by sight. Accordingly, the need to trust God fully, whatever the circumstances, is underlined yet again (cf. 6:6–10; 14:10–14), as Yahweh not only demonstrates his ability to provide, but also emphasizes the importance of obeying him by recalling the conse-quences of disobedience – a lesson the Egyptians learned the hard

way. By contrast, as their experience at Elim foreshadows, an obedient Israel could anticipate God's blessing both now and in the paradise that awaited them.

ii. Quail and manna in the Desert of Sin (16:1–36)
Context
Unfortunately, Israel's foretaste of such paradise was short-lived. Exactly one month after their departure from Egypt another crisis erupted, this time relating to a shortage of food. Again, the Israelites respond by grumbling, and again Yahweh turns the occasion into an opportunity to train them and develop their faith.

Comment
1–3. This incident took place in the *Desert of Sin*,[7] which lay between Elim and Mount Sinai. Although the two names are similar (both in Hebrew and English), the Desert of Sin and the Desert of Sinai are clearly distinguished from each other in the biblical narrative (17:1; 19:1–2; cf. Num. 33:12, 15). Possibly, however, Sinai refers to a particular region (close to the mountain of God) of the much larger Desert of Sin (Stuart 2006). Identifying the location of either place, however, is complicated by the major problems involved in reconstructing Israel's exodus itinerary (see Introduction 4c, 'The route of the exodus'). The fact that grumbling is mentioned even before the nature of the problem has been disclosed may imply that a predisposition to grumble has already taken root and spread like a noxious weed throughout *the whole community*, which is now implicated in such behaviour (cf. 15:24). Such grumbling is ostensibly directed against Moses and Aaron, who are deemed responsible for Israel's present crisis.[8] The fact that the grumblers ignore Yahweh's role

---

7 NB *Sin* in this geographical context transliterates a Hebrew proper noun which is unrelated to the English word or theological concept of sin.

8 It is unclear why Aaron should also be targeted in the criticism here yet not in the grumbling on either side of ch. 16 (cf. 15:24; 17:3). Possibly, however, this relates to the greater role he plays in this chapter as a

in their circumstances reflects a theological naïvety, as the subsequent verses will underline (cf. vv. 6–8). This is the first time the
Israelites express the sentiment that they would have been better
off perishing in Egypt (cf. 14:12), but not the last (cf. Num. 14:2).
The way it is expressed is telling: they consider it preferable to
have died 'by Yahweh's hand' (AT) in Egypt (i.e. suffered the fate
of the Egyptians) than face death by starvation in the desert.
The less-positive aspects of their former life are conveniently
overlooked, as is often the case when such negative comparisons
are made. Though we could infer from the numerous livestock
accompanying the Israelites that their present situation was not
absolutely dire (cf. 12:38), simply consuming all their animals
would certainly have been a rather short-sighted solution. More
importantly, unless Moses' earlier response to Pharaoh was deliberately misleading, the Israelites still had no idea how much of
their livestock, also in some sense redeemed, was required for
the worship of Yahweh (cf. 10:25–26). It is thus conceivable that
Moses had prohibited any consumption of the livestock prior to
their arrival at Sinai, and even afterwards any such consumption
may well have been restricted to a sacrificial context until Israel
had settled in the Promised Land (cf. Lev. 17; Deut. 12:20–27).
Accordingly, even if a food source was not strictly unavailable,
what was accessible for consumption seems to have been in
short supply – hence these negative comparisons between their
wilderness rations and the copious amount of food they enjoyed in
Egypt (16:3). The issue here relates to the *quantity*, rather than the
quality of the food they had at their disposal (cf. Num. 11:5; 20:5).
However, rather than crying out to Yahweh, the Israelites resort
to type (cf. 15:24; see also 5:21; 14:10–12) by again grumbling (v.
2) in such adverse circumstances against Yahweh's servants – the
recurring motif in this section of Exodus (cf. vv. 7–9, 11; 17:3).

4–5. Despite their inappropriate response, however, Yahweh
again responds with patience and grace: rather than reacting
negatively to such grumbling (as in the similar scenario of Num.

---

whole – in terms of both communicating on Moses' behalf (16:9–10)
and preserving a sample of the manna for posterity (16:33–34).

11), Yahweh promises to *rain down bread from heaven*. While the precise nature of this heavenly food is not disclosed at this stage, the rest of the chapter makes it clear that the primary reference is to what was subsequently called *manna* (cf. v. 31). Such food would be supplied and harvested for one day at a time, except for the sixth day, when twice the normal daily amount could be gathered. The double supply on the sixth day facilitated rest on the sabbath (cf. vv. 22–30), foreshadowing the full revelation of Yahweh's covenant requirements at Sinai. Indeed, as verse 4 highlights, the way this food was supplied would test the Israelites with respect to Yahweh's teaching – 'whether they will walk in my torah or not' (AT). Blackburn (2012: 68–69) again insists on translating the verb *nsh* as 'teach/train' rather than 'test' (cf. 15:25), but the connotation here may be wider, especially since two quite different possibilities ('whether . . . or not'; cf. Gen. 24:21) are expressly considered. Undoubtedly Yahweh is seeking to teach/train the Israelites to trust him for their daily and weekly provision; hence a crucial aspect of this 'test' was indeed the necessity of trusting Yahweh accordingly, and doing so one day at a time.[9] However, as well as this important training aspect, Yahweh also seems to use these circumstances to examine Israel's response to his commands (cf. vv. 17, 20, 27) – not because he was personally ignorant of Israel's natural inclinations, or of how some would behave, but rather so that he might instruct the Israelites further, even through their non-compliance.

6–8. When Moses and Aaron begin communicating this information to the Israelites, they emphasize that the true focus of Israel's grumbling was in fact Yahweh: it was he who had brought them out of Egypt.[10] This fact would be highlighted afresh by their anticipated experiences that evening and the following

---

9 'Israel is to be kept in a perpetual state of dependence' (Enns 2000: 326). This fact is probably alluded to in the petition for daily bread in the prayer Jesus taught his disciples (cf. Matt. 6:11; Luke 11:3).

10 Moses' speech in 16:8 elaborates what Moses and Aaron have said to the Israelites in 16:6–7, clearly reiterating the rationale (*because he has heard your grumbling against him*) for emphasis.

morning (v. 6). The former is merely alluded to in verse 6 but is fleshed out by Moses in verse 8: Yahweh will demonstrate his saving interest in Israel by an unexpected supply of fresh meat to eat. The glory of Yahweh that Israel would see *in the morning* (v. 7) is likewise elaborated by Moses in verse 8 as an abundant supply of bread.[11] Elsewhere in Exodus 'the glory of Yahweh' (AT) refers to a physical manifestation of God's presence (cf. 16:10; 24:16–17; 29:43; 33:12–23; 40:34–35). Here, however, in its first occurrence in the book, it refers to the manna that would demonstrate Yahweh's presence in his care for Israel. Rather than implying anything about the relative quantity of bread in relation to meat, the description of each (lit. 'meat to eat' and 'bread to satisfy') alludes back to how the Israelite complaint was expressed (v. 3). Thus understood, Yahweh was about to give the Israelites exactly what they longed for, so presumably they would have their fill of both – as the parallelism implies (Stuart 2006: 376–377).[12] These experiences would therefore enlighten the Israelites, just as Yahweh had formerly enlightened the Egyptians when he stretched out his hand against them (cf. 7:5; 8:22; 9:14; 11:7).

9–12. At this point the chronology of the passage becomes somewhat confusing.[13] Aaron is told by Moses to instruct the entire community to come before Yahweh (v. 9). While he is doing so, Yahweh manifests his glory in the cloud (v. 10). However, this manifestation of Yahweh's glory is not what Israel was told to anticipate *in the morning* (v. 7; cf. v. 8), but either some kind of physical change in the appearance of the already present cloud (so Stuart 2006), or the reappearance of this visual phenomenon for

---

11 While the Hebrew noun can refer to 'food' in general rather than 'bread' specifically, the context here (where it is contrasted with 'meat') suggests that 'bread' is a more appropriate translation at this point in the narrative (also, cf. v. 31).

12 However, while the manna was clearly an ongoing provision, the meat was apparently not so; cf. Num. 11:4–34.

13 While others may account for such duplication of material by recourse to source criticism, this does not explain its canonical arrangement.

the first time since chapter 14.[14] Most surprisingly, Yahweh then instructs Moses to impart information to the Israelites that Aaron and he have communicated to them already (v. 12; cf. vv. 6–8).[15] The most obvious way to make any sense of this is to assume that the material in 16:4–12 has not been arranged in chronological sequence.[16] The canonical arrangement seems to place emphasis on what Yahweh wanted Israel to learn from the experience: namely, to know that Yahweh was indeed their God.

13–15a. Israel's new food supplies came exactly as Yahweh had promised, with fresh meat in the evening followed the next morning by the substance the Israelites subsequently called manna (v. 31). The sudden influx of all these *quail* is not, in one sense, all that extraordinary. After all, these rotund, pigeon-like birds are easily exhausted during their long migration, and many tend to drop from the sky in the Sinai Peninsula region. However, while Yahweh may be providing for the Israelites through 'natural means' here, the timing clearly indicates that divine providence is nevertheless operative.[17] Nevertheless, the emphasis throughout the rest of this chapter suggests that Yahweh's provision of these

---

14 Either way, the glory of Yahweh here, as elsewhere, describes some visible manifestation of his presence.

15 Other than *twilight* (lit. 'between the evenings'; cf. 12:6) replacing 'evening', and the slightly different theological lesson (here, 'I am Yahweh your God'), there is little difference between this and the previous revelation to Israel in vv. 6–8.

16 The chronological sequence could be as follows (although this is admittedly conjectural): vv. 1–3; vv. 11–12; vv. 9–10; vv. 6–8; vv. 4–5. Interpretations which attempt to read the text chronologically are unconvincing. For instance, Hamilton's suggestion (2011: 252) that Yahweh's speech in vv. 11–12 is 'confirmatory' rather than 'revelatory' begs the question, 'When (and from whom) did Moses get the information communicated to the Israelites in 16:6–8?' Hamilton seems to imply that Moses was speaking 'prophetically', and Yahweh subsequently confirmed that this 'prophetic' word was spot on!

17 Unlike the later provision of quail (cf. Num. 11), there is no associated divine judgment here in Exod. 16.

quail was of secondary importance, apparently designed as a temporary measure to tide the Israelites over until the regular provision of manna began the following day.

The manna became visible only after the dew had evaporated in the morning (cf. Num. 11:9). Both the description given to it (*thin flakes like frost on the ground*) and the Israelites' reaction to its appearance (v. 15a) suggest that it was an unfamiliar substance.[18] Moreover, the fact that the manna was supplied almost daily, throughout the year, suggests that more was involved than simply some naturally occurring phenomenon such as the secretions of scale insects or plant lice. Whatever similarities there are between known phenomena and the biblical descriptions of manna, significant differences must not be overlooked or downplayed in the interests of either 'authenticating' or 'demythologizing' the narrative. Unfortunately, most naturalistic explanations fail to take the biblical narrative seriously, sometimes implying that massive exaggeration was introduced as the account became embellished by folklore. While there is no reason why Yahweh could not have used some natural substance to provide for his people (cf. the quails), if he did so in the case of the manna it appears that the natural substance was 'genetically modified' to some extent (e.g. its non-seasonal nature and its extraordinary absence one day every week).[19] While the text does not say so explicitly, there seems to be some connection between the question posed in verse 15 and the biblical name given to this unfamiliar substance (cf. v. 31). The use of the interrogative *mān* for 'What?' is certainly unique in the Old Testament,[20] but whether this reflects an archaic usage of the term (cf. the unusual use of *mah* as 'why' in 14:15 and 17:2) or later

---

18 Admittedly, like most of their wilderness experiences, the appearance of manna could have been something of a novelty for the Israelites because they were unfamiliar with this territory.

19 The honeydew secreted by plant lice is available for harvesting only in late May, June and July.

20 The normal Hebrew interrogative for 'What?' is *mâ*. In Semitic languages *mān* generally denotes 'Who?' – although it is used for 'What?' in late Aramaic and Syriac.

folk etymology (possibly involving wordplay) is unclear.[21] In any case, this unusual interrogative seems to explain the monosyllabic name given to the substance in the original (i.e. 'man' rather than 'manna'; v. 31). Elsewhere the LXX employs the disyllabic term 'manna', which is carried over into the New Testament and has obviously influenced Latin and English translations.

15b–18. In response, Moses identifies it as the bread that Yahweh has provided (v. 15b; cf. v. 4), and then communicates Yahweh's instructions (cf. vv. 4–5) for harvesting it (v. 16). While each person was apparently permitted to gather as much manna as considered necessary (lit. 'according to the mouth of his eating'), harvested quantities were subsequently measured out (an *omer* [cf. v. 36] per person) to ensure that everyone was adequately provided for. Thus understood, the specific measurement in verse 16b qualifies the otherwise open-ended policy of verse 16a, and what is then narrated in verses 17–18 is the implementation of this policy, not some kind of miraculous intervention in the collection and distribution of the manna.[22] Verse 18 therefore explains how, despite the variation in quantities of manna collected by individuals (v. 17), everyone ended up with a sufficient amount of manna. It is this principle of mutual support that Paul applies to Christian giving in his Corinthian correspondence (2 Cor. 8:15).

19–20. The prohibition on keeping any of the manna for the following day demanded faith in Yahweh's ongoing, daily provision: it was evidently to inculcate such faith that the manna was not to be stored up. Not surprisingly, it was this instruction that some of the Israelites found too challenging. By ignoring Moses' exhortation and attempting to 'stockpile' the manna, these disobedient Israelites not only foreshadowed the further and more serious rebellion that lay ahead (cf. ch. 32), but also betrayed the fact that they were living by sight, rather than by faith. Their

---

21 Wordplays suggested include *mennu*, an Egyptian word for 'food', and *man*, an Arabic word for plant lice.

22 *Pace* Hamilton (2011: 255) who, with several other commentators, infers that Yahweh miraculously downsized the portion of the greedier harvesters and upsized that of the unselfish.

attempt to do so, however, was thwarted by the rapid decompo-
sition of Yahweh's provision, which was clearly designed for just
one day at a time. While Moses was understandably angered by
their disregard for Yahweh's instructions (cf. v. 4), again foreshadowing what was to come (cf. 32:19), no punishment was imposed
– a further demonstration of Yahweh's patience and grace in this
period of Israel's instruction and training.

21–26. The fact that the prescribed amounts of manna had
to be collected early in the morning, before being melted by the
heat of the sun (v. 21), suggests that it had to be stored in the
shade before being prepared for consumption (cf. v. 23). Cooking
it, however, was apparently not simply the means by which the
additional manna collected on the sixth day was preserved for
the seventh. Had this been so, any astute Israelite could obviously
have preserved some on other days as well. Rather, the preser-
vation of the additional quantities collected on the sixth day (v.
22a) seems, like the provision of this additional manna, to have
been miraculous. Most likely it was the unexpected opportunity
to harvest twice as much on the sixth day that took the leaders
of the community by surprise and prompted them to approach
Moses for an explanation. Significantly, Moses had not yet
mentioned this aspect of Yahweh's instructions (cf. v. 5) to either
the leaders or the people in the preceding narrative. Moreover,
only now is the theological rationale for the double quantity of
manna on the sixth day introduced: the seventh day was to be
'a day of rest, a holy sabbath to Yahweh' (v. 23, AT). This is the
first explicit reference to the sabbath – notably prior to its official
promulgation in 20:8–11. Evidently this, like some other Israelite
observances (e.g. circumcision), was practised before the law was
given at Sinai. However, at this stage the concept was probably a
novelty for the Israelites, who had experienced no such weekly
stoppages in Egypt.

Obeying the instruction to save some of the manna on the
sixth day until the following morning (v. 23) again required the
exercise of faith, and this was rewarded the following day by the
discovery that the manna had not spoiled (as it had previously),
but remained fit for consumption on the sabbath, on which they
could expect no new manna to appear (vv. 25–26).

27–30. However, some of the Israelites, like Pharaoh, were slow learners. Despite being told that there would be none to gather on the seventh day (vv. 25–26), some insisted on going out in search of it (v. 27). Once again, such heady defiance does not bode well for a people who will shortly obligate themselves to doing everything that Yahweh says (cf. 19:8; 24:3, 7). Some of the people have tripped up over the very first hurdle. Whereas the previous act of disobedience had evoked the anger of Moses (cf. v. 20), this second evoked a strong rebuke from Yahweh himself (vv. 28–29). The seriousness of Yahweh's rebuke is underscored by the fact that the last time Yahweh asked such a question (i.e. *How long will you refuse . . . ?*, v. 28),[23] he was addressing the recalcitrant Pharaoh (cf. 10:3). These rogue Israelites were already in danger of becoming like Pharaoh by flouting the simplest of Yahweh's instructions. As Moses goes on to explain (v. 29), the sabbath had been given to them as Yahweh's gift, and he had facilitated its observance by supplying double the usual amount of manna on the sixth day. There were thus to be no further attempts to harvest any manna on the seventh day.[24] Whether by choice or simply through lack of incentive to do otherwise, sabbath rest was now dutifully observed (v. 30).

31–36. It appears that some (or possibly all) of this final paragraph is an editorial gloss, recording what subsequently took place (i.e. after the tablets of the law had been given at Sinai, and possibly after the ark of the covenant had been constructed; cf. v. 34). Verse 31 reads almost like a parenthetical comment, supplying further information about Israel's supernatural food supply. As mentioned above (see v. 15), the name they gave it apparently

---

23 The Hebrew plural subject (*you*) makes it clear that it is the Israelites (rather than Moses) to whom Yahweh is addressing this rhetorical question.

24 The 'going out' proscribed here relates to harvesting manna. Rabbinical interpreters, however, applied this to 'going out' in general on the sabbath. In conjunction with Josh. 3:4–5, this gave rise to the concept of a 'sabbath day's journey' (cf. Acts 1:12), the maximum distance considered permissible to travel on the sabbath.

derived from the question the Israelites asked when they first saw it. Evidently it was white in colour (i.e. the colour of coriander seed), crisp in texture (like wafers; cf. v. 14) and extremely sweet in taste (honey being a natural sweetener). Indeed, the association of honey with the Promised Land may suggest that in some respects the manna was a small foretaste of the blessing that awaited them.

However, it was also to serve as a perpetual reminder of how Yahweh had provided for his people after he had brought them out of Egypt (v. 32). Thus, largely for the benefit of posterity, a sample *omer* of manna was to be preserved in a jar and 'placed before Yahweh' (v. 33, AT). Aaron evidently interpreted the latter in terms of 'the Testimony' (AT; here anachronistically referring either to the covenant tablets or to the ark of the covenant in which they were subsequently placed), and presumably he did so as part of his official role as Israel's high priest. The following verse (v. 35) clearly constitutes a further anachronism – evidently an editorial gloss inserted after Yahweh's miraculous provision of manna had ceased (cf. Josh. 5:10–12).[25]

The final verse of the chapter (v. 36) is a parenthetical comment providing an equivalence measure for the benefit of later readers. Clearly by the time this note was inserted, an *ephah* (between 10 and 12 litres) had replaced an *omer* (just over 1 litre) as the more popular measurement. Nevertheless, the fact that the original account employed what had obviously become an archaic measurement is testimony to the tradition's antiquity.

Meaning
Though this new crisis involved food rather than water, the previous lesson still applied. However, rather than taking the lesson of the previous incident on board, it seems that the Israelites were both slow to learn and quick to forget. Once again, their incessant grumbling betrays not only ingratitude,

---

25 While such anachronistic comments demonstrate that the canonical form of the Pentateuch postdates Moses, they do not undercut the nuanced approaches to Mosaic compilation defended by contemporary conservative scholars (see Introduction 2, 'Composition and date').

but also their lack of faith, for which the barometer is obedience. Accordingly, as well as generously supplying the necessary food, on this occasion Yahweh actually tests their obedience. The first test, prohibiting any hoarding of manna, encouraged them to trust God each day, rather than relying on selfishness or their own resourcefulness – a lesson applied to Christians by the apostle Paul (2 Cor. 8:15). Unsurprisingly, some failed the test, drawing the ire of Moses (Exod. 16:20). The second test, prohibiting the collection of manna on the sabbath, encouraged them to trust in God's promise of a double provision one day per week. Again, some failed the test, evoking a rebuke from Yahweh (vv. 28–29). That following Yahweh's commands and instructions is somewhat problematic for Israel is no longer simply implicit (cf. 15:26), foreshadowing a significant problem with the covenant commitment they will later express (cf. 19:8; 24:3, 7). Nevertheless, despite Israel's failure, Yahweh proved faithful to the promises he made, ultimately through Jesus who – despite being tested like Israel in the wilderness – demonstrated humble dependence on God expressed through perfect obedience.

iii. Water from the rock at Rephidim (17:1–7)
Context
As Wenham (2003: 67) observes, 'The final episode in this trio of grumbling stories is clearly the most serious, often referred to in other parts of the Old Testament (e.g. Deut. 6:16; Ps. 95:8).[26] After the miraculous provision narrated in the two previous incidents, the community's impatient and hostile reaction to yet another water shortage seems quite inexcusable, and their insolent question – 'Is Yahweh among us or not?' (AT) – almost beggars belief.

---

26 In Ps. 95:7–11 and Heb. 3 – 4 it serves as a severe warning against hardening one's heart and disobeying God. The fact that a similar incident frames the wilderness period towards its conclusion (Num. 20:1–13) indicates that 'as a whole this is characterized as a period of rebellion' (Enns 2000: 329 n. 16).

Comment

1. This next incident in Israel's travelogue begins quite serenely, with the Israelites moving as Yahweh directed them – whether by the pillar of cloud, the leadership of Moses, or both.[27] This stage of their journey took them from *the Desert of Sin* (cf. 16:1) to *Rephidim*, their last stop before reaching Sinai (cf. 19:2), which was evidently quite close by (cf. 17:5–6; 18:5). From Sinai's proximity and the date suggested in 19:1 (i.e. between two and three months after the exodus), we may infer that this journey took several weeks (cf. 16:1). But however long and arduous it had been, the absence of fresh water at this new campsite would naturally have been a severe blow to their morale and a further test of their faith and confidence in Yahweh (cf. Ps. 81:7 [MT 8]).

2. Having made this unwelcome discovery, the Israelites again vent their frustrations, belligerently insisting that water be given to them (v. 2a). Rather than 'quarrelling' (NIV) – which suggests a heated social exchange – the idea of a contentious protest, involving or at least threatening physical violence (v. 4), better captures the nuance here.[28] As Moses' response (v. 2b) implies, they were apparently expecting God to fulfil *their* demands, and were thus 'putting Yahweh to the test' by demanding that he prove himself (cf. v. 7).[29] Such behaviour reflected gross arrogance in trying to make Yahweh answerable to them. Moreover, by reacting in this way they were hardening their hearts (as Pharaoh had) by ignoring the revelation they had already received (cf. Ps. 95:7–9). As the psalmist implies, Israel was thus already on

---

27 They journeyed, literally, 'by the mouth of Yahweh', the sole occurrence of this phrase in Exodus. In Numbers it is used to stamp a divine imprimatur on priestly practices. If used in a similar manner here, it may suggest that Moses' leading was divinely sanctioned.

28 The Hebrew verb (*rîb*) can denote violent conflict (cf. Ps. 35:1), as apparently so here in Exod. 17:2 where Moses feels himself physically threatened.

29 As before (cf. 16:6–8), Moses redirects their complaint heavenwards, again exposing what they are really doing.

a trajectory (from doubt to disobedience) that would eventually result in dire consequences (Blackburn 2012: 73).

3–4. Given their physical circumstances, Moses' protests fall on deaf ears. Incapable of seeing past the immediate crisis, once again they resort to grumbling against Moses, giving fresh expression to their previous accusation (cf. 16:3). Not only are they repeating their past mistake, but they are also forgetting everything that Yahweh had explicitly aimed to teach them (cf. 16:6–8). Not surprisingly, Moses responds with more than a little degree of exasperation, as well as an understandable fear for his personal well-being in these volatile circumstances.

5–6. Once again, however, Yahweh responds in grace, further demonstrating his ability to provide the Israelites with the sustenance they need. Some of the elders are to accompany Moses, presumably as witnesses to the extraordinary way in which Yahweh would supply the Israelites with water at Horeb. The visible manifestation of Yahweh 'standing before' Moses at Horeb was undoubtedly the pillar of cloud (cf. Ps. 81:7), which presumably settled beside or over the rock – the latter probably referring to Sinai's rock face rather than to a particular boulder or free-standing rock. This would certainly explain the otherwise anomalous use of the definite article here and might also lend scientific credibility to the spectacle about to take place. Thus understood, we should envisage water suddenly beginning to flow from a cliff face (i.e. like a covert spring or flash flood), rather than water suddenly gushing out of a solid boulder or the like. However, whatever 'naturalistic' explanation might be proposed, both the timing and the means by which this water appeared indicate that, like the previous two incidents, this should not be explained away in terms of some recognizable, natural phenomenon. Rather, as the utilization of Moses' staff so eloquently proclaims, this constituted a supernatural sign akin to those authenticating Moses' testimony to Israel (4:1–17) and those subsequently used to make Yahweh known to Pharaoh and the Egyptians (7:5).[30] Once again, Moses'

---

30 As Blackburn avers (2012: 72), the staff may thus assume the function of the 'I am Yahweh' statement in the previous two incidents.

staff was used to demonstrate Yahweh's unique ability to provide for his people. Paul figuratively interprets the water here (and the manna of the previous chapter) as a symbol of God's spiritual sustenance in Christ (1 Cor. 10:3–4).[31]

7. Only here is this location given the double name *Massah* (testing) and *Meribah* (contending), although on two occasions the names occur in poetic parallelism (Deut. 33:8; Ps. 95:8). Elsewhere, each name is used independently: Massah in the rest of Deuteronomy, and Meribah in Numbers and the rest of Psalms. Both names would serve as a perpetual reminder, not only for the present generation, but also for future generations, of their intrinsic tendency to walk by sight rather than by faith.

Meaning

As noted previously, the theme that unites all three crises narrated in 15:22 – 17:7 is Yahweh's ability to provide for the people he has redeemed. Once delivered from their Egyptian oppressors, the Israelites are not left to fend for themselves as they complete their trek in the wilderness. Rather, through each of the crises that arise on their journey, Yahweh demonstrates his sustaining grace and seeks to teach his people to trust him to provide. As Enns (2000: 325) observes:

The main purpose of sending manna and quail is certainly not just to test the Israelites or simply fill their stomachs. It is rather to teach them something about God, or as [16:6] puts it, so that the Israelites will 'know that it was the LORD who brought you out of Egypt' (see also [16:12]). That the Israelites will 'know' is

---

31 Paul's reference to Israel drinking 'from the rock that followed them' (AT) is often thought to draw on Jewish exegetical tradition that sought to explain how Israel was sustained between Exod. 17 and Num. 20. However, Paul evidently puts a Christological spin on this: rather than thinking in terms of a relocating rock or moveable well, Paul understands the replenishing rock spiritually rather than physically: the OT Rock (i.e. Yahweh) who accompanied the Israelites is equated by Paul with Christ (Ciampa and Rosner 2010: 450–451).

another echo of the departure narrative. God is not yet finished teaching his people who he is. In fact, he has hardly begun.

Unfortunately, however, as this third incident further illustrates, Israel is quick to forget what Yahweh has done and the lessons he has taught them thus far. Maintaining their trust in Yahweh, especially when faced with adverse circumstances, is clearly challenging, and repeatedly threatens to derail them. Still, like a patient parent, Yahweh continues to meet their every need, demonstrating not only his power to provide, but also his right to their trust and obedience. Nevertheless, as underlined by the rationale behind the naming of the location where this incident occurred, Israel's faithlessness has taken an ominous turn – testing God. As is clear from subsequent allusions to this incident (cf. Deut. 6:16; 9:22; Ps. 95:7–9), this is the Israelites' most serious misdemeanour to date.

B. Divine protection in the face of Amalekite aggression (17:8–16)

Context
As this next episode demonstrates, lack of food and water supplies was not the only problem the Israelites encountered at this stage of their journey: they also faced unprovoked hostility from the Amalekites. Unlike the three previous crises, on this occasion there is no mention of Israelite grumbling or anxiety, nor is there any suggestion that this incident constituted discipline for their previous behaviour. Rather, faced with an external threat involving unprovoked hostility, Moses seems to know precisely what to do,[32] and everyone falls into line. Indeed, Yahweh does not make an explicit appearance until the crisis is over. This particular crisis seems, therefore, to demonstrate once again how Israel, with Yahweh's assistance (attested by the use of Moses' staff), can overcome those who would oppose them and Yahweh's

---

32 As Hamilton (2011: 270) concludes, Moses may simply be applying the principle reflected in the previous crisis-handling directive (cf. 17:5–6).

purposes.[33] In so doing, it illustrates that Yahweh protects his redeemed people, as well as providing for them. Moreover, quite possibly it serves as a foil for the following account, which narrates how another non-Israelite met and (positively) responded to this pilgrim people.

Comment

8. The territory of the *Amalekites* is mentioned in Genesis 14:7, although that is surely an anachronistic description since these semi-nomads were descended from Esau (cf. Gen. 36:12, 16). While this may partly explain the animosity shown here towards the Israelites, it is more likely that they were simply attempting to capitalize on the vulnerability of these Hebrew migrants (cf. Deut. 25:18).[34] Their military superiority is illustrated by the fact that they dominated the Israelites except when Moses' arms were elevated (cf. 17:11). They later reappear when the Israelites are spying out the land (cf. Num. 13:29; 14:25, 43, 45), where their presence becomes a factor in Israel's prolonged stay in the desert. Even after the conquest, the Amalekites continued to oppose Israel (cf. Judg. 3:13; 6:3, 33; 7:12; 10:12), and were not finally defeated until the period of the monarchy (cf. 1 Sam. 15; 30). Whether as a result of this particular encounter recorded in Exodus, or an outworking of the earlier tensions between Jacob and Esau, a long-standing animosity developed between Amalek and Israel, finally climaxing in the Persian period, when Haman the Agagite (Esth. 3:1) attempted to annihilate the Jewish race by means of an officially sanctioned pogrom throughout the empire.

---

33 'Although the form of the danger is different . . . the threat is ultimately the same: Israel's existence is threatened, and the patriarchal promises endangered' (Blackburn 2012: 74).

34 From Balaam's oracle (cf. Num. 24:20) it may be inferred that the Amalekites organized themselves into some kind of national entity. While they are generally located much further north, perhaps this southern foray was considered a pre-emptive strike on those threatening to encroach on what they considered to be Amalekite territory.

9. *Joshua* appears here without formal introduction, indicating that such was quite unnecessary for Israelite readers. From elsewhere we know that he was Moses' younger assistant (cf. 24:13; 33:11) and designated successor (Num. 27:12–23),[35] whereas here his role is exclusively a military one: he is to select an ad hoc militia to repel these Amalekite marauders.[36] Given the nature of the pool from which the selection was made, it would be quite mistaken to infer that Joshua was responsible for forming some kind of elite fighting unit. Rather, his task would simply have been that of gathering able-bodied men who were willing to participate in the ensuing conflict. But regardless of their inexperience, the Israelites would actually have to engage the enemy and fight: on this occasion it was not a matter of simply needing to *be still* (cf. 14:14); now Israel was to have a much more active role,[37] which typifies how Israel will engage the Canaanites, and possibly also foreshadows Israel's more active participation in making Yahweh known in the following chapters (Blackburn 2012: 75–76).

The battle was not joined immediately, giving the Israelites a day to prepare for it.[38] Some infer from this that either there was a gradual build-up of Amalekite forces, or else the latter gave notice of their intent, possibly with accompanying terms (cf. 1 Sam. 11). However, if the Amalekites were content with sporadic raids on the stragglers (cf. Deut. 25:18), the initiative for a more formal conflict may well have been Israel's. In any case, the mention of *tomorrow* and Moses' *staff* also evokes memories of the plague

---

35 Joshua's future role as Israel's military leader is implied also here in 17:14.

36 Fittingly, however, his name means 'Yahweh saves', and is the Hebrew equivalent of the name Jesus.

37 However, as Blackburn notes (2012: 75), one should not infer from this that Yahweh somehow needs Israel's assistance (Fretheim 1991a: 193–194), or that this change of policy was determined by the relatively smaller size of Amalek's army compared to Pharaoh's (Propp 1999: 617).

38 Even if *tomorrow* belongs with 'I will station myself' (AT; as per MT's major disjunctive accent), the following verses make it clear that no military action was engaged until after Moses had done so.

narrative: there *tomorrow* was when God acted to punish Israel's enemies (cf. 8:23, 29; 9:5, 18; 10:4), and Moses' staff had been the instrument God had used to call forth divine judgments on those who opposed him and his people. It is thus not difficult to antici-pate the outcome of this particular conflict. Moreover, as Enns (2000: 344) observes:

> The mention of this battle here in the narrative performs a specific theological function. Just as certain elements in the previous passage foreshadow events in Israel's near future (Sinai and the giving of the law), the battle with the Amalekites foreshadows the ultimate goal toward which God is bringing his newly freed people: the conquest of Canaan.

10. Joshua's obedience models that expected of the Israelites in general, with whom he is increasingly contrasted as the Pentateuchal narrative progresses. While Aaron is by this stage already well known, *Hur* (like Joshua) is mentioned here for the first time and without genealogy – again implying that he was an equally well-known figure. Presumably it is this same Hur who reappears in 24:14, where again he and Aaron assist Moses. From elsewhere we learn that Hur belonged to the tribe of Judah and was the grandfather of Bezalel (cf. 31:2; 35:30; 38:22; cf. 1 Chr. 2:19–20).[39] Thus, as Enns infers (2000: 347), there may again be some foreshadowing here of subsequent events in the book of Exodus.

11–13. The assistance of Aaron and Hur is undoubtedly signif-icant, but unfortunately the precise meaning of this, and indeed of the raised hands of Moses, is unclear. While the latter is often interpreted in terms of a praying posture (cf. 9:29),[40] such is not

---

39 Assuming, of course, that all these texts refer to the same Hur. His father, Caleb, son of Hezron (1 Chr. 2:18), is probably not to be identified with his better-known namesake whose father is listed as 'Jephunneh' (Num. 13:6).

40 Cole 1973: 136–137. Others (e.g. Noth 1962: 142) have inferred some sort of magical rite.

explicitly mentioned here; moreover, the efficacy of prayer is surely unrelated to physical stance. More likely the elevation of the staff was some kind of symbolic gesture, drawing attention to the divine power that was key to Israel's success. Quite possibly it also served as some kind of military ensign (cf. vv. 15–16), bolstering the faith and courage of those engaged in the battle below. But whatever its precise significance, this action focuses attention primarily on the hilltop and not on the battlefield, suggesting that this was where the victory was truly won. As in the earlier conflict with the Egyptians, it was through Yahweh (as symbolized by the raised staff) that Israel prevailed. Perhaps the assistance that Moses received from these others foreshadows the additional help and cooperation that would be necessary in order to accomplish this divine mission (cf. the appointment of assistant judges in ch. 18).

14. This incident is followed by the first explicit reference to Moses recording something at God's command. While there are relatively few such references in the Pentateuch (cf. 24:4; 34:27–28; Num. 33:2; Deut. 31:9, 19, 22, 24), together these attest to Moses' contribution in the compilation of at least some of the material incorporated in the final form of the Pentateuch. What Moses recorded here was evidently the first written edition of the Amalek incident. The stated rationale for such a written 'memorial' (AT) was so that Joshua, Israel's military leader, would *hear* it (i.e. presumably as the account was read out publicly) and thus remember to mete out the divinely decreed punishment on the Amalekites – eradicating all 'memory' (AT) of them in due course (cf. Deut. 25:17–19).[41]

15. Surprisingly, Yahweh's command to record this incident for posterity is followed by narrating, not Moses' obedient compliance, but rather his erecting and naming of an *altar.* However, rather than this being a spontaneous act or reflecting a narrative gap of some kind, it seems reasonable to infer that this commemorative

---

41 Unfortunately, the pun in the original between 'memorial' (*zikkārôn*) and 'memory' (*zēker*) is lost in the NIV and NLT; cf. most other English versions.

altar-building was associated in some way with Yahweh's previous directive.⁴² It is clear that this altar was built to commemorate the aforementioned victory. As it is this altar that Moses names *yhwh nissî*, it seems clear that the traditional English translation (*The LORD is my Banner*) may be somewhat misleading. While the Hebrew word can denote a 'banner', it may simply refer to a pole (i.e. like a flagstaff).⁴³ Thus understood, possibly the altar here may have been more like an obelisk, and the name undoubtedly implies that it served as an enduring symbol of the role that Yahweh (as represented by Moses' staff) had played in the routing of the Amalekites.

16. Unfortunately, this verse is particularly cryptic. The first sentence literally reads: 'Because [?] a hand/memorial is upon/against/towards the *kēs* [?] of Yahweh,⁴⁴ a battle for Yahweh

---

42 As illustrated several times in the patriarchal narratives, the erecting of (apparently) non-sacrificial altars or pillars was a means through which dramatic encounters with Yahweh were memorialized (cf. Gen. 12:7–8; 13:4, 18; 26:25; 33:20; 35:7; cf. 28:18, 22). As Hamilton (2011: 273) notes, the closest parallel to the present altar-building scenario appears to be Gideon's action recorded in Judg. 6:24.

43 Cf. Num. 21:8–9.

44 The precise nuance of nearly every word in this clause is uncertain. The initial particle (*kî*), which I have rendered 'because', could arguably serve an exclamatory function here ('Indeed!') or simply introduce the reported speech. If *yād* is translated 'hand', it is unclear who it belongs to (Moses, Yahweh or Amalek) or what its precise significance is (e.g. does it refer to the enacting of an oath, or allude to the elevated arms of Moses or the action of the Amalekites who take up arms against God?). However, while normally meaning 'hand', *yād* clearly denotes a 'monument' or 'memorial' in several OT texts (1 Sam. 15:12; 2 Sam. 18:18; Isa. 56:5; cf. Ezek. 21:19 [MT 24], where it denotes a 'signpost'), and this could arguably suit the context here also. The Hebrew preposition *'al* has a fairly wide semantic range, the intended nuance normally being determined by the immediate context. The exegetical challenges of this clause alone are thus considerable. Comparison of the Targums, LXX and Vulgate suggests that ancient translators were equally puzzled.

against Amalek from one generation to another.[45] The word *kēs* appears only here, which many (following ancient versions) take as a shortened form of *kissē'* ('throne'). However, as some translations suggest (e.g. NAB; NJB; NRSV), the problematic word (*kēs*) may be a distorted form of *nēs*, the word traditionally translated 'banner' in the previous verse. Understood as such, Moses is here elaborating on the name given to the altar, although what he intends to convey by such is still unclear. It may be some kind of war cry (cf. NABRE; NJB; NRSV), or simply a statement of fact (NAB). Whatever the precise meaning, this much is clear: the commemorative altar serves to remind all subsequent generations of Yahweh's (and thus their) attitude towards the Amalekites.

Meaning
While this was the first time that the Israelites had a more active role to play, it is clear that Moses was relying, not on military prowess, but on divine assistance. Once again, therefore, Yahweh demonstrated his ability to take care of his people. Just as he has provided them with food and water, so now he makes them victorious over those threatening to impede their progress. This victory over the Amalekites serves as an example of the military strategy Israel was to employ in future conflicts, particularly those related to the conquest of Canaan. Moreover, the fate of the Amalekites clearly serves as a warning for all those who might dare to oppose Yahweh and his plans for his people.

---

45 Whatever this means, significantly the battle is primarily between Yahweh and Amalek, just as the celebratory song of Exod. 15 depicts the earlier contest being between Yahweh and Egypt.

7. THE RESPONSE AND ADVICE OF
JETHRO (18:1–27)

Context

Some scholars question the chronology at this point in the narrative, believing this next chapter to be out of its historical or logical sequence. There are two main reasons for this: (1) the chapter seems to assume that Israel was already encamped at Mount Sinai (v. 5); (2) the chapter also assumes that at least some of the Sinai legislation had already been disclosed (v. 16). Neither argument is compelling, since the context places the Israelites *near* (but not necessarily *at*) the mountain of God (cf. 17:5–6; 19:2)[1] and has also made clear that some of Yahweh's decrees and instructions were disclosed prior to Sinai (cf. 12:24, 49; 13:9; 16:4, 28). Therefore, unless the chronology of the narrative has been deliberately inverted at this point, the family reunion narrated in

---

1   As there is no preposition before *mountain of God* in 18:5, one must be supplied in English. However, 'near' seems just as appropriate as 'at' or 'beside'.

this chapter took place while the Israelites were still at Rephidim, in close proximity to Mount Sinai (cf. 17:5–6; 18:8; 19:2). This last episode before Israel's extraordinary experience at Sinai involved Jethro, Moses' father-in-law, whose formal reintroduction may be included to remind readers of how this non-Israelite had formerly welcomed a refugee (Moses) from Egypt. One of the reasons why the narrator has preserved a detailed record of this encounter is possibly because it contrasts so markedly with the previous incident.[2] As such, perhaps both stories serve as illustrations of the unfolding of the promise in Genesis 12:3 with respect to those who bless Abraham and those who treat him with contempt.

Comment
A. Jethro's response to testimony about Yahweh (18:1–12)

One interesting feature of this episode is the fact that Jethro's status as Moses' *father-in-law* is mentioned no fewer than eight times in verses 1–12. Clearly the narrator considered this significant, even though the focus is on much more than simply a family reunion, as the almost passing reference to Zipporah and the two boys illustrates. Possibly the emphasis on Jethro's status serves to bracket Moses' mission (cf. 4:18), which is about to reach the significant milestone alluded to back in 3:12 (cf. 18:12).

1. According to this opening verse, news of Yahweh's exploits and Israel's exodus had reached as far as Midian. We are not told how Jethro obtained this information; possibly we are meant to infer that Zipporah had told him – although this would depend on whether Moses sent his family away (cf. v. 2) before or after the exodus. Alternatively, news of what had happened in Egypt may have been spread orally by caravaneers, merchants or other travellers. In this case, Jethro may have heard some of the facts, which were subsequently filled out by Moses himself (cf. v. 8). It could also be argued, however, that this first verse in chapter 18

---

2   There is considerable verbal overlap between the two episodes, which
     serves to highlight this contrast (see Enns 2000: 367).

serves as a heading, summarizing the account that is narrated in detail in the following verses. In this case, Jethro (and possibly also Zipporah) heard all about Yahweh's actions from Moses himself (cf. v. 8). Obviously, a lot depends on the degree of overlap we are meant to infer between verses 1 and 8.

2–4. The present paragraph provides the backcloth for Jethro's visit: some time previously Moses had *sent away* Zipporah and their two sons. While the verb (*šlḥ*) is later used of divorce, it seems unlikely that such is the nuance here.[3] Jethro appears to be reuniting Moses with his family, and there is no indication that they were again 'sent away' with Jethro after this reunion (cf. v. 27). Zipporah and her sons may have returned to Jethro shortly after the circumcision incident recorded in chapter 4, or at some undisclosed time between Moses' confrontation with Pharaoh and the Israelites' escape from Egyptian territory. While it is also conceivable that Moses had dispatched his family only recently, around the time they arrived in Rephidim and were already in the vicinity of Midian, this seems most unlikely (cf. vv. 2, 6).[4] However, any such attempt to reconstruct the chronology of this family separation is purely conjectural. There is obviously a narrative gap here that the author has not seen fit to fill in for us. Just as we are not told when this happened, neither are we told what prompted Moses to do so; therefore, all attempts to explain the latter are necessarily speculative.

The mention of Moses' two sons, and particularly the statements concerning the rationale for both their names, is evidently significant, especially since the information about Gershom is technically redundant (cf. 2:22). The narrator clearly wants readers to reflect again on its significance, in conjunction with this

---

3   Hamilton (2011: 275) prefers to understand *'aḥar šillûḥêhā* as 'along with her dowry'. However, as well as involving a most unusual use of the Hebrew preposition, this does not balance quite so neatly with the 'sending away' of Jethro at the end of the chapter (cf. Hamilton 2011: 290).

4   The latter seems less likely in view of the contents of Jethro's communiqué recorded in 18:6.

new information concerning Moses' other, hitherto anonymous, offspring (cf. 4:20). Both names, it seems, focus attention on Yahweh's deliverance of Moses himself (cf. 2:11–15),[5] and possibly of Israel also, now that they share in Moses' experience. Eliezer is mentioned explicitly here for the first and only time, although it is clear from Exodus 4:20 that Moses had more than one son during his protracted stay in Midian.

5–6. Given the close proximity of Rephidim to Horeb (cf. 17:5–6), reference to *the mountain of God* here does not necessarily preclude Jethro's visit taking place prior to the last leg of the Israelites' journey to Sinai (cf. 19:2). As noted above, the absence of a preposition in the original means that English translations must supply such; different options are contextually possible, including 'near'. Since Moses knew exactly where he was headed (cf. 3:12), this rendezvous near Sinai was quite possibly pre-arranged to reunite Moses with his family (v. 6).[6] In any case, Zipporah and her sons quickly recede into the background and attention is focused exclusively on Jethro, highlighting the narrator's primary reason for including this episode in his account (see below).

7–8. The formalities narrated here (v. 7) highlight the congenial relations that existed between Moses and his father-in-law, further suggesting that Moses and Zipporah had parted temporarily and amicably. Several facets of this reunion resemble the analogous reunion that had taken place earlier between Moses and another relative, his brother Aaron (cf. 4:27–28), which may reflect a chiastic symmetry between Moses' first encounter with Yahweh and the encounter about to take place on Sinai (so Enns 2000). In any case, Moses' report to Jethro, like his earlier report to Aaron

---

5   While arguably alluding to one incident in particular (i.e. the official death warrant referred to in 2:15), deliverance *from the sword of Pharaoh* (18:4) may encapsulate a range of experiences that further attest to Yahweh being his helper.

6   While a pluperfect (*Jethro had sent*) may provide a smoother transition in 18:6 (NIV; Hamilton), it is only necessary if the previous verse is taken to suggest that Jethro and the others had already made their way into the Israelite camp.

(4:28), is theocentric in focus, highlighting Yahweh's deeds rather than his own. Unless 18:1 is simply a summation of the following events, there is clearly some overlap between Moses' testimony here and what Jethro knew already. It is possible, however, that Moses' report focuses more on what had taken place *after* the Israelites left Egypt, rather than on the exodus itself or the events that led up to it. Understood in this way, Moses is filling in the gaps in Jethro's knowledge – primarily by relating Yahweh's victory over Egypt at the Sea and his care for the Israelites up to and including their encounter with the Amalekites.

9–11. Contrary to scholarly theories such as the Kenite hypothesis,[7] the biblical testimony suggests that Jethro obtained his knowledge of Yahweh from Moses rather than vice versa. On hearing Moses' testimony about all that Yahweh had done, Jethro's reaction was one of jubilation and praise (vv. 9–10). Employing one of the book's key recurring motifs (cf. 5:2; 6:7; 7:5; 8:10; 9:29), Jethro's confession (*Now I know* . . ., v. 11) has heightened theological significance: Jethro is here acknowledging what others (such as Pharaoh and the Amalekites) have initially failed but eventually been forced to acknowledge – the supremacy of Israel's God.[8] As Enns (2000: 369) suggests, this highlights the central point of this story and why it has been included here:

---

7   According to the Kenite hypothesis, Moses had learnt about Yahwism from his father-in-law, a Midianite *priest*, and introduced this new form of religion to the Israelites. Admittedly, it is possible to infer that Jethro is merely coming to a fuller appreciation of the deity he already worshipped. Significantly, however, 'Yahweh' is not mentioned explicitly, either by or to Jethro, until now (cf. 4:18). Indeed, even here, after Moses' testimony and Jethro's personal acknowledgment (vv. 8–11), there is a marked preference for 'God' in all references to Israel's deity (cf. vv. 15–16, 19, 21, 23), which is somewhat strange if Jethro is a fully-fledged Yahwist.

8   Technically speaking, Jethro's confession (just like Israel's in 15:11) is henotheistic: Yahweh is acknowledged as the supreme deity, rather than the only one (monotheism).

Midian is the one nation that gives a proper response to God's deliverance of his own people. God's dealings with Pharaoh were so that 'my name might be proclaimed in all the earth' (9:16). The Hebrew word for 'proclaim' is *sipper*, which is used also in 18:8 (translated 'told' in the NIV). But it is Jethro, not Pharaoh or the Amalekites, who gives the proper response: praise.

12. As well as his verbal response to Moses' testimony, Jethro engaged in a voluntary, and apparently spontaneous, sacrificial ritual, presenting a *burnt offering* and *sacrifices* to God.[9] Since the former was entirely consumed on the altar, it appears that the *sacrifices* refer in particular to 'fellowship offerings', the only sacrifices that could be consumed by those who offered them (cf. Lev. 3). The fact that Jethro '*took* [i.e. presented] these offerings to God' (AT) may well suggest that a non-Israelite priest officiated at this ritual worship (although cf. Lev. 12:8). If so, this is hardly remarkable, since Israel's official priesthood had not yet been set up, and Jethro has expressed some kind of Yahwistic belief. Indeed, it is quite possible that the ritual here described constituted a covenant meal of some kind (i.e. that which ratified the establishment of a covenant between the parties involved; cf. 24:9–11; also Gen. 26:26–31; 31:43–54); as such, it was the ritual means through which Jethro expressed his affiliation with Yahweh and the Israelites, and through which the Israelites (represented by Aaron and Israel's elders) acknowledged their fellowship with Jethro. Although the text does not say so explicitly, the radical change in Jethro's theological convictions, together with his immediate participation in the worship of Yahweh, may thus imply that he was now, at least in some measure (cf. p. 209 n. 8), a worshipper of Yahweh. If this is indeed the case, Jethro serves here as an important model of hope for the nations (cf. Gen. 12:3).

---

9   No distinction between 'God' and 'Yahweh' is here intended, any more than such is implied in 24:10–11. Even so, the preference for 'God' over 'Yahweh' is again remarkable.

B. Jethro's advice to Moses (18:13–27)

The second main part of this chapter records a further response of Jethro, this time to the prevailing situation within the Israelite camp, as Moses attempts to settle all the people's disputes by himself. Similar episodes are recorded in Numbers 11:16–17 and Deuteronomy 1:9–18, which source critics tend to identify as 'doublets' (variants of the same episode deriving from different sources). Others attempt to harmonize the three accounts in terms of at least two distinct events, the one described here in Exodus 18, and a subsequent delegation of responsibility that took place later, after Israel's experience at Mount Sinai. In support of this, it may be noted that the parallels are far fewer, and Jethro's role is never mentioned in the Numbers passage. Moreover, while the latter is also true of the Deuteronomy passage, the timing of the incident related there is vaguer ('at that time'), so arguably it is that account which is out of chronological sequence. However, it is possible that Jethro's advice (given before Sinai) was implemented in stages (cf. 18:24–26), which would easily explain his absence in the otherwise similar episodes.[10] Understood thus, there is no compelling reason to question the chronological sequence of the Jethro encounters recorded here in Exodus 18.

13–14. There was nothing unusual about Moses, as leader, assuming the role of legal arbiter. Any such leader would have had such a responsibility in the ancient world. Moreover, this would have been the only model with which the people would have been familiar: apparently the Egyptian pharaoh would regularly make himself available for anyone to approach him in open 'court'. However, Moses' caseload was clearly unsustainable: the litigants *stood round him from morning till evening*, and even with this, apparently justice was not being served very efficiently (cf. v. 23). It was thus the logistics of Moses' administrative load rather than his role

---

10 Explaining the 'discrepancies' between these texts in terms of 'changes, deletions and additions' that might be expected over a forty-year hiatus (Hamilton 2011: 290) seems to raise more significant questions than it answers.

as judge which was the focus of Jethro's query: 'Why do you sit alone as judge?' (AT).

15–16. Moses' explanation of the current judicial system is primarily theological. It operated in this way because the litigants wanted to 'enquire of God' and because Moses could 'make known God's decrees and instructions' (AT).[11] As the mention of the latter again makes clear (cf. 15:26; 16:25–26), at least some of the law promulgated at Sinai had already been disclosed beforehand: presumably some such 'judgments' decreed by Moses are codified in the case laws contained in 21:1 – 23:19, the *Book of the Covenant* (24:7).[12] In any case, it was on the basis of his unique revelatory authority (i.e. his role as prophet) that Moses felt obliged to hear each individual case himself and thus act alone.

17–18. Despite the theological rationale put forward, Jethro remained convinced that the present policy could not possibly be in the best interests of either Moses or Israel, and, by implication, was not in God's best interests either. The fact that Jethro forthrightly rejects it as *not good* (cf. Gen. 2:18) – and this negative evaluation is allowed to stand unqualified by the narrator – suggests that the judicial system set up by Moses was probably ad hoc and without divine sanction. Jethro's argument was essentially pragmatic (i.e. 'the present arrangement is not really working and you are only wearing yourselves out'), highlighting the fact that the current one-man judicial system was impractical and unsustainable.

19–20. Significantly, Jethro's proposal addresses the theological problem that Moses has raised and not just the logistical concerns already underlined. Given his unique role as Israel's representative, Moses must continue to bring their disputes to God, and – (implicitly) in accordance with the revelation received – teach the people how to conduct themselves. There is no suggestion

---

11   While the use of the verb *dāraš* rather than *šā'al* for 'enquiring of God' may imply that Moses is functioning more in a prophetic than a priestly role (Hamilton 2011: 286–287), the difference here is arguably semantic.

12   The precise parameters of this *Book of the Covenant* will be discussed below.

that the replacement system will expedite justice by taking God out of the picture. Rather, God's *decrees and instructions* are still the foundation upon which Israel's judicial system is to be built.

21–22. The more innovative aspect of Jethro's proposal involved the establishment of a judicial hierarchy through the selection and appointment of suitably qualified (i.e. capable, God-fearing and honest)[13] officials to handle *simple cases* – cases that were straight-forward, presumably because relevant legislation already existed. Unlike Moses, these officials would be constantly available to serve as judges for each population level. This division of labour would thus radically reduce Moses' docket, by freeing him up to adjudicate only the more *difficult case*[s] (presumably those for which no case law existed already).[14]

23. It is not quite clear whether Jethro was simply offering Moses a piece of sage advice or speaking himself with divine authority. The fact that Moses *listened . . . and did everything he* [i.e. Jethro] *said* (v. 24) may admittedly lend some credence to the suggestion that this was more than simply Jethro's personal opinion, since this language is most often used in relation to Yahweh in Exodus.

The phrase *and God so commands* may be read as part of the 'if' clause (so NIV), part of the 'then' clause (so ESV), or as an inter-jection adding punch to the 'advice' (so NRSV). Possibly, since Jethro was a priest, he had personal experience in such matters;[15] this would also explain the detailed nature of his advice, and his confidence that it would be much more efficient than the present system. While grammatically possible, it seems rather unlikely that this Midianite priest would be giving Moses divine directives.

---

13 They were literally to be 'men of strength, fearers of God, men of integrity, haters of corruption'.

14 Rather than functioning simply as a court of appeal, Moses presumably functioned more as a supreme court establishing the law where there was no obvious legal precedent.

15 Admittedly, this assumes that the role of this Midianite priest was analogous in some respects to that of an Israelite high priest, to whom people could come for a priestly 'torah' (or ruling).

This being so, it is probably best to interpret Jethro's words here in accord with his earlier wish that God [*might*] *be with* [*him*] (v. 19).

24–26. Whatever the source of Jethro's advice, its wisdom and the fact that it did indeed have God's approval must have seemed fairly obvious. This is underlined by the way Moses' implementation of Jethro's counsel is reported in verses 25–26 almost verbatim. Perhaps there is a subtle indication here that Israel's laws, like Israel's judicial system, were not necessarily introduced by Moses *de novo*, but were informed by the best 'worldly wisdom' that was currently available (cf. the similarities [and differences] highlighted later in this commentary between other Ancient Near Eastern laws and many of those in Exodus 21 – 23).

27. Since only Jethro is mentioned, it seems fair to assume that Zipporah, Gershom and Eliezer remained with Moses. While Zipporah is never mentioned again, Gershom's descendants apparently served as priests (cf. Judg. 18:30) and the sons of both sons are listed in Chronicles (cf. 1 Chr. 23:16–17). We are not told when (or why) Moses married his Cushite wife (Num. 12:1). Presumably this refers to a wife other than Zipporah, although some ancient and modern commentators have suggested otherwise. An identification with Zipporah is possible only if 'Cush' in Numbers 12:1 refers to 'Cushan' (which parallels Midian in Hab. 3:7). However, it is unclear why Miriam would object to Zipporah only at this late stage, and the immediate context makes it more likely that this Cushite woman belonged to the 'mixed multitude' (Exod. 12:38, AT) that had recently caused problems (Num. 11:4).[16] Accordingly, it is impossible to infer anything from Numbers with respect to Zipporah.

This is also the final appearance of Jethro in the Pentateuchal narrative.[17] Having served as a positive model for the nations and helped pave the way for the successful implementation of Yahweh's statutes and judgments, Jethro departs to his own country, and so the stage is set for the climactic moment of Israel's journey: the encounter with Yahweh on Mount Sinai.

---

16   For further discussion, see Davies 1995: 118–119; Yamauchi 2004: 35–75.

17   However, see comment on 3:1.

Meaning

Following hard on the heels of Amalek's incursion and defeat, this chapter focuses on a more positive response to Yahweh and his people. Like Amalek, Jethro is apparently a distant relative of Israel (cf. Gen. 25:1–4). However, it is his connection to Moses that is repeatedly highlighted in both parts of the chapter (cf. vv. 1, 2, 5, 6, 7, 8, 12 [twice], 14, 15 [MT], 17, 24, 27). Rather than emphasizing his foreignness (which might arguably have been better served by repeating the information about him being *the priest of Midian* [v. 1]), his status as Moses' *father-in-law* emphasizes his ties of kinship. Such ties, however, ran much deeper than simply relations through marriage. Rather, having heard all about Yahweh's action on Israel's behalf, Jethro both properly acknowledged Yahweh's supremacy and formally affiliated himself with his people. Moreover, he took a genuine interest in their (and not just his son-in-law's) well-being (cf. v. 18), helping facilitate an important part of their responsibility as Yahweh's redeemed people: compliance with Yahweh's decrees and statutes. Jethro is thus the positive counterpart to both Pharaoh and Amalek (who opposed Yahweh's purposes), and a personal embodiment of a primary goal within Exodus: that the nations would come to know Yahweh. Thus, as Carpenter contends (1997: 92), this chapter serves as a theological linchpin of the book:

> It helps to emphasize and make clear two ways of knowing Yahweh, that are indeed complementary: (1) the knowledge of Yahweh available in and through the event of the exodus itself and its recitation . . . and (2) the knowledge of Yahweh found in the way . . . of Yahweh – his Torah.

PART 3: REVELATION AT SINAI
(19:1 – 40:38)

The third and largest part of Exodus focuses on the events that took place after Israel's arrival at Mount Sinai. The first section (19:1 – 24:18) narrates the revelation of the covenant law and the ratification of the Mosaic covenant; the next (25:1 – 31:18) focuses on how ongoing fellowship between a holy God and his sinful people could be maintained: God thus discloses his blueprint for the tabernacle, as well as instructions for the clothing and consecration of its priestly personnel. After the implementation of all this is temporarily derailed by Israel's idolatrous breach of the covenant (32:1 – 34:35), the closing chapters (35:1 – 40:38) focus on the tabernacle's construction and the realization of one of the stated goals for the exodus (cf. 29:46).

All the events narrated in this last part of Exodus took place in a period of around ten months (cf. 19:1; 40:2, 17).

8. PREPARATIONS FOR COVENANT-MAKING WITH GOD (19:1–25)

Context

Many scholars consider the next block of material in Exodus (19:1 – 24:18) to be quite disjointed, but structurally and thematically these six chapters clearly belong together.[1] In terms of structure, a chiastic arrangement has been suggested by some,[2] whereas others discern significant parallels between two main blocks of speech (19:2b–8a and 20:21 – 24:3).[3] But regardless of how its arrangement

---

1 For a very insightful and helpful discussion, see Alexander 2022: 302–330.

2 E.g. Sprinkle (2004: 242):

 A *Narrative*: the covenant offered (19:3–25)

 B *Laws (general)*: the Decalogue (20:1–17)

 C *Narrative*: the people's fear (20:18–21)

 B' *Laws (specific)*: the Book of the Covenant (20:22 – 23:33)

 A' *Narrative*: the covenant accepted (24:1–11)

3 E.g. Alexander 2022: 304; see also Williamson 2008: 94–95.

is perceived, this is arguably a unified block of text with a uniform focus: the ratification of the covenant between Yahweh and Israel. As such, these chapters constitute an important watershed in Exodus. Not only is a major milestone finally reached, but attention now shifts from what God has done for Israel to what he demands of Israel in response. Thus, here and in the chapters that follow Yahweh spells out his plans for Israel, elaborating to some degree the 'service' of which he spoke in the earlier part of the book.

Chapter 19 takes us a significant step closer to the climax towards which the narrative has been moving ever since 3:12. It introduces this new narrative block by setting the scene for the revelation of the law (chs. 20–23) and the ratification of the covenant (ch. 24). Each takes place in the context of an awe-inspiring manifestation of Yahweh's presence (i.e. a theophany) on Mount Sinai. In preparation for this theophany, the purpose of which is stated in 19:9, Israel must first embrace the covenant in principle (vv. 3–8), and Moses must implement a number of divinely decreed measures to ensure the people's safety and survival (vv. 10–25).

Additional note: the chronological sequence of Exodus 19 – 24

From the canonical arrangement of the text most readers will likely infer that the events narrated in Exodus 19 – 24 unfolded in the following chronological sequence: (1) Moses hears and transmits Yahweh's message about his plan for Israel (19:3–8); (2) Moses communicates Yahweh's message concerning the forthcoming theophany (19:9–15); (3) Yahweh commences his descent and manifests his presence on Sinai, during which a dialogue with Moses (still located at the foot of Sinai) takes place (19:16–19); (4) Yahweh summons Moses up the mountain, where he instructs him to go back down and warn everyone, including Israel's priests, against breaching the prescribed boundary line (19:20–24); (5) Moses does as instructed, and the Decalogue is proclaimed (19:25 – 20:17); (6) the terrified people implore Moses to mediate Yahweh's words to them, so Moses alone approaches the theophanic cloud to receive further instructions from Yahweh

(20:18—21); (7) Yahweh declares to Moses the detailed stipulations of the covenant (20:22 — 23:33) and instructions for his next ascent (24:1—2); (8) Moses descends, and proclaims and records these stipulations, to which the people have given their assent (24:3—4a); (9) the covenant is solemnly ratified by a blood ritual (24:4b—8); (10) a delegation of leaders then ascends with Moses to meet with God (24:9—11; cf. 24:1); (11) Moses ascends to God at the top of Sinai (cf. 24:2),[4] where he remains for forty days (24:12—18) and receives instructions regarding the tabernacle (chs. 25—31).

This linear sequence, however, has been questioned by numerous scholars, whether along source-critical or narrative-critical lines. The former seeks to explain perceived tensions by the composite (and thus disjointed) nature of the text, whereas the latter accounts for its more enigmatic features by the presence of literary devices such as 'resumptive repetition' (Chirichigno 1987).[5] Either way, the narrative sequence inferred from a linear/chronological reading of the material is discounted.

The canonical text is not necessarily so incoherent as often suggested (see Williamson 2008). Moreover, hypothetical rearrangements of the material could inadvertently obscure its theological significance (e.g. Moses' repeated movements serve to highlight his role as mediator). Even so, there are arguably some indicators that a linear sequence is not always intended (cf. 19:8b, 9b). This, and the possibility that some recourse to 'flashback' may be warranted (e.g. 20:18—20; cf. 19:16), cautions against rejecting any non-chronological reading of the material. Nevertheless,

---

4   While Moses is accompanied part of the way by Joshua (24:13), it appears that Moses alone entered the theophanic cloud (24:15—18; cf. 32:17—18, where Joshua's apparent ignorance of the conversation that had just taken place between Yahweh and Moses implies that this had taken place further up the mountain than Joshua was permitted to go).

5   For Chirichigno (1987), ch. 19 comprises three discrete sequences: 19:3—8b, 19:8c—20b and 19:20c—25, some of the details of which are unpacked by 'resumptive repetitions' (i.e. 20:18—21 [including 20:1—17; 22:1 — 23:33] and 24:1—9a [including 24:9—18]) which serve to underline that the covenant is conditioned by the people's obedience.

some such reconstructions seem insufficiently anchored to the text itself.

Building on Chirichigno's suggestion that literary flashbacks are interspersed in the narrative to elaborate more concisely narrated events, Sailhamer (2009: 374–399) proposed the following reconstruction of the chronological data: (1) Yahweh's plans are disclosed for Israel to be a kingdom of priests (19:3–8); (2) stipulations for the anticipated mountain-top meeting between Yahweh and all Israel are disclosed and implemented (19:10–15); (3) in response to the actual theophany, the terror-stricken Israelites refuse to ascend Sinai, and insist that Moses go in their place while they remain at the foot of the blazing mountain (19:16–18; cf. 20:18–21); (4) from there, Israel witnesses the dialogue between Moses and Yahweh, during which the following are disclosed to Moses (who has gone up Sinai): covenant stipulations (i.e. the Decalogue and the 'Book of the Covenant'), along with the need for priestly mediators (19:19–24; cf. 24:1–2); (5) Moses returns to the people at the foot of Sinai and declares what Yahweh has said (19:25 – 20:17; cf. 24:3).[6]

Sailhamer's reconstruction is based on observations which may help explain some of the more opaque features of the text; namely, the unexpected shift in focus between Israel as a kingdom *of priests* and as a kingdom *with priests*; the relationship between the qualified prohibition of 19:10–13 and the absolute prohibition of 19:20–24; the connection between the reaction recounted in 19:16 and in 20:18–21; the connection between 19:20–24, 24:1–2 and 24:9–18; the content of Yahweh's dialogue with Moses in 19:19 (i.e. both the words of 20:1–17 and the instructions of 20:22 – 23:33). However, a number of valid objections can be raised: (1) clearly it was Yahweh's intention from the beginning that Moses would function as covenant mediator and that his unique experience on Sinai would

---

6   Following midrashic tradition (Exodus Rabbah), Sailhamer (2009: 399)
     seems to suggest that the instructions for building the tabernacle are
     also out of chronological sequence (allegedly belonging after the golden
     calf incident). However, this seems unnecessary and rather unlikely (cf.
     24:12–18; 32:1–2, 7–8).

validate this role in the sight of the watching Israelites;[7] (2) given the size of the Israelite population,[8] it seems unlikely that Yahweh ever anticipated a meeting with more than a representative group up the mountain; (3) while supporting his reconstructed reading in part, the Hebrew grammar and syntax is not quite so conclusive as Sailhamer suggests.[9] Even so, it is possible to adopt some of Sailhamer's analysis without embracing all of his conclusions – such as his bifurcation of the Abrahamic and Sinaitic covenants, and his extremely negative evaluation of law-giving in connection with the latter. Admittedly, identifying resumptive repetition is more an art than a science, so any proposed rearrangement of the narrative threads warrants careful scrutiny. Nevertheless, as Sailhamer suggests, the canonical sequence of Exodus 19 – 24 does leave several issues unclear: What did Yahweh say to Moses in 19:19? Why was the additional warning of 19:20–24 necessary? When was Aaron to accompany Moses up the mountain (19:24)? Is 20:1–17 direct or reported speech, and how does 20:18–21 relate to it? If Yahweh's *words* have already been declared (20:1–17), why does Moses need to reiterate them in 24:3?[10] The answers to such questions clearly impinge on the interpretation of this very significant section of Exodus. We must therefore beware lest conservative blinkers blind us to reading strategies that sharpen rather than obscure the text's overall coherence.

---

7   Sailhamer's analysis seems to pay insufficient attention to the signifi-
    cance of 19:9 in the chapter as a whole.
8   This point holds even if a much smaller population than that implied
    by the text (cf. 12:37) is conceded: it is hard to envisage even tens of
    thousands ascending part way up Sinai together.
9   E.g. An *X-qatal* verbal clause would seem more appropriate in some
    of the places where an alleged 'flashback' or introduction to reported
    speech actually employs a *wayyiqtol*, which normally suggests sequential
    progression.
10 This assumes, however, that Yahweh's *words* in 24:3 refer to the
    Decalogue and not Yahweh's straightforward commands (rather than
    various case *laws*) within the Book of the Covenant (20:22 – 23:33).

Comment
A. Encampment at Sinai and Israel's 'declaration of intent' (19:1–9)

1–2. Although it is not exactly clear when they arrived at Sinai,[11] the Israelites remained there for almost a year (cf. Num. 10:11). The amount of narrative space devoted to what took place during this period is a clear indication of Sinai's significance within the Pentateuch as a whole. Despite the uncertainty over its precise location (see Introduction 4c, 'The route of the exodus'), it seems that its whereabouts remained known for several centuries at least (cf. 1 Kgs 19:8). The biblical narrator, however, is clearly more interested in recounting Israel's experience at Sinai than mapping out its geographical coordinates.

3. As the people encamped at the foot of the mountain, Moses made his initial ascent.[12] Apparently, however, he did not ascend to the summit on this occasion (cf. 24:15–18), since *the LORD called to him from the mountain* – presumably indicating the top of the mountain (cf. 24:1–2). Moses is tasked with communicating the essence of Yahweh's proposed covenant with Israel,[13] through which their unique relationship will be formalized by means of an enacted bilateral oath (cf. 24:3–8). Rather than establishing Israel as the people of God (cf. 3:7, 10; 5:23), the covenant formally ratifies their relationship, analogous to a modern marriage ceremony (for more on this, see Williamson 2007).

4. Significantly (cf. also 20:2), Yahweh prefaces the people's obligation to keep this covenant with a reminder of his own actions on Israel's behalf – 'a highly compressed account of

---

11 The Hebrew noun may mean 'month' or 'new moon', hence the subsequent 'on this day' (AT) could refer to either the 'first' or the 'fifteenth' day of the month.

12 For the significance of Moses' numerous ascents and descents, see Arichea 1989; cf. also Williamson 2008.

13 The synonymous parallelism in v. 3b ('say to the house of Jacob, declare to the sons of Israel', AT) draws attention to the significance of what immediately follows.

Israel's threefold experience to date' (Davies 2004: 38): *what I did to Egypt, and how I carried you on eagles' wings and brought you to myself.* The first clause obviously alludes to Yahweh's humiliation of the Egyptians through the sequence of supernatural disasters and the destruction of their elite chariot force at the Re(e)d Sea. The next clause, portraying Yahweh as an eagle carrying her young, encompasses both the deliverance of the Israelites and the first stage of their wilderness itinerary – the journey from Egypt to Sinai. Similar ornithological imagery is employed in Deuteronomy 32:10-12, where the emphasis seems to be on divine protection (see Peels 1994). Davies (2004: 39) quite rightly dismisses any idea that the fledging Israelites are learning to 'fly for themselves' as they become less dependent on God. The key point in both texts is that Israel's rescue and survival had been facilitated by Yahweh's action, intervention and protection. As Isaiah would later observe, unlike mute idols whose devotees must carry them, Yahweh carries his people (cf. Isa. 46:3-4). As the final clause indicates, this journey was not aimless. Rather, Yahweh had a clear goal in mind – which was not just to fulfil the sign he had earlier given to Moses (3:12), but, more importantly, to bring Israel to this close encounter with himself: Yahweh had brought them out of Egypt so that he would dwell among them (cf. 29:46). It is to these gracious actions of Yahweh that Israel is now called upon to respond. Thus, while the Sinai covenant is certainly bilateral, the obedience and covenant-keeping that Yahweh stipulates in the next verse is evidently not designed to secure Israel's salvation (which was achieved through the exodus), but to explain how the nation should 'serve' Yahweh and his purpose in the way that he intended.[14]

---

14 Contra Sailhamer (2009: 379), the faithful obedience on view here seems to anticipate the covenant stipulations that are about to be disclosed (cf. Exod. 20 – 23); even the Abrahamic covenant incorporated stipulations (cf. Gen. 17:1, 9–10; 18:19; 22:18; 26:5), therefore it is somewhat specious to pit the Abrahamic and Mosaic covenants against each other on the basis of 'faith' versus 'law'. The same may be said of Sailhamer's attempt to negate the Mosaic legislation on the basis of Jer. 7:22–23 and Ezek. 20:19–25.

5. As evident from the grammatical syntax of this verse (i.e.
'So now, if you indeed obey my voice and keep my covenant, then
. . .'), Israel's covenant obligations obviously impinge on Yahweh's
stated purpose for Israel; so, in that sense, the Mosaic covenant is
clearly conditional.

According to this verse and the next, Yahweh's plan for Israel
was twofold: it involved a unique privilege, and it entailed a special
responsibility. The former is set forth in verse 5. Israel's special
significance (as compared with the other nations) is reflected
in its depiction as God's *treasured possession* (Heb. *sĕgullâ*), a word
that sometimes denotes valued personal property (cf. 1 Chr. 29:3;
Eccl. 2:8, where it refers to a king's private treasure). Elsewhere
in the Old Testament (Deut. 7:6; 14:2; 26:18; Ps. 135:4; Mal. 3:17)
the term is used metaphorically, as here, to depict Israel's unique
status before God. The rest of verse 5, along with verse 6, further
explains Israel's unique status vis-à-vis the nations. The precise
meaning of the last clause in 19:5, however, is debatable (cf.
ESV; NIV; NRSV). The main problem concerns the nuance of the
Hebrew particle (*kî*) in the present context. The following options
are all possible:

1 Causal, providing the rationale for Israel's special status
('because all the earth is mine');
2 Concessive, qualifying Israel's special status ('although all the
earth is mine . . .');
3 Explanatory, elucidating the statement about Israel's status
('for all the earth is mine, but you will be . . .').

Adopting the causal interpretation, Fretheim infers from this
'a mission that encompasses God's purposes for the entire world.
*Israel is commissioned to be God's people on behalf of the earth which is
God's*' (1991a: 212; emphasis his).[15] However, the third interpre-

---

15 Similarly, Wright 2021: 340–344. A missional interpretation is also
advocated by DeRouchie (2017: 233), who defends this conclusion
through a distinctive syntactical analysis of Exod. 19:5–6, which he
translates: 'And now, if you will indeed listen at my voice and keep

tation above is arguably more in keeping with the Hebrew syntax (Williamson 2008: 101).[16] From the disjunctive conjunction at the beginning of verse 6, as well as the chiastic arrangement of verses 5b–6a, Davies (2004) cogently maintains that the second two lines simply unpack the first two, thus highlighting the privileged status that would be enjoyed by Israel in comparison to the rest of the world:

A   You will be my special possession
B   from all the peoples
B'   for all the earth is mine
A'   *but* you, you will be my priestly kingdom and holy nation (AT).

Thus understood, rather than offering an explanation or rationale for Israel's divine election, the last part of verse 5, along with verse 6, simply provides a fuller account of Israel's unique status.

6. By obeying God fully and keeping his covenant Israel will be a 'priestly kingdom' (AT) and a *holy nation.*[17] If *kingdom* is roughly synonymous with *nation*, as seems reasonable to infer, the second

---

my covenant *and be my treasured possession from all the peoples*, for all the earth is mine, *then you will be for me a kingdom of priests and a holy nation*' (emphasis added). However, as Gehrig (2024: 126 n. 75) points out, this is 'unlikely as it is rare for a noun to be preceded by a *vav* of apodosis . . . Furthermore, the parallel constructions in 19:5b (וִהְיִיתֶם לִי סְגֻלָּה) and 19:6a (תִּהְיוּ־לִי מַמְלֶכֶת) point to understanding the apodosis as beginning in 19:5b with both clauses indicating what Israel will become to Yahweh if they obey him and keep his covenant: a treasured possession and a kingdom of priests.'

16 For detailed discussion and critique, see Davies 2004: 55–60.

17 While the translation and interpretation of the latter is relatively straightforward, the same cannot be said of the unique Hebrew phrase *mamleket kōhănîm* ('priestly kingdom'), as attested by ancient citations (cf. 1 Pet. 2:9; Rev. 1:6; 5:10; 20:6), contemporary translations and scholarly debate (see Williamson 2008: 102–103; for more detailed analysis, see Davies 2004: 63–68).

word in each phrase denotes the kind of kingdom/nation that God is calling Israel to be (or become): priestly and holy. For several interpreters the concept of a 'priestly kingdom' implies a missional responsibility of some sort (i.e. like priests, Israel had a responsibility to teach/instruct others, i.e. the surrounding nations).[18] However, there are no obvious grounds in the text for restricting this priestly concept to the idea of mediating the knowledge of God to others. Rather, it seems more likely that it is a distinctive priestly *status* that is in view here: just as Israel's priests were distinct from the rest of the community, so Israel as a nation would be distinct from the other nations. Thus understood, 'priestly kingdom' and 'holy nation' are most likely overlapping expressions of the same principal idea: the notion of Israel's consecrated national status. God is thus holding out the prospect of a priestly or consecrated status to all his people, a status normally restricted in Ancient Near Eastern society to a religious elite. Through obeying God fully by keeping his covenant, Israel would thus become a nation distinct from all others. Like a priestly elite, the entire nation would live consecrated lives of service in the presence of their God. This ideal for Israel clearly foreshadows the classical Reformed doctrine of the priesthood of all believers: the insistence that every Christian has direct access to God through Christ and has been called to a life of devoted service to God.

By actually living such dedicated lives before God, the Israelites would also be expressing God's values and norms to the surrounding nations, thus advancing the missional mandate encapsulated in the ancestral promise (cf. Gen. 12:3; 18:18–19). As suggested by the New Testament application of the terminology to Christian readers (1 Pet. 2:5–9; cf. Rev. 1:6; 5:10; 20:6), a similar responsibility belongs to Israel's covenant heirs.

7–8. While one might infer from *all the words* something more substantial than what is recorded in verses 4–6, this may

---

18 Davies (2004) flatly denies this, rejecting the functional interpretation of Israel's special status in preference to a purely ontological interpretation.

simply be a means of emphasizing that Moses communicated verbatim what Yahweh had said, to which the Israelites unanimously gave their consent.[19] The latter may seem somewhat premature or naïve,[20] given their relative ignorance of the details of such covenant commitment at this stage. However, it is clear from the preceding chapters (esp. Exod. 18) that some of these stipulations were already familiar prior to Sinai. In any case, the Israelites' avowed commitment here is better understood as a 'declaration of intent' (Bruckner 2008: 174) – formally expressing their willingness to enter into the aforementioned covenant with Yahweh. Accordingly, their later consent (cf. 24:3, 7) is not simply a reiteration of this initial response, but an *informed* verbal commitment to all their covenant obligations, including those that had been disclosed to Moses and were recorded by him in the Book of the Covenant.

9. Yahweh's presence would again be made manifest by a cloud (cf. 13:21–22; 16:10), only this theophany would also involve some aural revelation. The stated purpose of this forthcoming theophany is to authenticate Moses as mediator of God's revelation for his people and thus encourage their ongoing trust in Moses as God's appointed leader. Such a prospect is further underscored by Israel's initial response, which Moses now reports to Yahweh.[21] As noted above, it seems clear from this verse that it was always Yahweh's intention to speak directly to Moses alone, but for the Israelites to witness and draw important lessons from this.

B. Consecration of the people (19:10–15)

10–15. The anticipated theophany necessitated adequate

---

19 Either the elders (v. 7) did so on behalf of the people, or else the people did so once the elders had set before them the message delivered by Moses.
20 So Calvin, cited in Sailhamer 2009: 381.
21 Rather than narrating strictly sequential events, 19:8b seems to anticipate the action of 19:9b. In any case, the effect of the repetition is to underscore that this was indeed the desired response and that the formal ratification of the covenant could proceed.

preparation to avoid contaminating God's holy presence; any
form of ritual impurity would impede immediate access to God
(cf. 3:5). In Israel's case two actions were required, foreshadowing
the subsequent legislation in Leviticus: the washing of clothes
(vv. 10, 14; Lev. 11:24–28) and temporary sexual abstinence (v. 15;
Lev. 15:16–18; cf. Deut. 23:10–11; 1 Sam. 21:1–6). Moses appears to
have drawn the latter inference from Yahweh's explicit command
to wash their clothes. As Hamilton (2011) notes, the unusual noun
for *clothes* most likely alludes to the previous plundering of the
Egyptians (cf. 3:22; 12:35); thus it is probably a ritual removal of any
trace of Egyptian uncleanness that is primarily in view here. The
prohibition on intercourse most likely ensures that their 'cleansed'
ritual status is not jeopardized prior to the actual theophany. In
other contexts bathing (cf. 29:4; Lev. 14:8–9; 15:5–27; 16:28; 17:15;
cf. also Exod. 30:17–21) or the application of oil/blood (28:41; 29:7,
21, 36) is explicitly involved in consecration ceremonies. While
neither is explicitly mentioned here, bathing may well be implied
(cf. the use of the Hithpael verb in 19:22 and its association with
'bathing' in 2 Sam. 11:2–4) – especially since sexual abstinence
was most likely intended to eradicate the trace of semen from the
body. In any case, ritual washing and sexual abstinence were the
means by which the people were to be ready for the theophany.

   The strict limits imposed around the mountain (v. 12; cf. v. 23)
emphasized Yahweh's absolute holiness (cf. 3:5). The life of anyone
or anything that trespassed on this holy ground would thus be
forfeit. As is clear from the very human means of execution (v. 13;
cf. vv. 22, 24),[22] this exclusion zone was initially enforced by the
Israelites themselves, although actual physical contact with any
trespassers was strictly forbidden – presumably on the grounds
that the same penalty would necessarily apply to those in direct
contact with the offending parties. The possibility that the people
may actually 'ascend' (AT) the mountain (v. 13b) seems to strike
a somewhat discordant note; thus some interpreters restrict this

---

22 According to Milgrom (1970: 5–7), the use of the Hophal rather than the
    Qal further indicates that the executioners are humans, although such a
    distinction applies mainly within the Pentateuch.

'ascent' to the foot of the mountain (so NIV's *approach*), or find here an allusion to the subsequent ascent of the people's representatives who were later permitted to go part of the way up Mount Sinai (cf. v. 24; 24:1, 9). Alternatively, Sailhamer (2009: 383–392) infers from this that initially everyone would have been permitted to ascend once God had given the signal to do so – but such permission was revoked when the Israelites refused to come any closer than the foot of the mountain. In support of this, Sailhamer notes that (1) the plural verb in Exodus 3:12b anticipates an assembly worshipping *on* Sinai; (2) the preposition in 19:13 suggests going up 'on' (not 'to') the mountain; (3) the statement in 19:12 is a temporal rather than an absolute prohibition;[23] (4) the prohibition is clearly qualified by the ram's horn signal (v. 13b).[24] However, while these are valid observations, a representative body seems more logistically plausible and is more in keeping with the Pentateuch's 'inclusiveness' elsewhere. In any case (contra LXX's 'when the voices and trumpets and cloud *depart* from off the mountain', v. 13), the blast of the ram's horn in the MT clearly introduces a new and contrasting scenario (cf. v. 16), in which the previous warning was at least temporarily suspended.

C. Yahweh's descent on Sinai and instructions to Moses (19:16–25)

16–19. As anticipated (cf. v. 11), Yahweh's descent on Sinai – signified by an awe-inspiring audio-visual display of theophanic sights ('lightning flashes' [AT] and *thick cloud*) and sounds ('thunderclaps' [AT] and *trumpet blast*) – began at daybreak on the third day (v. 16). The sound of the trumpet (cf. v. 13) signalled that it was now time to approach and ascend the mountain (v. 17),[25] where

---

23 As Sailhamer observes, an absolute prohibition would require 'from' (*min*) before an infinitive form of the verb (cf. Targum), or the negative particle 'lest' (*pen*) before 'you will go up'.

24 Cf. also Deut. 5:4, from which permission to 'go up' the mountain can be inferred.

25 Two different but synonymous Hebrew terms are used for what appears

God's continued presence was visibly manifest by fire, smoke and violent quaking.[26] However, rather than responding positively to this trumpet call, the Israelites were paralysed with fear, and remained at a distance while Moses approached God on their behalf (vv. 16b–19; cf. 20:18–21).[27] With the decibel level increasing still further as Yahweh got closer,[28] an extraordinary dialogue takes place between Moses and God – the precise nature of which remains unclear, at least certainly at this stage in the narrative. Genuine communication is clearly implied, although God may arguably have 'answered Moses with thunder' rather than with the articulate speech suggested by many English translations. Assuming the latter, many interpreters suggest that it was at this stage that the covenant law (i.e. the Decalogue reported in 20:1–17) was disclosed to Moses – an interpretation that necessitates a non-sequential reading of the material between 19:16–19 and 20:18–20. In any case, this dialogue appears to fulfil the promise of 19:9, validating Moses as a trustworthy mediator – someone who is clearly able to communicate an authentic word to the people from Yahweh himself.

20–24. Moses is here invited up the mountain for a more intimate encounter with Yahweh (v. 20), during which an absolute ban on ascending the mountain is apparently imposed on everyone except for Moses and Aaron (arguably alluding here to a select group rather than just these two individuals; see below). Whereas

---

to be a metaphorical trumpet/ram's horn 'blown' by Yahweh.

26 As with supernatural phenomena depicted earlier in the exodus narrative, those described here should not be confused with natural occurrences, such as a mere lightning storm or volcanic activity; biblical authors were obviously familiar with such phenomena but portray Israel's experience at Sinai in extraordinary terms.

27 Although it is admittedly unclear from 19:19 that Moses had ascended the mountain, this is arguably spelt out for the reader in 19:20–24 and 20:21 (see Additional note on the chronological sequence of Exod. 19 – 24).

28 The text figuratively refers to the trumpet 'walking' and 'growing louder and louder'.

trespassers previously faced execution by their fellow Israelites (vv. 12–13), now Yahweh himself would *break out against them* (i.e. execute them; cf. Lev. 10:1–2; 2 Sam. 6:6–8). Rather than an unfortunate anachronism (e.g. Childs 1974: 375; Durham 1987: 273), *the priests* referred to in these verses (vv. 22, 24) are better understood (e.g. Garrett 2014: 463; Wright 2021: 341 n. 12) as attesting to an already existing priestly order – arguably (so Garrett) of Levites (cf. 1 Sam. 2:27) over whom Aaron already presided as leader (cf. Aaron's designation as *the Levite* in Exod. 4:14). Alternatively, *priests* here in Exodus 19:22–24 may proleptically allude to the as-yet-unestablished Aaronic priesthood (Sprinkle 1994: 20–21 n. 1), anticipating the subsequent role Aaron and his sons would have in Israelite worship (cf. 28:1; a similar anachronistic reference appears in 38:8). In either case, the invitation for Aaron to accompany Moses here (v. 24; cf. 24:1) quite possibly relates to the ascent of Aaron (and others, including Nadab and Abihu) described in 24:9–11.[29]

Alternatively, these pre-Aaronic *priests* are the young men who conducted such a role in 24:5 – conceivably the firstborn who had been purified and consecrated by the Passover ritual (Gehrig 2024: 148 n. 20).[30]

Some of Yahweh's commands (and Moses' movements) in

---

29 Somewhat surprisingly, neither Alexander nor Gehrig argues that these priests in Exod. 19 refer to some of the Israelite firstborn, consecrated through the Passover ritual (see on Exod. 12 and 13 above) and thus qualified to carry out such a priestly role prior to the consecration of the Aaronic priesthood. While Alexander does raise the possibility (of these pre-Aaronic priests being firstborn or elders), he doubts that it is possible to ascertain either their precise identity or the basis of their appointment (2017: 384).

30 NB Though Gehrig does not actually discuss the identity of the priests in 19:22, he rightly acknowledges that there is no explicit association of the young Israelite men with firstborn sons in 24:5. Alexander (2017: 544) considers it more likely that the latter were 'ordinary Israelites, drawn from all of the tribes', there being 'no reason to assume that they were firstborn sons'. If, however, the firstborn were already consecrated by the Passover ritual (as Alexander and Gehrig maintain), no Israelites

these verses may seem rather redundant, as even Moses himself
observes (v. 23). This, and the fact that Yahweh appears here
to be descending on the mountain a second time (v. 20; cf.
v. 18), prompts readers to ask how this material relates to its
immediate and wider context. According to Sailhamer (2009:
394), verses 20–24 unpack the conversation of verse 19;[31] together
with verses 18–19, they thus focus on a single divine descent to
the top of Mount Sinai (cf. v. 20).[32] In contrast to the scenario
envisaged in verse 13, 'drawing near to God' is now restricted to
Israel's religious elite (Moses and the Aaronic priesthood), which
underlines the necessity – in view of Israel's fearful response to
the theophany (20:18–21) – of a priesthood (and tabernacle) to
commune with God. Some such connection between the conversation of verse 19 and that of verses 20–24 is admittedly possible,[33]
and could throw some light on the structure and cohesion of
the Sinai narrative as a whole. However, for the problems with
Sailhamer's analysis, see Additional note on the chronological
sequence of Exodus 19 – 24.

25. After his encounter with Yahweh, Moses returns to the foot
of the mountain, where he again communicates Yahweh's instructions. The Hebrew syntax at the end of verse 25 (lit. 'and he said
to them') is unusual: such a clause normally introduces reported
speech.[34] Some thus understand the following verses (20:1–17) as
Moses' report of what Yahweh said to him during the interaction

---

were conceivably more qualified to carry out such a priestly role prior to
the consecration of the Aaronic priesthood.

31 Sailhamer believes that the Decalogue and the material recorded in
the Book of the Covenant were also disclosed to Moses during this
conversation.

32 This avoids the obvious redundancy of an additional divine descent to
the top of the mountain (v. 20) that must be inferred from a sequential
reading of the material (cf. v. 18).

33 The related narrative in Deut. 5:22–31 may be similarly understood:
Deut. 5:22 is arguably the summary account, on which Deut. 5:23–31
then elaborates.

34 However, this is not necessarily the case, as the verb *ʾāmar* may

of 19:19, an inference further supported by 20:1 (*And God spoke all these words*) and the second person singulars of the Decalogue (Sailhamer 2009: 387). However, while such an indirect revelation of the Decalogue could well have achieved the stated objective (19:9) and elicited the people's fearful response (20:18–19), there is nothing to suggest that *the voice/*'thunder' of 19:19 refers to articulate speech (see comment on 19:16–19). Moreover, the biblical text clearly suggests that Yahweh addressed the Israelites directly (20:22–23; cf. Deut. 5:4–5, 22–27). Admittedly, however, the Hebrew syntax of Deuteronomy 5:4–5 is also unusual and could likewise suggest that while Yahweh communicated the Decalogue *audibly* to the people from the fire, this revelation was communicated to them *verbally* by Moses.

Meaning
The primary focus of this chapter is on Yahweh's plan for the people he had graciously rescued from Egypt and safely brought to himself at Sinai: to enter into a covenant with them through which they would become his unique people, with a privileged status that was normally the prerogative of a priestly elite. In preparation for their anticipated meeting with a holy God on Sinai (cf. 3:12), any trace of uncleanness was eradicated and a strict exclusion zone was enforced, thus avoiding the contamination of the sacred space where Yahweh would manifest his presence (cf. 3:5). Terror-stricken by the actual theophany on Sinai (vv. 16–19; 20:18a), the Israelites insist on keeping their distance from God's immediate presence (20:18b–21), hence the absolute necessity of a covenant mediator who would draw near to God on Israel's behalf. The key motif in this passage is therefore the unique authority of Moses as covenant mediator between Israel and a holy and awe-inspiring God.

Given the association of the theophany with lightning, trumpet blasts, clouds and quaking, there is certainly some foreshadowing here of the ultimate biblical theophany: the second coming of

---

sometimes denote 'to order; to give a command'; cf. Chirichigno 1987: 478 n. 42; Meier 1992: 67.

Christ. However, there may also be some foreshadowing of earlier events, such as the Day of Pentecost (Acts 2) and, in view of the emphasis on *the third day*, Christ's resurrection (cf. Matt. 28:2).[35] In any case, in many respects this chapter anticipates the fuller revelation that God has given in Jesus Christ, the ultimate covenant mediator (Heb. 9:15) and permanent high priest (Heb. 7:24), through whom God has delivered us and called us to be his special people (1 Pet. 2:9–10).

However, unlike the people of the old covenant, we may 'draw near to God' (Heb. 7:19) 'with a sincere heart and full assurance of faith' (Heb. 10:22, AT). Nevertheless, while we have indeed come to Mount Zion rather than Mount Sinai (Heb. 12:18–24), we too must 'worship God acceptably with reverence and awe, for our "God is a consuming fire"' (Heb. 12:28–29).

---

35 If so, this text may be one of those to which Paul alludes in his claim that Jesus rose 'on the third day according to the Scriptures' (1 Cor. 15:4).

9. ISRAEL'S COVENANT OBLIGATIONS DISCLOSED (I): THE DECALOGUE AND ISRAEL'S TERRIFIED RESPONSE (20:1–21)

This part of the book (chs. 20–24), its literary and theological centre, focuses mainly on Israel's covenant obligations: the general stipulations of the Decalogue or 'ten words' set forth in 20:3–17, and the more detailed stipulations in *the Book of the Covenant* (24:7) – a mixture of straightforward imperatives and scenario-based instructions (21:1 – 23:19). Rather than an adjunct to their previous commitment to *obey [Yahweh] fully and keep [his] covenant* (19:5),[1] these obligations spell out and illustrate how Israel's covenant commitment to God must express itself. The more detailed stipulations conclude with instructions relating to a successful journey to, and secure settlement within, the Promised Land (23:20–33).

---

1   Contra Sailhamer 2009: 379.

A. The Decalogue (20:1–17)

Context
The general stipulations of the covenant (20:3–17) are bracketed by
a narrative introduction which highlights the salvation-historical
context in which these obligations were disclosed (20:1–2) and a
narrative conclusion which underlines the community's terrified
response to this divine revelation (20:18–21). Israel's reaction to
what they witnessed (20:18–21) explains why the more detailed
stipulations were disclosed directly to Moses alone (20:21).
The Decalogue is thus generally understood as unmediated
divine speech (20:1; cf. 19:25), sharply distinguishing it from the
subsequent stipulations (20:22 – 23:33), which were clearly communicated through Moses (20:22; 21:1; 24:1). Admittedly, *all these words*
(20:1) could conceivably encompass not just the Decalogue itself,
but also the more specific stipulations that follow (cf. 24:3–4a).
However, the Decalogue's introduction (20:1; cf. 20:22; 21:1) and
isolation (20:18–21) from the more detailed covenant stipulations
suggest otherwise.
Less obvious is how 20:1–17 correlates with the preceding
material (in ch. 19); indeed, disagreement exists even among
those who reject any suggestion that the Decalogue is a much
later interpolation.[2] Though insisting on its integral place in the
narrative, not all conservative scholars read the material sequen-
tially.[3] Rather, though narrating what God said on Sinai, 20:1–17 is
understood by some as expanding on the preceding narrative. For
example, it is either unpacking 19:19 – spelling out exactly what
the people overheard God answer Moses – or it is filling in further
details which the author has deliberately 'blanked' until now. Thus
understood, 20:1–17 is a literary flashback, which further accounts
for the narrative resumption that immediately follows in 20:18–21.

---

2 For a concise discussion and critique of late dating of the Decalogue,
   see Alexander 2017: 392–397.
3 E.g. Sprinkle 1994: 21–22; Williamson 2008: 119–120; Wright 2021: 349;
   cf. Alexander 2017: 434.

Comment

While subsequently referred to as 'ten *words*' (*dĕbārîm*, 34:28), both Jewish and Christian traditions differ over precisely how these should be enumerated – depending on whether or not (1) verse 2 constitutes the first 'word'; (2) verse 3 and verses 4–6 should be isolated from each other; (3) verse 17 is treated as a single or two separate commands. The following comments reflect the traditional Protestant enumeration, which is arguably the most straightforward structural analysis of the material.[4]

The basic covenant stipulations (traditionally, *the Ten Commandments*) encompass the Israelites' responsibilities to both God (vv. 1–11) and one another (vv. 12–17). Rather than a strict legal code that could be enforced by human courts (which is clearly impossible in the case of coveting), it establishes the core theological and socio-ethical principles that are to undergird Israel's covenant life. Israel's obedience is to be motivated primarily by gratitude, love and reverence, hence the presence of motivational clauses rather than mere penalties.

1. The speaker here is explicitly identified as God, not Moses (cf. 19:25). As suggested above, 20:2–17 is possibly articulating what God had proclaimed in Israel's hearing (cf. 19:9, 19). In any case, the suggestion that it is Moses (rather than Yahweh) who is here addressing Israel stems from a misunderstanding of 19:25b and how this clause relates syntactically to 20:1. Exodus and Deuteronomy agree that it was *Yahweh's* proclamation of the Decalogue that prompted Israel's request for Moses to act as mediator (20:18–19; cf. Deut. 5:22–27). Accordingly, however we understand the precise timing of God's speaking here, it clearly precedes Israel's terrified reaction and the subsequent disclosure of the more detailed stipulations through Moses.

2. The covenant stipulations are firmly grounded in Yahweh's prior act of salvation. A typical Ancient Near Eastern treaty pattern is arguably reflected in how the introductory preamble (*I am the* LORD *your God*) and brief historical prologue (*who brought you out of Egypt*) immediately precede a statement of the

───────────────

4   For more on this, see Youngblood 1994.

general stipulations (*You shall have* . . .). If so, Yahweh is being presented here as Israel's great king, whose action on Israel's behalf commands their gratitude and allegiance. At any rate, Israel must observe these stipulations, not in order to become God's people, but rather because they already were so, and this was how those who belonged to him – those whom he had graciously rescued from oppression – should now behave (cf. 19:4–5).

However, perhaps the motivation expressed in verse 2 relates especially to the first 'word' (the prohibition of v. 3) rather than simply all of the Decalogue in general. This would correlate more closely with the next four commands, each of which includes its own rationale or motivating clause of some kind. Thus understood, verse 2 explains why, in particular, an Israelite worshipper should have no gods except Yahweh (the *me* of v. 3): he is the one who has liberated each of them from slavery in Egypt.[5] Accordingly, it is to him alone that they owe gratitude and worship.

3. The precise nuance of *'al-pānāy* (lit. 'upon my face', traditionally tr. 'beside' or *before me*) is debated, but worshipping other gods as well as Yahweh (rather than simply 'instead of' or 'ahead of') is most probably in view here (cf. 22:20; 23:13, 24, 33). As redeemer and covenant Lord, Yahweh demands his people's exclusive allegiance. This first command thus proscribes any form of theological pluralism, sharply distinguishing Mosaic Yahwism from its polytheistic Ancient Near Eastern milieu. Even though the conceptual reality of *other gods* is acknowledged here and elsewhere (cf. 15:11), this does not necessarily imply belief in their metaphysical existence – at least, other than in the minds of their devotees, or in the idolatrous images associated with such rival 'deities'. While some Old Testament texts use the terminology of 'gods' or 'mighty ones' with respect to celestial beings such as angels (e.g. Ps. 82:1), this is not necessarily evidence that undermines early Israelite monotheism (cf. Deut. 4:35, 39). The idea that Israelite religion evolved from some form of henotheism

---

5   Significantly, here and throughout the following 'words', the individual
    Israelite appears to be addressed (consistently singular rather than
    plural forms are used).

or monolatry to monotheism is at variance with the consistent testimony of the biblical text.[6] As Childs (1974: 403) insists: 'Israel did not gradually progress to a belief in one God, but this confession was constitutive to the covenant faith from the outset.'

4–6. The second 'word' may reinforce or complement the first by prohibiting both the manufacture and the use of idolatrous objects. However, since the first command seems implicitly to exclude the worship of other deities alongside Yahweh, this second may more logically apply to the worship of Yahweh in particular. In any case, these verses expressly forbid the manufacture and worship of all idolatrous objects – whether such images of things in the created order (*heaven above . . . earth beneath . . . waters below*) represented Yahweh or not.[7] Accordingly, this command further distinguishes orthodox Israelite worship from that of surrounding cultures, in which idolatry played an essential role in expressing a deity's presence and accessibility. The means by which Yahweh chose to manifest his presence to Israel made such idols not only redundant, but also inappropriate: as the prohibition's comprehensive scope (v. 4b) may imply, nothing created could adequately represent Israel's transcendent God (see below). Clearly this did not apply in the case of *created* heavenly beings such as cherubim, whose physical representations in Israel's tabernacle and temple were neither inherently inaccurate (Ezek. 10:20; cf. Exod. 25:18–20; 37:7–9; 1 Kgs 6:23–28) nor the objects of worship; rather, these were simply symbols of the heavenly realm, where such creatures served in God's presence continually.

---

6   While the OT clearly attests such polytheistic thinking and practices among ancient Israelites at various times throughout their history, this is always associated with unfaithfulness, disobedience or apostasy. It is thus no great surprise that such religious syncretism in ancient Israel is also reflected in the archaeological data (cf. Hess 2007).

7   An orthodox Israelite may not have discerned such a distinction; strictly speaking, any idolatry was the worship of another god. However, idolatrous Israelite religion could often have reflected some degree of syncretism, whereby they sought to acknowledge Yahweh by inappropriate means.

Accordingly, the prohibition on making sculptured images did not extend to these items, which were never considered nor used as idols in ancient Israel.

As well as not making any such idols (v. 4), the Israelites must also refrain from bowing down before or serving them (v. 5a) – further underlining the exclusive adoration and allegiance that Yahweh deserved (cf. vv. 2–3). The theological rationale underpinning the command here in Exodus is divine jealousy (i.e. God's loving and proper concern for his exclusive rights and interests, which he zealously protects). No further reason is offered at this point (cf. Deut. 4:15–19, which underlines the inherent difficulty in making an idol that accurately represents Yahweh's distinctive form, something that remained concealed from human view even on Sinai; however, cf. Num. 12:8).

The incentive to obey is twofold: the negative threat of cross-generational judgment, and the positive assurance of multi-generational love. The former may initially appear unjust, but probably attests either to the long-term influence (and consequences) of sinful behaviour, or to the fact that an extended family unit living together were all culpable and thus shared in the guilt of any household's idolatrous offence (e.g. Num. 16:31–34; Josh. 7:24).[8] Whatever the scenario envisaged, *those who hate me* (i.e. those who reject or are disloyal to Yahweh, their covenant God) most likely defines all those who are punished, just as *those who love me and keep my commandments* delimits all those encompassed by the positive counterpart.[9] The deliberate imbalance between *third and fourth* (v. 5) and 'thousands' (v. 6, AT) – emphasizing the breadth of God's love rather than its duration (cf. 34:6–7) – clearly indicates Yahweh's preference.

---

8   I.e. *Third and fourth generation* either defines the extent of direct influence any individual might possibly have or alludes to the largest conceivable extended family in a single household. In neither scenario are those being punished innocent victims, but in some way are participants in parental/familial misconduct, as *those who hate me* suggests (Boda 2009: 110, 118, 518).

9   For the covenantal associations of the terminology, see Moran 1963.

7. While the third word may seem straightforward, its precise interpretation is much debated. According to Imes (2018: 7), 'At least 23 distinct interpretations of Exod 20:7 have been proposed . . . in part because its three key words . . . exhibit such a wide range of meanings, depending on the context.'[10] Many recognize the ambiguity of this 'Name Command', some (e.g. Huffmon 2004) even considering it to be intentionally broad. Nevertheless, most interpreters assume that the conceptual idea of 'bearing/lifting up the name' is speech-related (i.e. 'on your lips' is implied). Interpreted in this idiomatic or elliptical manner, the Name Command concerns 'reverence for God, specifically the proper use of God's holy name' (Baker 2017: 61). Thus understood, it expressly prohibits any profane or blasphemous use of the divine name (e.g. Lev. 24:11–16).[11] As Baker goes on to illustrate (2017: 62–63; see also Imes 2018: 13–15), such frivolous or false use of divine names, especially with respect to oath-taking, was considered a serious offence elsewhere in the Ancient Near East. Nevertheless, just as the third commandment cannot be restricted to 'swearing falsely by Yahweh' (Lev. 19:12; cf. Lev. 18:21; 22:2, 31–32), its concerns may be significantly different (whether wider or narrower) from those reflected in a cultural milieu stretching across several centuries.

The elliptical interpretation is narrowed by numerous interpreters to the issue of oath-taking (texts such as Exod. 23:1; Lev. 19:12; Pss 24:4; 139:20; Zech. 5:4 are adduced in support), although this ignores the fact that Yahweh's name can evidently be profaned by several other means (cf. Jer. 34:16; Ezek. 20:9, 14, 22; 36:20; Mal. 1:6–14). Moreover, the exact idiom ('lifting up the

---

10 For a comprehensive review and appraisal of all the various interpretations, see Imes 2018: 9–45.

11 The idea that the Name Command prohibits *any* pronunciation of the divine name is clearly mistaken, given how often God's name is invoked in both the immediate and wider context; e.g. 3:15–16; 4:22; 15:1–18; 18:10–11; 19:8; 20:24; 24:3, 7–8; see also Num. 6:24–27; Deut. 6:13.

name') never appears in an oath-making context,[12] making its interpretation as an 'oath-making idiom' somewhat incongruous. Such an objection carries less weight for those who supply 'your hand' between 'lift up' and 'name', since an uplifted hand is explicitly associated with oath-making elsewhere in the Old Testament (Gen. 14:22; Exod. 6:8; Num. 14:30; Ps. 106:26; Ezek. 20:5, 15, 23, 42; 36:7; 44:12; 47:14; cf. Deut. 32:40; Dan. 12:7).[13] However, the suggested meaning remains unclear, unless an additional verb is also implied: 'You must not lift up (your hand *and speak*) the name of the Lord your God falsely/frivolously' (so Huffmon 2004: 207; emphasis added).

Admittedly, the only Old Testament text (other than the Decalogue) that expressly mentions 'bearing/lifting up a name' does relate to speech (Ps. 16:4).[14] However, unlike the Name Command, it does so explicitly, possibly to emphasize the psalmist's loyalty to Yahweh (i.e. 'nor will I [*even*] lift their names to my lips').[15] Accordingly, an explicit reference to speech in Psalm 16:4 should not be naïvely imported into the Name Command, which probably encompasses a broader issue.

Several contemporary scholars defend the suggestion that verse 7 concerns dishonouring God's name by *whatever means*.[16] This non-elliptical interpretation makes excellent grammatical

---

12 The closest correspondence is in Ps. 24:4, where 'does *not lift up* [*lōʾ-nāśāʾ*] to an idol [*laššāwʾ*] my soul' is used in parallelism with '*and does not swear* [*wĕlōʾ nišbaʿ*] by deceit' (AT).

13 Interestingly, in all but Gen. 14:22 it is in fact God or his heavenly representative who swears in this manner.

14 While Ps. 139:20 might seem like a further example ('your adversaries misuse [lit. 'lift up falsely'] your name'), the Hebrew text does not explicitly include the word *šēm* ('name'), and God's name is not necessarily the implied object here in any case. See further, Imes 2018: 110–112.

15 So Imes 2018: 24.

16 E.g. Harman 1988; Block 2011; Wright 2021: 364–366. For a comprehensive lexical and contextual defence of this non-elliptical interpretation, see Imes 2018 (esp. 46–181).

and syntactical sense of the text as it stands: the verb (*nāśā'*, 'to bear/carry') needs nothing extra to clarify its intended meaning; God's *name* denotes his reputation (Exod. 9:16) and ownership (cf. Deut. 28:9–10),[17] both of which are significant issues in Exodus and throughout the Old Testament; 'Yahweh *your God*' (AT) again emphasizes the covenantal setting; and the adverbially used noun (*šāw'*), with its basic sense of 'false, empty, ineffective', reflects the manner in which the activity referred to is carried out.

With its emphasis on bearing or carrying God's name in a misrepresentative manner (cf. the positive role of Israel's high priest in Exod. 28:12, 29),[18] the prohibition encompasses any kind of behaviour that would tarnish or sully God's reputation (cf. Exod. 19:5–6; Lev. 22:31a–33; Prov. 30:9), including (but not restricted to) speech-related offences such as invoking God's name to sanction unethical conduct, or to endorse deceptive oaths (Lev. 19:12). As such, its focus extends well beyond any 'pointless, misleading and even false *use*' of God's name (Durham 1987: 288; emphasis mine). Rather, it is an unpacking of Israel's commission in Exodus 19 to be God's representative people, hence the significance of tarnishing his holy name. Thus understood, the Name Command concerns the special status and role of Israel as God's image-bearers.

The seriousness of this prohibition is highlighted by its associated warning: failure to bear Yahweh's name appropriately incurs guilt, and thus punishment (cf. 20:5; 34:7). Alluding to both the second and third commandments, the latter text (34:6–7) again emphasizes that while such punishment for sin is inevitable, it is not what God, the one who 'bears iniquity and transgression and sin' (AT), ultimately desires. Nevertheless, Yahweh cannot simply acquit the guilty, as Israel's subsequent history so eloquently illustrates.

---

17 See Imes 2018: 47–87.

18 Following Harman (1988: 3–4), Imes plausibly argues that Exod. 28:12, 29 offers a much closer and more analogous parallel to the Name Command than those used to support an elliptical interpretation (see above).

8–11. This and the next (v. 12) are the only two commands in the Decalogue that are framed positively (rather than as prohibitions). Moreover, up to this point both Pentateuchal accounts of the Decalogue are almost entirely identical; however, the fourth word displays considerable divergence (cf. Deut. 5:12–15; AT):

Exodus 20	Deuteronomy 5
Remember the sabbath day by setting it apart.	**Keep** the sabbath day by setting it apart,
	just as Yahweh your God commanded you.
Six days you must labour and do all your work,	Six days you must labour and do all your work,
but the seventh day is a sabbath to Yahweh your God.	but the seventh day is a sabbath to Yahweh your God.
Do not do any work, you, or your son or daughter,	Do not do any work, you, or your son or daughter,
your male or female servant,	or your male or female servant,
or your livestock,	or **your ox or donkey, or any of** your livestock,
or your foreign resident in your community.[19]	or your foreign resident in your community,
	so your male and female servant may rest just like you.
For in six days Yahweh made the heaven and earth, the sea and everything in it; but he rested on the seventh day.	**So you will remember that you were a [forced] labourer in the land of Egypt and Yahweh your God brought you out from there with a strong hand and an outstretched arm.**
Therefore Yahweh blessed the sabbath day by setting it apart.	Therefore Yahweh **your God commanded you to observe [lit. 'do']** the sabbath day.

---

19 Lit. 'your foreign resident in your gates' – indicating a town or city rather than a family residence.

While some of these variations are more easily explained than others,[20] a different theological basis in each account is unexpected, and may possibly indicate that only one (or neither) of these two texts is presenting a verbatim account of what God actually said (cf. 19:9b; 20:1).[21] Thus understood, one or both of these motivational explanations for observing the sabbath are secondary additions, whether provided by Moses himself or by subsequent authors/editors of the canonical Pentateuch. When such additions may have been incorporated is a matter of scholarly conjecture, as is the related question of chronological priority.[22] While the latter might seem obvious,[23] since Exodus precedes Deuteronomy in both its narrative and canonical location, the issue is complicated by the vexed question of Pentateuchal composition (see Introduction 2, 'Composition and date').

For example, if 'the Book of the Law' (Josh. 1:7–8; 23:6) recorded by Moses (Deut. 31:9, 24–26; Josh. 23:6) refers to Deuteronomy 5 – 26 (or 5 – 30) rather than the entire Pentateuchal corpus,[24] then the rationale for sabbath-keeping in Deuteronomy might arguably predate that given in Exodus – assuming the latter was written by someone other than Moses or one of his contemporaries (cf. Josh. 24:26). However, if Moses was also responsible for recording the relevant material subsequently incorporated

---

20 Some of the additional elements in Deuteronomy typically reflect the book's hortatory emphasis.

21 While both these explanations could have been spoken by God, we must still ask why only one of them is selected for inclusion in each of the two parallel texts.

22 Like many historical-critical matters in the Pentateuch, arguments for chronological priority are often based on highly speculative reconstructions of underlying sources and stages of compilation. For more on this, see Introduction 2, 'Composition and date'.

23 Indeed, the presence of typical Deuteronomic emphases in Deut. 5:13–15 arguably confirms that this account of the Decalogue is the later of the two versions.

24 See Alexander 2022: 342–345, who nonetheless maintains the chronological priority of the Decalogue tradition preserved in Exodus.

in Exodus (Exod. 24:4; cf. 34:27–28), the rationale for sabbath-keeping given in Exodus is almost certainly earlier (cf. 31:17) than that recorded in Deuteronomy.²⁵

In any case, whether one or both explanations of the sabbath regulation are secondary, each is a valid (and inspired) reason for setting aside the sabbath day for rest: this regular day of rest recalls God's purpose in both creation (Gen. 2:1–3) and redemption (Deut. 5:15), thus foreshadowing the ultimate deliverance and rest that are experienced through God's new creation and redemption in Christ (Heb. 4:1–11).

Significantly, both accounts (v. 10a; cf. Deut. 5:14) state that 'the seventh day is a sabbath to/for Yahweh your God'. This clearly echoes its depiction back in chapter 16 (vv. 23, 25) where, prior to the revelation of the Torah at Sinai, the sabbatical structure of Israel's week had already been established by God's instructions for collecting manna (16:22–30).²⁶ Both there (16:27–30) and subsequently (cf. 31:12–17; 35:1–3) its importance is underlined. The seventh day is exclusively for Yahweh, which arguably implies not simply rest from work, but devotion to God (cf. Isa. 56:2–6; 58:13). While many have inferred from this that it mandates some kind of religious activity, such *compulsory* 'sabbath worship' is nowhere stipulated in the Old Testament (although cf. Lev. 23:3; 24:8; Num. 28:9–10; see also Ps. 92's suggestive title and Acts 15:21). Moreover, keeping (or profaning) the sabbath is consistently related in Exodus to the activity of work rather than to worship (16:29–30; 20:10–11; 23:12; 31:14–15; 34:21; 35:2–3; see also Num. 15:32–36; Neh. 13:15–22; Jer. 17:21–27; Amos 8:5). This emphasis on cessation of normal activity is further underlined by the related noun (*šabbātôn*), with which 'sabbath' is sometimes qualified (Exod. 16:23; 31:15; 35:2; see also Lev. 16:31; 23:3, 24, 32, 39; 25:4–5).

---

25 Non-conservative scholars would dismiss this possibility on source-critical grounds (Gen. 1:1 – 2:3 [P] being post-exilic), but the postulated dating (and contents) of putative sources is subject to radical revision and ongoing debate.

26 Ironically, the only 'sabbath' Israel knew prior to Exod. 16 was the one that so displeased Pharaoh (Exod. 5:5).

For in six days . . . (v. 11a) correlates neatly with the traditional six-day creationist interpretation of Genesis.[27] However, while certainly alluding to the Genesis creation narrative, the inspired author may well be reflecting a literary rather than a strictly historical perspective: that is, Israel is to emulate the *pattern* (as reflected in Gen. 2:1–3) of God's resting from all his work on the seventh day, which Yahweh has given to Israel as a holy day of rest. In any case, as Shead (2000: 746) points out:

> We should beware of the simple equation of the Seventh Day [Gen 2:2–3] with the first Sabbath day. The Sabbath mentioned in verse 11b is . . . the Israelites' weekly Sabbath, the subject of the commandment. The altered quotation compares the Israelite Sabbath to the Seventh Day, not in order to equate those two days in every respect, but rather to show that God's action of blessing and sanctifying applies equally to both. Verse 11b is a shorthand way of saying, 'which is why Yahweh blessed not only the seventh day, but also the Sabbath'.

After the Sinai covenant has been fully ratified, the sabbath is further described as a perpetual sign of Israel's consecration to God (31:13, 16–17). As such, Israel must remember it *by keeping it holy*, namely, by making this day distinct from all others: the entire Israelite community (including servants, livestock and resident aliens) is to cease from normal daily labour on the sabbath – further distinguishing them from all other nations and societies around them, none of whom had any such law or custom insofar as we can tell.[28]

While the bearing of the fourth commandment on the new covenant people of God remains a contentious hermeneutical issue in some Christian circles, most would agree that the *seventh* day has been superseded by the first day of the week, and recognize sabbath as an Old Testament type of the eschatological rest that Jesus secured through his death and triumphant

---

27 See Steinmann 2019: 59–62.
28 For a concise discussion, see Baker 2017: 72–73.

resurrection. Though many still conscientiously apply the underlying principle(s) of the fourth commandment to their weekly pattern of work and rest, the New Testament arguably suggests that, like circumcision, this is no longer a covenantal obligation (cf. Rom. 14:5; Gal. 4:10–11; Col. 2:16–17) for those not under law, but under grace (Rom. 6:14–15; Gal. 5:18).

12. Like the previous word (vv. 8–11), this one also is framed positively.[29] If we distinguish the two covenant tablets, understanding each to contain five rather than all ten words, the location of this fifth one, with its clear anthropocentric focus,[30] seems somewhat anomalous. Indeed, even when its theological significance is fully appreciated (see below), the uneven distribution of the Decalogue in terms of content remains a problem unless all ten words are reduced to hypothetical originals of uniform length. However, there is no need for any such speculative reduction if each tablet was identically inscribed with all ten words (see comment on 24:12 below).

Though popularly related to children rather than adults, this fifth word was never intended to be thus restricted. Like the rest of the Decalogue, it applied in the first instance to the entire community, not just minors or adolescents. Everyone in Israel was obliged to *honour* their parents – regardless of age or circumstances. While the precise application of this command might inevitably vary,[31] depending on a wide range of practical concerns, the principle remained unaltered, and thus clearly extended beyond mere filial obedience.

---

29 Though the parallel text in Deuteronomy again differs, the change of verb and the two additions ('as the LORD your God has commanded you' / 'that it may go well with you'; Deut. 5:16) reflect that book's distinctive emphases.

30 Generally, a twofold division assumes a theocentric versus an anthropocentric focus of the two halves, but the fifth word does not seem to fit such a neat division.

31 Cf. Lev. 21:11; Num. 6:7; Deut. 32:7; Ruth 2:11; 1 Kgs 19:20. See also Lev. 19:32, which is arguably a broader application of the principle underlying this commandment.

As is clear from its antonym (Piel *qll*, 'to curse/make light of'; cf. Exod. 21:17; 22:28; Lev. 19:14; 20:9; 24:11–15; Deut. 27:16; Judg. 9:27; 2 Sam. 16:10; 19:21), the Hebrew verb (Piel *kbd*, 'to give honour/weight') denotes giving someone appropriate respect (Lev. 10:3; 2 Sam. 6:22; cf. Deut. 33:9). Both the verb and its cognates are frequently associated with Yahweh (e.g. Deut. 28:58; 1 Sam. 2:30; Pss 22:23; 50:15; 86:9; Prov. 3:9), adding further weight to its theological significance here in the Decalogue: just as Yahweh deserves appropriate honour/respect as Israel's Father (Exod. 4:22–23; cf. Deut. 32:6; Mal. 1:6), so too do human parents (Lev. 19:3), who in an Old Testament setting are primarily responsible for ensuring that Yahweh's covenant requirements are passed on from one generation to another (Deut. 6:6–7, 20–24; 11:18–19; 32:7; cf. Prov. 1 – 7). Not surprisingly, therefore, this covenant obligation includes *both* parents (mother as well as father), making it fairly distinctive in the ancient world.[32] Moreover, given such theological significance, it is no surprise that breaches of this commandment attracted the death penalty (Exod. 21:15, 17; Lev. 20:9; Deut. 21:18–21).

Honouring parents thus involves showing them proper respect (cf. Lev. 19:3; Prov. 30:17; Mal. 1:6), obeying them when appropriate (Deut. 21:18–21; Eph. 6:1; Col. 3:20; cf. Ezek. 20:18)[33] and caring for them in old age (Ruth 4:15; cf. Gen. 45:9–11; 1 Sam. 22:3; Prov. 19:26; Ezek. 22:7). It clearly prohibits anything that would be disrespectful or harmful (cf. Exod. 21:15, 17; Lev. 20:9; Isa. 1:2;

---

32 Though not without any parallel (e.g. the Egyptian advice on supporting one's mother in the *Instruction of Ani* §7, *COS* 1: 46, p. 113), it was more common in ancient society for only the father or older men to command such support or respect. See further, Baker 2017: 84–92.

33 It is clear from these texts that this commandment does not demand blind obedience or unqualified respect; sometimes it is entirely appropriate to ignore parental instructions or desires, especially if these are inherently immoral or otherwise inappropriate. Nevertheless, '[t]he validity of the fifth commandment is not dependent on having perfect parents but on the role of parents as God's representatives in giving life' (Baker 2017: 96, citing Barth 1951: 251–257).

Mic. 7:6). However, this word involves not simply refraining from
negative behaviour, but acting positively to do them good (cf.
Matt. 15:3–6; Mark 7:9–13; 1 Tim. 5:4).

As Paul observes (Eph. 6:2), this is 'the first commandment
with a promise' – but in its Old Testament setting this promise
of long life in the land is national as well as personal (Deut.
4:10, 40; 11:9; 12:1; 32:47; cf. Prov. 4:10).[34] The land in question is
Canaan, where Israel's tenure was dependent on faithfulness to
the covenant. As noted above, parents had a key role to play in
communicating the covenant's requirements to their children,
which not only sheds light on the significance of this word in its
literary and historical context, but also explains why Paul likewise
highlights the importance of this commandment in a Christian
setting (Eph. 6:1–3) – where the promise is not applied nationally
and territorially, but individually and globally.

In the ancient Greek version of the Old Testament (LXX), the
next three commandments (vv. 13–15) follow a slightly different
sequence: adultery; stealing; homicide. However, an intention to
keep both family-related commandments (parental honour and
marital faithfulness) together (Thomas 1976: 208) only partially
explains this alternative order; perhaps stealing and homicide
were likewise reversed because of the association between the
latter and *false testimony* (v. 16; cf. 23:7). In any case, the anthropocentric focus (cf. v. 12) continues in these and all the remaining
words of the Decalogue, where attention has clearly shifted to the
second part of Jesus' twofold summary: loving one's neighbour as
oneself (Matt. 22:39).

13. The killing prohibited in this sixth word relates to unlawful
or unauthorized homicide, something condemned in most civilized
societies, ancient as well as modern.[35] Of the Hebrew words for
killing, *rāṣaḥ* is the least common (less than 50x), the vast majority

---

34 Technically, the second word (Exod. 20:6) ends not with a promise but
    a statement of theological fact. Here in the fifth word, the motivation
    clause is more clearly promissory.

35 For typical attitudes and legislation in the Ancient Near East, see Baker
    2017: 101–103.

of its occurrences being found in legislation for Israel's cities of refuge (Num. 35:6–31; Deut. 4; 19; Josh. 20 – 21). With one notable exception (Ezek. 21:22, where Nebuchadnezzar's bloodthirsty intent is underscored), the verb is never used in relation to killing in war (for which *hārag* is commonly used). The immediate and wider Old Testament context clearly shows that this prohibition did not apply to slaughtering (generally, *šāḥaṭ*) animals (whether for meat or sacrifice), or to capital punishment.[36]

It is clear from its Old Testament usage that such unauthorized killing encompassed more than just murder (i.e. premeditated or intentional homicide; cf. Exod. 21:14; Num. 35:16–21; Deut. 19:11–13); it also applied to unintentional killing such as manslaughter or involuntary homicide (e.g. Num. 35:11, 22–24; Deut. 4:42; 19:4–6; Josh. 20:5), whether resulting from excessive use of force (Exod. 22:2–3) or from criminal negligence (Exod. 21:29; Deut. 19:5).

Such unapproved killing of those made in the image of God was a capital offence (21:12, 28–32; Num. 35:31–34; cf. Gen. 9:5–6), although in some cases (i.e. those involving negligence or no malice aforethought), a warranted death sentence could be commuted through payment of the appropriate compensation (21:30; cf. Num. 35:31–32).

As is clear from elsewhere (Lev. 19:16–18; Deut. 22:8; see also Matt. 5:21–26), this sixth word has wider ramifications than simply committing intentional or unintentional homicide. It underscores the need to constrain anger, rage, hatred and animosity, as well as to take appropriate steps to mitigate responsibility for any avoidable fatality.

14. Whereas the sixth word protects the sanctity of human life, the seventh is designed to protect marriage. *Adultery* is sexual intercourse between a married or betrothed person and someone who is not their spouse (cf. Lev. 18:20; 20:10; Deut. 22:22–27).

---

36 While *rāṣaḥ* is used once in relation to the avenger of blood (Num. 35:27) and once in relation to capital punishment (Num. 35:30), this seems to be to underline the talion principle (cf. Exod. 21:23–25). Usually where capital punishment is lawfully carried out, the causative form of the verb *mût* (to die) is employed.

However, 'it is less clear whether the verb refers to extra-marital sexual relations involving exclusively married or engaged *women* . . . or refers to extra-marital sexual relations with *anyone, male or female*, who is married or engaged' (Alexander 2017: 417; emphasis mine). As Alexander further explains, while only the latter might conflict with the practice of polygamy in the Old Testament, the former creates a double standard: a married man commits adultery only with a married or betrothed woman, whereas a married woman commits adultery regardless of a man's relational status. This, and the Old Testament's generally negative portrayal of polygamy in practice, raises significant concerns over the former interpretation. While some Old Testament legislation (e.g. Exod. 21:10; Deut. 21:15–17;[37] cf. Deut. 25:5–10, where the surviving brother is likely unmarried) might appear to suggest that not all polygamy was prohibited by the seventh commandment, it more likely – like the Mosaic legislation on divorce in Deuteronomy 24:1–4 – attempts to manage problems of existing cultural practices without necessarily approving of such.[38]

However understood, adultery was clearly considered a heinous offence in the Ancient Near East (cf. Gen. 12:18; 20:9; 39:9), punishable in Israel by the execution of both parties involved (Lev. 20:10; Deut. 22:24). While modern Western society would certainly consider this excessive, if not outrightly immoral, such severe punishment emphasizes the extremely high value that God places on marriage, raising it in significance to the sanctity of human life. As Alexander (2017: 420) comments: 'By incorporating this prohibition into the Decalogue, YHWH recognizes that a promiscuous society will not be true to the covenant being ratified, because its fundamental spirit proclaims that faithfulness in relationships is not a core value of its members.'

The unfaithfulness involved in adultery thus makes it an

---

37 The common interpretation that both these texts permit polygyny (a man having more than one wife) is challenged by Alexander (2017: 418); cf. comment on Exod. 21:10 below.

38 I am indebted to David Firth (personal communication) for this explanation.

appropriate metaphor for Israel's subsequent covenant unfaithfulness to Yahweh (e.g. Isa. 57:1–13; Jer. 2 – 3; Ezek. 23:36–49; Hos.
1 – 3). Of course, the seeds of such adultery (whether spiritual or
physical) are planted well before the act; hence this command, like
the previous one, has ramifications beyond the mere letter of the
law (Prov. 5; Mal. 2:10–16; cf. Matt. 5:27–30; Jas 4:4–5).

15. The 'theft' (AT) proscribed in the eighth word arguably
encompasses all forms of stealing (cf. Exod. 22:2; Lev. 19:11a, 13),
rather than one particular type of theft.[39] As Meyers (2005: 177)
suggests, 'it is more likely that generic theft, which could rupture
the fabric of family and community life just as could murder and
adultery, is the intent'.

Though not fully endorsing the rabbinic distinction between
theft by stealth (*gānab*) and theft by force (*gāzal*), Hamilton (2011:
348) notes that the eighth commandment explicitly prohibits
gānab, which Leviticus (cf. Lev. 19:11, 13) apparently distinguishes
from *gāzal* – a verb denoting robbery involving force (cf. Gen.
31:31; Deut. 28:29, 31; Job 24:19) or exploitation (cf. Gen. 21:25;
Prov. 22:22; Mic. 2:2) but never used in Exodus. Whatever the
subtle distinction, however, in the eighth commandment *gānab*
clearly eschews all kinds of theft, including subsets that involve
force or violence (cf. Exod. 21:16; Deut. 24:7). While the latter
two texts might seem to validate restricting the eighth word to
capital offences involving theft (e.g. kidnapping),[40] this is unlikely
and reductionistic: kidnapping seems much too narrowly focused
to warrant specific mention in the Decalogue, which does not all
relate to capital crimes in any case. Moreover, the absence of a
specifying direct object in Exodus 20:15 strongly suggests that the
prohibition encompasses taking *anything* that God has entrusted
to someone else (cf. 22:1–12 [MT 21:16 – 22:11]). Moreover, the
underlying principle extends beyond grand larceny to all kinds of

---

39 Following Alt (1949), some understand the prohibition in terms of
    kidnapping people in order to sell or enslave them.
40 As Hamilton points out (2011: 348), out of its sixty-eight occurrences in
    the OT, *gānab* refers to kidnapping only these three times (once in Exod.
    21:16, and twice in Deut. 24:7).

petty or indirect theft as well (cf. Lev. 19:13, 35–36; Deut. 19:14;
24:14–15; 25:13–16). Accordingly, Paul's exhortation (Eph. 4:28) is
by no means restricted to burglars, muggers and scammers (cf. 1
Cor. 5:10–11; 6:10).

Its inclusion in the Decalogue demonstrates that theft was
a serious infraction of the covenant. Despite this, however, it
was not a capital offence – except where people-stealing (i.e.
kidnapping; cf. Deut. 24:7) rather than just property was involved.
Nor did theft in Israel ever incur extreme penalties such as bodily
mutilation. This, and the fact that the appropriate punishment/
financial restitution was the same for all offenders, regardless of
their social status (Exod. 22:1, 3), further sharpens the distinction
between Old Testament legislation and that of the ancient world
in general, where penalties included execution and amputation
of bodily parts, and where gender or class discrimination was
commonplace.[41] Theologically, this reflects the much greater value
that God places on people (made in his image) over property.

16. Unlike the third (cf. v. 7), the ninth word clearly relates, at
least in the first instance, to a legal setting (cf. 23:1–3, 6–7).[42] This is
strongly suggested by the Qal stem of *'ānâ* ('to answer'), followed
by the preposition (*bĕ*) on the next word.[43] Elsewhere this combination denotes legal or judicial testimony *against* someone (e.g.
Num. 35:30; Deut. 19:16, 18; 1 Sam. 12:3; 2 Sam. 1:16; Hos. 5:5; 7:10;
Mic. 6:3 [see e.g. CSB]; cf. also Ruth 1:21 and Prov. 25:18, which are
arguably judicial also). A legal setting is further suggested by the
phrase 'false witness/testimony' (*'ēd šāqer*) and the synonymous
'empty testimony' (*'ēd šāw'*) used in the parallel text (Deut. 5:20;
cf. Deut. 19:18; AT). In such legal settings, deceptive speech can
have dire consequences (Exod. 23:7; cf. 1 Kgs 21:7–14), hence

---

41 For illustrative examples, see Baker 2017: 123–125.

42 Accordingly, there are numerous Ancient Near Eastern parallels, where
    perjury was likewise a serious offence that incurred similar punish-
    ments. For a concise discussion, see Baker 2017: 134–135.

43 Though the phrase can denote a positive witness (Gen. 30:33), it more
    often conveys negative testimony.

the importance of corroborative witnesses and an appropriate deterrent/penalty for perjury (Deut. 19:15–21).[44] However, while the wording of this command undoubtedly suggests a legal setting (i.e. testifying in court) as the primary focus, the underlying principle encompasses the use of dishonest or deceptive language more generally (Exod. 23:8; Lev. 19:11–12, 16; Hos. 4:2).[45] Unsurprisingly, therefore, both the Old Testament and the New Testament apply this word to all kinds of deceptive speech (Lev. 19:11; Prov. 8:13; 22:21; Zeph. 3:13; Col. 3:9; 1 Pet. 3:10), encouraging speech that is reliable and trustworthy in various contexts (Zech. 8:16; Eph. 4:25), including telling the truth even when it may be easier to remain silent (Lev. 5:1; 2 Cor. 6:7).

Though open to debate, this does not necessitate telling 'the truth, the whole truth, and nothing but the truth' in every situation outside a legal setting. For instance, if doing so would endanger human life, a biblical case can be made for misleading someone, or at least being economical with the truth (cf. Exod. 1:15–21; Josh. 2:4–14). Still, this does not negate the principle enshrined in the ninth commandment; rather, it is the exception that proves the rule – in this case one on which the health and harmonious relations of any community are utterly dependent.

17. If all of verses 2–6 is enumerated as the first commandment, this verse must be split into two distinct commandments to have a total of ten words: accordingly, the first part (v. 17a) would

---

44 As Baker explains, the talion law articulated in Deut. 19:21 (and elsewhere in the OT) is simply 'a vivid way of expressing the principle that punishment should fit the crime' (2017: 137). See, too, commentary on Exod. 21:23–25 below.

45 *Pace* Meyers (2005: 177), who suggests otherwise. Myers also insists (2005: 178) that this prohibition is strictly limited to other members of the covenant community (*neighbour* referring to those with community ties to one another). While again this is admittedly the primary focus in its immediate context, other texts (most famously Jesus' parable of the Good Samaritan in Luke 10:25–37) suggest a broader application of the principle underlying this and other commandments; see also Exod. 23:4–5, 9.

thus apply the prohibition to coveting a neighbour's house (i.e. 'household'), whereas the second part (v. 17b–e) would prohibit coveting any of its constitutive elements in particular. Such a division could be inferred from the anomalous repetition of 'you must not covet/desire' (AT) in this verse, as well as in the parallel verse in Deuteronomy (Deut. 5:21), which the Hebrew text divides in two by an extra paragraph marker. This twofold division may arguably be further accentuated in Deuteronomy by the use of two different, albeit synonymous, verbs meaning 'covet/desire'.

A further complication, however, is that (in contrast with Exod. 20:17) in Deuteronomy 5:21 the first part focuses on the neighbour's 'wife', with the latter 'replaced' by 'house' (now meant literally rather than figuratively; so Baker 2017) at the start of the second part.[46] This different sequence might also correlate with the verse-splitting paragraph markers in Deuteronomy 5:21 (i.e. the nouns may have been switched around to distinguish a man's wife from just another possession). More likely, however, the switch reflects a decreasing scale of importance, with a wife being by far the most valuable (cf. Prov. 31:10–31). In any case, like the use of two synonymous verbs in Deuteronomy, neither location of wife/house constitutes a compelling argument for isolating two separate commandments within a single verse. The verse is perfectly comprehensible as two discrete parts of a single commandment.

This tenth word is widely recognized as the most distinct in the Decalogue;[47] in marked contrast to the preceding nine, its focus is internal, concentrating on the human heart/mind rather than on any action or behaviour. Some scholars dispute this (often in an

---

46 Deuteronomy also includes 'field' (AT) – something that was obviously irrelevant in the Sinai historical setting reflected in Exod. 20.

47 Not surprisingly, there is nothing truly analogous in any extant ancient law codes. Though explicitly mentioned in association with theft of property or seizure of a city, it was the action rather than the coveting that was considered to be the serious infringement. So Baker 2017: 141–145.

attempt to impose some perceived uniformity on the Decalogue), suggesting that the prohibition encompasses action as well as thought. Thus understood, the coveting in view here is more than simply unfulfilled thoughts or desires but is illicitly acted upon: the coveted item is taken from the neighbour, thus becoming an offence that can actually be witnessed and prosecuted. However, there is nothing in the tenth word itself that supports this more tangible interpretation.

Covet (*ḥāmad*) is a morally neutral word; like its Hebrew synonym (Hithpael *ʾwh*) in Deuteronomy 5:21 and its Greek equivalent (*epithumeō*), it can denote something positive (cf. Gen. 2:9; 3:6; Pss 19:10; 68:16 [MT 17]). However, here, as more often the case in Scripture, the connotation is illicit desire (e.g. Exod. 34:24; Deut. 7:25; Josh. 7:21; Prov. 6:25; Mic. 2:2a) motivated by greed and selfishness that betray a lack of trust in Yahweh as provider (cf. Heb. 13:5). This is clearly not an offence that any human court could prosecute, but left unchecked it inevitably produces more-visible fruit (Josh. 7:21; 2 Sam. 11 – 12; Mic. 2:2b; cf. Matt. 15:19; Rom. 7:7–11; 1 Tim. 6:9; Jas 1:14–15; 4:2), such as breaking other commandments, including the first two. Given its close association with greed, which Paul labels 'idolatry' (Eph. 5:5; Col. 3:5), this is hardly surprising. It is also a fundamental breach of the law of love (Rom. 13:8–10). Accordingly, covetousness is totally inconsistent with the essence of God's covenant law – the fundamental duty to love God wholeheartedly (Deut. 6:5; Matt. 22:37–38) and to love others as ourselves (Lev. 19:18b; Matt. 22:39; Rom. 13:9; Gal. 5:14; Jas 2:8). As Wright (2021: 380–381) insightfully observes of this final word:

> In addition to prohibiting something not liable to legal penalty, it prohibited something which could be 'realized' in practical deed without necessarily breaking the law. It was (and remains) possible to fulfill a covetous desire without doing anything technically illegal. The Tenth Commandment, therefore, provides that radical thrust to the Decalog [*sic*] which distinguishes it from mere legislation, for it indicates that, while having done nothing illegal by human standards, a person can nevertheless be morally guilty before God.

Meaning
Rather than furnishing the Israelites with a shortlist of criminal and/or capital offences, the Decalogue briefly outlines Israel's covenant obligations with respect to God and one another. Whether these distinct obligations were set out on each of two identical tablets, or on the different sides of each identical tablet, or – as traditionally understood – this dichotomy was expressed by two quite different tablets, the twofold emphasis on demonstrating love for both God and neighbour in the Decalogue's contents is undeniable.[48]

However, as highlighted above, this twofold obligation involves more than simply actions and words; it also encompasses thoughts and desires, ensuring that every human being (with one notable exception) falls far short of the mark reflected in the Ten Commandments.

B. The community's response (20:18–21)

Context
This short paragraph narrates the people's response to the Sinai theophany, particularly God's verbal revelation of the Decalogue (20:1–17). As suggested above, it is perhaps best understood as picking up the earlier narrative (i.e. ch. 19), after the necessary flashback recounting God's verbal revelation of the Decalogue. Thus understood, this passage, along with 20:1–17, picks up from and elaborates on the narrative of chapter 19, and serves to explain why the more detailed stipulations recorded in the Book of the Covenant (24:4, 7) were directly disclosed only to Moses.

Comment
18–21. Israel's trembling response to the theophanic display on Sinai (vv. 18–19) may seem somewhat incongruous with the warnings expressed in 19:20–24 – there is certainly no thought

---

48 Though extending beyond the content of just the Decalogue, familiar summaries in the NT (Luke 10:27–28; Rom. 13:8–10; Gal. 5:14) clearly endorse this twin focus of Israel's covenant obligations.

here of anyone forcing their way through the perimeter fence for a closer look (cf. 19:21); rather, overawed by what they had just witnessed, the terrified people maintain their distance and insist that Moses act for them as mediator of God's word. Accordingly, it seems reasonable to conclude that these verses further unpack the theophanic encounter narrated back in 19:16–19, during which the people heard God's voice from the fire (cf. Deut. 5:24). Rather than risk prolonged encounter with this awesome deity, the Israelites elect to have God communicate with them indirectly, via Moses (cf. Deut. 5:23–27).

Although the fear the Israelites expressed was to some extent irrational (cf. Deut. 5:24–26), Moses nevertheless insists that the objective of this first-hand experience of Yahweh's revelation (of the Decalogue) was to instil in them an appropriate fear of Yahweh, which would keep them from sinning (v. 20). The 'paradox' in this verse may thus be explained by two distinct kinds of fear (i.e. an abject terror, and a godly fear that facilitates obedience), although possibly it relates rather to the object of their fear: 'Do not be afraid [*of dying*]. God has come . . . so that the fear *of God* will be with you to keep you from sinning' (NIV; emphasis added).

Meaning
The Israelites' close encounter with Yahweh's theophany on Sinai evoked the kind of reverence for a holy God needed in order to keep them from sinning, and so take their covenant commitment seriously. Thus, as is more fully explained elsewhere (cf. Deut. 5:28–29), Israel's response here should not be considered wrong-headed, even though their fear of imminent death was unfounded: God had not come to harm them, but to instruct them. Even so, their decision to remain at a safe distance from such a holy God was theologically correct (Exod. 19:12, 21; Deut. 5:28; cf. Exod. 33:20).

10. ISRAEL'S COVENANT OBLIGATIONS DISCLOSED (II): THE BOOK OF THE COVENANT (20:22 – 23:33)

The stipulations in 21:1 – 23:19 may seem like a somewhat loosely arranged collection of absolute commands and specific case ('if . . . then . . .') rulings. Some of the content is clearly organized thematically (e.g. 21:2–9; 22:1–15), whereas other sections seem more fluid in content (cf. 22:16–20; 22:21 – 23:9). However, as will be explained below, this is no piecemeal collection; rather, there is a discernible structure and organization of the material that reflects undeniable literary skill and theological acumen. Though by no means an exhaustive application of the Decalogue to various practical scenarios or situations typically encountered in an Ancient Near Eastern agrarian community, the material evidently has such a context in view, and reflects the same dual emphases (love for God and for neighbour) as the ten words, which the Book of the Covenant is further unpacking or applying.

While some of the material in the Book of the Covenant could potentially be used within a judicial setting, it is doubtful if this was ever the primary intention. As Sprinkle (1994: 122) insists:

The unsophisticated nature of the biblical 'legal judgments' ought rather to be interpreted as evidence that this was not intended as positive law to be inflexibly applied, but as paradigmatic illustrations of the kinds of resolution of grievances that should take place in Israelite society.

Indeed, such was also true of Ancient Near Eastern law codes more generally; these literary collections served more to impress the deity and/or enhance the royal standing than to provide case laws to direct judicial decisions in a legal setting. Rather than labelling such collections a 'code', a more accurate label is arguably 'treatise': the exemplary verdicts served a more didactic function, modelling judicial wisdom rather than prescriptive law (see Walton 2006: 287–301).

Accordingly, to refer to the material in Exodus 21:1 – 23:19 as covenant *stipulations*, *precepts* and *rulings* is far preferable than *laws* or *code*.

A. Regulations for worship, manumission and social responsibilities (20:22 – 22:20)

Context

The more detailed Book of the Covenant is introduced, as was the Decalogue (cf. 20:2), with a further reminder of Israel's privileged position (20:22), which forms the basis for the instructions that immediately follow (20:23–26). This initial material, along with 23:20–33, brackets the stipulations introduced by the structural marker in 21:1 and concluded with the prohibition on cooking a young goat in its mother's milk in 23:19b (cf. 34:26).[1] These

---

1 That these two verses (23:19 and 34:26) are entirely identical, and that some of the preceding material in Exod. 34 (e.g. vv. 10–16) correlates closely with 23:20–33, strongly suggests that the so-called 'ritual decalogue' of Exod. 34:10–26 is a representative summary of the Book of the Covenant, which alone is recorded by Moses (Exod. 34:27; cf. 34:1). The unspecified *he* in 34:28b (who actually inscribes the ten words on the replacement tablets) would accordingly be Yahweh, as 34:1 leads readers to expect.

stipulations constitute three main subsections (21:1 – 22:20; 22:21 – 23:9; 23:10–19). The first of these (21:1 – 22:20) contains regulations concerning the manumission of Hebrew slaves and various social responsibilities.

Comment

i. Regulations for Israelite worship (20:22–26)

22–23. What the Israelites have recently witnessed (Yahweh's audible and awe-inspiring revelation of the covenant's general stipulations) is clearly the theological basis for the following commands concerning unacceptable forms of worship (v. 23; cf. Deut. 4:15–20). The latter serve here, however, not as a summary of the first two commandments, but as a foil for the legitimate and acceptable way to worship Yahweh that is set out in the following verses (vv. 24–26).

24–26. These altar laws – the prohibitions on both stonework and ritual exposure – distinguish Israelite cultic practice from that of others, including the Canaanites. However, they appear also to be preparatory for the covenant ratification ritual that is carried out subsequently (cf. 24:4b–8), involving both the use of such an altar (presumably) and the two types of sacrifice prescribed here. Accordingly, these verses are not simply part of the ritual *inclusio* that brackets the Book of the Covenant's judicial core (i.e. the regulations introduced in 21:1), but provide relevant instructions for significant aspects of the subsequent ratification ritual.

ii. Regulations for the manumission of Hebrew bondservants (21:1–11)

1. The superscription here marks the beginning of the so-called 'covenant *code*' or detailed stipulations, comprising specific rulings and commands.

The first collection of casuistic ('if . . . then . . .') rulings that follows (21:2–11) relates to indentured household servitude – a situation markedly different from the chattel slavery practised in more recent times and clearly forbidden in Israel (cf. 21:16). In the case of indentured servitude, people voluntarily sold themselves (and/or family members) into such a contractual arrangement in order to pay off debt or survive extreme financial crisis (Lev. 25:39; Deut. 15:12; cf. Gen. 47:13–25). This was normally a temporary rather than a permanent situation. The instructions here are intended to prevent such arrangements from being abused by either party; respective rights and obligations (mainly relating to terminating the relationship) are thus set out.

Significantly, to have this separate section on Hebrew servants distinguishes the latter from being mere personal property (cf. their absence from the property laws in 22:1–15),[2] thus highlighting their unique status as human beings – a recurring emphasis within the Book of the Covenant.

2–6. The initial subsection (verses 2–6) focuses on compulsory emancipation at the end of six years' service (v. 2), analogous to the mandatory sabbath rest at the end of the six-day working week.[3] Such release is without cost (lit. 'for nothing'; Heb. *ḥinnām*). This could possibly allude to money given by the master (cf. Gen. 29:15; Jer. 22:13), in which case no such payment is required here in Exodus (cf. Deut. 15:13–15). However, most likely the non-payment in verse 2 indicates that the servant is no longer in his master's debt (cf. v. 11b), and thus his emancipation requires no ransom payment (i.e. release fee).

The qualifying conditions attached to such mandatory release (vv. 3–4) seem designed to ensure that the master's financial investments (particularly in relation to his female servants) are not undermined, nor his generosity (in giving a servant a wife) exploited. Thus, mandatory freedom after six years' service was restricted to those who had effectively 'earned' it by completing

---

2   While some English translations of Exod. 21:21 suggest otherwise, this text literally says that 'the slave is his [master's] *silver*' – which in context seems to suggest that compensating a temporarily incapacitated slave is unnecessary because the short convalescence period only hurts the master's own pocket.

3   Despite this obvious analogy, the sabbath principle is not explicitly applied to this compulsory emancipation of slaves in Exodus. However, cf. Lev. 25:39–55, where it is implicitly applied.

the contract; accordingly, marriage to a master's female servant did not automatically secure her and her children's release also. The additional qualifications (vv. 5–6) thus address the situation where such a servant prefers to remain, along with his wife and children, in his master's service. To ratify such ongoing servitude, an ear-piercing ritual must be carried out. Where and before whom this was done is unclear. The Hebrew noun (*hā)ʾĕlōhîm* may arguably refer either to God or to the judges in the Book of the Covenant (cf. 21:13; 22:8, 9 [MT 7, 8], 28 [MT 27]), making its exact nuance occasionally ambiguous.⁴ Moreover, some envisage two distinct stages in the procedure here (v. 6): a declaration of the servant made before (*hā)ʾĕlōhîm*, followed by ear-piercing at the master's house (cf. Deut. 15:17). However, it is perhaps unnecessary to isolate these two actions quite so sharply; verse 6a may allude to a local altar, or verse 6b may have in view the *door* or *door-post* of the sanctuary. But wherever it was carried out, this ritual established such an indentured arrangement as permanent.⁵

7–11. The second subsection of this unit addresses a master's obligations to certain female servants – those who have been sold on the understanding that they will become a wife of either their master or his son (vv. 8a, 9a).⁶ Unlike ordinary household servants (v. 2; cf. Deut. 15:12), such female servants could not be released after six years (v. 7), presumably due to their 'betrothal' or 'quasi-marital' status (Wright 2021: 399). However, if the master subsequently voids the agreement, he must allow such a woman to be ransomed, or continue treating and providing for her as appropriate (vv. 9b, 10b). If he does not, she may go free without financial penalty (v. 11).

---

4   See further, p. 277 n. 36 below.
5   The Hebrew (*lĕʿōlām*) does not necessarily mean 'for ever', but here encompasses the life of either the servant or his master.
6   Presumably prompted by financial extremity, the father possibly sells his daughter in lieu of the anticipated bride-money he would ordinarily have received (cf. 22:16) and/or the dowry he would have normally been expected to provide.

These regulations are evidently designed to protect such a female servant from exploitation or deprivation. However, while the substance is fairly clear, some of the specifics are less so. To start with, there is the precise status of such a servant (Heb. *'āmâ*) in her master's household. Here she is apparently not simply the feminine equivalent of a male servant (Heb. *'ebed*); for such a 'handmaid'/'maidservant' – whose duties primarily concerned the master's wife (cf. Gen. 16:3; 32:22 [MT 23]) – a different noun is commonly used (Heb. *šiphâ*). In terms of domestic hierarchy, an *'āmâ* was possibly superior (cf. Exod. 11:5; 1 Sam. 25:41), though such a distinction does not seem to be clearly maintained in the Old Testament, possibly because it diminished over time.[7] More controversial, however, is her exact status: is she considered a concubine, a normal wife, or something in between (a betrothed or some kind of 'slave-bride')? The master's obligations and the woman's rights (vv. 9–10) seem at least to suggest some form of the latter.[8]

A related issue of debate is the master's actions and obligations towards such an indentured female servant (vv. 8–10): (1) If, for some unspecified reason,[9] she loses favour with the master who has selected her for himself,[10] he must permit her to be ransomed

---

7 Suggested to me by David Firth (personal communication).

8 For further discussion, see Alexander 2017: 475–476.

9 While the Hebrew clause (lit. 'if she is bad/evil in the eyes of her master') could denote some moral failure (cf. Gen. 38:7; Num. 32:13; Deut. 4:25), it seems in context to suggest that she has simply lost his favour (cf. Gen. 6:8; Exod. 3:21; 33:12; Deut. 24:1); hence he no longer wants her as a (potential) wife. Had she been guilty of moral failure, he could presumably have ended this marital contract by divorce, as Deut. 24:1 subsequently legislates (cf. Matt. 1:19).

10 There is also a text-critical issue in v. 8 (see NIV footnote), which reads either '. . . the master, who has *not* [Heb. *lō'*] designated her', or else '. . . the master, who has *for himself* [Heb. *lô*] designated her' – depending on whether the MT's *Ketib* ('what is written') is translated, or – as suggested by the LXX and most contemporary English translations – the phonetically identical *Qere* ('what is read') is preferred.

(i.e. by fellow Israelites, most likely her relatives). He cannot
'on-sell' her to foreigners (i.e. those outside the covenant), having
unilaterally ended (lit. 'in his dealing treacherously with her'; cf.
Mal. 2:14–15) their relationship. (2) If the master has selected her
for his son rather than himself (v. 9), he must act towards her
'according to the regulation of daughters' (AT) – which possibly
alludes to the ruling subsequently recorded in Leviticus 18:15 (see
also vv. 9–11, 17).[11] (3) If he (the master) marries someone else (lit.
'another', though possibly meaning 'alternative' here rather than
'additional'),[12] the rights of the ʾāmâ must not be reduced. Rather,
the same 'food, clothing and oil[?]' (AT) should be provided as
before. The third of these provisions ('oil') glosses a Hebrew noun
(ʿônâ) that occurs nowhere else in the Old Testament but is often
interpreted as 'conjugal rights' or the like.[13] However, this may
wrongly presume that the ʾāmâ had already attained the status of
a concubine or wife. Following Hugenberger (1994: 322 n. 167),
Alexander (2017: 477–478) insists that no such marriage had yet
taken place, hence 'conjugal relations' is the 'least likely' meaning
of ʿônâ. Nevertheless, while certainly clashing with the consonantal text of verse 8 (see n. 10), and the 'alternative' interpretation
of verse 10a (i.e. 'takes another' means marrying an 'alternative'
rather than an 'additional' wife), the status of the ʾāmâ as some
form of wife seems to be consistently assumed in these verses.
Even so, there is no compelling reason for inferring any allusion
to sexual intercourse; it is just as likely that ʿônâ refers to some
other essential provision (cf. Hammurabi §148; see also §178).
Thus understood, these marital duties are little different from

11 Whether such a ruling was already familiar (Exod. 18:15–20; cf. Gen.
    38:26), or simply not incorporated in the canonical record of the Book
    of the Covenant, is uncertain. In any case, Exod. 21:9 assumes its
    existence.

12 So Hugenberger 1994: 322, followed by Alexander 2017: 477.

13 Yet the triad here in Exodus corresponds closely, albeit in a slightly
    different sequence, to 'food, oil and clothing' in Hammurabi §178 (COS
    2: 347). Cf. also Old Babylonian ipru, piššatu, lubuštu (food, ointment and
    a garment), HALOT 3: 855.

modern alimony, and raise fewer issues for the traditional interpretation of the seventh commandment (see comment on 20:14).
Accordingly, it is unnecessary to exclude any typical provision of
care where such an indentured *wife* remains part of the master's
household.

Even though it is not entirely clear what *these three things* (v. 11)
refers to,[14] failure in any of the master's obligations is a breach of
agreement that constitutes the exception to the initial ruling (v.
7), thus allowing the *'āmâ* also to go out, free of charge (cf. 21:2).
In any event, and contrary to some feminist interpretation, this is
about protecting the most vulnerable, not imposing a lower status
on women.[15]

***iii. Regulations for various social responsibilities (21:12 – 22:20
[MT 22:19])[16]***
This larger block of material – mainly in the form of 'case laws'
dealing with physical injuries (21:18–36) and property loss (22:1–16)
– is bracketed by two much shorter sets of absolute commands
that focus on offences that always evoke the death penalty:
murder, kidnapping and parental assault (21:12–17); sorcery, bestiality and idolatry (22:18–20).[17] This arrangement underlines the
difference between capital and non-capital offences, something
that is further unpacked in the contents of this section, where the
penalties discriminate between various types of physical assault
and homicide, and prioritize people over property by placing the

---

14 While it may just be the three items mentioned in v. 10, it could possibly
   allude to all three secondary rulings listed in vv. 8–10, in which case the
   penalty in v. 11 constitutes a fitting *inclusio* for vv. 7–11.
15 I am indebted to David Firth (personal correspondence) for this
   observation.
16 In the Hebrew text, 22:1 is numbered 21:37, so 22:2–31 is 22:1–30 in
   the MT. This commentary will use the English verse numbers for this
   material but add the Hebrew verse numbers in parentheses where it
   might otherwise be confusing.
17 So Wright 2021: 410–411.

highest value on the loss of human life, whether through malice, accident or negligence.

The opening set of absolute commands (vv. 12–17) that bracket the larger section (cf. 22:18–20) highlights four discrete capital offences: deliberate homicide; physical assault on a parent; kidnapping; and verbal assault on a parent.[18]

12–14. Though any fatal blow (whether intended to kill or not) warrants a death sentence (v. 12), only premeditated or deliberate homicide demands such (v. 14). Unlike in the case of an unplanned homicide (v. 13), there is no leniency for anyone who has deliberately killed another person (v. 14). Deliberate and involuntary homicide are thus clearly distinguished: the designated place of refuge (v. 13b) was never intended as a way those guilty of planned or premeditated murder might escape justice (cf. Deut. 19:4–6, 11–13).

It is possible to infer from verse 14 that Yahweh's *altar*[*s*] (wherever located) temporarily served as such a designated place (at least prior to the establishment of cities of refuge; cf. Num. 35:6; Deut. 4:41–43; 19:1–3), though verse 14 may simply relate to the subsequent trial of the accused (i.e. 'before God/the judges'; cf. 21:6; 22:8, 11; see also Josh. 20:6) rather than to the period of temporary asylum.[19] Admittedly, Yahweh's altar was occasionally clung to by those hoping to escape an immediate threat of execution (1 Kgs 1:49–53; 2:28–34), demonstrating that the sanctuary/temple altar was considered a place where one might appeal for leniency. However, unlike our text here in Exodus, the issue in Kings was not justice but mercy – something extended to Adonijah but denied to Joab.

15–17. It is technically ambiguous (see NIV footnote) whether the offence in verse 15 refers to any physical blow, or only to

---

18 The consistent use of a present participle (cf. NIV's 'Anyone who . . .') to begin, and an identically worded penalty clause (Heb. *môt yûmāt*, 'must certainly be killed') to end each primary instruction (vv. 12, 15, 16, 17), marks off these verses as a discrete unit.

19 So Alexander, who correctly notes that '[a] guilty party is unlikely to be clinging to the altar [until] his case is finally decided' (2017: 481).

striking that causes death (v. 12; cf. 2:11–12). However, given
that verse 12 has already stated that any fatal blow warrants the
death penalty, it seems more likely that verse 15 encompasses any
physical assault on a parent – regardless of injury inflicted. Like
verse 17, this is thus a practical application of the fifth (rather
than the sixth) commandment, demanding that parents be given
the honour which (like God) they rightly deserve (cf. 22:17; Lev.
20:19).

Bracketing such a serious offence as kidnapping between what
might initially be construed as more minor offences against parents
might seem rather odd for modern readers, especially if *curse* (v.
17) evokes for us only the connotation of psychological harm.
However, in the light of the power/significance of both blessing
and cursing in Israel and the ancient world (cf. Gen. 9:25–27;
14:19; 27:33; 48:9–20; 49:2–28; Exod. 12:32; Num. 22:5–12; 23:7–12;
2 Kgs 2:24), disassociating such verbal assault from serious harm
is arguably mistaken. In any case, even if the verb in Exodus 21:17
is understood simply in its etymological sense of 'making light of
someone' (i.e. disdaining or disrespecting them),[20] this constitutes
a very serious offence against parents in ancient Israel (Ezek. 22:7;
cf. Prov. 20:20). Accordingly, all three scenarios in verses 15–17
involve an affront to the respect that others deserve, and this sufficiently explains why these offences are so serious in Israel: it is a
capital offence, not simply to strike, but even to disrespect a parent,
and both are just as offensive to God as kidnapping someone for
financial gain (i.e. stealing someone else's life).

18–19. The following case rulings (vv. 18–36) continue the
preceding focus on personal injury or death, but concentrate now
on that which results from excessive force or negligence, rather
than malice. The primary concern is thus the kind of offence
alluded to in verse 13, not the kind described in verse 14. The
material may be divided into two subsections, focusing primarily
on (1) injury resulting from excessive force (vv. 18–27); and (2) injury

---

20 Such disrespect would obviously include denying parents appropriate
financial support or care in their old age, but there seems to be no
reason to restrict the offence here only to that.

resulting from human negligence (vv. 28–36). Inflicting physical harm on others, whether intended or otherwise, carries significant consequences. This is illustrated by each of the scenarios depicted in the following verses.

The first scenario (vv. 18–19) underlines that, regardless of who starts a fight, an assailant is personally responsible for injury they inflict with either an instrument or a fist.[21] Unless such an injury proves fatal (v. 18; cf. v. 12), the assailant will not face physical punishment (v. 19a); nevertheless, they must compensate the incapacitated person for any losses during the latter's convalescence, and ensure a full recovery (vv. 19b–20).

20–21. Unlike the first scenario, the second reflects a clear power imbalance. Significantly, however, the person who has the power (and superior status) is nevertheless held to account – regardless of the status or gender of their victim. If excessive force results in homicide, the victim 'must certainly be avenged' (AT). Unfortunately, many English translations unhelpfully make the master the subject here (the one who beats his servant *must be punished*). It is not stipulated here what such justice will involve, but even if it were only financial compensation to spouse or family (cf. v. 21b; v. 32), this would distinguish the Book of the Covenant from similar Ancient Near Eastern law codes.[22] If, however (as seems more likely the case), such an offence is implicitly avenged by death here, this stipulation is unique in the ancient world, again emphasizing the significance of human life above all else.

There is no need for any avenging, however, when injuries inflicted are only temporary (incapacitating the slave for just a day or two), since 'the slave is his silver' (v. 21b). This is often

---

21 Traditionally translated as *stone* or *fist*, the Hebrew noun (*'egrōf*) may possibly denote a 'tool' (cf. NIV footnote; however, cf. Isa. 58:4).

22 Cf. the class distinction in the analogous rulings of the Laws of Hammurabi (*COS* 2: 348): 'if he (the victim) is a member of the *awīlu*-class [the Babylonian upper class], he [a fellow *awīlu* assailant] shall weigh and deliver 30 shekels of silver [§207] . . . If he (the victim) is a member of the commoner-class, he shall weigh and deliver 20 shekels of silver' [§208].

interpreted as signifying ownership (i.e. the slave is merely part of the master's property), but probably the clause subtly alludes to the master's self-imposed financial loss (due to this recuperating slave's unplanned break), which renders compensation quite unnecessary.

22–25. This next scenario seems to be another case of unintended injury (v. 13), where a pregnant woman becomes the victim of collateral damage (v. 22). This should not be confused with the contrasting scenario in Deuteronomy 25:11–12, where a man's wife intentionally intrudes in such a fight and deliberately commits a culpable offence. Here in Exodus, there is no suggestion that the victim is anything other than an innocent bystander.

The precise nature of the 'harm' (AT; Heb. *āsôn*) alluded to in verses 22–23 has generated considerable controversy,[23] especially in view of the modern abortion debate. It is unclear whether (1) premature (but viable) birth or miscarriage is in view in verse 22; and whether (2) 'harm' (in v. 23) relates to the mother, the infant(s)[24] or both. While certainly not definitive, analogous Ancient Near Eastern regulations suggest the focus is on miscarriage and any further consequences suffered by the mother.[25] Verse 22 can be interpreted as encompassing both mother and

---

23 The noun is used elsewhere in the OT only in relation to the harm that Jacob fears might come to Benjamin in Egypt (Gen. 42:4, 38; 44:29).

24 The Hebrew (both verb and noun) is plural, which might allow for potentially more than one infant in the mother's womb. Alternatively, the phrase may simply allude to the premature/miscarried infant and the afterbirth.

25 E.g. Hammurabi (*COS* 2: 348) stipulates that, 'If an *awīlu* strikes a woman of the *awīlu*-class and thereby causes her to miscarry her fetus, he shall weigh and deliver 10 shekels of silver for her fetus' (§209), but 'if that woman should die, they shall kill his [the assailant's] daughter' (§210). Financial compensation, though reduced, also applies in the case of a woman who is commoner-class (5 shekels, §211) or a slave (2 shekels) who miscarries (§213), or 30 and 20 shekels respectively should the commoner (§212) or slave (§214) die as a result. Equivalent Hittite laws (*COS* 2: 108) compute the financial penalty for such miscarriages

child – especially if the wording of the talion principle in verses
23b–25 (*life for life, eye for eye, tooth for tooth* . . .) necessarily excludes
such injury to either in the previous verse. However, this logic
applies only if verse 22 depicts premature (but viable) birth rather
than a preventable miscarriage/stillbirth. In the case of the latter,
serious injury (NIV) relates exclusively to the postnatal condition
of the mother who has lost her child. The obvious objection to
this interpretation is twofold: (1) the logical inference that such
loss of a child does not constitute *serious injury* – a hurtful and
undoubtedly offensive idea for such an unfortunate mother; (2) the
implication that a miscarried child/dead foetus is not considered a
human being – warranting more than financial compensation (cf.
21:12, 18). However, in response to these objections the following
observations should be noted: (1) These verses primarily focus on
serious harm/injury rather than death. (2) The passage concerns
accidental and unintended consequences, and thus in relation
to homicide, the scenario equates more with 21:13 and 21:29–30
than 21:14 and 21:20. (3) The financial compensation demanded
is implicitly significant and commensurate with the loss involved
(v. 22b; cf. 21:30–32). Accordingly, there is no justification in these
verses for deliberate homicide or for suggesting that a child in the
womb is not considered a human person. Even if no additional
harm is done to the mother, the assailant must pay adequate
compensation (as determined by the husband's claim and a court's
judicial ruling) for the loss of the child. The ruling thus places a
high value on all human life, even life in the womb.

The second issue raised by this text relates to the retributive
principle (the law of talion), expressed formulaically in verses
23–25.[26] As often observed, this is perhaps one of the most

---

by the trimester involved (§17, §18). The class distinction in these texts
is again foreign to the Book of the Covenant.

26 Once again, Hammurabi (*COS* 2: 348) contains analogous rulings,
although in this case actual mutilation is implied. No financial alternative is offered for an *awīlu*'s offence against another *awīlu*, although
this arguably was an advance on earlier fixed monetary penalties that
were no big deal for well-off offenders (Alexander 2017), and class

misunderstood regulations in the Old Testament. Rather than encouraging vendettas and personal revenge, its objective was to curtail such, ensuring that no more (or less) is exacted than justice requires (i.e. 'one eye – not *two* – for an eye . . .'; cf. Lamech's boast in Gen. 4:23–24). Moreover, as the context makes clear (cf. vv. 13, 19, 26–27, 30, 34), the stated principle (vv. 23–25) was not to be applied literally (i.e. in terms of physical mutilation) in Israel.[27] Deliberate homicide was an obvious exception (21:14, 23b; cf. Num. 35:31), but in many other cases even capital punishment could be commuted to the payment of an appropriate financial penalty (cf. 21:30; Num. 35:32).

26–27. Significantly, there is no analogous legislation in extant Ancient Near Eastern law codes, suggesting that these laws in Exodus conferred on slaves a unique status in the ancient world (Alexander 2017: 289).[28] Though non-fatal beatings of slaves carried a less severe penalty (cf. v. 20), inflicting serious injury bore a significant financial cost. To compensate for any irreparable bodily damage to a household servant (a destroyed eye/tooth is

---

discrimination is unashamedly explicit: 'If an *awīlu* should blind the eye of another *awīlu*, they shall blind his eye' (§196). 'If he should blind the eye of a commoner . . . he shall weigh and deliver 60 shekels of silver' (§198). 'If he should blind the eye of an *awīlu*'s slave . . . he shall weigh and deliver one-half of his value' (§199).

27 The only punishment suggesting mutilation in the OT relates to the contrasting third-party scenario (Deut. 25:11–12) outlined above (see opening comment on 21:22). However, as Wright (2021) opines, even in this case physical mutilation may not necessarily be in view (the normal word for 'hand' is used in v. 11, whereas the word for 'palm' is used in v. 12, which could possibly be euphemistic for genitalia [i.e. her ability to conceive]). Such non-literal[?] 'cutting off' correlates more closely with the implied/potential consequence of her physical offence – the emasculation of her male victim.

28 As Alexander further notes, 'the present arrangement of the material [vv. 18–25] makes good sense . . . Having stated the principle of "an eye for an eye" . . . in vv. 23–25, we now see how this applies in the case of a slave who is harshly beaten by a master' (2017: 489).

presumably representative here for any such permanent damage
to the slave's body), the master must grant his/her emancipation.
Such a ruling not only makes financial provision for those who
have been incapacitated in some way, but also acts as a strong
deterrent to any unruly or excessive use of physical force.

28–32. Moving on from injuries caused by human violence, the
next set of rulings (vv. 28–36) deals mainly with cases that involve
'culpable negligence': the loss of human or animal life resulting
from lack of due diligence and care.

Where a dangerous animal (e.g. a bull or ox) is solely responsible for the death of a man or woman (v. 28), it must be stoned
to death[29] and its meat must not be consumed – the intrinsic
value of human life is highlighted not only by the necessity of
the animal's death (cf. Gen. 9:5–6), but also by the permanently
unclean status of its flesh (cf. Lev. 11:39–47). The bull's owner,
however, is not held accountable, unless personal negligence is
also involved: that is, though well aware of the potential danger,
the owner took no preventative measures to ensure the personal
safety of the community (v. 29). In this case, the life of the human
offender is also forfeit unless financial compensation is preferred,
in which case the owner must pay whatever sum is demanded (v.
30). This applies whether the victim was an adult or a child (*a son
or a daughter*, v. 31). In the case of a slave, however, such compensation is fixed at thirty shekels of silver (v. 32), possibly suggesting
that the compensation demanded in the other cases was likewise
commensurate with the victim's intrinsic value. In any case, even
in the case of a slave, the animal must be stoned to death – a detail
implicitly suggesting that a slave's life (whatever their net financial
worth) was still of equal value to that of every other human being.

33–34. The final verses of this chapter shift the focus from
human to animal death. In this first example, the fatality is again
the result of human negligence: someone has uncovered or dug a
pit, but failed to cover it afterwards, making it a lethal hazard for

---

29 Significantly, analogous Ancient Near Eastern laws (cf. Hammurabi
§250–252; Eshnunna §53–54) do not suggest executing an ox responsible
for the death of a human.

roaming livestock such as an ox or donkey (v. 33). Consequently, in line with the principle set out in verses 29–30, the negligent party must compensate the animal's owner for the loss and take the dead animal in exchange (v. 34).

35–36. Where the killing of one beast by another is involved (v. 35a), both owners must share the financial loss between them (v. 35b), unless the incident could possibly have been prevented by the owner of the aggressive animal (v. 36a). In this case their neighbour gets the living beast, and the negligent owner takes the dead one in exchange (v. 36b). Significantly, in both these cases where only animal life is lost, there is no mention of execution – whether for the negligent person or the offending animal.

22:1–4. The focus switches now to property regulations (22:1–17) – in particular, when property or income is lost or damaged due to the actions of others. Though the headings in the NIV suggest otherwise, this opening section of the chapter includes verses 16–17, where the focus is primarily on the potential financial loss involved in such an illicit sexual liaison.

The opening verses of the chapter (vv. 1–4) focus on simple theft (stealing someone else's livestock), and the compensatory damages that such incurred. The latter depended on the relative value of what was stolen (v. 1b),[30] and whether such loss was permanent (v. 1a) or only temporary (v. 4) – in which case the compensation was reduced. In either case, however, such compensation exceeded the net worth of what had been illicitly taken. The discussion of burglary (vv. 2–3a) in the midst of this opening subsection is due to the fact that livestock normally lived in part of an ancient home, thus stealing such might be the burglar's primary objective.

During a night-time burglary (v. 2a), striking such a home invader does not necessarily constitute excessive force – even if it results in their death. Under such circumstances the homeowner's defence of their family and themselves is perfectly reasonable, since the nature of the threat posed by the intruder is uncertain. Accordingly, the homeowner's violent reaction cannot be equated with culpable homicide (v. 2b). During daylight, however, the

---

30 An ox was clearly more valuable than a sheep.

motive behind such home invasion would be more obvious, and killing someone attempting to steal an animal would be dispro-portionate, making the homeowner guilty of bloodshed (v. 3a) and presumably subject to the appropriate penalty (cf. 21:12, 23). Significantly, such protection for the life of a thief is elsewhere unknown in Ancient Near Eastern law. The relative worth of human life – even that of a criminal – is thus further underlined here in the Book of the Covenant.

When thieves have no financial means to make the mandatory restitution, they are not executed (as per Hammurabi, §8) but rather sold into indentured servitude (v. 3b), presumably remaining in such until the debt is fully paid or until the designated year of release (cf. 21:2).[31]

What especially stands out in these four verses is that, compared to elsewhere in the Ancient Near East, the penalty for simple theft was more lenient, and involved neither execution nor physical mutilation;[32] clearly the loss of property was not considered nearly as significant as the loss of human life.

5–6. Two further examples of culpable negligence (cf. 21:28–36) rather than malicious intent are now provided,[33] but here the regulations are not concerned with any loss of life (human or beast), but with damage done to adjacent property (grass or crops) by straying livestock or an uncontrolled fire. The fact that the

---

31 *Pace* Sprinkle (1994: 132–133), such debt most likely correlated with the compensation stipulated in vv. 1 and 4 (cf. Philo, *On the Special Laws* 4.1.2–5).

32 Cf. Hammurabi's insistence that if a thief has nothing with which to repay his victim, he must be killed (§8); that a hired hand who steals seed or fodder must have his hand cut off (§253); and that an apprehended burglar or robber (i.e. theft involving physical threat or violence) must be executed (§21 & §22).

33 Both verses employ either the same verb (Hiphil *b'r*) with different nuances (graze, burn), or (more likely) two different verbs (i.e. homonyms) that share the same letters but have entirely different meanings. The absence of any (malevolent) motive suggests the damage done to the neighbour's property was accidental.

same two issues are also addressed by the Hittite Laws (in reverse order; §105–106, §107) may suggest that these scenarios were fairly commonplace, not merely hypothetical.[34] Other than ensuring that the property owner was not disadvantaged by receiving something of inferior quality (v. 5b),[35] the stipulated compensation simply equated to whatever loss/damage was experienced; no additional restitution was necessary, given the absence of any criminal intent.

7–15. Attention shifts in these verses to loss or damage while property was temporarily entrusted to someone else (vv. 7, 10, 14). The first two scenarios (vv. 7–9 and vv. 10–13) respectively concern goods or livestock temporarily handed over for safekeeping; the third scenario (vv. 14–15) concerns borrowed or hired livestock. Where theft by a third party is involved, the thief must *pay back double*, that is, compensation plus the normal damages (v. 7b; cf. v. 4). However, if no thief is apprehended (v. 8a), the guardian must be 'brought before God' (AT; lit. *hā'ĕlōhîm*),[36] who will determine

---

34 Hammurabi includes only such regulations on grazing (§57–58), but also includes negligent damage caused by flooding (§55–56), a concern shared by other ancient law codes but evidently less of an issue in Anatolia and Palestine.

35 SP and LXX include additional material, but this seems to be a later, clarifying expansion (see Baker 2009: 59 n. 41). In any case, neither reading insists on punitive damages, which in such cases would be inappropriate (Baker 2009: 62).

36 In v. 8 [MT 7] it is grammatically impossible to tell exactly who is intended, as the plural noun without any verb could refer to either God or human authorities. In the very next verse this noun attracts a *plural* verb ([*they*] *declare guilty*), possibly suggesting that both these verses envisage a trial before human judges. While the use of a plural verb with (*hā*)*'ĕlōhîm* is not unprecedented in relation to God (cf. Gen. 20:13; 31:53; 35:7), some of these verses may arguably be reflecting or accommodating a polytheistic mindset – but this would certainly be problematic in the case of the inspired narrator (Gen. 35:7). For Baker (2009: 67), the analogous stipulation in the Laws of Eshnunna (*COS* 2: 334–335) – in which 'the owner of the house shall swear an oath to satisfy him

whether or not they have appropriated the owner's property (v. 8b [MT 7b]). This naturally segues into the problem of conflicting claims of ownership (v. 9). In this case both parties must present their case before God, and whoever God declares guilty (of theft) must pay the other person back double (compensation plus damages; cf. v. 7b).

However, where an animal entrusted for safekeeping dies, sustains an injury or is taken *while no one is looking* (v. 10), the guardian must swear an oath of innocence before Yahweh,[37] which the owner must accept and carry the loss themselves (v. 11). But if the animal was stolen from the guardian (i.e. while they were present but did nothing to prevent or catch the thief), they must compensate the owner (v. 12). If the owner's livestock was mauled by a wild animal, the guardian must supply clear evidence of such misadventure and thus will not be liable to pay compensation (v. 13).

If an animal is injured or dies while borrowed (vv. 14–15), the borrower must make full restitution (i.e. pay for the stricken animal), unless the owner was present (thus no negligence was involved) or the animal was contracted for hire (hire costs covering any potential damage/loss).

Each of these cases thus underlines that people cannot be held responsible for loss or damage to another's property, unless they are complicit in illicit action or derelict in their duty of care. Moreover, even where there is such culpability, the penalty is simply paying the appropriate financial compensation, since property is replaceable.

16–17. Even though the nature of the 'property' and 'theft' envisaged here is significantly different, the case-law framework

---

[the depositor] at the gate of (the temple of) the god Tishpak' (§37) – confirms that God's temple is also in view here and elsewhere in the Book of the Covenant. In any case, v. 11 implies that in any such court procedure God was most certainly involved.

37 The LXX includes such an oath also in v. 8 [MT 7], but this may be an unnecessary harmonization, making explicit what is already implicit in the Hebrew text.

links these two verses with the preceding material (vv. 1–15), rather than with the three capital offences that immediately follow (vv. 18–20). The scenario in verses 16–17 involves a man who seduces a non-betrothed young woman who implicitly assents to his advances. This distinguishes the situation from Deuteronomy 22:23–24, where the consenting woman is already betrothed, so both parties are guilty of adultery,[38] and also from Deuteronomy 22:28–29, where a non-betrothed and non-consenting female is raped. Here in verses 16–17 neither adultery nor rape is involved; rather, this is simply a matter of consensual premarital sex. Clearly such casual intercourse is being strongly discouraged: the girl's paramour must pay the normal betrothal/marriage present (cf. Gen. 34:12; 1 Sam. 18:25; see also Deut. 22:29), whether or not the father permits the couple to marry.[39] This ensured that the girl's father was not cheated out of his conventional payment or forced to take a reduced amount since his daughter was no longer a virgin, and thus provided for the woman's ongoing support, something that would often be challenging in a subsistence economy. Moreover, it excludes any notion of 'free love' – sexual intercourse involving no formal commitment.

18–20. Matching 21:12–16, the literary *inclusio* closes with more capital offences. These are not only incompatible with Yahweh's and Israel's holy status, but also exemplify the behaviour for which the Canaanites would soon be judged (cf. Lev. 20:22–26). Sorcery (cf. 7:11; Deut. 18:10) encompasses any manipulation of power that belonged exclusively to Yahweh. Since practitioners included men as well as women (cf. 7:11; Mal. 3:5), the gender specificity here is possibly designed to deny any leniency even to the fairer sex (so Alexander 2017: 500). Bestiality not only defiled the offender

---

38 Cf. Deut. 22:25–27, where only the man is guilty, because there was no female consent.

39 It seems to be assumed here that the paramour is willing and intends to marry the man's daughter, whereas the rapist in Deut. 22:28–29 has no such intention – and so must permanently provide for his victim by marrying and never divorcing her.

but was a perversion of natural sexual relations (cf. Lev. 18:23).[40]
Sacrificing to other gods showed utter disregard for Yahweh's
basic covenant instructions, and accordingly invoked the same
judgment (offenders would be set apart for 'total destruction')
that would subsequently be carried out on the morally reprobate
Canaanites.[41]

Meaning
Like the Decalogue, the Book of the Covenant begins by
highlighting the covenant community's responsibility to love
God (in terms of how he alone must be worshipped, and how
such worship must be carried out) before focusing on their
responsibilities to one another (masters and servants, physical
injuries, property loss). The bracketing of the latter by a mixture
of capital offences, however, underlines that the overarching
focus is not simply on honouring the respective rights and obligations of one another, but ensuring that such conduct is exercised
within a theological framework: that is, it is an outworking
of their covenantal responsibility to serve Yahweh. As such,
these commands and rulings in the Book of the Covenant are
more theologically orientated than merely reflecting humanitarian interests: by conducting life in this manner, Yahweh's holy
nation will be honouring him by giving concrete expression to
his ideals for human society. Moreover, as subsequently noted in
Deuteronomy, by showcasing Yahweh's priorities in this manner
God's people will also manifest their 'wisdom and understanding
to the nations, who will hear about all these decrees and say,
"Surely this great nation is a wise and understanding people"'
(Deut. 4:6).

---

40 The Hittite Laws include similar – albeit more specific (cow, pig or dog)
    – injunctions (§187; §199).
41 The cognate noun of the verb used here is *ḥerem* (cf. Lev. 27:29), a
    concept frequently associated with the fate of the Canaanites (see esp.
    Deuteronomy and Joshua).

B. Reflecting God's care for the oppressed (22:21 – 23:9)

Context
Bracketed by yet another *inclusio* (cf. 22:21 and 23:9),[42] this material comprises three distinct parts: obligations to the weak and disadvantaged (22:21–27), obligations to God (22:28–31) and obligations to act justly and fairly (23:1–9). While the mix is certainly broad,[43] the presence of vertical obligations sandwiched between horizontal responsibilities highlights that no 'secular–sacred' dichotomy exists within the Mosaic covenant, because duty to God and duty to fellow human beings are inextricably linked. Moreover, as will be highlighted below, the moral values instilled throughout this collection of instructions are those demonstrated supremely by Yahweh himself – the God to whom the Israelites must offer their unreserved commitment.

Comment
i. Loving the disadvantaged (22:21–27)
21. Isolated from kith and kin, a 'foreign resident' (AT; Heb. *gēr*) is obviously more vulnerable to exploitation. As the Israelites had learnt from bitter experience, even people groups can fall victim to such; they should thus know better than most why such

---

42 While such closely overlapping (in both content and grammar) texts alone suggest that 22:21 – 23:9 constitutes a new section, this is confirmed by the fact that (1) the presentation style (less formal and more personal) differs from that of the preceding material; (2) no humanly enforceable penalties are included; and (3) the focus and emphases have changed – leading Alexander to label this material as 'moral exhortations' or 'precepts', rather than the kind of detailed 'rulings' reflected in the *mišpāṭîm* (2017: 508–510).

43 Discerning a unifying theme for all the material bracketed between these two verses is admittedly challenging (cf. 22:28–31; 23:4–5), but the inclusion of seemingly 'intrusive' material makes sense when this section is interpreted holistically (see below).

maltreatment (23:9; cf. 3:9) should not be tolerated (cf. Deut. 10:18;
24:17–18).[44]

22–27. Yahweh's active concern for the weak and disadvantaged, implicit in verse 21 (cf. 1:11–12), is explicitly articulated in
the rest of this subsection; indeed, here Yahweh's intolerance of
any such oppression is not just a theological fact, but a sombre
warning for any heartless Israelites (vv. 23–24, 27). Unfortunately,
Yahweh's chilling warning (v. 24) was subsequently ignored by the
nation (cf. Isa. 1:17), so the threat here eventually became a terrible
reality (cf. Lam. 5:3).

The two specific prohibitions (vv. 25–27) make it clear that
there are more subtle forms of oppression which Yahweh equally
disdains, such as charging interest for charitable loans (i.e. treating
acts of compassion *like a business deal*). As Baker (2009: 257)
helpfully puts it, 'Any loans should be made as one family member
lending to another, not as a [professional] moneylender seeking
to profit from a business transaction.' This contrasts sharply with
standard Ancient Near Eastern practice, where charging interest/
fees for charitable loans was an assumed right, and creditors could
impose relatively high rates by modern standards.[45] The second
example of more subtle oppression proscribed here is withholding
an essential item 'taken in pledge' for a loan (i.e. caring more
about one's financial risk than the extremity of others). While the
exact meaning of the verb (Heb. *ḥābal*; usually translated 'taken
in pledge') has generated some debate,[46] here it clearly denotes
an item given or agreed upon as the security for a loan. In both
these prohibited scenarios (v. 25b and v. 27b), wealth is prioritized

---

44 Significantly, such protection of foreign residents is unique to Israel in
    Ancient Near Eastern legislation.
45 For more details, see Baker 2009: 253–257.
46 It sometimes refers to property handed over by a defaulting debtor at
    the end of a loan period (e.g. Job 24:9; Prov. 20:16), leading some to
    understand the verb as denoting the *forcible seizure* (i.e. distraint) of a
    debtor's property. However, as Baker (2009: 270) observes, handover
    of a pledge by a defaulting debtor does not necessarily involve physical
    force, which is expressly prohibited in Deut. 24:10–11.

over people, and compassion is stymied. As before, Yahweh's compassion for such people should encourage genuine philanthropy and munificent benevolence.

ii. Living to please God (22:28–31)

28–31. The precise relationship between the initial prohibition in verse 28a and the one that follows (v. 28b) is debatable. As before (cf. 21:6, 22; 22:8–9), *'ĕlōhîm* (the common Old Testament term for God) could be interpreted here as 'court/judges' – though even the NIV plausibly prefers *God* in this instance, where only the latter half of the verse clearly concerns a human leader.[47] Perhaps the second part of this verse relates to the consequences that would inevitably fall on Israel's human leader should the people dishonour God (cf. Mal. 2:2). More likely, however, the second injunction in verse 28 simply links divine authority with human authority within the covenant community (cf. comment on 20:12).

In any case, the disrespect/dishonour (cf. 21:17) envisaged in verse 28 transcends mere speech, and is exemplified in the Israelites withholding from God what he demands (vv. 29–30; cf. 13:2, 11–16; Lev. 23:9–14), and failing to maintain their status as God's holy people by consuming food that ritually defiles them (v. 31; cf. Lev. 11 and Deut. 14 for a more comprehensive list). Thus understood, the prohibitions in verses 29–31 are all theological in nature and offer an illustrative sample rather than an exhaustive list of behaviours that would dishonour God and curse their leader – both of whom should rather be respected and obeyed.

Given the overall significance of holiness in Exodus (see Introduction 5, 'Theological themes in Exodus'), it is no coincidence that 'people of holiness you must be to me' (v. 31; AT) is pivotal in this section (22:21 – 23:9) which structurally unites Israel's divine and human obligations: 'this precept encapsulates all that God desires Israel to be' (Alexander 2017: 515). Israel's social and religious distinctiveness (expressed in how they relate

---

47 Significantly, the Hebrew noun (*nāśî'*) consistently describes Israel's human leaders elsewhere in Exodus (cf. 16:22; 34:31; 35:27), suggesting its (pre-monarchic) antiquity.

to God and other people) is thus an intrinsic mark of such a holy
people.

iii. Maintaining justice (23:1–9)

This third subsection of 22:21 – 23:9 discourages any perversion
of justice – whether by sharing false testimony (vv. 1–2), showing
partiality (v. 3), making false allegations (v. 7) or accepting a bribe
(v. 8). But refraining from hurting one's neighbour in these ways is
clearly not enough; Israel is also called to assist others when they
are in need (vv. 4–5). Active intervention, not just passive restraint,
is therefore strongly encouraged.

The two sets of prohibitions in these verses (vv. 1–3, 6–9)
are separated by two positive exhortations calling for impartial
compassion in verses 4–5. Some consider the style and content
of the latter two verses anomalous (suggesting they originally
belonged with earlier case rulings such as those in 21:18 – 22:17),[48]
but their current location between verses 3 and 6 – albeit as an
excursus emphasizing impartiality – makes perfectly good sense
where partiality is consistently being discouraged.

1–3. The first set of prohibitions concerns truth-telling, elaborating on the ninth commandment (20:16); this is summarized in
terms of 'spreading a false report' (v. 1a, AT). Possible reasons for
doing so are suggested in verses 1b–3: malevolently conspiring
with someone else (v. 1b); siding with the majority due to peer
pressure (v. 2); or natural empathy for the 'little guy' (i.e. the
impoverished person; v. 3). However, no such rationale justifies
propagating a lie.

4–5. Sandwiched between verses 3 and 6, the second part of
this subsection (23:1–9) has a positive emphasis: displaying impartiality, even in the most unlikely situations – where personal bias
or animosity might evoke a negative response. In both scenarios
(coming across an adversary's 'lost' or 'exhausted' beast of burden;
AT), the enemy should be treated as a friend; their property should
be returned (v. 4; cf. Deut. 22:1–3) or rescued (v. 5; cf. Deut. 22:4).

---

48   Unlike these earlier case laws, however, 23:4–5 does not include punish-
     ments (Alexander 2017: 516).

Again, these are simply illustrations of the type of impartiality Yahweh expected his people to exemplify in their treatment of others.

6–9. The final part of this subsection returns to prohibitions, with a clear emphasis on not denying justice to the disadvantaged. While the overarching emphasis reflects a judicial context in particular, the underlying principles undoubtedly applied more widely. As in verses 1–3, the basic precept is stated first (v. 6a), followed by three specific examples of such (assisting with false allegations/execution of the innocent, v. 7a–b; being influenced by bribes/gifts, v. 8a;[49] oppressing resident foreigners, v. 9a), along with the rationale bolstering the prohibitions (Yahweh will not acquit those guilty of injustice, v. 7c; bribery obscures and distorts the truth, v. 8b; Israel's experience in Egypt should have taught them empathy, v. 9b). The *inclusio* of verse 9 (cf. 22:21) brings this section of the Book of the Covenant to an end.

Meaning

As noted previously, like several ancient law codes (e.g. Hammurabi's) Israel's covenant 'code' was more a royal manifesto than a legal textbook. Rather than providing Israel's future judges with some practical examples of judicial case law, it was designed, first and foremost, to make a statement about Israel's God and the kind of society that showcases what truly reflects and honours him.

Accordingly, despite the numerous similarities with other Ancient Near Eastern collections, in significant respects Israel's covenant stipulations stand out as very different from all others: the priority of people over things; the sanctity of human life; the inherent human equality of all people, regardless of gender or social classification; and, as underlined especially in 22:21 – 23:9, striking the right balance between the exercise of compassion and the execution of justice to reflect God's holiness *and* his care for the oppressed.

---

49 As Alexander (2017: 517) observes, the Hebrew noun (*šōḥad*) may refer simply to a gift, not necessarily to something illicitly designed to influence legal proceedings (i.e. a bribe).

Like the Decalogue, this material in the Book of the Covenant is clearly designed to reflect, inculcate and proclaim *Yahweh's* distinctiveness and values – not simply for the cohesion and well-being of Israelite society, but ultimately as a witness to and for the blessing of the nations (cf. Gen. 18:18–19; 26:4–5).

C. Israel's ritual obligations (23:10–19)

Context
Attention shifts once again (cf. 22:29–31) here to cultic obliga-tions: (1) Israel's sabbatical year and day (vv. 10–12); and (2) Israel's mandatory pilgrimage festivals each year (vv. 14–19). These are separated by what appears to be a bridging verse (v. 13), under-lining the most important aspect of Israel's cultic obligations: an exclusive focus on Yahweh their God (cf. vv. 14, 15b, 17, 19). Along with the details outlined in 20:22–26 (esp. vv. 24–26), this section (23:10–19) is part of the cultic frame that encases the more general obligations (21:1 – 23:9) in the Book of the Covenant.

Comment
i. The sabbatical year and sabbath day (23:10–13)
10–11. The sabbatical year, like the weekly sabbath on which it is patterned (v. 12; cf. Deut. 5:14), is here chiefly an expression of humanitarian and ecological concern (v. 11), not an attempt to maximize productivity by crop rotation. Though not explicit, some suggest that a staggered cessation of agricultural activity for any given field may be envisaged here, rather than the nationwide stoppage of all such activity during the weekly sabbath and the Year of Jubilee (cf. Lev. 25). However, the latter passage clearly suggests otherwise (cf. Lev. 25:20–22). Although the relevance of Leviticus 25 might be discounted on the basis that it reflects subsequent practice, this is typically premised on the late dating and questionable historical veracity of Leviticus.[50] Unless such

---

50 E.g. its claim that 'these are the decrees, the laws and the regulations that [*Yahweh*] *established at Mount Sinai* between himself and the Israelites *through Moses*' (Lev. 26:46; emphasis added; cf. 7:37–38; 27:24; see also

a negative premise is uncritically assumed, Leviticus leads us to conclude that the sabbatical year demanded great confidence in Yahweh's promised provision from its inception, and also anticipates that this will indeed be a perennial problem (Lev. 26:32–35). Interestingly, there is no biblical record of the sabbatical year actually being observed, and the Chronicler implies that it was quite frequently (some seventy times) ignored (2 Chr. 36:21).

12. Given its significance as the covenant's *sign* (cf. 31:13, 16–17), some mention of the weekly sabbath (v. 12) in the Book of the Covenant (and its subsequent summary; cf. v. 21 in 34:10–28) is unsurprising. Here, however, it specifically relates to agricultural labour (v. 12b; 34:21b),[51] as befits the benevolent concerns of its immediate and wider context.

13. From its context here, this verse might seem to anticipate the allure of Canaanite fertility worship: the temptation to worship the deities of the indigenous population in order to secure good harvests. However, it is more likely that verse 13 serves as a bridging text, serving to reiterate the people's (*you* in this verse is plural) fundamental covenantal obligation: to obey and worship Yahweh exclusively (cf. 19:5–6; 20:3; 23:20–33). Moreover, as Wright suggests (2021: 440), sandwiched between regulations for agricultural labour and religious festivals this bridging text addresses both, and further undercuts any notion of a 'secular–sacred' dichotomy (cf. 22:18–20).

ii. Annual pilgrimage festivals (23:14–19)

14–16. This paragraph, which outlines Israel's mandatory pilgrimage festivals (*Unleavened Bread, Harvest* and *Ingathering*),[52] and the next (vv. 17–19) are structurally parallel: both are introduced

---

25:1; cf. 4:1; 5:14; 6:1, 8, 19, 24; 7:22, 28; 8:1; 11:1; 12:1; 13:1; 14:1, 33; 15:1; 16:1; 17:1; 18:1; 19:1; 20:1; 21:1, 16; 22:1, 17, 26; 23:1, 9, 23, 26, 33; 24:1; 27:1).

51 Elsewhere in Exodus, '*any* work' is proscribed: 20:10; 31:14–15; 35:2–3.

52 Different labels for these three festivals are used elsewhere: Unleavened Bread is sometimes called Passover; Harvest is sometimes referred to as Weeks (or Pentecost); Ingathering is also known as Tabernacles.

with a basic instruction (*Three* . . ., vv. 14, 17),[53] supplemented by
the specifics that immediately follow (vv. 15–16, 18–19).
The celebration of all three festivals further anticipates Israel's
settlement in the Promised Land (cf. 3:8; 6:8; 12:25–27) and
the typical agricultural programme that this will facilitate (cf.
23:10–12). As explained in detail back in 12:1–28, *Unleavened Bread*
includes *Passover* (cf. 34:18, 25; Lev. 23:5–8; Num. 28:16–25; Deut.
16:1–8), which here is simply assumed rather than (allegedly)
unknown.
Though each of the three pilgrimage festivals can in some
way be connected with the agricultural calendar,[54] only Harvest
and Ingathering are actually agricultural festivals (v. 16; cf. v.
15b).[55] All, however, are premised on God's promise of *a good and
spacious land* (3:8). By making such pilgrimage three times each
year, and bringing such appropriate offerings, the Israelites will
acknowledge Yahweh as the God who not only saves, but also
abundantly provides. Accordingly, *no one* should *appear before [him]
empty-handed* (v. 15b).[56]

17–19. Like the previous paragraph, a basic command (v. 17)
is supplemented by four specifics (vv. 18–19), with which the
detailed covenant stipulations formally conclude (cf. 34:25–26).

---

53 Though the Hebrew phrases used at the start of vv. 14 and 17 are not
    identical, they are synonymous in meaning.

54 Despite some association with the spring lambing season, Unleavened
    Bread/Passover has the most tenuous agricultural connection: 'Abib'
    (AT; 'green ears of grain'; cf. 9:31) is the month when the barley heads
    emerged and firstfruits (Lev. 2:14) were offered, but this only *anticipated*
    the spring barley harvest. Here and elsewhere in the OT Unleavened
    Bread is consistently associated with Israel's deliverance from Egypt;
    unlike the others, it is not a harvest festival. For more on the festival of
    Passover/Unleavened Bread, see comments on Exod. 12.

55 In v. 16b *at the end of the year* refers to the end of the agricultural year; the
    first month of Israel's calendar year was in spring (12:2), not autumn.

56 As Alexander (2017: 523) contends, the switch from second to third
    person 'suggests that the comment . . . is a parenthetical remark, relating
    to all three festivals (cf. Deut. 16:16–17)'.

These four specific instructions, concerning sacrifices and offerings, may apply particularly (though not necessarily exclusively) to the three annual festivals stipulated in verses 14–16.[57] Since the first two instructions (v. 18) are elsewhere closely associated with *Unleavened Bread/Passover* (12:8–10, 15–20), and the third (v. 19) has links with *Harvest* (cf. *firstfruits* also mentioned in v. 16a), the prohibition on boiling a kid in its mother's milk may conceivably relate to *Ingathering* (so Alexander 2017). However, any such link must remain tentative, since the rationale for this concluding taboo remains uncertain. Though much debated, there is still no scholarly consensus regarding its meaning or significance. Some think it alludes to a fertility ritual, as might possibly be inferred from its reiteration at the conclusion of the syncretistic golden calf episode in 34:26. Its only other Old Testament occurrence – at the very end of a long section on clean/unclean food (Deut. 14:1–21) – may imply that it relates to the maintaining of ritual cleanness, a very significant matter in the context of acceptable worship (cf. Exod. 19:14, 22; 29:4; 30:17–21; 40:12). Others suggest that it refers simply to a violation of the natural order – a mother's milk, which sustains the life of its offspring, should not be associated with its death. However, without any further light from its Ancient Near Eastern context, these and the many other speculative explanations offered must remain tentative for now.[58]

Meaning
Throughout the decrees and rulings in the Book of the Covenant, there has been a subtle but clear emphasis on the theological relationship between love for God and love for neighbour, and the fact that there is to be no sacred–secular dichotomy in God's covenant community. While here in this final section of regulations the focus is chiefly on Israel's cultic duties (sabbaths and festivals), two important facts must not be overlooked: (1) As their

---

57 Cf. Hamilton 2011; Alexander 2017; Wright 2021.
58 For further suggestions and a critical appraisal, see Alexander 2017: 525–526.

bracketing function for the Book of the Covenant highlights (cf. the *inclusio* with 20:24–26), these cultic obligations again reiterate the twofold emphasis of the book of the covenant as a whole: Israel's duties to others must not be interpreted in isolation from their duty to God. (2) As the bridging function of 23:13 underlines, Israel's cultic duties must not be viewed as an end in themselves or isolated from their primary function, which is to honour God in faithful, divinely decreed worship.

D. Hortatory epilogue (23:20–33)

Context
The *Book of the Covenant* (cf. 24:7) concludes with a more hortatory epilogue, focusing primarily on Israel's occupation of the Promised Land. Though dismissing the critical division of this material into two different sources, Childs (1974) considers it to be a much later (Deuteronomistic) interpolation. However, as Alexander (2017) demonstrates, key details – such as its consistent historical (pre-settlement) perspective and its conditional promissory elements – strongly support both its literary integrity and its covenantal context here in Exodus.

There are two subsections, each with two discrete parts: (1) Yahweh's trailblazing angel (vv. 20–23) and Israel's loyalty to Yahweh (vv. 24–26); and (2) Yahweh's removal of human obstacles (vv. 27–31) and Israel's responsibility to complete the task (vv. 32–33). Clearly there is a renewed emphasis here on Yahweh's covenant promises, particularly that of giving Israel *a good and spacious land* (3:8) – which is clearly assumed within the Book of the Covenant.

Comment
i. Yahweh's trailblazing angel and Israel's loyalty (23:20–26)
20–23. The opening focal marker ('See!', AT; Heb. *hinnē*) plus a concentration of first person singular verbs (*I will . . .*) draws explicit attention for the first time since 19:5–6 to Yahweh's obligations to Israel: in particular, how he will secure the fulfilment of his promises through a variety of means. The first of these is his *angel*/'messenger', who will lead the Israelites *to the place I*

[*Yahweh*] *have prepared.*[59] The authority of this messenger to forgive sins, along with the fact that God's *Name is in him* (v. 21), negates the suggestion that he is none other than Moses (Janzen 1997: 179–180). Moreover, his words and actions are closely associated in these verses with God himself, just like the heavenly being who appears elsewhere in Exodus (cf. 3:2; 14:19; 32:34; 33:2). While some infer from this that the angel is simply a manifestation of Yahweh himself (e.g. Durham 1987: 335; Stuart 2006: 542), a subtle distinction between this angel and Yahweh must surely be maintained (cf. 32:34; 33:2–5). Nevertheless here, as elsewhere (cf. Josh. 5:13–15; Judg. 2:1–5; 6:11–24), Yahweh's angel clearly speaks and acts with divine authority; thus, submission to him (Exod. 23:21a) guarantees divine assistance and success (vv. 22–23), whereas to ignore or rebel against him is to court disaster (23:21b). The use of the same Hebrew verb (*šāmar*; to keep/guard) to describe both the angel's 'protecting' (v. 20) and the Israelites' 'taking heed' (v. 21) further underlines such reciprocity.

On the list of indigenous inhabitants in the Promised Land, see comment on 3:8.

24–26. Following the explanation of what Yahweh will do, Israel's responsibility to worship Yahweh exclusively in the Promised Land is now articulated: rather than assimilating any Canaanite deities or the practices associated with such worship, Israel was to demolish their idols and cultic pillars (v. 24) and serve Yahweh (v. 25a; cf. 20:3, 23), on whom their sustenance, health, fertility and full lifespan truly depended (vv. 25b–26). Accordingly, every vestige of the Canaanite fertility cult must be eradicated. Unfortunately, however, this was something Israel patently failed to do (attested by both subsequent Old Testament testimony and archaeological excavations), ultimately choosing death over the life that Yahweh promises both here and elsewhere.

---

59 Though most interpret this as the Promised Land, it possibly refers more specifically to Yahweh's sanctuary (see 15:17; cf. Isa. 2:2; Mic. 4:1). As Alexander (2017: 533) insightfully observes, 'In the light of such an expectation the subsequent construction by the Israelites of a portable tabernacle for YHWH fits well with the larger narrative.'

ii. Yahweh's promise and Israel's task (23:27–33)

27–31. These verses return to the topic of *how* Yahweh will deal with the current inhabitants of Canaan (cf. v. 23b). Rather than exterminate them, he will *drive them out* (Piel *grš*; cf. Gen. 3:24; 4:14; Exod. 34:11) before Israel (vv. 28–30), an expulsion achieved by means of his *terror* (v. 27a), *the hornet/*'wasp' (v. 28a) and his chosen people (*you* . . . , v. 31b).[60] The relationship between the first two (*terror* and *hornet*) and Yahweh's aforementioned *angel* (vv. 20–23) is not spelt out, but it seems safe to assume that Yahweh's *terror* (*'êmâ*) refers to a dread of Yahweh that will evoke panic and confusion (15:16; Josh. 2:9; see also Exod. 14:24, which reflects the same verb [*hāmam*] as here), securing success for Israel.[61] The word translated *the hornet/*'wasp' (*hāṣṣir'â*) explains how Yahweh will drive out the indigenous nations before Israel, but its precise nuance is debated. Many interpret it literally, some suggesting that the singular noun with a definite article here is generic – 'the hornets' (cf. ESV; NET; NJB; Houtman 1996; Propp 2006). Others interpret the term metaphorically (e.g. an invading army) or suggest an alternative meaning (e.g. 'despair'; 'pestilence'; 'plague'; 'panic-terror') for this noun, which occurs only here and in two closely related texts (cf. Deut. 7:20; Josh. 24:12). Though its intended meaning remains uncertain, it is distinguished explicitly from the Israelites (v. 28) and implicitly from the aforementioned *terror* (v. 27). It seems also to be distinguished from Yahweh's angel (vv. 20–23) but may arguably allude to his activity (cf. 33:2). As such, it is a significant aspect of the agency through which Yahweh will achieve his purpose for Israel.

However, the indigenous population – the list of verse 23 is abridged here (v. 28) to just three – will be displaced only gradually

---

60 While the *you* is singular here, it is clearly referring to the people as a whole (cf. vv. 20–24, 25–30) rather than individual Israelites.

61 Though the idiom ('I shall give all your enemies to you *by the neck*') is generally understood as signifying their retreat (i.e. turning and fleeing from Israel; so LXX and EVV), Alexander (2017: 535) tentatively suggests that it implies their defeat/Israel's victory over them (e.g. Gen 49:8) – possibly also reflected in 2 Sam. 22:41; 2 Chr. 29:6; Ps. 18:40 [MT 41].

(vv. 29a, 30a). The rationale for this – Israel's numerical size is insufficient to cultivate the land and protect themselves from wild animals (v. 29b; so also Deut. 7:22; cf. Lev. 26:22; 1 Sam. 17:34–37; 2 Kgs 18:25–26; Ezek. 14:15) – differs sharply from other texts, which underline Israel's disobedience/idolatry as the major reason (e.g. Judg. 2:10 – 3:6), and seems to imply a much smaller population than in 12:37. However, any perceived discrepancy is more apparent than real. The two different rationales are not mutually exclusive; indeed, the one offered here in Exodus seems to reflect the pre-settlement context and is arguably the earlier of the two traditions. For the numerical size of the exodus population, see comment on 12:37.

Though it might take longer than presently anticipated (v. 29a), Israel's full possession of the Promised Land would indeed be realized (vv. 30–31) – as underlined by the extensive boundaries specified both here and elsewhere (cf. Gen. 15:18; Num. 34:3–12; Deut. 11:24; Josh. 1:4). While this became a reality for Israel only briefly (mainly in the 'Golden Era' of David and Solomon), the territorial promise finds its ultimate fulfilment in the new creation (Williamson 2000).

32–33. Israel's role in fulfilling God's plan is again reiterated (cf. vv. 24–26). To secure their possession of the Promised Land, the religious influence of its current inhabitants had to be eradicated. This could be achieved only by the same zero-tolerance policy towards them and their gods being rigorously maintained. Rather than an expression of racism or xenophobia, the strict prohibition on covenants involving the Canaanites and their gods, as well as their removal from the Promised Land, was crucial for Israel's survival as God's holy people. Unfortunately, the warnings here were subsequently ignored, culminating eventually in Israel's expulsion from the land as well.

Meaning
The closing literary bracket (23:20–33; cf. 20:22–23) again highlights the special focus and distinctive nature of Israel's worship, and thus the exclusive allegiance that Yahweh demands. It is clear from this hortatory epilogue in the Book of the Covenant that Israel's unique status as the redeemed people of God comes

with important caveats: to enjoy the future blessings that God promises, they must not be rebellious but pay careful attention to God's demands; and while Yahweh will facilitate their settlement in the land promised to Abraham, Israel's tenure there is implicitly dependent on their ongoing devotion and loyalty to Yahweh, who demands exclusive worship.

11. THE SEALING OF THE COVENANT
(24:1–18)

Context

Finally, the Sinai narrative has reached its climactic point (24:1; cf. 19:24): the fulfilment of the sign God gave Moses back in 3:12, and the sealing of the covenant between Yahweh and Israel. After everything disclosed to Moses (20:22 – 23:33) has been communicated to the Israelites (24:3), three stages in the formal establishment of the covenant are now described: a ritual ratification of the covenant by enacted oath (24:4–8); a fellowship meal with God for Israel's leadership (24:9–11); and Moses' ascent to receive the two stone tablets of the covenant law (24:12–18).[1]

---

1   As becomes clear in the following chapters, Moses would first receive instructions relating to the tabernacle and how God's objective to dwell with his people (29:45–46) will be facilitated (chs. 25–31).

Comment
A. The covenant-making ceremony (24:1–11)

1–2. The subject (i.e. *the LORD*; cf. NET; NIV; NLT) of the opening clause is implied rather than explicitly identified (cf. MT; LXX; and most EVV), suggesting that these two verses are not some kind of literary flashback (*pace* Chirichigno 1987; Hamilton 2011), but continue the divine speech that began in 20:22. Thus understood, before Moses descends the mountain, Yahweh gives Moses specific (and arguably additional; see comment on 19:24) instructions for his next ascent, which will involve others also: on this occasion Moses must bring along Aaron, two of his sons, and seventy Israelite elders. Aaron's inclusion with Moses has already been anticipated back in 19:24, but this duo is now considerably expanded. Presumably Nadab and Abihu are included because they were the oldest of Aaron's sons (cf. 6:23; 28:1). The *seventy . . . elders* seem to be a representative group drawn from a larger number of elders (3:16; 19:7; cf. 4:29; 12:21; 18:12; Num. 11:16, 24). Together, this party represented Israel's leadership or nobility (v. 11), but even this privileged delegation must not get too close (v. 2), worshipping only *at a distance* (v. 1c). To Moses exclusively belonged the invitation to approach Yahweh. Thus, like the portable divine dwelling place soon to be constructed (the tabernacle), the mountain of God is here divided into three distinct parts, reflecting different gradations of holiness. At its base, where the Israelites were encamped, was its 'outer court'; further up, where this delegation could ascend to worship God, was its 'holy place'; and right at the top, where the glory of God *settled* or 'tabernacled' (v. 16), was its 'most holy place'.

3–4a. Prior to assembling this representative group and leading them up to meet God, Moses follows the instructions Yahweh issued back in 20:22 and 21:1. In view of the latter, all Yahweh's 'words and rulings' (AT) may arguably refer here only to the speech recorded in 20:22 – 23:33, and exclude the Decalogue which Yahweh had already communicated to the Israelites directly (cf. 20:1, 18–19). Further support for this interpretation may be adduced from inclusion of both kinds of material (straightforward commands/prohibitions, as well as specific case rulings) in 20:22 – 23:33 (Alexander 2017: 543).

However, most interpreters suggest that here in 24:3 Yahweh's 'words' refers to the Decalogue and his 'rulings' refers to the material contained in 20:22 – 23:33. The strength of this position lies in the fact that, otherwise, there is no explicit record in Exodus (cf. Deut. 5:23–33) of the Israelites formally agreeing to the Decalogue, which seems particularly strange in the immediate context of the covenant's ratification, which formally concludes with the reception of the two stone tablets on which it is inscribed (24:12; cf. 31:18; 34:28).

As previously (cf. 19:7–8), the people respond positively to 'everything Yahweh has said' (AT) – which presumably includes the Decalogue. It seems entirely plausible, therefore, that *the Book of the Covenant* mentioned in 24:7 actually contained the Decalogue as well as the material now located in 20:22 – 23:33. However, even if it was only the latter material that Moses subsequently records and reads to the people (vv. 4a, 7a), 24:12 confirms that official copies of the Decalogue have already been made for the people's instruction.[2]

The terms of the covenant, to which the people have now given their assent, are thus duly recorded (v. 4a; cf. v. 7) – as was typical when ratifying a covenant in the ancient world. This also explains what happens the next morning (v. 4b), which might otherwise take the reader a little by surprise.

4b–8. Rather than setting off with the aforementioned delegation to worship God, Moses first presides over an elaborate ceremony involving altars, pillars, sacrifices and the ritual sprinkling of blood. While there are obvious connections with the instructions Moses previously received (20:24–26), the cultic ritual carried out here in chapter 24 is in some ways unique. It is clear from the liturgy employed in verses 7–8 that this was a sealing of the covenant forged between Yahweh and Israel. The covenant partners seem to be represented respectively by the *altar* and the

---

2   The two stone tablets contained only 'the ten words' (cf. 34:28; Deut. 5:22; 10:4).

twelve stone pillars (v. 4b).[3] While such pillars were prohibited if associated with idolatry and related ritual (23:24; Lev. 26:1; Deut. 7:5; 12:3), here these pillars signify Israel and have nothing to do with fertility gods.[4]

The *young Israelite men* (v. 5) clearly perform the role of priests here. Significantly, they are not identified as such here (cf. 19:24), so presumably they had not functioned as such previously (otherwise they could simply have been described as priests). Though Gehrig does not actually discuss the identity of the priests back in Exodus 19:22, he tentatively suggests that these young Israelite men (24:5) may have been Israelite firstborn, despite no such explicit association being made in the text (2024: 175 n. 169). Alexander (2017: 544), however, considers it more likely that the young men here were 'ordinary Israelites, drawn from all of the tribes', there being 'no reason to assume that they were firstborn sons'. While possibly a representative selection was made from all twelve tribes, it seems more likely that those performing this priestly role were drawn from the clans of Levi – possibly limited only to Aaron's actual sons (cf. 6:23; 28:1), whose official role as tabernacle priests would be formalized subsequently (28:41; 29:1–44; Lev. 8:1–36).[5]

The function of the *burnt* and *fellowship offerings* (v. 5), mentioned together for the first time back in 20:24, is not explained. However, their general purpose can be deduced from Leviticus. The whole burnt offering was a means of atonement (Lev. 1:4) and signifies complete consecration of the worshipper to God.

---

3   Some English translations (e.g. ESV; NET; NIV; NLT) make this explicit; others more accurately reflect the MT's '*for* the twelve tribes of Israel'.

4   Still, the antipathy towards such sacred pillars in Israel's later history (cf. 2 Kgs 18:4; 23:14) arguably suggests the antiquity of this and other such traditions in the Pentateuch (cf. Gen. 28:18–22; 36:9–15).

5   Though some suggest that the Israelites may have had a functioning priesthood already, this runs counter to Genesis, where no such priestly mediation was considered necessary. During their oppression in Egypt no such sacrificial worship was apparently carried out by the Israelites (cf. Exod. 8:26) or, if it was (cf. 1 Sam. 2:27–28), it is not mentioned in Exodus.

The fellowship offering, which was made for a variety of reasons (cf. Lev. 7:12, 16), was distinctive in that some of its meat could be consumed by the worshipper (Lev. 7:15, 16–21), and it expressed harmony and restored relationships. Here in Exodus 24, these offerings arguably concern Israel's consecration to God's service and their special relationship with him. In keeping with this, the blood-sprinkling ritual (vv. 6–8) might also be an ordination ritual for Israel, similar to the one relating to the Aaronic priesthood (cf. 29:15–46). Accordingly, 'here all Israel is being ordained to the service of Yahweh; this is a commissioning service for Israel to be the priestly kingdom and holy nation God spoke of back in chapter 19' (Williamson 2008: 117).

However, this blood-sprinkling ritual may well have served a dual purpose. In the ancient world covenants were often sealed in blood, and the dual sprinkling (some on the altar, some on the people), separated by a further recital of the covenant obligations and Israel's assent (v. 7), suggests such a significance here. Thus understood, the splattered blood symbolized the death of the covenant-makers should they become covenant-breakers (Meyers 2005: 206; Williamson 2008: 117). This ritual was therefore an enacted oath, through which the covenant was formally sealed, paving the way for the next stage of covenant ratification.

9–11. Having sealed the covenant in blood, Moses and Israel's representatives now make their way up the mountain as instructed by Yahweh in 24:1 and experience an extraordinary encounter with God. The text categorically states that they *saw the God of Israel* (v. 10a, 11b),[6] perhaps implying that they lifted their gaze above the bright blue platform on which God was enthroned (cf. Ezek. 1:22–28).[7] However, it is most unlikely that they saw God's

---

6   The use of this rare expression in the Pentateuch (cf. Gen. 33:20; Num. 16:9) is especially fitting here in the context of Israel's covenant ratification and communion with Yahweh.

7   Given the pharaonic obsession with making bricks in Exod. 1 – 5, it is perhaps significant that these Israelites get to see this lapis lazuli brickwork that far exceeds any human construction (Alexander 2017: 547).

face – his non-reflected glory (cf. 33:18, 20).[8] Nevertheless, this was
clearly an exceptional experience, emphasized by the fact that no
harm came to them: 'but upon these pillars of Israelite society he
did not stretch out his hand' (v. 11a, AT; cf. 3:20; 9:15). While some
take *ate and drank* (v. 11b) as further underlining their survival, this
phrase most likely alludes to some sort of fellowship or covenant
meal (cf. 18:12; see also Gen. 31:54). As such, this is the capstone of
the covenant ceremony, signifying that Israel's special relationship
with Yahweh has now firmly been established.

B. Moses' ascent to receive the covenant tablets (24:12–18)

12. The final stage in the ratification of ancient treaties
normally involved depositing their terms in the temples of the
treaty partners. This arguably elucidates God's instructions here
and offers the best explanation for why *two* tablets of stone
were necessary (cf. 31:18),[9] and why the presentation of these to
Moses is prefaced with detailed instructions to build the tabernacle – beginning with the chest (ark) in which these engraved
tablets would subsequently be deposited (25:16). Though only the
handover of the two stone tablets is explicitly mentioned in verse
12, the command for Moses to ascend the mountain and 'remain
[lit. 'be'] there' (AT) makes clear that much more than a simple
hand-off would be involved.

13–14. Taking his cue from this, Moses clearly anticipates a
significant absence. He thus delegates his judicial authority (cf.
18:15–26) to Aaron and Hur, while he and Joshua are otherwise
engaged (vv. 13–14). This is the first time that Joshua is described
as Moses' 'aide' (AT; cf. 33:11; Num. 11:28; Josh. 1:1), but the second
occasion when all three men (Joshua, Aaron and Hur) assist
Moses in implementing Yahweh's instructions (cf. 17:10–13). Here,

---

8   Though Yahweh spoke to Moses *face to face* (33:11), this is an idiomatic
     expression that must not be interpreted literally (cf. 33:20, 23).
9   It is clear from the subsequent narrative (34:1, 28; cf. Deut. 4:13; 5:22;
     9:10–11) that these two tablets contained the Decalogue, here described
     as the *law* (*tôrâ*; i.e. instruction) and 'commandment' (AT; *miṣwâ*).

however, their roles are reversed: Joshua accompanies Moses (for part of the ascent; cf. 32:17),[10] while Aaron and Hur remain below to handle any disputes – foreshadowing the crisis that will unfold in chapter 32 under Aaron's leadership.

15–18. As before (cf. 19:16–19), Yahweh's manifest presence was accompanied by a blanket of *cloud* and what appeared to be *a consuming fire on top of the mountain* (vv. 16–17; cf. 3:2). As well as underlining, for the Israelites below, that Moses was again meeting with God (cf. 19:9), this settling of the cloud and Yahweh's glory on Sinai foreshadows its subsequent settling over and in the tabernacle, demonstrating God's abiding presence with his people (cf. 40:34–38). That Moses must wait seven days before entering the cloud (v. 16) further accentuates Yahweh's holiness, possibly alluding to the need for due caution and appropriate consecration (cf. 19:10–11, 22–24; see also 29:35); not even Moses can rush into or casually enter God's holy presence (cf. 3:5).

Meaning

This chapter constitutes the climax of the Sinai narrative (Exod. 19 – 24), which culminated with a select group of Israel's leadership – and subsequently Israel's appointed mediator by himself – ascending Mount Sinai to meet and commune with Yahweh. Before these ascents, the Israelites formally agreed to their covenant obligations, solemnly sealed by an enacted oath – the self-maledictory ritual depicted in verses 4b–8. That only the altar (representing Yahweh; cf. the twelve pillars representing Israel) is

---

10   This seems to be the first and possibly the only occasion when Joshua accompanied Moses up Mount Sinai. No explanation is given, but Moses may possibly have assumed that help would be needed to carry the stone tablets on the way down. It appears, however, that the tablets were not too heavy (or too large) for Moses to handle on his own. This, and the fact that they could fit into a relatively small box (cf. 25:21), suggests that the tablets were neither as heavy nor as large as often depicted. Like the two inscribed clay tablets I once saw Alan Millard holding in the palm of his hand to illustrate this possibility, they could have been much smaller than we usually imagine.

explicitly blood-splattered may be significant (cf. the somewhat similar ritual in Gen. 15), perhaps implying that Yahweh would bear the punishment for breach of covenant. However, unless understood primarily as a consecration ritual (see Alexander 2017: 545–546), the fact that some of this blood was also sprinkled on the people (v. 8) suggests otherwise. In any case, the sacrifice and ritual at the foot of the mountain was necessary and preparatory for what followed, when the significance of the fellowship offerings becomes more apparent. Evidently some of this meat was taken up the mountain for a fellowship meal, expressing the special relationship into which this covenant had brought Yahweh and Israel: each could now draw near the other more safely (cf. the situation in Exod. 19), because sin had been atoned for (cf. the burnt offerings of v. 5) and by eating sacrificial meat Israel had arguably been consecrated as God's holy people (Alexander 2017: 549). All that remained was the final stage of its formal ratification; namely, the reception (and safekeeping) of the official depository of its stipulations – hence Moses' personal invitation to ascend the summit to receive these very special tablets (vv. 12–18).

As is clear from the New Testament, the ratification of the covenant here in Exodus 24 serves as a paradigm for understanding the new covenant, as highlighted by Jesus' echo of Moses' solemn declaration (24:8) at the new covenant's inauguration during another sacrificial meal: 'This is my blood of the covenant, which is poured out for many' (Mark 14:24; cf. Matt. 26:28; Luke 22:20; Heb. 12:24). Moreover, as one greater than Moses, Jesus has ascended on high and 'given us of his Spirit' (1 John 4:13), through whom God's covenant law has been inscribed on 'tablets of human hearts' (2 Cor. 3:3).

12. DIVINE INSTRUCTIONS FOR WORSHIP (I): THE TABERNACLE'S DESIGN (25:1 – 27:19)

The next major block of Exodus (25:1 – 31:18) focuses primarily on the tabernacle and the priestly ritual that will facilitate Yahweh's dwelling among his people. The importance of this moveable sanctuary is underscored by the copious space devoted in Exodus to (1) instructions regarding its construction and personnel (chs. 25–31) and (2) the subsequent implementation of these instructions after the covenant has been renewed (chs. 35–40). The account of the tabernacle is 'interrupted' by the golden calf episode – which, among other things, serves to highlight further the only legitimate and proper worship that Yahweh demands from those who serve him.

Context

Chapter 24 has focused mainly on the ratification of God's covenant with Israel. As mentioned above, there were three aspects to this. The first was the sacrificial ritual at the foot of the mountain, in which the obligations of the covenant were sealed by blood. The second was the extraordinary meal that took place further up the mountain, where Israel's leaders not only saw God, but enjoyed a fellowship meal in his presence. The third, in keeping with Ancient Near Eastern tradition, was the depositing of the terms of the covenant in the divine sanctuary of both covenant partners. This helps explain why, after Moses ascends to receive the tablets of the covenant law, instructions for building a mobile sanctuary become the priority.[1] However, as well as housing the covenant law, this special structure will in some sense be a dwelling place for God himself,[2] and ensure that Israel's experience of God at Sinai can be sustained as they make their onward journey to the Promised Land.

Comment
A. Collection of the raw materials (25:1–9)

1–7. Yahweh's instructions begin with the raw materials to be voluntarily donated by the Israelites as an offering to God. Some of this material, such as the silver, gold and possibly the linen, had been given to them by the Egyptians (cf. 12:35–36), but other items may have been salvaged from flotsam (cf. 14:30) or the battlefield (17:8–13), or even acquired through peaceful trading with nomads.[3] In any case, such materials were clearly not in short supply: the Israelite 'freewill offerings' surpassed the actual requirements (cf. 36:5–7). Both Yahweh (and later Moses; cf.

---

1 For a helpful summary and critique of the historical-critical perspective on the tabernacle, see Alexander 2017: 556–565.

2 As Alexander (2017: 565, 582) notes (following Hendrix 1992: 126; cf. also Meyers 1996, 2008), the use of two designations for the sanctuary in these chapters (Exod. 25 – 30), viz. 'tabernacle/dwelling' and 'tent of meeting', seems to suggest that the first block of detailed instructions (25:10 – 27:19) focuses on it as a divine dwelling place, whereas from 27:20 its role as a 'meeting place' comes more to the fore.

3 The precise meaning of *taḥaš* (NIV: *another type of durable leather*) is uncertain. While often understood as the hide of sea-cows, it is unlikely that such ritually unclean material would have been used on the sanctuary (Garrett 2014: 553).

35:4–9) initially mention some items (the light; the anointing oil; the fragrant incense; the ephod and breastpiece) without explanation. This seems to indicate that these concepts were at least vaguely familiar to the original audience, possibly due to similar items in an Egyptian setting. In any case, an explanation of these and other items is subsequently supplied in the more detailed instructions for the tabernacle, its furnishings and its priestly personnel that follow.

8–9. At this stage, however, it is only the purpose of this *sanctuary* or holy place (Heb. *miqdāš*) that is spelt out: it is to facilitate Yahweh's 'dwelling' (Heb. *šākan*) among them (v. 8). Accordingly, this tabernacle or 'dwelling' (Heb. *miškān*, a cognate of *šākan*) and all its furnishings must conform to the divine blueprints – a pattern (Heb. *tabnît*) as yet undisclosed (v. 9b; cf. 25:40; 26:30; 27:8). While this may simply imply that the divine blueprints are implicit in the instructions that follow, one should probably infer that God showed Moses a pattern or model which underpinned the instructions he gave to Moses. However, rather than any suggestion that the Mosaic tabernacle was patterned after some heavenly edifice, the author of Hebrews insists that it is a copy (i.e. reflection) of heaven itself (Heb. 9:24). Moreover, it is significant that Moses is repeatedly said to have been shown this pattern *on the mountain* (Exod. 25:40; 26:30; 27:8). When he entered the cloud on top of the mountain, Moses effectively entered the Most Holy Place; the gradations of holiness on the mountain are subsequently reflected in the earthly tabernacle, suggesting that the pattern Moses saw was manifest on Mount Sinai itself. This may also explain why, when later pressed to make a representation of God, Aaron made a golden calf (32:1–4; cf. Ezek. 1:7); he and the other leaders were possibly inspired by what they had seen while up the mountain: the calf-like feet of the cherubim below God's majestic throne (24:10; Ezek. 1:22–26).

B. Gold furniture and accessories (25:10–40)

Unlike the account of its actual construction (chs. 35–40), Yahweh's instructions for the tabernacle commence with its most precious furniture and accessories. Yahweh subsequently tells Moses to place these items (26:33–35) within the tabernacle, and it is undoubtedly their intended location (in the Most Holy Place or the Holy Place) and theological significance that explains why they are prioritized here.[4]

i. The ark (25:10–22)

10–22. The first piece of tabernacle furniture mentioned is undoubtedly the most important – not only because this was where the tablets of the covenant law would thereafter be stored (v. 16), but also because of its special location and theological significance. The ark was a fairly small (approx. 1,200 x 720 x 720 mm),[5] gold-plated, rectangular wooden box or chest (the meaning of both the Hebrew noun *'ārôn* [cf. Gen. 50:26; 2 Chr. 24:8–11] and the archaic English word 'ark'), with four feet to keep it off the ground and an ornate *cover* or 'lid'. The precise meaning of the Hebrew noun (*kappōret*), generally interpreted as a cognate of the verb 'to atone' (*kipper*), is debated. While certainly associated with atonement by its smearing with blood on the Day of Atonement (Lev. 16:15), a suggested morphological connection with a similar-sounding Egyptian word meaning 'sole of the foot' (Milgrom 1991: 1014) may point to its biblical connotation as God's footstool (cf. 1 Chr. 28:2; Pss 99:5; 132:7). The ark's cover was made of pure gold (though not necessarily from a single lump; Garrett 2014: 554 n. 16) and adorned with carved representations of two cherubim, symbolizing the awesome creatures most fully described by Ezekiel (cf. Ezek. 1:5–14; 10:1–22). Here on the ark their posture is one of reverent awe in the presence of Yahweh himself (v. 22). The ark was the only item of furniture located in the Most Holy

---

4   For the omission of the golden incense altar at this point, see comments on 27:20 – 30:38 below.

5   An exact measurement depends on whether the *cubit* (the length between elbow and tip of middle finger) referred to in Exodus was about 450 mm (the typical measurement) or about 520 mm (the royal [or Egyptian] 'cubit', probably alluded to in 2 Chr. 3:3 with respect to the Solomonic temple).

Place (40:20–21),[6] and was to be carried by two gold-plated rods – inserted on either side through the rings attached to its four feet – to avoid any direct contact by humans (cf. 2 Sam. 6:6–7; 1 Chr. 13:10). Indeed, other than the high priest, it is likely that few Israelites ever set eyes on it, as it was covered by the veil any time the tabernacle was disassembled (cf. Num. 4:5–6).

In terms of its theological significance as God's footstool, the ark represented the place where heaven and earth met, and it was thus from above its cover/footrest that Yahweh would meet and communicate with Moses (v. 22).

ii. The table (25:23–30)

23–30. This and the following item of furniture (the lampstand) were designed for the Holy Place. The table was the same height as the ark (*c.*720 mm), but shorter (*c.*920 mm) and narrower (*c.*480 mm). Like the ark, it was made of gold-plated acacia wood, and was similarly designed to be carried by two gold-plated rods inserted through the two rings on either side. The rim and gold moulding around its edges were probably not just decorative; they also served a more practical function: to keep its gold utensils (plates, dishes, pitchers and bowls) from falling off and being defiled while the tabernacle was in transit (cf. Num. 4:7–8) or when the priests were carrying out libations with such utensils or arranging the *bread of the Presence* on the table top (cf. 37:16; Lev. 24:5–9).[7] From Leviticus 24:5–9 we learn that this bread was in fact twelve baked loaves set on the table in two stacks of six each – apparently representing each of Israel's tribes (cf. Exod. 28:9–12) – that were replaced with fresh loaves every sabbath day. Both (the bread and the sabbath) are described as 'an everlasting covenant' (Exod. 31:16; Lev. 24:8; AT), suggesting a theological relationship

---

6 However, see comment on Exod. 30:6.

7 While such drink offerings were prohibited on the altar of incense (30:9), they clearly were poured out elsewhere (viz. on the altar of burnt offering; 29:38–42). The fact that such utensils were kept on the table in the Holy Place does not necessarily imply that they were for exclusive use *within* the tent of meeting.

between them: the God who gives rest to his people is also the
God who gives them nourishment (Garrett 2014: 462). In further
contrast to the typical (daily) provision of food for Ancient Near
Eastern deities, this bread was not intended to feed God (cf. Ps.
50:12), but to be consumed by Israel's priests (Lev. 24:9; cf. 1 Sam.
21:2–6). Thus, the bread symbolically represented, not Israel's
provision for their God, but rather Yahweh's provision for his
covenant people, including their priests.

iii. The lampstand (25:31–40)

31–40. Like the atonement cover, the seven-branched 'menorah'
or *lampstand* was to be hammered out of solid gold, the amount of
which (v. 39; cf. 2 Sam. 12:30) suggests that it was probably around
the same height as the incense altar (almost 1 metre according to
30:2). Three branches, each featuring three decorative *cups* (i.e.
blossoms) shaped like almond flowers, extended from each side
of the central stand, which itself had four such cups, one at the
base, and one above each pair of extending branches. In contrast
to the typical menorah familiar from Judaism today,[8] there is
little in Exodus to suggest that the branches on either side should
extend in exact parallel with one another or that their lamps
had to be at the exact same height.[9] Rather, this seven-lamped
menorah is arguably depicted as a flowering almond tree. While
possibly symbolic of the tree of life in the Garden of Eden, it more
likely alludes to the burning bush (3:2), a theophany associated
elsewhere in Exodus with the mountain of God (3:1; cf. 3:12)
and the revelation of God's holiness (3:5; cf. 19:23). Accordingly,
as well as serving the practical function of providing light in the
Holy Place throughout the night (25:37; cf. 27:21; Lev. 24:2–4),

---

8   I.e. one with symmetrically balanced branches extending each side, as
    famously depicted on the Arch of Titus in Rome or by the more angular
    statue outside the Knesset in modern Jerusalem.

9   While Exod. 39:37 may imply such with *its row* [Heb. *maʿărākâ*] *of lamps*
    (NIV; cf. Lev. 24:6), the term may simply denote 'arrangement' here (so
    NASB). Admittedly, however, it is generally used to denote an orderly
    arrangement, such as military battle lines.

the menorah also bore theological significance – indicating that the tent of meeting was holy ground where God would manifest his presence, be worshipped and make himself known. Thus understood, the menorah served more than simply a utilitarian or aesthetic function (Garrett 2014: 562).[10]

In the light of the menorah's probable associations with the burning bush, the latter may be further alluded to in the final verse's reference to 'the pattern [Moses] was shown on the mountain' (v. 40, AT), as Robinson (1997: 119–121) argues on the basis of 'the *appearance* Yahweh showed Moses' referred to in Numbers 8:4. In any case, while the final caution (v. 40) may strictly apply only to the lampstand and its equipment, the *inclusio* with 25:9 suggests that, by extension, it encompasses all three main items of tabernacle furniture mentioned thus far.

C. The sacred tent (26:1–37)

1–37. The focus now shifts from the precious furniture to the special tent that will house it.[11] Despite numerous attempts to visualize this structure (whether by artistic drawings, scale models or even life-size replicas), there are insufficient details in the text to do so with absolute confidence. For example, the tent apparently had a flat roof with perpendicular (or perhaps very slightly angled) sides rather than the inverted V-shape roof of a modern ridge tent. There is also some debate over the precise shape and size of its wooden framework.[12] Because the information simply lacks sufficient detail, any reconstruction of the tabernacle must necessarily be tentative. Even so, the essential structure is fairly straightforward.

The divine dwelling place was a rectangular tent (13.5 metres

---

10 *Pace* Garrett, the 6 + 1 pattern reflected elsewhere in Exodus seems somewhat forced here.

11 In ch. 26 *tabernacle* (Heb. *miškān*) strictly relates to the divine residence (i.e. the 'tent of meeting') rather than the entire area including its outer courtyard (for the latter, see 27:9–19; cf. 35:11).

12 For a concise discussion, see Alexander 2017: 556.

long, 4.5 metres wide and 4.5 metres high) that consisted of a
gold-plated wooden skeletal structure (consisting of uprights set
in silver bases and crossbars joined to the uprights by gold rings),
covered with four layers of different materials (linen, woven goat
hair, and two types of animal hides). On the basis that no dimensions are provided for what is typically understood as the two
outer layers, Wright (2021: 497) speculates that these may actually
have been large leather sacks for transporting the other materials
when the tabernacle was in transit. However, the terminology
(covering, Heb. *miksê*; and 'above'/*over*, Heb. *milmā'ēlâ*) arguably
suggests otherwise (cf. 25:21; 36:19; 39:31; 40:19, 20), and inferences
from any lacunae in the tabernacle instructions are problematic
in any case.

The two innermost layers (sheets of specially woven linen and
sheets of goats' hair, respectively about 13 metres and 14 metres
long) were draped over the wooden frames to form the roof and
sides of the tent, with some surplus material shutting off the rear
of the tabernacle from external view (v. 12). The two outer layers
were made of more weatherproof material (leather),[13] and thus
probably served a more utilitarian purpose. However, the fact
that both these coverings came from *dead* animals may suggest
a theological significance as well: the danger of death that the
presence of/proximity to a holy God posed (cf. 19:10–24).

The tent was divided into separate compartments (v. 33) by
two entrance curtains, attached with gold hooks to additional
gold-plated wooden posts that supported them. Like the other
tent posts, the four supporting the inner curtain had silver
bases, whereas the five supporting the outer curtain were set
in bronze – an indication of gradation between the two rooms:
one of these curtains closed off access into the Most Holy Place
(a 4.5-metre cubic room), whereas the other facilitated entry into
the 9-metre-long outer room, the Holy Place. Both entrance
curtains were made of linen woven together with blue, purple

---

13 The reddening of the ram skins would have resulted from the tanning
process. The precise identity of the other animal skins (often identified
as dugongs/manatees) is debated.

and scarlet thread, but the curtain that sealed off the Most Holy Place was also expertly weaved with cherubim (v. 31),[14] like the long linen sheets joined together to form the innermost sides and roof of the tent (v. 1). These woven cherubim presumably reflected what Israel's leaders had seen up the mountain (24:10; cf. Ezek. 10:20), and evidently served to remind Israel of the holiness of the one who had chosen to dwell among them (cf. Gen. 3:22–24).

Once again (cf. 25:9, 40), the importance of making sure everything conforms to the revealed plan is underlined (v. 30), although here this especially relates to how the divine dwelling place is set up and its furniture is arranged (vv. 31–37) – which almost certainly explains why a different noun (*mišpāṭ*; cf. 1 Kgs 6:38) is now employed.

D. The bronze altar (27:1–8)

1–8. Chapter 27 focuses mainly on what lay outside the divine tent, beginning with the most imposing and significant item: the bronze altar. Measuring 2.3 metres wide and 1.4 metres high, this was essentially a very large, portable barbeque for roasting various offerings (cf. 38:1). It comprised a square wooden frame overlaid with bronze,[15] into which a bronze network with rings at each corner was inserted, making it possible to transport the altar with two bronze-overlaid poles (v. 7). The altar's bronze utensils included *meat forks* (v. 3). Presumably these were for extracting cooked meat for human consumption (cf. the illicit action of Eli's sons in 1 Sam. 2:12–17), this being the only legitimate source for beef, lamb and goat meat under levitical law (cf. Lev. 17).

---

14 The word *ḥōšēb* (which NIV translates in 26:1, 31 as *skilled worker*; cf. 28:6, 15) refers to the most complex art of weaving, involving figure-work such as cherubim. Less intricate weaving (but using different colours) and basic weaving (using only one colour) were carried out by a *rōqēm* (e.g. 26:36; 27:16; 28:39) and an *ōrēg* (e.g. 28:32; 35:35) respectively.

15 For more on the critical study of the bronze altar, see Averbeck 1996: 888–908.

The purpose of the horns at each corner is not explained here, but these were certainly not for tying down live animals to the altar; in Mosaic ritual the animals were killed *near*, but not *on*, the altar (Lev. 1:11; 3:13), and even whole burnt offerings were cut to pieces before being placed on the altar (Lev. 1:6–9). Subsequent references to the horns on this altar or those of the altar of incense (cf. 30:1–10) associate them with the death (symbolized by the blood) of the sacrificial victim (29:12; 30:10; cf. Lev. 4:7; 9:9) or the consecration of the altar (Lev. 8:15; 16:18); hence their function was primarily ceremonial.

The bronze plating over the acacia wood obviously served a functional purpose: namely, to protect the flammable material underneath from combusting. As Garrett (2014: 577) notes, unless whole burnt offerings were first dissected (Lev. 1:6–9), the heat generated would have been too intense in any case. However, as well as serving this utilitarian purpose, the use of bronze for the altar and its utensils (as well as the other items in the courtyard) signified a space that was much less sacred and significant than that inside the actual tent.

The nature and function of the bronze grating is more debatable. Although often understood as the altar's grill or fire pan, its location (towards the bottom/halfway up the altar) makes this problematic: the heat generated by such would almost certainly have consumed the wooden frame. For this reason, Garrett suggests that this bronze network had a strengthening and stabilizing function for the hollow altar, although his assumption that the network had four legs beneath it is not validated by the text. Perhaps the network sat at the bottom of the altar but had perpendicular sides which were fitted under the bronze shielding (v. 4) to halfway up the wooden frame, or it had several tiers to hold the firepans (so Bruckner 2008: 251). Admittedly, this is equally speculative given the lack of such specific details in the text. In any case, such a bronze lattice base or insert would have made the altar much more stable (and transportable), especially if the latter was filled with sand or rocks when in use (cf. 20:24–25).

The importance of following the divine pattern is again underlined (v. 8; cf. 25:9, 40; 26:30). *Just as you were shown on the mountain* (lit. 'just as *he showed you* on the mountain') may possibly allude back to 20:24–26, where the Lord gave Moses specific instructions regarding the type of altar the Israelites must build.

E. The courtyard (27:9–19)

9–19. To establish a courtyard around the tabernacle (i.e. the divine dwelling place), a large fence (approx. 2.3 metres high, 45.7 metres long and 22.9 metres wide) was to be erected. This would comprise twenty evenly spaced posts on each side (i.e. north and south), ten along the back (west) and three on either side of the entrance at the front (east). These wooden posts, with silver caps (signifying special or holy space, and perhaps also protecting the tops of the posts against rot; cf. 38:28), were to be set in bronze bases (cf. the silver bases used for the tent posts; 26:19, 21, 25, 32) to support the plain (off-white) linen curtains that were attached to the posts by silver bands and hooks, and to the ground by bronze tent pegs (v. 19).[16] Together these formed the perimeter of the sanctuary complex. Four more posts were used to support the more colourful curtain (v. 16; cf. 26:36) that sealed off entry into the courtyard enclosure. This perimeter fence corresponds to the limits that were earlier set up at the foot of Sinai to mark it out as holy ground that posed great danger to any trespassers (19:12, 21–24). Accordingly, the tabernacle complex is to be understood in a similar manner, with only the tent itself (and especially its Most Holy Place) exceeding this.

Meaning
With several commentators, Wenham (2003: 73–76) notes that the tabernacle

> resembled a royal palace with its throne-room, the holy of holies, right at the heart of the structure. It thus expressed the idea that Israel's king dwelt among his people. Its drapes of

---

16 The fact that no tent pegs are mentioned in relation to the tabernacle itself may indicate that the coverings were simply draped over the framework and held in place by the sheer weight of the leather.

purple suggested royalty and its blue curtains suggested heaven. The sequence of metals, from bronze in the outer court, silver around the base of the tent, and pure gold covering the furniture inside the tent, indicated increasing nearness to the divine king.

The overarching significance of the tabernacle (as Yahweh's royal dwelling place within Israel's camp) is thus clear,[17] but this is less so with respect to all its various details, few of which receive specific attention elsewhere in the Old Testament.[18] Consequently, the meaning of the tabernacle has sometimes been obscured by rather speculative or fanciful interpretations of its component parts, usually with particular focus on Jesus and his atoning sacrifice, but with little or no exegetical grounding in the text and theology of Exodus. Such suggested meanings are thus often more allegorical in nature, and in danger of skewing or missing the legitimate typological connections implicit in the biblical text. With respect to such allegorical interpretations, the following ditty immediately springs to mind:

Wonderful things in the Bible I see,
Some of them put there by you and by me![19]

In order to avoid this, we must pay careful attention to the symbolic significance of the tabernacle suggested in Exodus itself.

---

17 As such it bears striking resemblance to 'the Battle of Qadesh reliefs of Rameses II, whose tabernacular, fenced-off tent was in the middle of a rectangular camp' (Kitchen 1993: 123); cf. the similar structure of the Hebrew camp depicted in Numbers. This may thus be another example of what Currid (2013) labels 'polemical theology' in Exodus.

18 From this Webb cautiously infers that 'while the OT does clearly support a typology of the tabernacle as a whole, it does not appear to support a typology of its individual parts' (2008: 169).

19 This parody of the 1871 hymn 'I Am So Glad That Our Father in Heaven' (Philip P. Bliss, 1838–73) was a gentle reproof when someone in my former church circles in Ireland strayed too far in their interpretation from the biblical text.

First and foremost, the tabernacle and its furnishings signify theological facts about Yahweh, and how his holy presence in the midst of the Israelites may be facilitated. Only when such symbolism in Exodus is properly understood can we draw legitimate typological threads from the tabernacle to what God has done for us in Christ.[20]

As noted above, the most important significance of the tabernacle is its relationship with Yahweh's presence – one of the overarching motifs in the book of Exodus as a whole. The tabernacle's *raison d'être* was that Yahweh might dwell (as divine king) in Israel's midst (25:8).

The various features of the tabernacle help signify this reality, and how the Israelites might survive such an experience yet give Yahweh the worship he demanded. The graded holiness of the complex is reflected not only in the names given to its three enclosures (courtyard, Holy Place, Most Holy Place), but also in the increasing value of the precious metals used, and the cherubim-adorned curtains that symbolically guarded the entrance to each part. The outer furniture (the bronze basin and sacrificial altar) signified how Yahweh could be safely approached only through ritual cleansing and the appropriate sacrificial offering, whereas the furniture within the outer tent (Holy Place) signified Yahweh's life-sustaining presence and the sweet-smelling savour of acceptable worship. Within the inner sanctum (Most Holy Place) Yahweh's cherubim-covered ark was not only the repository for holy things (the all-important covenant stipulations of the Decalogue), but also, as a divine footstool, it symbolically linked heaven and earth. In the light of these facts, it is not difficult to see how the author of Hebrews and other New Testament authors could extract from the tabernacle and its furnishings a typological significance that finds its antitype in the new covenant's Immanuel, the Lord Jesus.

However, in addition to this, as Webb (2008: 159–160) observes:

---

20 For more on this hermeneutical principle with respect to typology, see especially the insightful discussion in Webb 2008.

If we take the programmatic statements of the first part of Exodus as our cue ('Let my people go that they may serve me' [7:16; 8:1, 20]), then the tabernacle, and the 'service' associated with it, is the real, vital centre of the Pentateuch. The journey to Sinai is a journey towards this kind of service, the happenings at Sinai are the establishment of it, and the journey on from there is the living out of it. In theological terms, we might say that what the tabernacle material of Exodus teaches is that the worship of God is both the goal and foundation of the redeemed life.

13. DIVINE INSTRUCTIONS FOR WORSHIP (II): THE PRIESTHOOD (27:20 – 30:38)

Context

Further instructions relating to the lampstand (27:20–21) are somewhat surprising at this point, as one might have expected such to have been incorporated with the relevant instructions at an earlier (25:31–40) or later (30:22–38) stage in the narrative. Moreover, this unexpected little section is immediately followed by a fairly lengthy section dealing with the Aaronic priests rather than the tabernacle or its furnishings.

However, the instructions in 27:20–21 actually provide a natural segue into the following material focusing on the tabernacle's priestly personnel, whose role involved ritual activities in both the outer court and the Holy Place. Moreover, special attention to matters relating particularly to the priests continues right through to the end of chapter 30. Thus, although the somewhat sudden shift in focus might initially make the narrative seem somewhat disjointed, chapters 28 and 29 are actually bracketed by matters that concern, in particular, the special role of Aaron and his descendants (27:20–21;

30:1–10).¹ Accordingly, the switch in focus to the priests, their clothing and their consecration to service is not nearly so abrupt or 'oddly placed' as might initially appear.

Comment
A. Oil for the lampstand (27:20–21)

20–21. Top-quality oil (pressed rather than crushed olives) was used to fuel the *lamps* (i.e. receptacles with wicks) that were at the end of each branch of the menorah (cf. 25:37). Such bowls were normally made of clay, but in this case, like the rest of the lampstand, they were made of gold (37:23). The fact that these lamps were to remain lit in the Holy Place throughout the night (27:21; cf. 1 Sam. 3:3), and that this was a *lasting ordinance* that the priests must observe, suggests that this light in the tent of meeting served a symbolic rather than a utilitarian purpose: like the royal ensign raised over Buckingham Palace in London, it indicated that the monarch was actually in residence.

B. Vestments for the priests (28:1–43)

The narrative in chapters 28–29 switches from the tabernacle itself to its priestly personnel. As Garrett (2014: 580) suggests, the considerable space devoted to the Aaronic priesthood here (more verses than in the account of Israel's rescue and celebration at the Sea) reflects its theological significance. The major focus is on the special clothing – particularly, that of the high priest (28:3–39) – and how Aaron and his sons should be consecrated for priestly service (29:1–37). Given the absence of any explicit divine selection, possibly Aaron and his sons had already assumed the role of Israel's de facto priests (cf. 19:24; 24:5); in any case, here they are being equipped and set apart to serve as priests in the tabernacle, thus assuming 'a new identity and rank' (Garrett 2014: 593). The final verses (29:38–46) outline the regular (twice-daily) burnt offerings

---

1   Nearly all the material in ch. 30 especially concerns Aaron and his descendants, but only the golden altar (30:1–10) and its associated incense (30:34–38) are exclusively connected with the Holy Place.

(29:38–42a) and the dual function of the consecrated tabernacle as both a tent of meeting (29:42b–43) and divine residence (29:44–46).

i. General instructions for the priestly garments (28:1–5)

1. The grouping of Aaron's four sons in two pairs both here and previously (6:23) may anticipate the events recorded in Leviticus 10. Only Nadab and Elihu were mentioned back in chapter 24 (vv. 1, 9) in connection with the extraordinary experience up the mountain, and where all four sons are subsequently named (and likewise paired) in the Pentateuch, it is in explicit association with the incident recorded in Leviticus (Num. 3:2, 4; 26:60–61).

2–5. Significantly, the high priest's garments were to be skilfully woven with the same dyed linen materials as the tabernacle curtains, and were designed to express the same holy status of Aaron (as explicitly underlined by the inscription on his turban) – hence the *dignity and honour* the priestly vestments would confer on Aaron (v. 2) and his sons (v. 40). Rather than additional strands of gold being woven (like thread) into the priestly material, the gold 'strips' (AT; see 39:2, 8) may simply be for making the gold elements of the ephod, breastpiece and turban (28:36) – braided chains, filigree settings, rings, bells and the ornamental inscription – that were skilfully fitted to the woven material. The Hebrew wording is ambiguous (cf. different English translations), but there is good reason to take the final phrase, 'finely twisted linen' (AT), as explicative, and thus referring only to the coloured (linen) fabric and not the strips of gold.[2] The design and function of the six items listed here (v. 4), as well as of the priests' linen underwear (v. 42), are elaborated in verses 6–43. The ephod is described before the breastpiece, not because it was the most important item, but because the breastpiece (given double the attention) was borne by it.

ii. The ephod (28:6–14)

6–8. The ephod was an ornate apron-like outer garment worn by the high priest. It was held on by two shoulder pieces and a

---

2   For the *skilled workers*, and a *ḥōšēb* in particular (28:6, 8, 15), see p. 311 n. 14 above, and comment on 31:1–11.

woven waistband (vv. 7–8).³ The latter suggests that it extended at least to the upper thighs, if not to the knees.

9–12. Two onyx stones, each engraved with the names of half of Israel's tribes, in order of their birth, were attached to the shoulder pieces, symbolizing Aaron's representative role for all Israel (v. 12b) and serving as a reminder (*zikkārôn*) to God to keep his covenant promises (cf. Gen. 9:14–15). The identity and colour of these stones is debated, but they may arguably have been red like carnelian (see *HALOT*).

13–14. Two braided chains of pure gold were also attached to the ephod's gold filigree settings for holding the breastpiece in place.

iii. The breastpiece (28:15–30)

15–21. The breastpiece was a unique, folded piece of the same richly coloured material as the ephod. Folded double, it measured around 23 centimetres square and was decorated with four rows of three precious stones (each of the twelve engraved with the name of one of the twelve tribes) mounted in gold lace settings. Again, the exact identity of all these various stones is uncertain (cf. English translations), but their significance lies more in their splendour and value, arguably underlining that Israel was indeed God's 'precious possession' (cf. 19:5; Ps. 135:4; Mal. 3:17; AT).

22–28. Braided rope-like chains of pure gold on the breastpiece were attached with blue cord to the gold rings on the ephod in order to keep the former in place over the priest's heart/chest.

29–30. The theological rationale is similar to that given before (cf. v. 12b) – symbolizing Aaron's representative role before Yahweh. Its association with decision-making (*breastpiece of decision*, v. 29) stems from its function as a pouch (the reason it was folded double, v. 16) to hold the *Urim* and *Thummim* – Israel's only legitimate means of divination (cf. Num. 27:21; Deut. 33:8; 1 Sam. 14:41–42; 28:6; Ezra 2:63). While there are several theories, the precise nature of these two objects or how they were used to determine divine rulings in specific situations (Num. 27:21; 1 Sam.

---

3   Lit. 'the weave of his/its *'ăfuddâ*' (i.e. the skilful work of its *woven waistband*).

28:6; Ezra 2:63 || Neh. 7:65) remains unclear. They may have been
two or more stones or flat pebbles with different coloured/marked
sides, offering various answers (yes, no or wait) when drawn out
as lots or flipped like coins, possibly a number of times (so Kitz
1997). However, they could have been more akin to dice, if stones
at all. The lack of any explanation in the text could indicate that
they were already familiar items that were in use before the ephod
and breastpiece were made (so Garrett 2014: 591), yet this could
simply be yet another literary gap in the narrative, whose intended
readership required no such explanation.

iv. The robe (28:31–35)

31–32. A blue-coloured robe, possibly extending as far as
Aaron's calves or ankles, was to be worn directly underneath the
ephod. Its material is not stipulated here or in the Hebrew text of
39:22 (cf. LXX and SP), but linen (symbolizing purity, as for the rest
of the priestly garments) is much more likely than wool, which
induces sweat.

The hole in the middle of this robe (more like a long poncho
than a sleeved pullover) was reinforced with a woven edge to
prevent tearing. Unfortunately, the illustrative simile (lit. 'like the
mouth/opening of a . . .') is somewhat cryptic, as the key term
(*taḥrāʾ*) is employed only here and in 39:23. It evidently alludes to
something familiar to the Israelites, quite possibly the protective
leather collar worn by Egyptian charioteers (so Sarna 1991: 182). In
any case, the stitched hem of the high-priestly robe was to protect
the garment rather than its wearer.

33–35. Its lower hem was decorated with braided pomegranates
(symbolic of something desirable and beautiful; cf. Num. 13:23;
20:5; Song 4:13; 6:7), interspersed with functional gold bells.
The practical function of these bells most likely emphasizes the
inherent danger involved in approaching Yahweh, and implicitly
warns that any unauthorized tabernacle activity would almost
certainly result in death (v. 35; cf. Lev. 10).[4]

---

4   For other suggestions, see Houtman 1990.

v. The emblem (28:36–38)

36–38. An engraved gold emblem (Heb. *ṣîṣ* means 'flower' or 'blossom') was attached with blue cord to the front of the high priest's linen turban (cf. v. 39; 29:6; 39:30; Lev. 8:9) and served as a reminder of Aaron's special status ('holy to Yahweh', AT), thus ensuring that he could officiate safely before God despite offering sacrifices that were defiled by Israel's sin. His priestly role in bearing such guilt on Israel's behalf ensured that their iniquity would be removed and that they and their sacrifices were acceptable to Yahweh. Thus here, as the author of Hebrews underlines, we have a foreshadowing of the work of the ultimate High Priest who would do so once and for all through the sacrifice of himself (Heb. 8 – 10).

vi. The tunic and sash (28:39–41)

39. The tunic (worn under the blue robe, 29:5) and turban for the high priest were to be made of fine linen. An embroidered *sash* would fasten the blue robe and linen tunic around the priest's waist.

40–41. Similar, albeit plainer, items designed for Aaron's sons had the same theological purpose (cf. v. 2). Wearing such garments, both Aaron and his sons would be anointed, ordained and consecrated as Israel's official priesthood. For more on these three actions to be carried out by Moses, see commentary on Exodus 29, where these are discussed in greater detail.

vii. The undergarments (28:42–43)

42–43. The final item of priestly clothing mentioned is their underwear. In contrast to the overt sexuality reflected in typical Ancient Near Eastern fertility religion, Israel's priests were to keep their genitals covered and avoid exposing themselves during any of the cultic ritual in which they engaged (cf. 20:26). Failure to comply with such was a sacrilege which, like several other priestly offences (see 30:19–21; Lev. 10:6, 9; 16:2, 13; 22:8–9; Num. 4:15, 17–20; 18:3), was punishable by death. Significantly, like maintaining the lights of the menorah (27:21) and other distinctively priestly responsibilities (e.g. 30:7–10, 17–21), wearing the designated vestments when carrying out priestly duties in the tabernacle was non-negotiable – a *lasting ordinance* for both Aaron and his descendants.

Notably absent from this list of priestly garments is any mention of footwear. From this omission, coupled with divine instructions elsewhere (3:5; 30:19; cf. Josh. 5:15), it seems reasonable to infer that Israel's priests carried out their duties in and around the sacred tent barefoot.

C. Consecration of the priests (29:1–46)

Although focusing mainly on the consecration of Aaron and his sons, this chapter also includes related instructions regarding the consecration of the bronze altar and the tent of meeting. The consecration of the priests involved several stages: (1) ritual washing, robing and (in the case of the high priest) anointing (29:4–9a); and (2) ordination, involving (a) a sin/purification offering of a young bull (29:10–14), (b) a burnt/food offering of a ram (29:15–18) and (c) a fellowship/ordination offering of a second ram, incorporating wave offerings of both bread and meat (29:19–34).⁵ The latter stage (ordination) was a more prolonged affair (taking place over seven days, 29:35; cf. Lev. 8:33), during which a separate sin offering made each day would consecrate the altar (29:35–37).

The instructions that follow (29:38–43) relate, not to the initial consecration of the priests or the altar, but to the regular (twice-daily) burnt offering to be made thereafter. This would facilitate the ongoing consecration of the tent of meeting by the glorious presence of God, and thus the ultimate objective of the exodus (29:44–46).

1–3. God's instructions begin with an inventory of materials needed for the consecration ritual: a young bull, two rams and three different varieties of unleavened bread (cf. Lev. 7:12).

---

5   The use of unleavened loaves in association with the second (ordination) ram, and the stipulation that nothing be left over for consumption on the following day, identifies it as a special kind of fellowship offering (cf. Lev. 7:11–15).

4–9. After Aaron and his sons were brought to the tent of meeting (presumably to the basin outside the entrance to the Holy Place; cf. 30:17–21), they must undergo ritual washing (v. 4; cf. 19:10, 22) before being robed in their priestly attire (vv. 5–9). Once robed, Aaron's head must be anointed with the special anointing oil (v. 7; cf. 30:22–33; Lev. 8:12; Ps. 133:2).[6] The sacred garments of Aaron and his sons were mandatory for the service they would perform (cf. 28:43), emphasizing that the priesthood was theirs by lasting ordinance (29:9). Suitably attired in these priestly vestments, their 'ordination' would then begin (v. 9b). The underlying Hebrew expression (lit. 'fill the hand of . . .') used in verse 9b and subsequently denotes exclusive dedication to God or cultic activity (cf. 32:29; Judg. 17:5; 1 Kgs 13:33). Perhaps the Hebrew idiom stems from the fact that, during their consecration, the hands of priests were literally filled with various wave offerings (cf. 29:24).

As noted above, the priests' ordination would involve three distinct sacrifices: a sin/purification offering, a burnt offering and a fellowship offering. Sin/purification offerings are sometimes associated more with ritual defilement than with sinful behaviour (e.g. see Lev. 12:6; cf. also Num. 6:14, 16). As Hamilton (2011: 500) infers, the absence of any punitive or absolution language (cf. Lev. 4:20, 26, 31; 5:6, 11) suggests that ritual purification is likewise the focus at this point in Exodus 29.

Verse 9b is open to different interpretations (cf. EVV), but what follows in the rest of the chapter suggests that ordination *followed* the preliminary stage of their consecration recorded in verses 4–9a.

10–14. The young bull for the sin/purification offering (v. 14; cf. Lev. 4:3–12) was to be presented, like the priests (v. 4), at the front of the tent of meeting (i.e. outside the Holy Place). By laying their hands on its head (v. 10; also vv. 15, 19), Aaron and his sons were identifying with the animal before it was slaughtered and its blood smeared on the horns or poured out at the base of the

---

6 While Aaron's sons were also to be anointed (cf. 28:41), this took place subsequently as part of the ordination ritual (cf. Lev. 8:30).

altar (v. 12). Subsequent to priestly ordination (cf. Lev. 4:6–7), such blood was also taken inside the Holy Place and daubed on the golden altar, not just on the bronze altar in the courtyard. But clearly this was impossible before the anointed priest was ordained and consecrated for the task.

The purpose of this purification ritual was primarily to make atonement for and to purify the altar (cf. Lev. 8:15, 30), presumably its horns and base (like the priestly extremities; see below) representing the whole. Verse 36 provides the same rationale for the additional sin offering made on each of the seven days of priestly ordination. Significantly, there is nothing said (either here or in Lev. 9) to suggest that this purification offering removed priestly guilt or defilement that would have disqualified them from the task to which they were appointed.

Rather than referring to all internal organs (cf. NIV), the 'inner parts' (v. 13a, AT; Heb. *qereb*) probably encompass only those (i.e. the entrails) which required washing (Lev. 1:9, 13) due to dung deposits (so Hamilton 2011: 497). As was typical for such offerings (cf. Lev. 4:8–12), the fatty coated entrails must be burnt on the altar (29:13b), while everything else must be burnt outside the camp (v. 14) – at the place where altar ashes would be dumped, according to Leviticus 4:12. This signified the removal and disposal of impurity. For the typological fulfilment of the latter in the crucifixion of Jesus (as the ultimate sin offering) outside Jerusalem's walls, see Hebrews 13:11–12.

15–18. The first of the two rams constitutes a whole burnt offering (v. 18), subsequently described as providing atonement for the worshipper (cf. Lev. 1:3–9) – as was almost certainly the case here also. Without this ceremonial removal of priestly guilt, the ordination process could advance no further. Once again, the priests must personally identify with the animal before it was slain and its blood splashed on the sides of the altar (vv. 15–16). This time, however, after ritual dissection and washing, the entire animal was to be burnt on the altar as a pleasing fragrance to Yahweh (vv. 17–18). There is some debate over the precise meaning of the final phrase; traditionally understood as 'it is an offering made by *fire* to Yahweh' (for a defence of this interpretation, see B. Levine 1989: 7–8, 201 n. 24), some take the key term (*'iššê*) simply to mean 'offering' or 'food gift' (e.g. Milgrom 1991: 161–162).

19–34. The second ram served a different and exclusive purpose – namely, priestly ordination (v. 22) – and thus involved some distinct ritual after the priests had identified with this animal also: (1) some of its blood was to be smeared on the priests (v. 20a), some splashed on the altar (v. 20b) and – together with anointing oil – some sprinkled on the priests and their garments (v. 21; cf. 24:6–8); and (2) only select parts of the ram (v. 22),[7] together with each kind of unleavened loaf (vv. 23–25; cf. v. 2), were to be offered to Yahweh (v. 25). Why some parts were waved before Yahweh is not explained, but they arguably represented the choicest cuts (cf. Gen. 4:4; Lev. 3:16; 1 Sam. 9:24; Isa. 1:11), as well as being the most combustible and aromatic (Exod. 29:18, 25; Lev. 4:31; 17:6; Num. 18:17; Isa. 43:24). On this unique occasion (Aaron's ordination) the breast would be allocated to Moses – as the officiating 'priest' (v. 26; cf. Lev. 8:29) – and the rest of the animal would be consumed by Aaron and his sons (v. 27).

No explanation is given but smearing the blood on the priests' extremities (their right ears, thumbs and big toes) in verse 20 is most likely synecdochal – representing the consecration of their entire self, and as Hamilton (2011) avers, most likely alludes to a change of status. The only other occasion where blood is smeared on bodily extremities is in the case of someone healed of an infectious skin disease (Lev. 14:14, 25), that is, moving from an unclean to a clean state. This parallel, along with explicit atonement language (i.e. *kipper 'al*) in both contexts, may point to an analogous transformation here: priests are being cleansed from any kind of impurity and transitioning to a holy/consecrated status.

The second blood ritual – being sprinkled with blood from the altar and with the sacred anointing oil (v. 21; cf. 30:22–33) – sealed such consecration for both the priests and their vestments

---

7   As well as the fat on the entrails, the long lobe of the liver and both kidneys with the fat on them (cf. 29:13), *the fat, the fat tail* and *the right thigh* of this ordination ram were included in the portion offered up to Yahweh.

(v. 21; Lev. 8:30). In the execution of the priestly ordination (Lev. 8:22–30), the consecration of the priests and their garments directly *follows* the smearing of the priests' extremities and their wave offerings (Lev. 8:22–29). Given the repeated emphasis in Leviticus 8 on doing everything 'as Yahweh commanded', it seems clear that the sequence reflected in Exodus 29:19–21 was neither intended nor interpreted in a narrow chronological sense. Both passages agree, however, that the climax of the ordination ceremony was the fellowship meal and remaining at the entrance to the tent of meeting for seven days (Exod. 29:31–37; Lev. 8:31–35).

The aside in 29:27–28 explains how the normal practice of consecrating (setting aside) and donating the breast and right thigh of fellowship offerings to the priests (cf. Lev. 7:28–36) carries on from this ordination rite. This is followed by a further aside (vv. 29–30), again looking beyond the initial ordination ceremony of Aaron and his sons; here the issue is high-priestly succession, and the formalities involved: namely, being ordained in the sacred garments and wearing them for seven days straight – clearly identifying the participant as the heir to this office.

In verses 31–34 the focus returns to the initial ordination ceremony – in particular, the cooking and priestly consumption of the remaining meat of the ordination ram, as well as the rest of the unleavened bread. Despite what some translations suggest, the verb (*bāšal*) has a much wider semantic range than 'boil' (cf. Deut. 16:7 and Exod. 12:9), and arguably means 'cook' here in 29:31 (so, too, 1 Sam. 2:15), since no liquid (e.g. water or milk) is explicitly mentioned. By consuming this consecrated ram with which they had identified, the priests themselves are likewise consecrated to Yahweh. Significantly, the requirement to burn rather than consume any leftovers (v. 34; cf. Lev. 7:15; 8:32) echoes similar such legislation for the Passover (12:10), arguably suggesting that these two fellowship meals had much more in common than has been generally understood (see *Meaning* at the end of this section).

35–37. The process of priestly ordination would last a total of seven days (v. 35), during which Aaron and his sons must remain at the entrance of the tent (cf. Lev. 8:33–35). Other than the daily sin offering of a bull to make full atonement (v. 36),[8] what happened on each of these days is rather unclear. While the entire ritual may have been repeated daily, the ordination process could have taken several days to complete, as was apparently so for the purification and consecration of the altar (vv. 36–37). The latter was presumably a one-off event, rather than something to be repeated at the consecration of every successive high priest.

38–44. Attention shifts here to the perpetual priestly responsibility of presenting twice-daily sacrifices of a year-old lamb, along with flour, oil and wine offerings – a ritual necessary for the tent's ongoing functional use as a divine–human meeting place.[9] Rather than consecrating the tent of meeting (cf. v. 43), these perpetual burnt offerings would ensure that the tent would be consecrated by Yahweh's glory as he manifested his presence there and met with his people.

45–46. The tabernacle is no mere addendum to deliverance from Egypt, but rather expresses the ultimate significance and goal of the exodus: that Yahweh would be known as the one who had delivered his people from Egypt so that he might dwell among them.

Meaning
In order to function as priests in the tabernacle, Aaron and his sons had to be suitably equipped and consecrated. Like the tent of meeting itself, with which there are several parallels, the priests' garments had symbolic significance. This is particularly so of the high priest's clothing, which highlighted not only his holiness but also his role as Israel's chief representative in the worship of God.

The preliminary stage of priestly consecration involved the removal of any defilement (washing), investiture with sacred garments, and what was most likely an indication of divine selection: anointing.[10] The next stage involved three sacrificial

---

8   As suggested by Hamilton (2011: 499), the plural Hebrew noun here is most likely intensive.

9   Possibly all three regular priestly activities (cf. 27:20–21; 30:7–8) were conducted consecutively at the same time each day (Hamilton 2011).

10 In some places being anointed with oil is closely associated with an

rituals culminating in a special meal, all of which share a number of parallels with the previous rituals concerning the nation as a whole. As Alexander (2017) and Gehrig (2024) contend, this is especially so in relation to the Passover ritual, suggesting that the latter served an analogous purpose: to purify and consecrate the Israelites whose firstborn had been ransomed from death by a substitutionary sacrifice (see comments on Exod. 12 – 13).

Whatever the precise significance of all the ritual described, the most important thing to note is that Aaron and his sons are to take on a role that is not only exclusively theirs in perpetuity (29:9, 29) but is essential for the tabernacle to fulfil its purpose and function as Yahweh intended (29:42–46). As we know from the New Testament, all this reaches its eschatological fulfilment in the superior High Priest of the new covenant, our Immanuel, 'who through the eternal Spirit offered himself unblemished to God . . . [and] by one sacrifice . . . made perfect for ever those who are being made holy' (Heb. 9:14; 10:14).

D. Priestly service in the tent of meeting (30:1–38)

Context
This chapter is somewhat disjointed in nature, with what look like miscellaneous instructions concerning furniture, a poll tax, and recipes for sacred oil or incense. Such a lack of cohesion is further suggested by the repeated use of the phrase *Then the* LORD *said to Moses*, both here and in the following chapter: the previous appearance of this structural marker was back in 25:1, suggesting that both 25:1 – 30:10 and the paragraphs that follow (30:11–16, 17–21, 22–33, 34–38; 31:1–11, 12–17) are all discrete literary units.[11]

---

endowment of the Spirit (e.g. 1 Sam. 10:1–10; 16:13), but in Exodus the latter is expressly mentioned only in connection with Israel's skilled craftsmen (31:3; 35:31), who were apparently not anointed at all (cf. also Judg. 3:10; 6:34; 11:29; 13:25).

11 The Hebrew phrase used in 30:34 and 31:12 is slightly different but is likewise used throughout Exodus as a structural marker commencing a new section or subsection.

The overarching focus, however, is arguably on matters 'essential to priestly service in the tabernacle' (Bruckner 2008: 269), an emphasis that could explain why further instructions concerning tabernacle furniture are given here, rather than back in chapters 25 or 27, where the other furniture inside the tent of meeting (cf. Exod. 37) or in the tabernacle courtyard (cf. Exod. 38) was introduced. However, this anomaly may also be explained by a twofold literary emphasis in the larger block of text: for example, Milgrom's (1991: 236–237) distinction between 'the tabernacle in blueprint' (26:1 – 27:19) and 'the tabernacle in operation' (27:20 – 30:38), or the more likely distinction Alexander (2017: 565) notes – on the basis of the two primary designations used for the sanctuary within these chapters – between its function as a divine 'dwelling place' (25:8 – 27:19) and its function as a 'tent of meeting' (27:20 – 30:38).

The focus on incense (vv. 1–10, 34–38) that brackets the contents of this chapter may further suggest at least some degree of overall cohesion.

Comment
i. The golden altar (30:1–10)
For the introduction of more tabernacle furniture at this point, see *Context* above.

1–5. While similar in design to the bronze 'altar of burnt offering' (27:1–8), this altar is a third of the size (*c.*480 mm long and wide, and 960 mm high), is overlaid with pure gold (rather than bronze), and has a pedestal-like top (v. 3) rather than any kind of network grating (cf. 27:4–5).

6. It is located inside the tent of meeting rather than within the surrounding courtyard. However, its precise location is complicated by the fact that, contrary to most interpreters of the Pentateuch (including Josephus), the author of Hebrews places it *within* the Most Holy Place (cf. Heb. 9:4), rather than directly outside it. *In front of the curtain . . . before the atonement cover* (30:6; cf. 40:26) is somewhat ambiguous, but most interpreters consider it more natural to indicate a location just outside the curtain that separated off the Most Holy Place. Admittedly, the appositional statement (*before the atonement cover that is over the tablets of the covenant* *law*) and the relative clause (*where I will meet with you*) might suggest a location between the veil and the ark of the covenant (i.e. inside the Most Holy Place), and the appositional statement could possibly have been omitted from some manuscripts (see *BHS* critical apparatus) due to its similarity with the preceding clause. However, while a location inside the Most Holy Place conforms with the placement of such an altar in the Solomonic temple (1 Kgs 6:22; although not with its location in the Holy Place of the Second Temple in the first century; cf. Luke 1:11), and arguably better serves its utilitarian function of providing a smokescreen for the atonement cover (cf. Lev. 16:13), it remains difficult to square this with Hebrews 9:7 in view of the regular high-priestly duties prescribed in Exodus 30:7–10.

7–9. Twice daily – while attending to the lamps in the Holy Place – the high priest was to replenish the sacred incense offered up in smoke on this altar. It is unclear if censers were to be used for such (cf. Num. 16:17–18), rather than burning the incense directly on the top of the altar or in some kind of receptacle permanently placed there. While nothing is said here about the theological significance of this incense, elsewhere it is associated with turning away God's wrath or seeking divine favour (Num. 16:44–50; Ps. 141:2; Rev. 5:8; 8:3, 4). For the unique recipe for this incense, see verses 34–38. Other than this, nothing else was to be burnt or offered on this altar, further emphasizing its special status (cf. v. 10). Significantly, the timing implies a theological relationship between the burnt offerings on the bronze altar (29:38–43), the incense offered up on the golden altar, and the burning lamps of the menorah that symbolized God's presence.

10. Annually, on the Day of Atonement, this altar (like the bronze altar; cf. Lev. 16:18–19) was reconsecrated by the atoning blood of the purification offering, which was smeared on its four horns by the high priest.

ii. Atonement money (30:11–16)

11–16. Stipulations for a census tax may seem rather intrusive in the context of tabernacle furniture and other accessories, but like everything else in this chapter, it is its association with priestly responsibilities (see 38:21, 25–28; Num. 1:3; 26:1; cf. 2 Kgs

12:4–16) that explains its relevance here. The initial census tax, collected from everyone twenty years old or more (cf. 38:26),[12] provided some of the raw materials for the manufacture of the tabernacle (cf. 38:27–28). The regulation here,[13] however, apparently applies not just to that initial census (taken prior to the tabernacle's construction; cf. 38:25–26), but also to any subsequent census (cf. Num. 1; 26), to provide funds for ongoing tabernacle expenses (30:16). However, as well as providing for such practical needs, this poll tax served a twofold theological purpose: (1) it highlighted the danger inherent in any such census (v. 12; cf. 2 Sam. 24:1–17); (2) it was a symbolic reminder that each redeemed person (regardless of social status) owed their life to Yahweh.

iii. The bronze basin (30:17–21)

17–21. This bronze basin, set on a bronze pedestal, was to be located in the courtyard between the bronze altar and the entrance to the Holy Place. It held the water which priests used to wash their hands and feet (whether ritually, practically or both) before entering the tent or burning food on the bronze altar. The importance of such washing is emphasized by the reiterated purpose clause *so that they will not die* (vv. 20–21), as well as by the observation that this is yet another *lasting ordinance* (v. 21; cf. 27:21; 28:43; 29:9, 28) which Israel/the priests must observe.

Subsequent reference to the source of the bronze used in its construction (see 38:8) throws little light on its actual size or dimensions – construction details which are strangely absent

---

12   It is generally assumed that those included in this census were exclusively male, but this is inferred from a gender-specific interpretation of the 603,550 figure at the end of the verse and a similar interpretation of Exod. 12:37, which (along with the nature and scope of the census reflected in the figures of Num. 1:46 and 2:32) Alexander (2017: 240–243, 602–603) has recently challenged. See comment on 38:25–26.

13   On the basis that the conditional particle (*kî*) in administrative legislation such as Exod. 30:12a should be translated 'If . . .' rather than 'When . . .', some (e.g. Garrett 2014: 604 n. 71) insist that the taking of such a census is not a divine imperative.

here. This further underlines that even the prescriptive chapters concerning the tabernacle (i.e. Exod. 25 – 31) primarily serve a theological rather than a practical purpose.

iv. Anointing oil (30:22–33)

22–33. While this anointing oil has been mentioned previously (25:6b; 29:7), only now are its precise ingredients and formula disclosed. Unlike the pure olive oil used as fuel for the lampstand (cf. 27:20), the anointing oil contained large quantities of aromatic ingredients (around 6 kg of myrrh resin,[14] 3 kg of cinnamon spice, 3 kg of reed-spice[15] and 6 kg of cassia),[16] which were expertly blended into about 4 litres of olive oil (v. 24). This unique recipe, like the *sacred . . . oil* itself, was exclusively for the consecration of the tent of meeting, its furniture, accessories and priestly personnel. Any other usage was absolutely prohibited (vv. 31–33). The holiness it conferred was transferrable (v. 29) – in the sense that any unauthorized contact with items thus consecrated would result in death (cf. 2 Sam. 6:7). Unauthorized use of such anointing oil or profane use of its formula would also have dire consequences (v. 33; cf. 12:15).

v. Incense (30:34–38)

34–38. The incense to be burned on the golden altar inside the tent (vv. 1–9) was a unique blend of spices and gum resin (vv. 34–35).[17] It was to be used exclusively for cultic purposes (v. 37); as with the anointing oil, any profane use of its unique formula

---

14 *Liquid myrrh* (NIV; cf. ESV; NRSV) is potentially misleading, as the qualifying word (*dĕrôr*) denotes how it is extracted as tree sap rather than its solidified state when stored or used (Garrett 2014: 605 n. 72).

15 As several EVV suggest, this arguably refers to calamus, a spice derived from a reed.

16 The precise meaning of the Hebrew noun, appearing only here and in Ezek. 27:19, is uncertain, but most English translations follow the Vulgate in identifying the substance as cassia (similar to cinnamon in flavour).

17 The meaning of the first-named spice is unknown; the next two are

was strictly forbidden (v. 38). The reason for the incense being *salted* is unclear: while possibly used to increase the burn rate or to preserve a large batch of it, the salt may simply have been symbolic (cf. Lev. 2:13). Its *most holy* nature (v. 36b; cf. v. 32) stems from the fact that this ground-up incense was to be burned in such close proximity to the ark of the covenant law, from where God would communicate directly with Moses (v. 36; cf. 25:22; 30:6).

Meaning

Bracketed by an *inclusio* that focuses on incense (the altar of incense in vv. 1–10; the incense itself in vv. 34–38), this material is clearly concerned with ensuring that any activity within the tent of meeting could be conducted safely, and that the strict separation between Israel's sacred and profane (i.e. non-sacred) actions would in no way be compromised. Accordingly, those who approached the (bronze) altar to burn a sacrifice or who entered the tent of meeting could only do so after the appropriate purification (washing hands and feet). Direct contact with the most holy altar of incense was clearly to be avoided (cf. its carrying poles and holders). Nothing other than specifically designed oil and incense could be used for tabernacle ritual; moreover, any profane use of this unique oil and incense, including the recipes, was strictly prohibited. While the poll tax provided additional funds for the tabernacle (and, subsequently, its ongoing service), it highlights the inherent risk in any such census and further reminds the ransomed community that they owed their lives to Yahweh.

Though the ransomed people of God's new covenant community certainly have greater 'confidence to enter the Most Holy Place by the blood of Jesus, by a new and living way opened for us through the curtain, that is, his body . . . having our hearts sprinkled to cleanse us from a guilty conscience and having our bodies washed with pure water' (Heb. 10:19–22), this Exodus text foreshadows the fact that we too 'were bought at a price' (1 Cor. 6:20) and, accordingly, 'belong to the Lord' (Rom. 14:8).

---

generally understood as onycha and galbanum. These are to be mixed in equal amounts with *frankincense* (i.e. olibanum gum resin).

14. DIVINE INSTRUCTIONS FOR WORSHIP (III): THE SKILLED WORKERS, THE SABBATH AND THE COVENANT TABLETS (31:1–18)

Context

Now that the requirements for the tabernacle, its various items of furniture and its priestly investiture are completed, attention shifts to those divinely equipped to complete, teach or oversee the skilled craftsmanship involved in the manufacture of the tabernacle and its various accoutrements. While only two artisans are named (Bezalel and Oholiab), several others are alluded to, all of whom have been divinely equipped for their specific tasks.

The material that follows, which concludes the instructions given to Moses on the mountain top (cf. 24:12–18), deals with the *sign* of the Sinai covenant (31:13, 17). Coming at the climax of the covenant's establishment, just before the reception of the *tablets of the covenant law* (31:18), suggests that the instructions relating to Israel's worship (25:1 – 31:12) are also an intrinsic part of the covenant, and thus part of Israel's response to Yahweh.

Comment
A. Bezalel and Oholiab (31:1–11)

1–5. The first artisan named is apparently the more significant one: a short genealogy is supplied for both Bezalel and Oholiab, yet only Bezalel is said to have been 'called by name' (AT), and spiritually endowed with the requisite skill sets. Undoubtedly God gave Oholiab 'skill' (lit. 'wisdom'), like the rest of the skilled workers (v. 6; cf. v. 3), but the master craftsman was apparently Bezalel, who is subsequently singled out for attention in 37:1 and arguably in the bulk of what follows (some EVV remove the ambiguity by translating the *singular* third person pronoun of the Hebrew text as 'they').

Bezalel's credentials (*filled . . . with the Spirit of God*, i.e. a divine endowment with *wisdom, understanding* and *knowledge* that made him proficient in all kinds of skills; v. 3; cf. 35:31) highlight how Yahweh has prepared and equipped him for the various tasks at hand (cf. 28:3; Deut. 34:9). Bezalel's expertise includes artistic metalwork, gem-cutting and setting, intricate woodwork and numerous other artistic crafts (vv. 4–5; cf. 35:31–33). We subsequently learn that Oholiab's (more limited?) speciality was engraving, design and weaving intricate patterns with fine linen (38:23).

6. Perhaps Oholiab, Bezalel's divinely appointed assistant, was his protégé, although each man seems to have particular expertise in different areas (see above), suggesting that their working relationship was of a more complementarian nature; in any case, both were able to pass on at least some of their expertise to others (cf. 35:34) – one of the ways God equipped *all the skilled workers* for this special assignment (cf. 35:35; 36:1).

7–11a. The manufacture of the tabernacle, its furniture, the priestly garments, the special anointing oil and the fragrant incense would thus be undertaken by suitably skilled personnel, with different tasks obviously being assigned or delegated according to particular skill sets (e.g. spinners and weavers, tanners and dyers, metallurgists and woodworkers, jewellers and perfumers) and carried out under the supervision of Bezalel and his assistant (cf. 36:8 – 39:31).

11b. Possibly the expertise of Bezalel and his team of skilled workers enabled them to 'fill in' any significant practical 'gaps' in the divine instructions communicated through Moses. Indeed, at least some of the missing dimensions (e.g. the lampstand's height and thickness, or the size of the bronze basin and its stand) may have been determined more by the amount of raw material prescribed (cf. 25:39) or provided (38:8) than anything else. We should probably be very cautious about reading Exodus 25 – 30 as a precise architectural drawing or draughtsman's blueprints in any case. The important point to note is that everything must conform to the divine instructions, and Moses subsequently confirms that this was indeed the case (cf. 39:32–43).

B. Sabbath rest (31:12–17)

12. This climactic section of the tabernacle instructions – underlining the theological significance of sabbath rest – appropriately begins with the seventh occurrence of a divine speech formula (cf. 25:1; 30:11, 17, 22, 34; 31:1, 12). However, while such a creation-week pattern is subsequently alluded to in the setting up of the tabernacle (ch. 40), it is less obvious in the account of its construction (chs. 35–39).

13–16. Complete cessation of labour on the sabbath was a symbol and perpetual reminder of Israel's holy status. Just as Yahweh had set one day apart from all the rest, so also he had set one people apart from all others. Desecration of the sabbath thus invoked the death penalty: here (v. 14) and occasionally elsewhere the death penalty is equated with 'being cut off from his/their people'. As noted previously (cf. comment on 12:15), one can infer from this that the latter concept refers to much more than simply temporary or even permanent expulsion from the community.

17. See comment on Exodus 20:11. By following Yahweh's lead,[1] the Israelites are in some sense participating in and pointing forward towards the goal of creation: enjoyment of God's rest. This

---

[1] The idea of God having to 'refresh himself' or 'catch his breath' (Niphal *npš*) is a bold anthropomorphism (cf. 23:12; 2 Sam. 16:14).

is further suggested by the prominence of sabbath observance in both sections dealing with the construction of the tabernacle (i.e. closing the first; beginning the second; cf. 35:1–3); as expressions of divine rest, the sabbath and the tabernacle are two sides of the same reality, anticipating the rest in which Yahweh wants Israel – and, ultimately, all nations – to share.

C. Reception of the covenant tablets (31:18)

18. Returning to the narrative of Exodus 24 and the rationale for Moses' trip up Sinai, this narrative block (24:12 – 31:18) concludes by refocusing on the final part of the covenant's ratification: the reception of the tablets of the covenant law (24:12) that were to be deposited in the ark (25:16). These two *tablets of stone* were not necessarily large or heavy, despite being engraved (*front and back*, 32:15) with the covenant law. This was apparently just the Decalogue (cf. 34:1, 28) rather than all the additional material already recorded by Moses (cf. 24:4). The *finger of God* is understood by some interpreters as a bold anthropomorphism (cf. 8:19; Luke 11:20), which simply highlights the divine (as opposed to human) origin or inspiration of the covenant law. Others, however, interpret the text more literally – referring to a supernatural engraving process (cf. 34:1, 27–28) – understanding Yahweh to be consistently the one responsible for the engraving of these tablets. For a defence of the latter, see comments on 34:1 and 34:28.

Meaning
It is clear from the start of this chapter that as well as revealing his plans to his people, Yahweh also facilitates the implementation of such by raising up the necessary personnel and equipping them with the required skill sets. Accordingly, however extraordinary, God's commands are not impossible to obey; rather, with the help of his Spirit, people are equipped not only to know God's will, but to carry it out, however imperfectly, in a way that honours him and attests to his greatness.

Keeping the sabbath, for Israel, is clearly of particular importance – a point further underscored by its description as a perpetual covenant *sign*, as well as by the priority given to it after the covenant has been broken and remade (cf. 35:1–3). The fact that the sabbath requirement is repeated just before work on the tabernacle commences highlights that even with respect to the latter,[2] covenant faithfulness is the priority – a truth that Israel was unfortunately slow to learn and quick to forget.

With the reception of the covenant tablets, we reach the climax of the covenant's ratification, again highlighting the essence of Israel's covenant responsibility, but, given its immediate context, also underlining the gravity of the 'great sin' that will be narrated in the section that follows.

---

2   This is further suggested by the contrastive particle (*'ak*) that prefaces the exhortation in 31:13b.

15. THE COVENANT BROKEN AND RE-ESTABLISHED (32:1 – 34:35)

A. Israel's 'great sin' with the golden calf (32:1 – 33:6)

The focus now shifts abruptly to events in the camp below during Moses' absence (24:18) – which was much longer than anyone in the community had anticipated (32:1). Israel's behaviour during this period constituted a flagrant breach of the covenant, thus jeopardizing the fulfilment of Yahweh's plans for Israel (ch. 32). Indeed, it was only after the consequences of Israel's folly were fully spelt out, and Moses had persistently interceded on Israel's behalf (ch. 33), that the covenant – and with it, the rationale for the tabernacle – could be graciously reinstated (ch. 34).

i. Israel's idolatry and Yahweh's response (32:1–10)
Context
With the reception of the tablets of the covenant law (31:18), we expect the narrative to move immediately to the communication and implementation of God's detailed instructions for the tabernacle (chs. 25–31). However, rather than moving directly to this

(chs. 35–39), the narrative switches attention to what was taking place at the foot of Sinai during Moses' absence (24:18). Before his ascent, Moses had delegated responsibility for settling disputes – presumably the hard cases (cf. 18:22, 26) – to Aaron and Hur (24:14). However, his protracted absence evoked a leadership crisis at the foot of the mountain. Instead of maintaining order in the camp, one of his two deputies led the Israelites in an act of rebellion, one that has aptly been understood as 'Israel's fall' – echoing that of humanity back in Genesis 3. On the people's insistence, Aaron manufactures a graven image in the shape of a young bull.[1] While he understood this graven image as somehow representing Yahweh (cf. 32:4–5) – and therefore not technically a breach of the first commandment – the repeated use of *gods* (along with plural verbs) ironically shows otherwise. It clearly foreshadows the sin of Jeroboam I (1 Kgs 12:26–28); thus later readers can infer that the Israelites have broken both the first and second commandments.

Comment

1–4. So far as we know, Moses had not remained on the mountain overnight before, and now he has been up there for nearly six weeks (24:18) – a delay that was much too long for those below. Prompted by Moses' prolonged absence, the hostile mob that gathers *round* [or 'against'; Heb. *ʿal*] Aaron dismissively refers to *this fellow Moses*, crediting him alone with their departure from Egypt (v. 1; cf. 19:4). What is less clear is precisely what they meant when they demanded that Aaron make *gods who will go before us*. Were they insisting on some kind of replacement(s) for Moses, Yahweh or both?

That they wanted someone or rather some*thing* to replace Moses is obvious – his prolonged absence is the presenting problem; indeed, this was the catalyst behind their insistence on having some visual representation of deity to go before them. Moreover, as soon as Aaron accedes to their request, this visual

---

[1] 'Bull' is a better translation of *ʿēgel* than 'calf'; the idea is of a one- to three-year-old fully grown animal, not a suckling calf.

representation of deity is credited with what had earlier been
credited to Moses: *These are your gods, Israel, who brought you up out
of Egypt* (v. 4; cf. v. 1). That this golden bull has taken the place
of Moses is thus beyond doubt. But has it also taken the place of
Yahweh? In one sense it clearly has, in that it was really Yahweh
who had brought them up out of Egypt (16:6; 20:2) and gone
before these people to lead them (13:21–22). Moreover, the very
wording of the people's demand and their subsequent response
to Aaron's handiwork is theologically revealing: 'Make us *gods*
who will go before us'; '*These* are your *gods* . . . who brought you
up out of Egypt.' The author is making it quite clear here that the
Israelites were breaking the first commandment as well as the
second. This golden bull was usurping not only the role of Moses,
but also – and more significantly – the role of Yahweh.

   Yet this is not necessarily how the Israelites themselves would
have perceived the situation, despite the polytheistic language
used in the text. Possibly the latter is simply a literary device
intended to highlight the full consequences of their actions; it's
doubtful that they saw themselves being in flagrant breach of the
first commandment, or that they viewed this idol as a replacement
for Yahweh. More likely it was understood as a means to represent
and manifest God's presence – ironically, in that they were doing
this at the very time that Yahweh was giving Moses instructions
regarding the tabernacle, for which their gold would have been
more appropriately used. Far from securing Yahweh's presence
among them, this idol and rival system of worship actually
forfeited it. Nevertheless, that was hardly their intent. They were
arguably seeking not to replace Yahweh, but simply to represent
him in some way. Indeed, the golden bull may well have been
conceived as a pedestal upon which Yahweh stood.

   Thus understood, the Israelites viewed Aaron's golden bull as
little more than a visual aid through which they could acknowledge
their faith in Yahweh and express their devotion. Certainly, this
was Aaron's take on what was going on. Perhaps, therefore, the
ambiguity of the people's demand is intentional and underlines
their own theologically confused rationale. But whatever their
intentions, they were effectively replacing *both* Yahweh and Moses
with this dumb idol which they could control. As suggested

above, there is thus a strong allusion here to the much later sin of Jeroboam I (1 Kgs 12:28–33), who notoriously led Israel astray (2 Kgs 17:21–22).

5–6. However the people may have understood what was going on, Aaron evidently did not see this idolatrous image as representing some other deity or alternative religion. Rather, for him (at least) it was specifically designed to facilitate the worship of Yahweh. Presumably this is why Aaron was willing to collaborate in this enterprise in the first place, and it may also explain why the worship festival he organizes bears notable similarities to the genuine worship of Yahweh. However, while this may explain Aaron's involvement, it does not exonerate him (cf. v. 21). Despite having some semblance of legitimacy, the worship of Yahweh (namely, *burnt offerings* and 'peace offerings', AT), that organized by Aaron was a grotesque parody of the real thing, and quickly degenerated into something entirely different (v. 6b); this *revelry* possibly involved sexual misconduct (cf. Gen. 39:14, 17), making Yahwism into little more than another fertility cult – typical of what the Israelites had been instructed to eradicate when they reached their final destination (23:24–26).

7–10. Not surprisingly, this terrible turn of events evoked God's wrath. Significantly, Yahweh disowns them here: just as they had credited *Moses* with their deliverance (v. 1), so now Yahweh pointedly does likewise. There is no ambiguity in Yahweh's assessment of the situation: these people have 'corrupted themselves' (v. 7, AT; cf. Gen. 6:11–12), having turned away from God's express instructions (v. 8; cf. 20:3–4, 23). As the psalmist puts it, 'They exchanged their glorious God / for an image of a bull, which eats grass' (Ps. 106:20). The folly of this act is astonishing, especially so soon after they had repeatedly promised to do 'everything that Yahweh had said' (19:8; 24:3, 7; AT). Used here for the first time, *stiff-necked* (v. 9; cf. 33:3, 5; 34:9; Deut. 9:6, 13) alludes to Israel's natural propensity (cf. Deut. 10:16) to disobey God's explicit commands (cf. Deut. 31:27; 2 Kgs 17:14; Neh. 9:16–17; Jer. 7:26; 17:23; 19:15). Israel's entire future was now in serious jeopardy (v. 10). Though they were acutely unaware of this as yet, the threat of annihilation was hanging ominously over them: God was threatening to wipe them out and start afresh with Moses. And presumably this is exactly what would have happened had Moses not sought God's favour and, as the psalmist puts it, 'stood in the breach before [God] / to keep his wrath from destroying them' (Ps. 106:23). Nevertheless, Yahweh is clearly prodding Moses into action here; the events that unfold – including Moses' initial response – neither take God by surprise nor are beyond his sovereign control or redemptive plan.

Meaning
Up until chapter 32, salvation history has been moving along steadily, though not without hiccups or unexpected delays even after the Israelites escaped Egypt. Their trek in the wilderness has been punctuated by several crises; there's been a tendency to grumble at every opportunity – to fixate negatively on the circumstances rather than focus confidently on the Lord. But however serious and inexcusable their earlier expressions of unbelief may have been, these pale in significance when compared with the present episode – this notorious incident involving idolatrous worship. Here, at what is a critical juncture in redemptive history, we encounter a potentially catastrophic event. As Fretheim puts it, 'It is Genesis 3 all over again' (1991a: 227). The gravity of this incident is highlighted by the fact that Israel's entire future is left hanging in the balance. Indeed, were it not for Moses' intercession, prompted by Yahweh's threat of destruction, here Israel's history might well have ended, and a somewhat different account of salvation history might apparently have begun. However, as soon becomes evident, this was not really what God, who prefers that no-one should perish, ultimately desired.

ii. Moses' intercession and Yahweh's forbearance (32:11 – 33:6)
Context
While some have sought to explain the canonical arrangement of this and the subsequent material (33:7 – 34:35) in terms of different literary sources or even resumptive repetition, a sequential reading can be sustained with little difficulty. Other than the brief but contextually significant flashback in 33:7–11, the sequence of events – involving a series of interactions between Moses and Yahweh – is clear and underlines the seriousness of the dilemma that both Yahweh and Israel now faced. As Bruckner explains

(2008: 278–279), four major decisions provide a framework for the extended narrative, with the long process of dialogue and action highlighting Yahweh's anguish over the situation. Yahweh's first decision was whether or not to annihilate the people; his second decision was whether to accompany them to the Promised Land; his third decision was whether or not to forgive them; and the fourth related to how he would accomplish his intended goal. Exodus 32:11 – 33:6 resolves the first of these issues but ends with the second still unresolved.

Comment

11–13. The narrative focus now switches to Moses' response: here in verses 11–13 it is his reaction to what Yahweh has just told him; subsequently (vv. 15–29), it is his reaction to what he witnesses first-hand on his descent. Moses' initial response is to plead for mercy and so avert the threatened disaster. Moses employs three persuasive arguments: (1) As Israel belongs to Yahweh (*your people*; cf. v. 7), who has dramatically rescued them from Egypt, it would make absolutely no sense to destroy them (v. 11). Moses is reminding Yahweh of the very thing that God himself so often enjoins Israel to remember: that Yahweh has gone to considerable lengths to deliver these people from Egypt. So why go to all this trouble, only to destroy them? Why undo Israel's deliverance so quickly? While the people's overturning of salvation history is terrible, for God to do so is unimaginable and intolerable. (2) Israel's annihilation by Yahweh would be totally misinterpreted by the Egyptians, who would view this as proof of divine caprice (v. 12) or impotence (cf. Deut. 9:28). Surely this would undermine everything Yahweh had done so far to make himself known. The Egyptians would surely jump to the wrong conclusions. The basic point is simply this: God's own reputation was at stake. Moses is thus challenging God to think through the implications of his proposed judgment. (3) Yahweh's proposed action (v. 10) was not in keeping with the spirit of his ancestral promise; he had promised to multiply the descendants of Abraham, Isaac and Israel (v. 13): to give them the Promised Land as their forever inheritance. Moses ultimately bases his argument here on the very element that God seems to have discounted in the previous verses:

God had promised to bless Abraham's descendants, not destroy them. In other words, Moses is insisting here that God be true to his word. Clearly Moses did not consider God's proposal in verse 10 to be in keeping with the spirit of this promise. Moses is thus not prepared to stand back and let God annihilate Abraham's descendants and heirs. Moses therefore insists that God fulfil the obligations of the ancestral covenant.

14. Not surprisingly, Moses' arguments prove successful. However we understand the theological complexities of this divine–human exchange, Moses' intercession has the desired effect. As Enns (2000: 589) puts it, 'Without Moses, the tabernacle would get no further than the architect's plans, cast aside on a drawing room floor.' In between Israel and God stood a mediator – one who wrestled with God and stood in the breach; one who shielded Israel from God's justified wrath and secured for his people a future hope, despite their sinful rebellion. The basic idea of the verb translated *relented* is 'to feel sorrow' or 'have compassion'. Thus divine wrath is now tempered with mercy; the first crisis – the immediate threat of annihilation – has been averted by Moses, who here foreshadows the ultimate mediator, the Lord Jesus (cf. 1 Tim. 2:5; Heb. 7:25).

15–16. Having stopped the catastrophe by dissuading God from annihilating Israel, Moses makes his descent from the summit, with the two tablets of the law in his hands. Significantly, the narrator now describes these two tablets in considerable detail. In particular, however, he stresses their divine origin (v. 16; cf. comment on 31:18). Whether the language here is literal or metaphorical, the important point to grasp is that these tablets were extremely special – the kinds of objects that today would be covered with protective bubble wrap and have 'Handle with care' stamped prominently on the packaging – making Moses' subsequent action (v. 19) all the more dramatic.

17–18. At some unspecified stage of his descent Moses is reunited with Joshua who, unlike the people below, has been waiting patiently. The two men complete the last stage of the journey together. Once within earshot of the camp, they hear the sound of great commotion – what Joshua took to be the sound of battle but was probably more akin to the raucous singing associated with a sports stadium rather than a church; there was certainly nothing godly about it, as soon became evident when they entered the camp.

19–20. Moses was obviously horrified and incensed by what he saw, and his immediate reaction (*his anger burned*) is now surprisingly similar to Yahweh's (cf. v. 10). As such, his enraged destruction of the tablets should not be viewed as Moses spontaneously losing his temper or self-control, but as a deliberate act intended to highlight the serious consequences of Israel's apostasy: Israel had broken the covenant and thus exposed themselves to God's wrath, both of which were symbolized by the shattered stone tablets.

Having broken the tablets, the next priority was to destroy the idol (v. 20). The destruction of the golden bull reflects standard procedure for desecrating such an image in the ancient world: first it was burnt; then it was ground to powder; and finally it was scattered in the field or in the water supply (cf. Deut. 9:21). Accordingly, the last aspect of the ritual should probably not be understood in terms of Numbers 5:18–22, in which the rationale was to determine guilt. Here it serves simply to desecrate the idol (by making it excrement) and highlight the folly of worshipping such an object.

21–24. The seriousness of this incident is further underscored by Moses' description of it as a *great sin* (v. 21; cf. vv. 30, 31) for which Aaron is personally responsible. Like Adam, Israel has flouted a direct command of God and jeopardized the divine–human relationship for which they had been created. Aaron's assessment of the people (v. 22) is certainly valid; however, he minimizes his own involvement and culpability: though he begins almost verbatim with what the narrator has already reported (cf. v. 1), when it comes to his own role he departs noticeably from the official script (cf. vv. 4, 35). Contrary to his somewhat comical 'spin-doctoring' (v. 24), Aaron's handiwork is stamped all over the idol. Moreover, it's clear from elsewhere that, like Israel, he would be in serious trouble had Moses not sought God's mercy (cf. Deut. 9:20).

25–29. Moses now turns his attention to the situation in the camp, where there was pandemonium as the people *were running wild* and *out of control* (v. 25). The meaning of the final clause in this verse is uncertain, as the feminine noun (*šimṣâ*) appears only here in the Old Testament (cf. Job 4:12; 36:14, where its masculine cognate denotes a 'whisper'). While the standard English translation may be correct – *and so become a laughing-stock to their enemies* (NIV) – something more sinister than this might possibly be intended; it could mean that they had become 'a menace to any who might oppose them' (TNK). Understood thus, this riotous mob posed a threat to those who stood against them (i.e. those loyal to Yahweh). Only the Levites, however, were willing to separate themselves from the rest and declare themselves unequivocally for Yahweh (v. 26); thus they alone were charged with restoring order in the camp (vv. 27–29). This was not a random slaughter, but rather a 'surgical strike', apparently targeting the relatively small number (*three thousand*, v. 28) who remained out of control and possibly persisted in the aforementioned revelry (v. 6; cf. Num. 25:8). In any case, behaviour which threatened the life of the community had to be stopped, so the camp had to be swiftly purged of those who were putting it at risk by their refusal to repent.

On account of their willingness to restore order to the camp, the Levites experienced the blessing of being *set apart* (cf. sons of Aaron, 28:41) for special service to Yahweh, the slaughter of their fellow Israelites functioning as a kind of ordination rite.

30–35. Moses' earlier intercession had secured a stay of execution (v. 14), but Yahweh had said nothing about forgiving Israel for this great sin. How Moses proposed to *make atonement* is not spelt out, but his self-sacrificial offer (v. 32) is arguably not intended as some form of penal substitutionary atonement. Rather, Moses is categorically rejecting Yahweh's earlier offer (v. 10) and is willing to suffer the consequences with Israel should their sin remain unforgiven. The *book* alludes to a heavenly register of the living, akin to ancient census records. Psalm 69:28 (cf. Isa. 4:3; Dan. 12:1; Mal. 3:16) describes a similar metaphorical concept as 'the book of life', as do several New Testament texts (Phil. 4:3; Rev. 3:5; 20:12–15; 21:27; cf. Luke 10:20).

Though not committing himself at this stage to forgiveness, Yahweh is clearly unwilling to blot out anyone except those who have sinned (v. 33). All Moses has secured so far, therefore, is a further stay of execution – the threat of divine judgment continues to hang perilously over this people (v. 34c), despite Moses' reiterated charge to lead them to *the place* [*God*] *spoke of* (v. 34a; cf. 3:8–9, 17; 23:23), and the confirmation concerning Yahweh's trailblazing angel (v. 34b; cf. 23:20, 23). The latter could further hint at this clear and present danger Israel faced (cf. 23:21–22); however, the angel's role here in 32:34 appears to be more positive and is not specifically associated with the punishment that ensues (v. 35). The latter appears to be a partial fulfilment of the punishment anticipated in the previous verse, rather than alluding to any subsequent punishments the exodus generation will experience (cf. 1 Cor. 10:5–10).[2]

33:1–3. This chapter ostensibly begins on a positive note, with Yahweh expanding on his instructions to the Israelites (cf. 32:34) to leave Sinai and proceed to Canaan, in fulfilment of the covenant promise to their ancestors (v. 1). Moreover, Yahweh again repeats his promise to send an angel before them to drive out the current inhabitants (v. 2; cf. 23:20–23). Though referred to here as *an angel* (cf. 23:20), this is arguably the same one referred to in 32:34 as *my angel* (cf. 23:23). While this angel is very closely associated with Yahweh, he is nevertheless distinguished from him both here and elsewhere. There is thus no contradiction between 33:2 and 33:3.

Despite Yahweh's renewed promise concerning Israel's territorial inheritance, it quickly becomes evident that a major problem remains unresolved: Israel's sinfulness is impeding Yahweh's plan to accompany them (lit. 'to go up in your midst', v. 3b). Given its express purpose (cf. 25:8; 29:44–46), any plans to erect a tabernacle have thus been shelved; rather than constructing this accommodation for Yahweh, Israel is to break camp and continue their journey at once. They will be accompanied *only* by Yahweh's angel (v. 2; cf. 32:34; see comment on 23:20), rather than by Yahweh

---

2   It is possible that in 1 Cor. 10 Paul is alluding to Exod. 32 in v. 7 *and* in v. 8, in which case the 23,000 who died (v. 8) should be distinguished from the 24,000 who died in the later Baal Peor incident recorded in Num. 25:9.

himself (v. 3). Not surprisingly, the rationale for this radical change relates to the obstinate nature of the Israelites (*stiff-necked*; cf. 32:9), and the threat which Yahweh's presence would thus pose (v. 3). As Alexander observes (2017: 628), such incompatibility between Yahweh's holiness and Israel's sinfulness 'marks a return to the situation that existed prior to the sealing of the covenant in ch. 24'.

4–6. The focus here shifts to the people's distressed reaction to Yahweh's decision, and to the enforced removal of their remaining 'jewellery' (AT; elsewhere *ornaments* [Heb. *ʿădî*] refers primarily to jewellery, as apparently so here, the only place the word is used in the Pentateuch). This was probably booty they had taken from Egypt, so in one sense these items were tokens of their emancipation. Now Yahweh insists that they be removed (vv. 5b–6), though the rationale for this is not spelt out. Perhaps it was because, as the booty taken from Egypt, these items were symbols of their redeemed and privileged status as God's people. Or possibly it was because such items were closely associated with idolatry (cf. Gen. 35:2–4), especially the manufacture of the golden bull (Exod. 32:2–4), and thus removing them symbolized repentance and/or eradicated a further stumbling-block. Or maybe it was because such items might no longer be needed for the construction of God's tabernacle, given the present circumstances. But whatever the reason(s), donning such jewellery was clearly considered inappropriate in the current situation, and so the people followed Yahweh's instructions (vv. 4b, 6). By depicting Yahweh in something of a quandary (v. 5c), Israel's perilous predicament is further underlined: the nation finds itself in a kind of spiritual limbo, facing an uncertain future.

Meaning

While Israel's previous conduct or attitude is often far from exemplary (cf. 14:12–13; 15:24; 16:2, 27–30; 17:2–3), this time their offence is much more serious, highlighted particularly by Yahweh's angry response (32:10) and Moses' breaking of the covenant tablets (v. 19). Israel's *great sin* (vv. 21, 30–31), as Yahweh points out to Moses (v. 8), was *to turn away from what [he] commanded them and [make] themselves an idol cast in the shape of a calf* (cf. Rom.

1:23). Yahweh's covenant commands had 'exposed sin in its true colors and thereby invoked the inevitable consequences – death' (Wright 2021: 568).

Rather than securing God's presence, Israel's idolatrous activity jeopardized it, as well as their special relationship with him. As Moberly (2011: 62) suggests, they effectively committed adultery on their wedding night, and thus dissolved their marriage before it had fully begun. In view of their propensity to sin, Yahweh seems prepared to eradicate them and begin afresh with Moses. And yet it is clear that he is not only reluctant to do so, but is also willing to pay attention to Moses' protests and respond favourably to his intercession on Israel's behalf. As such, Yahweh's sovereign will prevails.

However, there is no suggestion in this passage of cheap grace or easy forgiveness. Rather, Yahweh is portrayed as being on the horns of a dilemma; while prepared to show mercy, he must nevertheless execute justice. Israel's great sin cannot simply be swept under the proverbial mat but must be punished – and indeed it will be punished in due course. Moreover, while God must keep his covenant promises, Israel's sinfulness puts them in great danger in view of Yahweh's holiness. How can he possibly dwell in the midst of such a people without destroying them? Such is the acute dilemma with which this subsection ends, but thankfully the narrative (and Moses' intercession for Israel) continues.

B. Moses' mediation and the covenant restored (33:7 – 34:35)

Whereas the first half of this narrative block focuses on the Israelites' great sin and Yahweh's punitive response (32:1 – 33:6), the second part is much more positive, focusing on Moses' special relationship with God, through which the present crisis is resolved and God's covenant relationship with Israel is restored. Significantly, two passages (33:7–11 and 34:34–35) – both highlighting Moses' intimate relationship with Yahweh – frame this account of Moses' persistent mediation and Yahweh's subsequent restoration of the Sinaitic covenant (33:12 – 34:33).

i. Moses' tent of meeting (33:7–11)

Context

Many scholars, especially source critics, consider these verses to be awkwardly placed in the immediate context. However, others insist that they are an integral part of the narrative, despite the likelihood that they digress from the immediate *sequence* of events. Most scholars agree that the *yiqtol* (and *weqatal*) verbs here should be interpreted in an iterative ('Moses *used to* take a tent . . .') or frequentative sense ('Moses *would* take a tent . . .'). Thus understood, this passage describes something Moses had been doing for some time, rather than action adopted only now, in direct response to the current crisis.[3] What is less clear is whether there was some kind of hiatus – especially in terms of the visible manifestation of Yahweh's presence – until the situation was resolved. If so, this would certainly throw significant light on Moses' otherwise unexpected request to be shown Yahweh's glory (33:18), and on his immediate response after such glory had been partially manifest (34:9). In any case, this short interlude, focusing on Moses' recurring encounters with Yahweh at this *tent of meeting* outside the camp, is not a literary intrusion. Rather, it serves to highlight Moses' regular practice and clearly illustrates how his unique intimacy with Yahweh facilitated his intercession on Israel's behalf.

Comment

7–8. Given the present circumstances (v. 3), this may now be the only *tent of meeting* that Israel is likely to have – very inferior to the grandiose one which God had planned (cf. 30:36).[4] Rather

---

3   *Pace* Enns (2000: 579), for whom this *tent of meeting* is 'an alter-native "tabernacle" in which at least Moses can have access to God'. Stuart (2006: 695) likewise understands it as an emergency response, a 'substitute "tent of meeting" that would never have been invented or needed had not the idolatry of chap. 32 taken place and the close presence of God been withdrawn from Israel as a result'.

4   Significantly, both 'tents of meeting' are described by the exact same Hebrew phrase: *'ōhel mô'ēd.*

than being erected in the midst of the camp, this tent was set up outside the camp; rather than the ornate construction described in chapters 25–31, this was a much simpler affair; rather than being staffed by consecrated priests, this tent was frequented only by Moses and guarded by Joshua in his absence (cf. v. 11b). Yet it clearly performed an important function: it served as the meeting place between Yahweh and Moses, through whom the Israelite community had access to God. This tent of meeting is thus the most likely venue for the following dialogue between Moses and Yahweh (33:12 − 34:3).

9–11. The pillar of cloud was the visible manifestation of Yahweh's presence, and its location at the entrance to the tent was indicative of the divine–human communication that took place between Yahweh and Moses, as acknowledged by the people's response (v. 10). The other significant point highlighted here is that this communication between Yahweh and Moses took place *face to face, as one speaks to a friend* (v. 11). As Stuart (2006: 699 n. 111) suggests, 'the expression "face to face" . . . is an idiom', here suggesting intimacy (cf. 'person to person' or 'heart to heart') rather than visual perception (cf. v. 20, where seeing God's face would prove fatal). Yet here and elsewhere Moses is said to encounter God in an up-close and personal manner that makes him very special (Deut. 34:10; cf. Num. 12:8). It may thus be inferred that, despite the great gulf presently separating *Israel* and their God, there was still hope so long as they had such a mediator (v. 11).

Meaning

As suggested above, this pericope – which some dismiss as intrusive or inappropriate in a context which stresses Yahweh's withdrawal and absence – actually provides significant insight into the resolution of the present crisis. As well as highlighting how Moses' intimate relationship with Yahweh facilitated his role as mediator, it also draws attention to the significance of the cloud as a manifestation of Yahweh's presence – something that had been jeopardized by Israel's *great sin*. This may help explain why Moses persists in his requests (33:18; 34:9), even after the problem of Yahweh's accompanying presence seems to have been resolved

(33:14, 17). Along with the closing bracket (34:33–35), this literary *inclusio* draws our attention to Moses' personal experience of Yahweh's presence and glory: initially, the cloud that stood outside the tent of meeting and facilitated Yahweh's speaking to Moses *face to face* (33:9–11); and finally, how Moses' radiant face reflected Yahweh's glory after subsequent encounters in the tent (34:34–35). One might reasonably infer from this that what Moses requested (and was safely granted) was not simply a verbal assurance of Yahweh's presence, but a renewed and ongoing manifestation of such, not simply for his own benefit, but also for that of the Israelite community. In any case, we see here in Moses a foreshadowing of the one whose intimacy with the Father and whose persistent intercession for his people is even greater.

ii. Moses' request to see Yahweh's glory (33:12–23)

Context

With Moses' privileged status now clearly in view, the following verses (vv. 12–23) pick up where 33:1–6 left off: with the threat of Yahweh's absence particularly in focus. Though Moses again begins the conversation (cf. 32:31), once again it is important to see that God remains open to persuasion (cf. 33:5). Rather than altering God's sovereign plan and purpose, Moses' mediation is again a key factor in its implementation.

Comment

12–13. Moses' confessed ignorance in verse 12 of who will accompany him may seem strange in the light of Yahweh's previous revelation (33:2). Admittedly, the identity of the angel appears more vague in 33:2 (cf. 32:34), although this seems purely stylistic (cf. 23:20, 23). The issue now, however, is apparently not the trailblazing angel who will go *before* them. Rather, it is whom Yahweh will send *with* Moses. As Yahweh's response to this question (v. 14) makes clear, Moses' concern is with Yahweh's reluctance to accompany this stiff-necked people lest he destroy them on the way (v. 3). What Moses claims in verse 12b comes as news to the reader; this privileged status has not been explicitly expressed previously in Exodus. Given that such narrative 'gapping' is not uncommon elsewhere in Exodus, it is arguably unnecessary to suggest that Moses is simply drawing an inference from what Yahweh has explicitly said to him (e.g. 32:10). In any case, Yahweh confirms the veracity of Moses' status just a few verses later (v. 17). On the basis of this fact, Moses requests a fuller knowledge of Yahweh himself and his intentions (lit. his 'way') so that he might continue to find grace in his sight – primarily, it would seem, in relation to his pleadings for Israel. While the LXX makes the latter more explicit ('and so that I may know that this great nation is your people'), presumably reading the Hebrew imperative consequentially, most translations interpret the final clause in verse 13 as an exhortation directed to Yahweh. Either way, Moses is implicitly reminding Yahweh once again of Israel's unique status in God's plan.

14–16. Clarifying his intentions as Moses had requested, Yahweh appears here to have changed his mind – *my Presence* [lit. 'face'] *will go* (cf. v. 3) – thus guaranteeing a successful outcome: *rest* (i.e. secure settlement) in the land. In view of this, Moses' response here is rather surprising. While this anomaly can be explained by taking *you* (sing.) in verse 14b to refer only to Moses (hence his implicit inclusion of Israel in the 'go with *us*' of v. 15; emphasis added),⁵ Moses may simply be insisting that this promise of divine accompaniment take effect immediately. Indeed, quite possibly Moses has particularly in mind God's earlier revelation concerning the tabernacle (cf. 25:8; 29:45–46). In any case, Moses now emphatically includes the people along with himself (note the twofold *me and your people*). The special status of Moses and Israel hinges on the fact that God is with them; thus, for Moses, this is really non-negotiable.

17. Once again, Yahweh accedes to Moses' request, reversing his earlier intention (v. 3b). Significantly, Yahweh relents here because he is *pleased with* and knows Moses *by name* (cf. vv. 12b, 13a). As is clear from 34:9, Israel's proclivity to sin remains a significant issue for Yahweh, though the divine revelation prompted by

---

5 NB The *with you* (v. 14) and *with us* (v. 15) supplied in ancient and modern translations is not reflected in the Hebrew text.

Moses' next request (v. 18) places emphasis on the possibility of forgiveness (v. 19; 34:6–7).

18. Despite Yahweh's concessions thus far, Moses is clearly still not satisfied. Rather, as his subsequent petition in 34:9 demonstrates, the issue of forgiveness – whether for past (cf. 32:32–34) or future (33:3) rebellion – remains unsettled. In view of this, it seems mistaken to read Moses' new request here (*show me your glory*) as something more personally orientated. Rather, it seems intrinsic to the larger issue at hand; Moses is effectively asking for a demonstration of the assurance just given. Previously, Yahweh's glory had been manifest in the pillar of cloud (cf. 16:7, 10) and in the fiery cloud that had descended on Sinai (cf. 24:15–17). Moreover, Yahweh had promised that the tabernacle would be sanctified by this glory (29:43), and subsequently this is precisely what happens (40:34–35). Significantly, 33:7–11 has made explicit the connection between the presence of the pillar of cloud and Yahweh speaking to Moses *face to face* (33:11), and the following chapter concludes by highlighting the glorious effect speaking directly with Yahweh has on Moses' *face* (34:29–35). It can reasonably be inferred, therefore, that here in 33:18 Moses is requesting an experience similar to what he had enjoyed previously – some kind of theophanic encounter with Yahweh. This seems to be confirmed by Yahweh's immediate response, in which an extraordinary theophany is certainly anticipated (vv. 19–23).

19–23. Rather than denying Moses' request, Yahweh in some measure complies (v. 19), while taking necessary steps to ensure Moses' personal safety and survival (vv. 20–23). Accordingly, Yahweh promises some form of theophany (causing *all my goodness to pass in front of you*) and, in keeping with the request of verse 13, further insight into Yahweh's *name* and character (cf. 34:6). Whatever the difference between full exposure (seeing God's *face*; v. 20) and partial exposure (seeing God's *back*; v. 23) to Yahweh's *glory* (v. 22), Yahweh is clearly willing to accede to the spirit of Moses' request, as attested by Moses' experiences in the following chapter.

Meaning

This passage is primarily concerned with Yahweh's express reluctance to accompany the Israelites any longer. However, as Moses correctly insists (v. 16), this is an essential feature of Israel's distinctive identity as the people of God, those with whom God is truly pleased. Accordingly, Moses places significant emphasis here on their unique identity (vv. 13b, 16) as he pleads with Yahweh to accompany them and to demonstrate his intention to do so by a further theophany (v. 18). Rather than something that Yahweh denies, this actually receives a positive response, albeit with an important caveat concerning the safety limits imposed. Thus understood, what Moses is requesting here is not a deeper personal experience of divine glory, but rather a better understanding of God (cf. v. 13) and a visible manifestation of his glorious presence, as had been experienced previously on Sinai and would subsequently be demonstrated with respect to the tabernacle (40:34). This, above all else, was what Moses and Israel most needed at a time when the nature of the promised accompaniment still remained in doubt.

iii. The covenant re-established (34:1–28)

Context

Significantly, the theophany anticipated at the end of the previous chapter (34:5–7; 33:19–23) is here set in the context of a reissuing of the law and remaking of the covenant. Rather than reiterating all the covenant stipulations previously disclosed (chs. 20–23), the emphasis in the synopsis here (34:11–26) is on Israel's obligations with respect to worship – which is entirely appropriate in the light of their covenant breach involving idolatry. While certainly offering theological grounds for hope, Yahweh's self-disclosure (vv. 5–7) does not set aside the covenantal framework and responsibilities of Israel's relationship with Yahweh. Rather, the latter stipulations further imply that however compassionate and gracious he may be, Yahweh will *not leave the guilty unpunished* (v. 7).

Comment

1. Reference to the *two stone tablets* of the covenant law (cf. 24:12; 31:18) heralds the final stage in the resolution to Israel's great sin: Yahweh will re-establish the covenant which the Israelites had broken. However, while Yahweh will again be responsible for inscribing the tablets (cf. 31:18b; 32:16), this time Moses must *chisel*

out the replacements for those he had smashed (32:19). This, and the fact that elsewhere Yahweh is also said to have engraved these replacement tablets (cf. Deut. 10:4), strongly suggests that the writing subsequently done by Moses (cf. 34:27) was limited to the material recorded in 34:11–26. Thus, unless the *I will write* here in verse 1 is understood figuratively, the unspecified subject in verse 28b must surely be Yahweh rather than Moses. As with their direct communication to the Israelites (cf. 20:1), their supernatural inscription on the two tablets elevates the covenantal significance of the ten words.

2–4. Yahweh's instructions to Moses (vv. 2–3) echo those given previously – before both the initial theophany (ch. 19) and the ratification of the earlier covenant (ch. 24), further underlining the abrogation of the latter; Israel's situation had reverted to that reflected in chapter 19, where it was incumbent on all except Moses to maintain a safe distance lest they encroach on Yahweh's holiness and face the inevitable consequence (v. 3a; cf. 19:12). The mandatory preparation for Moses (v. 2; cf. 19:11, 15), as well as the prohibition including livestock (v. 3b; cf. 19:13a), signals that another theophany is about to take place on Sinai, with similar covenantal significance (i.e. Yahweh is re-establishing the covenant that Israel had broken, as signified by the replacement stone tablets and their divine inscription with the Decalogue). Compliance with Yahweh's instructions (v. 4) reintroduces a significant motif in the book as a whole (cf. 7:6, 10, 20; 16:16–17, 34; 36:1) and especially its final two chapters.

5–7. This is clearly the theophany anticipated in 33:19–23, manifested in response to Moses' request to see God's glory. What Moses sees (vv. 5–6a), however, is almost totally eclipsed by what he hears (vv. 6b–7). Using a kaleidoscope of divine attributes (vv. 6b–7a), Yahweh proclaims his *name*, underlining the full extent of his *goodness* (cf. 33:19), though not at the expense of his justice (34:7b). As Stuart (2006: 715) observes:

> Moses had sought to know that Yahweh would be with him and Israel as they left Sinai to head toward the promised land, and knowing Yahweh – knowing who he really was and what he would be like in reference to his people – was what Moses craved. Yahweh's self-proclamation would provide that.

Accordingly, the attributes listed here are primarily positive, emphasizing Yahweh's mercy, love and grace. Yahweh is *compassionate*, reflecting merciful concern; he is *gracious*, giving people what they do not deserve; he is *slow to anger*, demonstrating great patience towards sinners; he is 'great in covenant love' (loyalty) (AT; Heb. *ḥesed*) and *faithfulness*, utterly reliable and faithful to all his promises; indeed, he 'maintains covenant loyalty [*ḥesed*] to thousands' (AT), which here suggests indefinitely (so Stuart [2006: 716], thousands meaning generations rather than individuals; cf. 20:5–6), and forgives all sorts of sinful behaviour (*wickedness, rebellion* and *sin* being more a representative summary than a definitive list; Stuart 2006: 716). The only caveat in all of this is the reminder that Yahweh *does not leave the guilty unpunished* (cf. 20:7; 32:34–35), but *punishes the children . . . to the third and fourth generation* (v. 7b; cf. 20:5b–6). However one understands the latter (see commentary on 20:5–6), it clearly serves here as a corrective to 'cheap grace' – an attitude that assumes God's mercy and underestimates the consequences of sinful behaviour.

Moses is thus, as he has previously requested (cf. 33:13), given very significant insight into Yahweh's 'way' or character, offering significant assurance (as well as an implicit warning) in the present situation. Not surprisingly, this theological revelation becomes a mainstay in Moses' subsequent intercession (Num. 14:18) and Israel's ongoing relationship with God (cf. Neh. 9:17, 31; 2 Chr. 30:9; Pss 86:5, 15; 103:8–10; 111:4; 145:8; Joel 2:13; Jon. 4:2; Mic. 7:18; Nah. 1:3), where similar emphasis is unsurprisingly placed on Yahweh's abundant mercy and forgiveness, rather than his retributive justice.[6]

8–9. Capitalizing on Yahweh's self-proclamation, Moses again presses home his petition that Yahweh forgive Israel and keep on

---

6   Outside the Pentateuch the emphatic 'certainly not acquitting the guilty' relates to a foreign nation (Nah. 1:3), although the Hebrew text leaves open the possibility that the warning to Nineveh applies also to the wicked in Jerusalem. In any case, there are several partial citations of the phrase elsewhere (cf. Prov. 6:29; 11:21; 16:5; 17:5; 19:5, 9; 28:20; Jer. 30:11; 46:28), so it would be mistaken to conclude that only the positive facet of Exod. 34:7 was applied to the covenant community.

accompanying and embracing them as his inheritance as originally planned. Whether in spite of or because of Israel's proclivity to sin (being a *stiff-necked people*), Moses acknowledges here that God's forgiving nature is their only hope.

10. After the prolonged and intense dialogue that has occupied most of the previous two chapters, the resolution to this crisis is now expected. This materializes, as anticipated in the first part of the present chapter, with the re-establishment of the covenant that had been annulled by Israel's apostasy (vv. 10–28).

Yahweh now persists in his original intentions (cf. 19:4–6), with the Sinai covenant being reinstituted rather than revised; as 34:1 has already indicated, the following verses (vv. 11–26) should not be understood as a new or modified Decalogue replacing the original. Rather, the detailed covenant stipulations highlighted here in chapter 34 are a pointed synopsis, introduced in verse 10 by a future rather than a past orientation: what Yahweh *will do* rather than what he *has done* already (cf. 20:2). The impact these unprecedented *wonders* will have on surrounding nations, however, would be the same as that of those performed previously (in and with Egypt): through such awesome deeds Yahweh's greatness will be impressed upon a watching world.

11–26. Though the content of these verses is an abridged form of the obligations previously listed in the context of the covenant's inauguration (i.e. a summary or synopsis of the instructions in chs. 20–23), there is a particular emphasis here on how the Israelites should conduct their worship. As such, these laws are especially pertinent in the context of Israel's recent idolatry, when they had broken the covenant by adopting worship practices typical of other nations. Thus understood, the function of these cultic laws is to underline, in particular, Israel's covenant obligation to worship Yahweh *only* as he has prescribed.

This reiteration of the covenant's stipulations is introduced by a summary command to obedience (v. 11), significantly prefacing a further reiteration of successful settlement (cf. 23:23; 33:2), but now mentioning *Yahweh's* action (rather than the aforementioned angel). This is followed (vv. 12–16) by specific instructions with respect to the current inhabitants of the Promised Land. No covenants should be made with them (v. 12; cf. 23:32–33), lest the

Israelites be ensnared and compromise their exclusive reliance on Yahweh. Canaanite cultic and idolatrous paraphernalia must be destroyed (v. 13),[7] as Yahweh – who insists on being the sole focus of Israel's worship (v. 14) – is a jealous God who guards his unique significance (cf. 23:24–26). As Stuart maintains (2006: 724), *jealous* (Heb. *qannā*) should probably not be understood here as another divine name (cf. *whose name is Jealous*; so most EVV), but rather as an attribute of Yahweh (cf. CSB footnote's 'being jealous by nature') – particularly significant here in the context of illicit worship. Though either interpretation is grammatically feasible, the emphasis here is to convey an important facet of Yahweh's *character*, rather than to disclose the name by which he is known (cf. 3:15).

In the light of Yahweh's jealousy, even personal covenants – such as marriage – with those who live in the land are thus prohibited, for those who *prostitute themselves to their gods* (the plurality suggests gross infidelity, hence the prostitution metaphor here) will inevitably lead Israelites to do the same (vv. 15–16). These warnings against adopting the idolatrous practices of other nations conclude (v. 17) with a prohibition on making any 'cast idols' (AT) – something in which Aaron's golden bull (32:4, 8) had set an unfortunate precedent that would regrettably be repeated in Israel's subsequent history, most notably by Jeroboam I (cf. 1 Kgs 12:28; 13:34).

The following verses (vv. 18–26), focusing primarily on how the Israelites should worship Yahweh, generally repeat material from 23:14–19, albeit with a different structure and emphasis. Here in Exodus 34, particular emphasis is placed on the festival of Passover/Unleavened Bread (vv. 18, 25), with more details (echoing chs. 12 and 13) about how Passover should be commemorated and certain firstborn should be ransomed. Neither donkeys nor humans were eligible as a sacrifice to Yahweh; thus firstborn

---

7   Strictly speaking, *Asherah poles*, mentioned here for the first time in the OT, were carved representations of Asherah, the female consort of the Canaanite fertility god Baal. However, here (see also Deut. 7:5; 12:3; 16:21) the *masculine* plural form of the noun may refer to *any* carved symbol of such pagan religion (so Stuart 2006: 723).

donkeys must either be ransomed or have their necks broken, but human firstborn must always be ransomed (cf. Num. 18:16–17). The insistence that *no one . . . appear before [Yahweh] empty-handed* clearly bars any exceptions to the latter, while also encompassing the less specific application reflected in 23:15.

Yahweh's instruction on weekly sabbath rest is again reiterated (cf. 20:8–11; 23:12), but now with an emphasis on cessation from work even during busy periods such as ploughing and harvest time (v. 21). The latter naturally segues into Israel's two harvest festivals, Weeks and Ingathering (v. 22), which – along with Passover/Unleavened Bread – constitute the three mandatory festivals in Israel's cultic calendar (v. 23; cf. 23:17). The thrice-yearly pilgrimage obligation for Israelite men is now elaborated with reassurance regarding Israelite property during such festival absences (v. 24).[8] The final instructions in this section (vv. 25–26), specifying the suitable offerings for these festivals, repeat verbatim the material in 23:18–19 (see comments there).

27–28. The recording of Israel's covenantal obligations in these two verses further emphasizes the reinstatement of the Sinai covenant. There is significant debate, however, over precisely what Moses is commanded to *write down* (v. 27) and the identity of the subject responsible for inscribing the new tablets with the 'ten words' (v. 28, AT). Though it is possible to equate *these words* (v. 27) with 'the ten words' mentioned in verse 28, thus understanding Moses to be the scribe in both verses, contextually it is more likely that *these words* in verse 27 refers to the covenant stipulations just listed in the preceding verses, which constitute a summation of the Book of the Covenant (Houtman 2000: 716; Alexander 2017: 649). Thus understood, as in 24:4, here in 34:27 Moses is responsible for recording material that *supplements* the covenant's general stipulations (the ten words). The latter become the focus only in verse 28, where the subject of the Hebrew verb (*wayyiktōb*; 'and he wrote') is not specified. Moses is unquestionably the subject of all three preceding verbs in this verse, and there is no clear

---

8   *Pace* Stuart, only males (Heb. *zākûr*) were obligated to attend the central sanctuary for these special occasions.

syntactical marker of any subject change in the second part of the verse. Accordingly, one might logically infer that Moses is the subject throughout verses 27–28. However, this is difficult to reconcile with both 34:1 and the tradition reflected elsewhere (e.g. Deut. 10:2, 4) that Yahweh was solely responsible for engraving the ten words on each occasion such tablets were inscribed. So unless such emphasis on Yahweh's unique role in engraving the tablets (cf. *the finger of God* in 31:18; Deut. 9:10) is interpreted metaphorically (i.e. Yahweh engraved the tablets *by the hand of* Moses), the wider context certainly suggests that two distinct writers are involved: Moses records the more detailed stipulations (v. 27; cf. 24:4), whereas Yahweh inscribes 'the ten words' on the stone tablets (v. 28; cf. 24:12; 31:18; 32:16; 34:1; Deut. 10:2, 4). As Alexander (2017: 649) observes, the latter scenario (two distinct writers) is certainly more

> consistent with the distinction that is drawn in chs. 20–24 between the Decalogue (spoken directly by God to the people and later inscribed by him on stone tablets) and the Book of the Covenant (mediated through Moses to the people and recorded by Moses).

The reason for Moses' forty-day period of fasting in the presence of Yahweh is not spelt out here, but as already noted above, this period repeats significant aspects of the original reception of the covenant law (chs. 24–31), one of which is its duration (cf. 24:18). Deuteronomy (9:25 – 10:5) associates Moses' forty-day fasting with his intercession for Israel, which took place just prior to the occasion depicted here in Exodus 34, although the precise chronology reflected in Deuteronomy is not altogether clear (cf. Deut. 10:10), possibly due to it purposefully conflating the sequence of events depicted in Exodus 33 – 34.

Meaning
Since the beginning of chapter 32 readers have been awaiting the resolution of the crisis that unfolds there, one serious enough to abrogate the freshly minted covenant between Yahweh and Israel, and thus to put in jeopardy his plan to dwell among these people

he has rescued from bondage in Egypt. At last we discover light at the end of this dark tunnel: not only will Yahweh keep his ancestral promise to bring Abraham's numerous descendants back to Canaan (Gen. 15:13–21), but – despite their proclivity to sin – he will accompany them precisely as planned, and also demonstrate his amazing 'grace, compassion and mercy' by forgiving every kind of sin that would otherwise make this ongoing proximity to God utterly impossible.

Accordingly, a chapter that begins with a broken covenant ends with it gloriously restored, with Moses not only receiving the two newly inscribed tablets of the covenant testimony, but also regularly meeting with Yahweh in his glorious presence and reflecting this as he relayed Yahweh's instructions to the Israelites (vv. 29–35) – thus setting the stage for the faithful implementation of these divine instructions in the chapters that follow.

However, while the primary thrust of this chapter is positive, focusing on Yahweh's covenant faithfulness and amazing grace, there is also a theological undertone that readers dare not miss: this God of love and mercy is also a jealous God, and a God of justice – who therefore *does not leave the guilty unpunished*, but *punishes the children and their children for the sin of the parents to the third and fourth generation* (v. 7).[9] Thus, this remaking of the covenant with Israel should not be misconstrued as a licence to sin; rather, Israel's covenant obligations are reinstituted, and their core duty to serve Yahweh alone, and as he himself has clearly stipulated, is emphatically made clear. While Israel's tabernacle worship clearly foreshadows how Yahweh will ultimately not leave the guilty unpunished, it also underlines the obligations Yahweh demands of those who are in covenant relationship with him.

iv. Moses' radiant face (34:29–35)
Context
After his further forty-day period on Mount Sinai (34:28; cf. 34:4; Deut. 9:9–10; 10:10), Moses returns with divinely engraved

---

9   As noted above (see comment on 34:5–7), both aspects of this seminal text become significant OT motifs.

tablets for the second time. On this occasion (cf. ch. 32), however, Aaron and the Israelites are far more subdued – intimidated by the novel effect this most recent theophany has had on Moses' face. This becomes a key focus of attention in this literary unit, which together with 33:7–11 brackets the material that recounts Moses' successful intercession and the restoration of Yahweh's covenant and presence with Israel. However, as the context makes abundantly clear, the overarching point relates not to Moses' shining face, but to its theological significance.

Comment

29–32. Like the original set (31:18; 32:15), the divinely engraved replacements are described as 'the two tablets of the testimony' (v. 29a, AT). As Stuart (2006: 736 n. 236) explains, unless elliptically referring to the actual tablets (e.g. 25:16, 21), 'the testimony' (Heb. *hā'ēdût*) alludes either to the ark in which they would subsequently be kept (cf. 16:34; 27:21; 30:6) or, as here and elsewhere, to the covenant/its stipulations.

The fact that Moses was unaware of any change in his physical appearance (v. 29b) suggests that it was less obvious (at least to Moses) than sometimes portrayed. The verb used in verse 29 (*qāran*) to describe 'the skin of Moses' face' is closely related to the Hebrew noun (*qeren*) meaning 'horn', unfortunately giving rise to a tradition that Moses had grown horns (as reflected in some medieval and Renaissance artwork, such as Michelangelo's sculpture of Moses). However, the more likely interpretation of the Qal verb here is that something (perhaps rays of light) was emanating from Moses' face. This reflected glory of Yahweh was the visible sign, not only of Yahweh's restored presence with Israel, but also – and perhaps more importantly here – of the divine authority with which this appointed mediator of the covenant spoke, both now and subsequently (cf. vv. 34–35).

The reaction of Aaron and the Israelite community (v. 30) clearly echoes that reported back in chapter 20 in response to Yahweh's unmediated revelation of the Decalogue. There the object of their fear was Yahweh; here it is his servant Moses. Significantly, however, both texts serve to underline Moses' unique role as mediator of the covenant. Indeed, this is the major focus of what follows in Exodus 34, as first the leaders, and then the Israelite community, approach him, and Moses resumes his ministry as covenant mediator, communicating all that Yahweh had spoken to him on Sinai (vv. 31–32).

33–35. These final verses of the chapter describe how Moses customarily (as in 33:7–11, the verbs indicate iterative/frequentative action) performed this role, distinguishing between that as covenant mediator and his more mundane activity in the community; when addressing the Israelites in the former role, Moses did so with his glowing face unveiled, whereas otherwise he kept it covered. Periodically covering Yahweh's reflected glory with a veil was implicitly for the benefit of those who were reluctant to look at it directly (cf. 2 Cor. 3:7). Yet Paul further suggests that this also concealed from Israel the transient nature of this reflected glory (2 Cor. 3:13) – an inference drawn on in 2 Corinthians 3:7–18 to contrast the temporary glory of the old covenant (which brought condemnation) with the surpassing and lasting glory of the new covenant (which brought righteousness). However, there is no suggestion in Exodus 34 that Moses deliberately intended to conceal from the Israelites that the glow on his face was fading. The precise nature of Paul's interpretation is thus debated, with some commentators (e.g. Wright 2021) dismissing any exegetical basis whatsoever and understanding it as an entirely figurative reflection on the text. Others (e.g. Garrett 2014), however, seek to clarify and defend Paul's interpretation (see Additional note on Paul's interpretation of Moses' veil), or simply focus on the Exodus text and entirely ignore the use made of it by Paul.

Given its obvious significance here in the concluding section of the golden calf episode – setting forth its full resolution and Moses' customary practice from this time onward – it seems most unlikely that Paul is implying any degree of duplicity on his part. Accordingly, some way of reconciling these two texts that does justice to the intended meaning of each seems preferable to dismissing Paul's interpretation as fanciful or arbitrary. This is demonstrably possible, so long as the conventional understanding of 2 Corinthians 3 is not uncritically adopted, and closer attention is paid to Paul's grammar and argument (see Additional note on Paul's interpretation of Moses' veil).

Meaning
The crisis precipitated by Israel's apostasy with the golden bull has now been fully resolved. The threat of Yahweh's absence is gone, replaced by this new and continued intimacy with Moses, Israel's covenant mediator, whose divine authority is evident in his radiant face. As well as demonstrating the glory of the Sinai covenant (as noted by Paul in 2 Cor. 3), Moses' status as Israel's divinely appointed leader is thus elevated, paving the way for the overarching emphasis on their obedience to God's mediated instructions in the chapters that follow.

Additional note: Paul's interpretation of Moses' veil

As noted above, Paul's use (2 Cor. 3:7–18) of the periodic veiling of God's reflected glory by Moses (Exod. 34:33–35) has evoked scholarly debate, some finding this impossible to defend in terms of grammatical-historical exegesis, especially if one concludes from the latter that Moses' veiling action was for the benefit of those around him. The conventional translation of what Paul says in 2 Corinthians 3 seems to suggest, rather, that Moses was seeking to hide something from them – namely, the fact that this glory on his face was fading away. Accordingly, Paul's interpretation would appear to clash with a straightforward reading of these verses in Exodus, and present Moses as acting in a duplicitous rather than in a magnanimous manner.

However, as Garrett (2014: 667–676) demonstrates at length, this hermeneutical problem can be resolved by paying closer attention to the vocabulary Paul uses, and the contextual flow of his argument. According to Garrett, 'nullify/abolish' more accurately reflects the meaning of the Greek verb *katargeō* (conventionally rendered 'destroy/come to an end/fade away'), consistently used here in 2 Corinthians 3 (vv. 7, 11, 13, 14) to describe the nullification of the *old covenant* in Christ. Rather than suggesting the glory on Moses' face was *fading*, Paul is simply drawing attention to the fact that the very great glory of the old covenant (as reflected on Moses' radiant face) was *destined* to be surpassed by that of the new covenant. Yet, just as the veil on Moses' face covered this glory of the old covenant from the ancient Israelites who were disturbed by it, the surpassing glory of the new covenant remained 'veiled' from those who were fixated on the old covenant. Thus understood, Paul's interpretation is in perfect exegetical accord with Exodus 34, and in no way impugns the character of Moses.

16. MANUFACTURE OF THE TABERNACLE AND PRIESTLY GARMENTS (35:1 – 39:43)

With Israel's serious breach of the covenant fully resolved, the narrative returns to the communication and implementation of the cultic instructions God had given to Moses beforehand – clearly indicating that the plans Israel had jeopardized were finally back on track.

While closely corresponding to the contents of chapters 25–31, this implementation section differs in (1) its focus on the actions of Moses, the Israelite community and the skilled workers;[1] (2) its more logical arrangement (the manufacture of the tabernacle comes first, followed by its internal and external furniture, the surrounding courtyard, and finally the priestly garments); and (3) its inclusion of some additional details (e.g. the use of guy-ropes,

---

1   Significantly, the expert craftsmen have a much more prominent position (near the start rather than near the end) in the implementation section. Given their crucial role in the implementation of the project, this is hardly surprising.

35:18; the origin of the bronze used for the laver, 38:8). Even
so, much of the material may well seem overly repetitive, if not
entirely redundant, to a modern reader, including commentators
– who often pay it only glancing attention or simply subsume
these final chapters along with their comments on chapters 25–31.
However, in addition to emphasizing that the divine instructions were carefully followed (cf. the repeated refrain *as the LORD
commanded*), the repetition highlights the tabernacle's theological
importance in the structure and message of the book as a whole.

A. Sabbath regulations (35:1–3)

Context
These verses record Moses' communication of the divine instructions given back in 31:12–17. This is the sixth time that Exodus
highlights Israel's weekly sabbath requirement (cf. 16:22–30;
20:8–11; 23:12; 31:12–17; 34:21), further suggesting its importance
for the covenant community.

Comment
1–3. Any work on the sabbath was a serious covenant infraction,
punishable by death (v. 2b; cf. 31:14–17). Presumably, the prohibition of 35:3 serves as an illustration of such work, but it is unclear
(1) why this example in particular was selected; (2) if it refers to
burning fires or simply kindling them; (3) whether it encompasses all domestic fires or only those lit for labour purposes (e.g.
smelting metal). While the immediate context could suggest the
last of these (Alexander 2017: 654), the case of the sabbath-breaker
in Numbers 15:32–36 seems to suggest a wider application.[2]
Though not entirely prohibited on the sabbath (cf. Exod. 29:38–
43), the use of such fires within Israelite dwellings for cooking
purposes would have been unnecessary before settlement in the
Promised Land (cf. 16:23).

---

2   The offender in Num. 15 is 'gathering [Polel *qšš*] wood/sticks',
     presumably to light a fire (cf. 1 Kgs 17:10, 12; cf. Exod. 5:7, 12).

Meaning

While sabbath observance would certainly have applied to the construction of the tabernacle, this brief reiteration of the sabbath regulation serves mainly to highlight the resolution of the covenant crisis (which, along with 31:12–18, it frames) and the tabernacle's theological significance in terms of experiencing 'rest' in the presence of God (see comment on 31:12–17).

B. Preparations for construction (35:4 – 36:7)

Context

Having emphasized the priority of sacred time, the next subsection begins with an almost verbatim report of the divine instructions given to Moses (35:4–9; cf. 25:2–7), listing the raw materials to be provided by the community. Just as they had formerly donated their jewellery for the manufacture of Aaron's idolatrous golden calf, they now give much more generously and enthusiastically towards the manufacture of Yahweh's tabernacle and all its accoutrements.

Comment

i. Materials for the tabernacle (35:4–29)

4–9. As before (25:2), emphasis is placed on the fact that any such 'contribution' (Heb. *těrûmâ*; elsewhere denotes food gifts rather than building materials; cf. 29:27–28) offered to Yahweh should be spontaneous (v. 5b) rather than coerced – each verse uses a form of the same Hebrew root, *ndb*, with reference to a 'ready' or *willing* heart.

10–19. The inventory of raw materials is followed by what might be considered a summary statement of the more technical instructions recorded in 25:8 – 31:10. Unlike the preceding inventory, there are no corresponding instructions at this point in the earlier material (cf. 25:8–9); however, there is some overlap with 31:6–11. Since Bezalel and his colleagues later made everything according to the prescribed specifications (cf. 36:8 – 38:20), Moses must have communicated much more information either at this point or subsequently. In any case, the focus is now on how the voluntary donations are to be deployed by those with the requisite skills (cf. 31:6b–11) to make the various elements for the tabernacle. Significantly, the list of items here corresponds with the order of the manufacture and inspection of them in 36:8 – 39:43.

20–29. The community response was not just enthusiastic, but overwhelming (cf. 36:2–7). It would be quite mistaken to infer from the repeated emphasis on anyone *whose heart moved* [or 'carried'] *them* (vv. 5, 21, 22, 26, 29; cf. 36:2) that there was any lack of generosity or commitment to Yahweh within the community. Rather, the entire Israelite community (v. 20), including its women (vv. 22, 25–26, 29) and its leaders (v. 27), generously supplied all that was required for making the tabernacle and its various accoutrements. Among the gifts supplied by these leaders were olive oil for the tabernacle's intricate lampstand or menorah. However, the ongoing responsibility for this (i.e. after the tabernacle was operational) was assigned to all Israelites (Lev. 24:2). Whether through donations of gold jewellery, yarn, linen, goat hair, animal skins, silver, bronze, wood, cloth, precious stones, spices, oil or expertise, each person made a significant contribution to the project as a whole.

ii. Designated skilled workers (35:30 – 36:3a)

35:30 – 36:3a. The need for skilled personnel was noted previously (35:10); now Moses explains the particular roles God has assigned to Bezalel and Oholiab (cf. 31:1–11). Moses does not repeat here the specific items listed in 31:1–11, having already enumerated these in 35:10–19. While Bezalel's credentials are stated exactly the same as before, Oholiab's role (31:6) is now elaborated in terms of the ability he shares with Bezalel to teach others the requisite skills (35:34; cf. 38:23). These two experts would thus be assisted by an undesignated number of apprentices, whose skill/wisdom (Heb. *ḥokmâ*) to perform the various tasks is likewise accredited to Yahweh (35:35 – 36:2). As well as further emphasizing the tabernacle's special status – requiring highly skilled artisans as well as costly materials – this emphasis on divine selection and equipping underlines that it was much more than a product of human ingenuity or creativity. Rather, God was intimately involved in the execution of this project from start to finish, and this was key to the successful human workmanship.

iii. Restrained generosity (36:3b–7)[3]

3b–7. With the divinely equipped workforce assembled, and the people's voluntary donations handed over (vv. 2–3a), this next development is somewhat unexpected: the people kept on giving. Evidently the jewellery demanded for the manufacture of the golden calf (32:2) had been only a fraction of the 'booty' received from the Egyptians (12:34–36; cf. 33:4–6). After all, this was the most likely source for much of what they were now giving so generously to Yahweh, though perhaps some of the materials (e.g. timber, animal hides, spices, oil) may have been obtained through trade with the Midianites or other nomadic groups. Such enthusiastic giving had thus to be stopped, because they had exceeded the necessary requirements (only the skilled workers could determine when they had given *more than enough*, vv. 4–5). But however excessive, this generosity of the community was certainly an appropriate response to the amazing grace and mercy they had experienced from God (cf. 2 Cor. 8:9).

Meaning
With respect to the construction of Yahweh's tabernacle, three important things are highlighted here: (1) the significant cost involved, both in terms of material goods and manpower; (2) the overwhelming nature of the community's generosity, reflecting both their gratitude to Yahweh for all he had done for them, and their eagerness to worship him in the way that he had disclosed; (3) the way that God uniquely equips his people for works of service, ensuring that they all can carry out the tasks, however challenging, that he has commanded. Accordingly, this material serves as a great encouragement for later readers, whether Old Testament temple-builders in the physical sense or New Testament temple-builders in the spiritual sense.

---

3   Garrett (2014: 679 n. 100) correctly notes that since Exod. 36:3b commences with an offline (*we-X-qatal*) clause that provides background for the subsequent narrative, it should be understood as commencing the next textual unit.

C. The manufacture of the tabernacle and its furniture (36:8 – 38:31)

Context
From here to the end of chapter 38 the focus is on the construction of the tabernacle and its accoutrements, ending with an inventory of the gold, silver and bronze that was involved. As noted above, a logical sequence is reflected here, with work on the tabernacle itself prefacing work on the furniture that this construction will subsequently house (cf. Exod. 25).

Comment
i. The ornate tent of meeting (36:8–38)

8–38. This unit recounts the implementation of the instructions given in 26:1–37, differing from the latter mainly in the use of indicative rather than imperative verbs, although some of the earlier instructions (e.g. 26:9, 12–13, 33–35) were obviously irrelevant (and thus ignored) until the assembling stage of construction (cf. ch. 40). The verbatim repetition in this and the subsequent units implicitly underscores that Yahweh's instructions for the tabernacle were all precisely followed, as explicitly expressed in the 'as Yahweh commanded Moses' refrain of the following chapters (chs. 39–40, AT). Thus, this block of text should certainly not be dismissed as redundant repetition. It is underscoring Israel's faithful obedience, in sharp relief to Israel's great sin (32:21, 31) which the previous section underlined.

In verse 10, while the NIV's *they* rightly gives the impression that this was a collaborative enterprise (cf. v. 8), here and throughout the following verses (vv. 10–38) the Hebrew text employs a third masculine singular form ('he'), presumably referring to Bezalel (cf. 37:1; 38:22), the master craftsman responsible for all the handiwork. While explicitly the subject only in 37:1, Bezalel is also the most likely subject of the same third person singular verb (*he made*) in 37:2 – 38:9.

ii. The ark of the covenant (37:1–9)

1–9. Bezalel (see previous comment) likewise oversees the production of the ark; thus again the main difference with the original instructions (25:10–20) relates to the verbal forms and the necessary postponement of some matters (25:21–22) until the tent was initially set up (cf. 40:20–21). The emphatic instruction on keeping the carrying poles inserted (25:15) is not expressly reflected in the implementation section, but it is arguably assumed by the fact that there is no mention of removing the poles after the ark has been placed within the Most Holy Place (40:20–21).

As the symbol of Yahweh's presence ('enthroned between the cherubim'; cf. 1 Sam. 4:4; 2 Sam. 6:2; 2 Kgs 19:15; Pss 80:1; 99:1; Isa. 37:16), but not an idolatrous object, the ark was the legitimate alternative to Aaron's golden bull (cf. 32:4, 8).

iii. The table for showbread (37:10–16)

10–16. Though not mentioned explicitly (see NIV footnote and my comment on 36:10 above), Bezalel also oversees the construction of the table and all other tabernacle furniture. Once again, the instructions of 25:23–29 are implicitly followed, but placing it within the tent and showcasing the bread of the Presence (25:30) is obviously postponed until later (40:22–23).

iv. The seven-branched lampstand (37:17–24)

17–24. This again closely follows the earlier material (25:31–40), other than ignoring the instructions for how the lampstand should be installed within the Holy Place. As with other sacred furniture, the lampstand will subsequently be set up in the tent as divinely directed (cf. 40:24–25).

v. The incense altar (37:25–29)

25–29. While listed out of logical sequence earlier (30:1–10), here the construction of the incense altar (along with the manufacture of anointing oil and incense) is more logically described alongside other items of furniture located in the Holy Place. Once again, instructions with respect to its location in the tent and subsequent use (30:6–10) must obviously be deferred until after the tent has been erected (40:26) and the priests have been ordained (Lev. 8 – 9).

vi. The altar for burnt offerings (38:1–7)

1–7. The focus shifts now from items placed in the tent of meeting to those placed in the courtyard – the construction of which immediately follows (vv. 9–20). Other than omitting the reason for its bronze pots (cf. 27:3) and the command to make the altar *just as you were shown on the mountain* (27:8b), the details here reiterate the instructions in 27:1–8.

vii. The basin for washing (38:8)

8. The earlier instructions regarding the making and use of this basin (30:17–21) are simply assumed, with no dimensions for this piece of furniture being provided here either. However, additional and somewhat cryptic information is given about the source of the metal used; ancient mirrors were often made of highly polished bronze. The duties performed by these *women who served at the entrance to the tent of meeting* (cf. 1 Sam. 2:22) are unclear. This has led to speculation over the legitimacy of their activity there, even though there is no suggestion in Exodus that they were guilty of behaviour (e.g. prostitution or some other infraction) that resulted in the confiscation of their property. Hamilton (2011: 609) infers such confiscation from the parallel Greenstein (2000: 171–173) draws between these women's utensils and the censers reappropriated in Numbers 16:37–39. However, the parallels are inexact: there is no hint in Exodus that the women's items were forfeited; moreover, their service at the entrance to the tent of meeting (as yet unassembled) seems to refer to a legitimate role undertaken *after* the tabernacle was operational (cf. 1 Sam. 2:22), rather than engagement in the kind of illicit or inappropriate behaviour for which Eli's sons are later condemned.

Since the same verb (Heb. *ṣābā'*, 'to perform a duty') is later used to describe the duties of the Levites (Num. 4:23; 8:24), there is good reason to conclude that some sort of more mundane work associated with the tabernacle is in view here also: possibly it involved washing utensils, replenishing the water and other practical tasks that would ensure the smooth operation of Israel's cult. In any case, given the positive tone of this section as a whole, we should undoubtedly conclude that these ladies willingly donated small but not insignificant possessions for the service of God. In other words, this is a further example of the spirit of generosity towards this project reflected by the Israelite community as a whole (cf. 35:29).

viii. The surrounding courtyard (38:9–20)

9–20. The final step in the creation of Israel's sacred space was the manufacture of the perimeter fence to enclose the courtyard surrounding the tent. Again, the previous instructions (27:9–19) are closely followed, although additional information is supplied regarding the height of the entrance curtain (38:18b) and the silver caps on its posts (38:19b), and there is no mention of the other bronze *articles used in the service of the tabernacle* referred to in the parallel instructional section (27:19a). These minor differences, however, do not detract from the main point: that every detail in the manufacture of the tabernacle, including its perimeter fence, followed Yahweh's instructions to the letter.

ix. The official inventory (38:21–31)

This is an official record of the gold, silver and bronze collected for the tabernacle which supplements the more generic inventory recorded previously (cf. 35:21–29). While the silver is associated here (38:25–28) with a census or poll tax (cf. 30:11–16), this was nevertheless an offering (Heb. *tĕrûmâ*) to Yahweh (30:13–15; 35:21), albeit not a *wave offering* (Heb. *tĕnûfâ*; cf. 35:22; 38:24, 29). The tallies of precious metal recorded here are certainly substantial, but not extraordinary for ancient temple structures (Kitchen 2003: 275–280). In any case, the point of this inventory commissioned by Moses was not simply to have an official record of the quantity of materials donated (38:21), but to provide details of how Bezalel and Oholiab (v. 22) utilized such large contributions in the work they had undertaken. Thus, unlike previously, the emphasis here is less on the community's generosity, and more on the honesty and integrity of those involved in the distribution and deployment of the materials provided.

21–24. *The tabernacle of the covenant law* is a description Exodus uses only here of the tabernacle/tent of meeting (cf. Num. 1:50; 10:11). It highlights another aspect of its covenantal significance: it served as the depository for the stipulations that gave expression to Israel's divine–human relationship.

25–28. A census or poll tax (see 30:11–16) was apparently taken at some undisclosed point prior to the tabernacle's construction. Since this provided the silver that was used in its posts and their bases (vv. 27–28), the census alluded to here in Exodus must be distinguished from the one recorded in Numbers 1, which Yahweh commanded one month after the tabernacle had been erected (Num. 1:1; cf. Exod. 40:17). In contrast to the voluntary offerings mentioned previously (35:4–29), this poll tax for each adult person was a compulsory contribution (38:26). As Alexander observes (2017: 664), there is no stipulation either here or back in 30:11–16 that this poll tax applied only to adult *males*. However, whether such a gender qualification applied to the census figures in Numbers 1 (or in Num. 26) is more debatable, especially since 'male' (Heb. *zākār*) and the other stipulation reiterated there ('going out to war'; Heb. *yōṣē' ṣābā'*) elsewhere apply exclusively to going out in a military capacity, as distinct from *lišbō' ṣābā'* (meaning 'to enter service' in a cultic capacity, where the latter is almost always spelt out). Thus, while Alexander's suggestion provides an attractive solution to the extremely large numbers in Exodus, it seems to run into difficulty in Numbers.

Significantly, however, the amount of tax collected (301,775 shekels,[4] 38:25) correlates with the 603,550 head count (half a shekel per person). Not surprisingly (see comment on 12:37–28), therefore, a literal interpretation of this large number has not gone unchallenged.

29–31. The mirrors donated by the serving women (v. 8) had possibly been donated specifically for the laver and its stand (in accord with their possible tabernacle responsibilities – see comment on 38:8). Accordingly, there was no reason to include it here along with the other objects made from this bronze wave offering (v. 29).

---

4   NB 100 talents = 300,000 shekels.

Meaning
The primary emphasis of this subsection on the manufacture
of the tabernacle and its furniture is the skilled workers' use of
all the material donated as Yahweh intended. Accordingly, they
played a very significant part in ensuring that the sanctuary would
be built according to God's design (cf. 25:9, 40) so that his plan
to safely dwell among them (cf. 25:8–9) would indeed be realized.
However, as emphasized again by the detailed inventory (38:21–31)
– throwing further light on how the gold, silver and bronze were
obtained – everyone played an important part in this project, a
community effort in the fullest sense.

D. The priestly garments (39:1–31)

Context
As in the instructions section (cf. 28:1), the focus now shifts (cf. ch. 28)
from the manufacture of the tabernacle itself to the special garments
required for its priestly personnel. Here, however, the transition is
smoother (cf. 27:20–21), moving almost seamlessly from how precious
materials were used for the tabernacle to how they were used for the
various priestly garments (39:1). Like the subsection recounting the
manufacture of the tabernacle (36:8 – 38:20), this material differs from
the relevant divine instructions (ch. 28) in (1) replacing imperative
with indicative verbs; (2) focusing on construction rather than use
(e.g. no mention is made of the Urim and Thummim, and the breastpiece is not referred to as 'the breastpiece of judgment'; cf. 28:15,
29–30, AT); and (3) reflecting abridgement in places and a slightly
different order (e.g. leaving the gold emblem of Aaron's turban to last).

Comment
i. Production of the priestly garments (39:1)
    1. The sevenfold refrain that commences here ('as Yahweh
commanded Moses', AT; cf. vv. 5, 7, 21, 26, 29, 31) explicitly
highlights the degree of Israel's compliance with Yahweh's design.

ii. The ephod (39:2–7)
    2. As previously (see comment on 36:10), the skilled artisans
apparently work under the supervision of Bezalel, the most likely

subject of the verb here (once again, the Hebrew has a third person sing., as do vv. 7–8 and 22). However, the collaborative nature of the enterprise is clearly reflected in the third person plural verbs that dominate this section (cf. vv. 3–4, 6, 10, 15–21, 24–31).

3. This information, unparalleled in the divine instructions, is traditionally understood (see English translations) to explain how an unusual blend of both fabrics and gold (cf. 28:6–8) was accomplished by making thin strips of gold 'thread'. However, as suggested previously (see comment on 28:2–5, p. 319), these strips of gold plate may possibly have been a more functional feature sewn into the ephod and breastpiece, rather than a merely decorative element delicately woven throughout the fabric.

4–7. The details here are an abridged form of the earlier instructions, with the requisite change in the subject and mood (indicative rather than imperative) of the verbs. The repeated use of the refrain (vv. 5, 7) in these verses dealing with the ephod further highlights its theological significance.

iii. The breastpiece (39:8–21)
8–21. Other than the omission of the functional instructions (see 28:29–30), the requisite change in verbal subject and mood, and the addition of the closing refrain, this unit matches the earlier instructions.

iv. The robe (39:22–26)
22–26. This likewise correlates closely with the parallel section (see 28:31–35), again omitting the more functional details (28:35).

v. The tunics, turban, caps, undergarments and sash (39:27–29)
27–29. Apart from omitting the functional aspects and reflecting a slightly different order (caps, undergarments, sash), this unit also corresponds with the original instructions (28:39–43).

vi. The sacred emblem (39:30–31)
30–31. This item is discussed immediately after the robe in the earlier instructions to Moses (28:36–38). Presumably it is the last item here because it was not attached to the turban until after the

latter had been made. However, its climactic location here may also allude to its theological significance.

Meaning
Building on the previous two subsections, this one further emphasizes that God's instructions were carried out to the letter. It does so implicitly by means of the (otherwise redundant) repetition (as in 36:8 – 38:20), but also explicitly by its sevenfold refrain 'as Yahweh commanded Moses'. Just as Israel's failure to trust and obey God is a recurring theme in earlier sections of the book, so their confidence and compliance is the recurring theme in these final chapters.

E. The workmanship inspected (39:32–43)

Context
Now that all the preliminary work on the tabernacle and its accoutrements has been completed, it is presented to Moses for inspection and approval. In doing so, Moses was demonstrating his complete obedience to the personal instructions God had given him (cf. 25:9, 40; 27:8).

Comment
32. Along with verses 42–43, this verse forms a literary bracket (or *inclusio*) that underlines the main point of this unit: namely, that the Israelites did 'everything/all the work just as Yahweh commanded' (AT). Here and in the following chapter (40:2, 6, 29) the construction is referred to as 'the tent of meeting residence' (AT), an unusual combination that underlines its twin purpose as a place of residence and a place of revelation.

33–41. It may again seem rather unnecessary to list everything they had manufactured, but the point of such repetition (as in the previous section) is to draw further attention to the fact that every item they had made was according to the divine design.

42–43. Moses now carries out an inspection to ensure that everything has indeed been manufactured according to Yahweh's explicit design (cf. 25:9). Satisfied that this was indeed the case (39:42–43), Moses *blessed* the people. While possibly echoing God's blessing of the seventh day after his work of creation (cf. Gen. 2:1–3; Exod. 20:11),[5] this may also serve to remind the Israelites where true blessing is to be found: in fully trusting and obeying Yahweh (20:24; 23:25; cf. 12:32).

Meaning
As throughout this long section that deals with the manufacture of the tabernacle, its furniture and the priestly vestments, this final unit strongly emphasizes the faithfulness of Moses and the Israelites in following God's instructions. Their track record may certainly have been one of failure, but their present response was one that clearly held out the prospect of God's continued presence and blessing.

---

5   While several commentators note this and several other verbal similarities (in the closing two chapters of Exodus) to the Genesis creation account, the parallels are inexact, and we should probably be cautious about inferring too much from them.

17. THE TABERNACLE ERECTED AND FILLED WITH YAHWEH'S GLORY (40:1–38)

The closing chapter of Exodus narrates the final stage in the construction of the tabernacle: setting everything up for the first time. Yahweh's instruction to erect the structure and position all its furnishings as specified is followed by the additional instruction to consecrate everything – including its priestly personnel – with the special anointing oil (40:1–9). However, the implementation of only the first of these instructions is narrated here (40:16–33), with the closing verses highlighting the significance of the Sinai theophany within this portable divine dwelling for both Moses and Israel (40:34–38). The implementation of the other instructions is not narrated until Leviticus 8:5–30, although the time-lapse between the setting up of the tabernacle and the consecration of both it and its priests was apparently minimal (cf. Num. 7:1). However, Exodus 40 is much more focused on the theophany (vv. 34–38; cf. Num. 9:15–23).

A. Yahweh's final instructions to Moses concerning the tabernacle (40:1–16)

Context

Ever since 35:1 Moses has been the primary speaker, with the community and particularly Bezalel being the key respondents. Now that Moses has communicated God's instructions to the Israelites and ensured that everything has been manufactured according to the divine pattern (chs. 35–39), the narrative returns once again to divine speech directed to Moses – with instructions to set up the tabernacle some twelve months after the exodus.

Comment

1–8. While God's instructions unsurprisingly focus more on the location of the sacred furniture than on the erection of the tent (v. 2) and its surrounding courtyard (v. 8), the sequence here is identical to that of 36:8 – 38:20. According to the date mentioned in verse 2 (i.e. the *first day of the first month* [*in the second year*; cf. 40:17]), the tabernacle was initially set up almost twelve months after the exodus (cf. 12:2, 6) and between nine and ten months after Israel's arrival at Sinai (19:1).

9–11. Once the tent had been set up with its furniture in the designated location (vv. 3–8), Moses was to *consecrate it and all its furnishings* with the special *anointing oil* (cf. 30:22–33), thus setting it apart for sacred use. While not actually narrated in the present chapter, Moses faithfully carried out this action also (cf. Lev. 8:10–11; Num. 7:1).

12–15. Likewise, this command for Moses to anoint and consecrate (i.e. set apart) *Aaron and his sons* to serve as priests, in keeping with the ritual more fully prescribed in chapter 29, is only later narrated (Lev. 8).[1] The detailed description of this ordination service given in Leviticus 8 suggests that Exodus 40:17–35 is a concise summary and abridgement of events that transpired over several days, if not weeks (cf. also Num. 8:1–4).

---

1   The book of Exodus is thus clearly designed to be read as part of a larger narrative that includes Leviticus (Alexander 2017: 672).

16. The Hebrew (MT) concludes the first section of the chapter with Moses' response to Yahweh's instructions: 'So Moses did; according to everything Yahweh had commanded him, thus he did' (AT). This transitional summary is then elaborated in more detail in the section that follows.

Meaning

Just as God commanded creation into existence in Genesis 1, he now commands this new beginning into existence, albeit using human instruments to do the creative work on this occasion. However, it is important that this 'new creation' is not an addendum to God's saving work but reflects the ultimate goal of the exodus: God's intention to 'dwell with the Israelites and be . . . their God' (29:45–46, AT). Setting up this consecrated dwelling place, along with its furniture and priestly personnel, not only facilitates and makes this possible, but also foreshadows the ultimate reality of new creation, when God will dwell with his redeemed people for ever (Rev. 21:3–4).

B. The faithful implementation of Yahweh's instructions (40:17–33)

Context

The traditional Jewish structural division of this chapter (see note on v. 16) is supported by the Hebrew syntactical marker with which verse 17 begins. However, this next section clearly elaborates on the observation of verse 16, highlighting once again – but now emphasizing more explicitly (cf. 36:8 – 38:20) – how Yahweh's instructions for the tabernacle were faithfully carried out. In chapter 40 there is less repetition or direct overlap between the divine instructions and their human execution, the refrain now performing the function of such repetition in the initial implementation account (36:8 – 38:20; cf. 39:1–31).

The inclusion of *the second year* (v. 17) not only clarifies the date alluded to at the start of the chapter (v. 2), but also helps establish the time frame for everything that took place between the erection of the tabernacle and Israel's departure from Sinai less than two months later (Num. 10:11).

Comment
Verse 16 has already reintroduced the familiar refrain used seven
times in relation to the making of the priestly garments (Exod. 39).
This is now used seven more times in the present unit in relation
to the setting up of the tabernacle. However, in contrast to the
previous emphasis – where Bezalel and his artisans made everything
'as Yahweh commanded Moses' – this text now stresses the key role
and faithful obedience of Moses himself: 'Moses did everything . . .
[v. 16] as Yahweh commanded him' (vv. 19, 21, 23, 25, 27, 29, [32]).
Although his contribution may well have been mainly supervisory
– obviously he did not do all this heavy lifting by himself – it was
clearly important, as underlined by Moses being credited with
having *finished the work* (v. 33; cf. 1 Chr. 21:29; 2 Chr. 1:3). Because
of Moses' faithful communication of God's instructions and his
role in their execution, the architecture of the tabernacle (as well
as the design and location of each item of its furniture) perfectly
conformed to the pattern shown to him on the mountain (cf. 25:40).
Accordingly, in contrast to Aaron's golden bull, this structure would
much better serve the purpose for which it was intended.

17. Here, in what appears to be a summary account of what
follows, *the tabernacle* most likely refers to both the tent of meeting
and its entire enclosure (cf. v. 33). Apart from the additional
inclusion of the year,[2] the repetition of the date (cf. v. 1) would
be redundant. However, it clearly underscores that Yahweh's
instructions were followed, and thus foreshadows the refrain in
the verses that follow.

18–19. In contrast to the preceding (summary) verse, here and
in the following verses *the tabernacle* primarily refers to its most
significant part, the *tent of meeting* (v. 22; cf. v. 1). As expected, the
procedure starts with the erection of this tent, with the bases
being set in place prior to the framework, which is then covered.

20–21. Again, the order is a practical one, with the tablets
inserted into the ark before its poles and lid are attached, and the

---

2　Unusually inserted between the month and the day (the typical Heb.
sequence is year–month–day), suggesting that the month is fronted for
emphasis (cf. 40:2).

shielding curtain hung up only after the ark has been placed inside the Most Holy Place.

22–23. Likewise, the table is set in position before the bread is set on it.

24–25. While the order of the actions here is again most logical, elsewhere it is Aaron who carries out this task (Num. 8:1–4). Possibly we are meant to understand that Aaron carried out this task at Moses' directive (cf. Num. 8:2) and thus, like several other actions attributed to Moses here in Exodus 40, there were other people involved. In other words, Moses is seeing to it that everything is set up as Yahweh commanded, rather than doing everything himself. Alternatively, Moses was responsible for setting up the lampstand initially, but instructed Aaron on how he must do so on all subsequent occasions (Num. 8:2).

26–27. The immediate context (cf. vv. 20–25) makes it abundantly clear that within the tent of meeting the incense altar was indeed located in the Holy Place (along with the lampstand and table) rather than in the Most Holy Place along with the ark (see comment on 30:6). While Moses may well have burned the incense on this altar himself (i.e. prior to the consecration of the official priesthood; cf. Lev. 8:6–30), it is equally possible that it was Aaron who did so – after he had been duly consecrated (cf. 30:7–8; Lev. 9:23). Possibly it was such priestly action and its aftermath (Lev. 9:24) that emboldened Nadab and Abihu to burn some incense and so offer unauthorized fire before Yahweh (Lev. 10:1).

28–29. With everything arranged inside the Holy Place as it should be, the tent of meeting is closed off with its entrance curtain, and the bronze altar is set up outside. As noted above, for Moses to officiate prior to the consecration of Aaron is also attested elsewhere (cf. Lev. 8:6–30).

30–32. The location of the bronze water basin directly outside the tent of meeting is clearly important (cf. 30:17–21). Such ritual washing symbolizes the need for the removal of anything potentially defiling before humans can enter the presence of a holy God. This applies not only to the priests as they go about their sacred duties (cf. 19:22), but to everyone (cf. 19:10, 14), including Moses himself (cf. 3:5; 24:16).

33. Finally, with the erection of the perimeter fence and its entrance curtain, Moses *finished the work* – possibly (although cf. Alexander 2017: 672) a further echo (see comment on 39:43) of God's creation week (cf. Gen. 2:2).

Meaning
The main point underlined here, as in the previous narrative block (35:1 – 39:43) and the opening section of this final chapter, is that Yahweh's instructions were fully obeyed. Whereas previously this emphasis on faithful obedience had concluded with the blessing of Moses (39:43), here it is immediately followed with the manifestation of God's glorious presence, which fully consecrates his dwelling place (cf. 29:43). The key to such fellowship with a holy God, as the latter half of Exodus has so consistently emphasized, is faithfulness to his covenant commands.

Although Moses and the Israelites have finally managed some measure of success in doing so, it won't be long before we see further lapses into faithless disobedience and further rebellion. Thus we must read this more positive section in Exodus against its wider literary and historical context, lest we draw the wrong theological conclusions. Against the wider canvas of the Pentateuch, and of the Old Testament as a whole, the tabernacle that Moses constructed was merely a symbol and shadow of a greater reality still to come – ultimately, the new Jerusalem into which 'nothing impure will ever enter . . . but only those whose names are written in the Lamb's book of life' (Rev. 21:27), namely, those who by God's grace 'keep God's commands and hold fast their testimony about Jesus' (Rev. 12:17).

C. Yahweh's glorious and guiding presence (40:34–38)

Context
With the work on the tabernacle fully completed (v. 33b), attention now shifts to how Yahweh set his seal of approval on what his people had constructed at his command. Here the threat of 33:3 is reversed as God's guiding presence or glory cloud manifests itself over and within this specially constructed divine residence. As Meyers (2005: 283) notes, the mention of this cloud in each

verse here underlines the divine presence as the key idea at the conclusion of the book.

Comment

34–35. The people are now blessed with the visible manifestation of Yahweh's guiding and directing presence among them. The theophanic *cloud* that had directed Israel's journey out of Egypt (13:21–22; 14:19–20, 24; 16:7, 10; 19:9; cf. 17:1; 18:12) and manifested God's glorious presence on top of Mount Sinai (cf. 19:16–19; 24:15–18) now *covered* [or 'resided over'] *the tent* and *filled the tabernacle* – not only sealing this project with Yahweh's approval but, more importantly, further answering Moses' earlier petition (cf. 33:15–18) and giving concrete expression to the ultimate goal of the exodus (cf. 29:44–46). Significantly, the cloud is said to 'settle/dwell' (Heb. *šākan*; cf. its cognate noun, *miškān*, meaning 'tabernacle/dwelling place') on the tent of meeting (cf. 24:16; 25:8; 29:45–46; see also John 1:14; Rev. 7:15; 21:3).

There may be an implied contrast between the new situation here, where *Moses could not enter the tent of meeting* because Yahweh's glory had filled it, and the previous situation, where Moses had entered his more mundane *tent of meeting* while the pillar of cloud remained outside (cf. 33:9). However, such exclusion for Moses was likely only temporary, since the impression given elsewhere is that on some occasions Moses did enter the tent (cf. v. 32; Num. 1:1), although not the Most Holy Place (cf. Lev. 16) from which Yahweh would have addressed him. In any case, the main point here is that such was the intensity of Yahweh's visible presence on this occasion that not even Moses could safely enter the tent of meeting.

36–38. This final subunit moves beyond the immediate occasion – the tabernacle being filled with the manifest presence of God – to the significance of this theophanic cloud for Israel's subsequent itinerary. Like the more developed statement in Numbers 9:15–23, the perspective here is clearly a future one (looking back over Israel's post-Sinai itinerary), and the point is the same: from Sinai onwards Israel's itinerary was directed exclusively by the manifest presence of the God who had promised to accompany them (33:14) and lead them safely to the Promised Land (3:8, 17; 6:8; 23:20).

Meaning
The climax of Exodus is the fulfilment of the promise that has driven the latter half of the book (19:5–6; 25:8; 29:45–46), but which was placed in jeopardy by Israel's sinful attempt to represent and worship God their own way (cf. 32:1–6, 10; 33:3b, 5, 15–16). At last God makes his dwelling with Abraham's descendants permanent, leading and accompanying them on their way to the Promised Land.

While not confined to the tabernacle, as the moveable pillar of cloud and fire so clearly demonstrated, God's presence was more immanent there than anywhere else on earth. And so a book that began with the apparent absence of God ends with his glorious presence in the midst of his redeemed people, foreshadowing the time when this finds its full and final realization – when 'God's dwelling-place is . . . among the people, and he will dwell with them. They will be his people, and God himself will be with them and be their God' (Rev. 21:3).

.

www.ingramcontent.com/pod-product-compliance
Lightning Source LLC
Chambersburg PA
CBHW041919011025

33429CB00004B/11